CW00685866

Mothering Sundae

Raising children in a changing world

Ruth Maddock

Disclaimer: I am not a medically qualified doctor or health practitioner and I do not intend that this book should provide specific medical advice or be used as a basis for diagnosis and choice of treatment. In fact I have no medical or scientific qualifications whatsoever. The information contained in this book has come about as a result of my personal journey. I hope that you too will take your own personal journey of discovery. However you should always consult your own qualified health professional before changing your medication or attempting to self-treat any conditions.

Copyright © Ruth Maddock 2013

Ruth Maddock asserts the moral right to be identified as the author of this work.
A catalogue record for this book is available from the British Library.

First published in the UK in 2013 by Maddock House Publishing
16 Market Square
Bromyard
Herefordshire
HR7 4BP
www.motheringsundae.co.uk

All rights reserved. No part of this book may be reproduced in any form, except brief excerpts, without the written permission of the author.

Printed by: imprintdigital.com

ISBN 978-0-9926923-0-8

Scripture verses used are from the King James Version (KJV), the New Revised Standard Version (NRSV) and 'The Message' (THE MESSAGE).

Scripture quotations from the New Revised Standard Version Bible, copyright © 1989 National Council of the Churches of Christ in the United States of America. Used by permission. All rights reserved

Scripture quotations from **THE MESSAGE**. Copyright © by Eugene H. Peterson 1993, 1994, 1995, 1996, 2000, 2001, 2002. Used by permission of NavPress Publishing Group.

Web sites accessed and correct in July–September 2013.

Many thanks to my friend Sylvie for copyediting. What a joy it is to have such talented friends. For professional copyediting service contact her at sylviejay@homecall.co.uk. My thanks too to Mark Stibbe—www.thescriptdoctor.org.uk—for his invaluable advice. My husband Mark and friends Bob, Sarah, Mo, Ann, Sue, Angie, and Shirley, who read through the proof copies and gave me their comments, also helped me to hone this book further. Any spelling mistakes, inconsistencies and inaccuracies are entirely my own work.

For Mark without whom this great adventure would not have been possible and the children we love dearly—David, Rosannagh, Elisia and Christopher.

And in memory of Nathan who . . .

'shall grow not old, as we that are left grow old:
Age shall not weary *him*, nor the years condemn.
At the going down of the sun and in the morning
We will remember *him*.'[1]

---

[1] For The Fallen (1914), Laurence Binyon (personalized)

CONTENTS

Intro

I always intended to be the perfect mother. After all, how hard could it be? Coming to motherhood late, I'd had many years of watching my friends and family raise their kids. And I was pretty sure I could do just as well or perhaps even better!

Baby was going to come with me everywhere and experience the full, rich life that I would lead. I would breast-feed him for at least eighteen months: he would be plump and healthy and days would be full of sunshine and laughter. The way I saw it, child-rearing would be filled with trips to feed the ducks, picnics in the park, and days of creativity: painting, sticking, and generally recycling all the empty cereal packets. Yes, I was going to be the sort of mum that kept them all: neatly stored on an organized shelving system, in an immaculate and highly creative house.

It was a good plan and I would have really enjoyed it if it had worked out that way. But these plans held no place for mind-numbing exhaustion, no place for temper tantrums in Tesco, no place for all the stuff that must go with you everywhere and certainly no place for size 16—or dare I even whisper it—size 18 dresses. In my plans the baby didn't cry all night or want feeding when it wasn't convenient—I once spent the whole evening feeding baby Rosannagh in the toilets at a restaurant, I even had my meal there. In these plans poo always stayed where it was meant to be—inside the nappy— rather than managing somehow to completely fill the babygro from top to bottom: how do they do that? All this fun and laughter wouldn't have to take place alongside that nagging feeling that it was about time that I cleaned the loo, changed the sheets, did the washing, paid the bills, weeded the garden, and even perhaps had an evening out with their father. I wouldn't have to look after baby while I was throwing up with a migraine. And these plans always—but always—included bank accounts that were nicely in the black rather than hopelessly in the red. On top of that the pictures in the dream always included a house that was a 'real home': full of understated 'chicness'—rather than a half-finished decorator's nightmare! It would never rain, I would be constantly full of energy, baby would be a little bundle of joy and happiness all the time, and it would all be just perfect.

I know now—oh what a double-edged sword is the wisdom of hindsight—that although babies arrive crying, helpless, and naked, they don't arrive empty-handed waiting for life to write nice things on all their blank pages. They arrive with a full set of emotional luggage, that they will stack haphazardly on top of yours, and that they will gradually unpack—presenting you as parents with some of life's greatest joys, frustrations, and challenges.

Being a mother has been an emotional roller-coaster ride: juggling my own needs and issues with the needs of the five little people that God called me to love. I have lunged from first birthday parties and nativity plays to the funeral of a son and the possibility of my own death from cancer. From that first 'I love you mummy' to 'I'm leaving home'. From combing the hedgerows for food because we had run out of money, to laughing in the waves on family holidays.

Through all these happy times and through the desperately sad times the foundation in my life has been my relationship with Jesus. Without this relationship I don't think I would have made it this far. Following him is my focus, my guide is the Holy Spirit, and my manual for the journey is the Bible.

The Bible is an amazing book. There just seem to be layers upon layers of truth contained within it. I know of no other book that gives us such a detailed glimpse of events that will take place in the future. Written nearly 2 millennia ago it accurately predicted a global focus on the tiny reborn state of Israel, a world that is increasingly becoming one global community with a unified monetary system, and a numerical system for personal identification that can be implanted into a person's body.

From it we learn that the world's system is racing headlong towards a climactic end, and that we are nearer to that end than any generation before us. Indeed we and our children will almost certainly live to see the dramatic changes in the economic, political, global, and environmental landscape that it forecasts.

And our babies—with all their baggage—will grow up to be fully fledged citizens of this brave new world. A world coloured by a history that has turned it into a maelstrom of conflicting and often hostile forces. From the very beginning of their lives these forces will try to shape them, mould them, and make them conform to their own characteristics.

This history began in perfection with a creation at one with God and his purposes. When our first ancestors Adam and Eve turned away from this perfection they gave control of the earth to Satan and his plans for chaos, disorder, and distress.

Once King and Queen in a world full of God's goodness: Adam and his wife Eve were reduced to the status of servants and labourers in a world pregnant with thorns and thistles, sweat and tears, suffering and death. It was this legacy that they handed down to their children, their children's children, and to you and me and our children. Gee—thanks Grandpa and Grandma!

Satan having executed a masterstroke of planning was now en route to his ultimate goal of world domination. He began to set about changing mankind, their world, and their societies into his likeness so that his kingdom would increase. Through their worship of him he would become a god.

And so the history of the world is one that is replete with all his characteristics. War and hostility, pain and distress, beguiling but false religions, sickness, disease, famine, and all manner of disasters have been the lot of mankind since that fateful day when Adam and Eve ate the 'apple'.

Into this chaos came one who, though born in a stable and placed in a manger, was the legitimate king by virtue of his royal lineage. As heir to Adam's crown through Mary, Joseph, and their ancestors back to Adam he could have claimed this crown during his time on earth just as some of his followers wanted. By dying Jesus made a way for us to step out of our natural inheritance from Adam and Eve so that we can share in his inheritance. When we put our faith in Jesus we become children of God and 'joint heirs with Christ'.[2] Because we are then 'adopted' into God's family we have a right to inherit from him and we lose the right to inherit from our birth family—Adam and Eve. Even today an adopted child has no legal rights to inherit from his or her birth family—so even if I knew who he was—I, as an adopted child, could not claim on my birth father's estate when he dies.

We who follow Jesus live in a time of overlap: whilst we live as co-heirs with Christ we also see Satan's plans nearing fruition. The Bible makes it clear that in the last days of this age Satan will be behind the push to create a global empire that will be fronted by his man the Antichrist. The word 'anti' comes from the Greek word which means against and opposed to but also 'in the place of'. Whilst we have seen many forerunners of this man, the last Antichrist to come on the world stage will embody both of these characteristics as he sets himself up in opposition to God and also take the place of Christ the King.

Nimrod, who set up the first post-flood world empire, was one of these forerunners. At Babel God judged this initiative and separated the people-groups by causing a confusion of languages. It has taken mankind some four thousand years to get back to the place where a global government is a real possibility. Characteristics that we see in Nimrod's kingdom are beginning to emerge once again;

- *Rebellion against God*: The literal translation of the name 'Nimrod' means 'rebellion' and may have been used as a nickname. Society today is a society in rebellion.
- *Hero worship*. Because the world was a dangerous place in the time of Nimrod he drew people around him who wanted protection. One of his titles was 'Shepherd', which in the Chaldean language was He-Roe. Hero worship is endemic in our society, and this sets us up for the emergence of a hero to save us from economic, political, and environmental ruin.

---

[2] Rom. 8: 17, NRSV.

- *A unified religious system*: Nimrod and his wife Semiramis set up a religious system devoted to sun worship. As a tyrannical leader he forced people to turn from the worship of the one true God to this new religion. It is from this one religion that all the world religions emerged. Today there are many agendas aimed towards a re-merging of all world religions. This can be seen in programmes such as the 'Earth Charter' a United Nations initiative which is an 'alternative' to the Ten Commandments. The Earth Charter is a New Age and Humanist charter for society. It promotes the creation of a one-world religion underpinned by the belief that there are many ways to Heaven. The charter has been housed in the 'Ark of Hope' which is modelled on the biblical Ark of the Covenant.[3]
- *The encouragement of sexually deviant behaviour and the breakdown of family life*: Nimrod and in particular his wife Semiramis encouraged sexually deviant behaviour and even added it into their religious system. We see echoes of this in the current push by world leaders to redefine marriage and legitimise other sexual practices.
- *The worship of the global leader as god and king*: Nimrod was worshipped as the sun god and his worship continues in various forms to this day. The new world leader will almost certainly be voted in on a wave of euphoria as he appears to save the world from military, political, economic, and even environmental ruin. He may be very charismatic with amazing speaking skills and persuasiveness. He may be very attractive, having the appearance of goodness, and he may even profess some sort of faith. A military genius, he will go on the rampage as he tries to bring all countries under his domination. But not until the final years of this age will Satan's game plan fully emerge as this man sets himself up as a god to be worshipped.

We can see that these characteristics in society are on the increase and as we race headlong into an even more godless society the task of raising our children, whole, healthy, and loving Jesus may well become increasingly difficult for us as Christians.

But for many people the stress and busyness of their day-to-day lives mean that God and faith find no place. He is dead, extinct, non-existent, a figment of other people's imagination, or at best just marginalized as a vague influence on the edge of reality. He's something to be thought about later—one day—when there's time.

In the Westernized world that we inhabit most adults live with boring predictability, like hamsters on an endless treadmill, chained to the pay packet by mortgages, loans, spiralling living costs, and peer pressure to conform. Our homes must be fully colour coordinated, we must have up-to-the-minute labour saving devices. We must keep our houses squeaky clean and

---

[3] http://www.arkofhope.org/.

smelling of synthetic lemons, with an ever-glossy kitchen floor, in a garden plot that would put Eden to shame. Within this environment we must live happy, clean lives, with immaculate children, who are only ever cute and never disgusting, inappropriate, rude, or ill. We must look constantly as if we've walked off the front cover of a glossy magazine, and wear expensive creams and make-up to keep age at bay. If we are ill we can go to see our busy doctor who will prescribe pills to make us instantly well and happy again. We must have a partner and a rampant sex life. We must be calm, self-assured, in control and have successful careers with large salaries in order to repay our debt mountains. We will take holidays in the sun where we will laugh a lot, showing off our perfectly straight, white teeth. And just in case we might be aware of some gaping hole in our lives—if we have the time to think at all that is—we can gather a few bits of a pick-and-mix religion to fit in with our lifestyle and give it meaning and hope. To be really successful we must make sure that our children follow in our footsteps. Later we will be forced to sell all our hard-earned assets in order to pay for care as we sit dribbling in some nursing home waiting for death (or perhaps euthanasia) to release us.

As someone who believes in Jesus I don't want to become entangled in the values and principles of this fallen world. Nor do I want to train my children to conform to these patterns. I belong to a world where God our Father like a designer at his drawing board has made plans—plans for each one of his kids. Knowing the forces that would shape us, he has planned our lives giving each of us a unique purpose and a unique relationship with himself. He has plans for each one of my children. He has plans for each one of your children. 'Like an open book, you watched me grow from conception to birth: all the stages of my life were spread out before you, the days of my life all prepared before I'd even lived one day.'[4]

Because God's nature is one of love we know that these plans are good, but they also have a way of being completely unique, upside down, inside out and back to front.

'You are old, Father William,' the young man said,
'And your hair has become very white;
And yet you incessantly stand on your head—
Do you think, at your age, it is right?'[5]

As parents we believe—and rightly so—that it's our task to be good role models for our children and to lead them to God. But when he said: 'whoever does not receive the kingdom of God as a little child will never enter it'[6] Jesus made it abundantly clear that being a parent is a two-way street and that we absolutely must learn from our children even as they learn from us.

---

[4] Psalm 139: 16, THE MESSAGE.
[5] Lewis Carroll, *Alice's Adventures in Wonderland* (1865).
[6] Mark 10: 15, NRSV.

Jesus said a lot of other things that turn our world-view on its head. Consider, for instance, his teachings that we call 'the beatitudes'. They really do challenge us and highlight the difference between the way we think and the way God thinks.

This is what he said:

'You're blessed when you're at the end of your rope. With less of you there is more of God and his rule.

'You're blessed when you feel you've lost what is most dear to you. Only then can you be embraced by the One most dear to you.

'You're blessed when you're content with just who you are—no more, no less. That's the moment you find yourselves proud owners of everything that can't be bought.

'You're blessed when you've worked up a good appetite for God. He's food and drink in the best meal you'll ever eat.

'You're blessed when you care. At the moment of being "careful," you find yourselves cared for.

'You're blessed when you get your inside world—your mind and heart—put right. Then you can see God in the outside world.

'You're blessed when you can show people how to cooperate instead of compete or fight. That's when you discover who you really are, and your place in God's family.'[7]

These sayings point to how things work in his Kingdom. At the end of this age Jesus will come back to earth, oust the usurper—Antichrist—and reign on earth. He will take his place as the global leader: the King of kings.

Because we are so face-up with the reality of the world's system and way of doing things we often find it difficult fully to grasp the reality of the Kingdom of Heaven. But even though most of us struggle with having a foot in both camps, as Christians we inhabit this kingdom now. All too often we conform to the world's way of doing things: but our aim must be to bring this Kingdom into our reality and experience more and more. Faith is the mechanism by which this happens. 'Without faith it is impossible to please God, for whoever would approach him must believe that he exists and that he rewards those who seek him.'[8]

As parents we are going to model this relationship with God and we are going to be the book from which our children learn. Which world are they going to see into as they read from us?

---

[7] Matt. 5: 2–9, THE MESSAGE.
[8] Heb. 11: 6, NRSV.

Born out of my own struggles, health issues, and mistakes, and out of the struggles of my family, this book is about the things I've discovered along the way and the things I wish I'd known before embarking on this journey. I have written primarily to those who are raising children within the context of a Christian family. However, I hope that those who are caring and nurturing in a much wider sense will also find this book helpful.

Although the content of this book contains more background information than precise 'recipes for success', you will probably have noticed by now that I have also 'snuck' in a few of my knit and crochet designs. I hope that some of you will enjoy making these projects and that they will serve as a reminder that the things we hear from Jesus should always have a practical and creative outcome. We are called to do the things he says and not just to hear them. Knowledge just makes us proud.

I hope also that you won't see what I've written as yet another parenting burden—another set of rules. We don't need another set of rules. For at the heart of our desire to be good parents lies the love that we have for our children. Jesus considered love to be the most important of all God's laws. When asked about this he replied: 'love the Lord your God with all your heart, and with all your soul, and with all your mind.'[9] Not only does this reply show us that love is at the heart of God's dealings with us, it also points to the fact that we humans, being made in God's image have three parts to our personality.

I have a similar three part approach in this book. So often we focus on what we can see and feel and hear, but our personality is made in the image of God and like God consists of three parts: body, soul and spirit. If we focus our parenting skills on only one or two of these parts then we do our children a disservice. They may grow up out of balance and unable fully to take hold of their calling and destiny.

My journey remains just that—a journey—it has begun but it hasn't finished. I don't profess to know it all, or to have perfect understanding. If that were the case my journey would have ended, and where would the fun be in that? Nor do I profess that we have put it all into practice, but we are seeking to do so more and more. As time goes by I anticipate that I will hear more, learn more and understand more. I hope, though, that this little snapshot will be of help and that those of you who have struggles may find the information contained in this book increases your faith for the future, your hope and your direction.

---

[9] Matt. 22: 37, NRSV.

'May God himself, the God who makes everything holy and whole, make you holy and whole, put you together—spirit, soul, and body—and keep you fit for the coming of our Master, Jesus Christ!'[10]

---

[10] 1 Thess. 5: 23, THE MESSAGE.

Nesting Baskets

SIZES

The Large Basket is 20 cm (8 in) diameter and 9 cm (3½ in) high.
The Small Basket is 15 cm (6 in) diameter and 6 cm (2½ in) high.

MATERIALS

For 1 large and 1 small basket you will need: 3 x 50g balls of Rico Essentials Soft
Merino Aran – 100% Virgin Wool (100m per ball).
Size 5.5 mm (USI/9) crochet hook for the large basket or size 4.00 mm (USG/6)
crochet hook for the small basket.
Approx 1 m x 1 cm of ribbon to match for each basket.

Nesting Baskets

TENSION

The Large Basket: 13 htr and 10 rows=10 cm (4in) square on no 5.5 mm hook and double thread. The Small Basket: 17 htr and 14 rows=10 cm (4in) square on no 4 mm hook and single thread.. Change hook if necessary to achieve size given.

ABBREVIATIONS

See page 305.

LARGE BASKET

Base of Basket

Using no 5.5 mm hook and two strands of yarn work as follows;

Round 1: Make a magic circle and into this work 2 ch, (counts as 1 htr), and 7 htr. Pull up tight to close circle and join with ss worked into 2nd of 2 ch at beg of round. (8 htr)

Round 2: 2 ch, (counts as 1 htr), 1 htr back into 1st htr, 2 htr in each htr to end of round. Join with ss worked into 2nd of 2 ch at beg of round. (16 htr)

Round 3: 2 ch, (counts as 1 htr), 1 htr back into 1st htr, 1 htr in next htr, * 2 htr in next htr, 1 htr in next htr, rep from * to end of round. Join with ss worked into 2nd of 2 ch at beg of round. (24 htr)

Round 4: 2 ch, (counts as 1 htr), 1 htr back into 1st htr, htr in each of next 2 htr, * 2 htr in next htr, 1 htr in each of next 2 htr, rep from * to end of round. Join with

ss worked into 2nd of 2 ch at beg of round. (32 htr)

Round 5: 2 ch, (counts as 1 htr), 1 htr back into 1st htr,1 htr in each of next 3 htr, * 2 htr in next htr, 1 htr in each of next 3 htr, rep from * to end of round. Join with ss worked into 2nd of 2 ch at beg of round. (40 htr)

Round 6: 2 ch, (counts as 1 htr), 1 htr back into 1st htr, 1 htr in each of next 4 htr, * 2 htr in next htr, 1 htr in each of next 4 htr, rep from * to end of round. Join with ss worked into 2nd of 2 ch at beg of round. (48 htr)

Round 7: 2 ch, (counts as 1 htr), 1 htr back into 1st htr, htr in each of next 5 htr, * 2 htr in next htr, 1 htr in each of next 5 htr, rep from * to end of round. Join with ss worked into 2nd of 2 ch at beg of round. (56 htr)

Round 8: 2 ch, (counts as 1 htr), 1 htr back into 1st htr, 1 htr in each of next 6 htr, * 2 htr in next htr, 1 htr in each of next 6 htr, rep from * to end of round. Join with ss worked into 2nd of 2 ch at beg of round. (64 htr)

Round 9: 2 ch, (counts as 1 htr), 1 htr back into 1st htr, htr in each of next 7 htr, * 2 htr in next htr, 1 htr in each of next 7 htr, rep from * to end of round. Join with ss worked into 2nd of 2 ch at beg of round. (72 htr)

Sides of Basket

Round 10: 2 ch, (counts as 1 htr), *1 htr into next htr working into back loop of st only, rep from * to end of round. Join with ss worked into 2nd of 2 ch at beg of round.

Round 10 forms the pattern. Repeat this row six more times.

Round 22: 2 ch, (counts as 1 tr), * 2 ch, skip 2 htr, 1 tr into next htr, 3 ch, skip next 2 htr, 1 tr into next htr, rep from * to last repeat 2 ch, skip 2 htr, 1 tr into next htr, 3 ch, skip next 2 htr, ss to 3rd of 3 ch at beg of round. (Place marker in 12th tr from the beg of round)

Round 23: 1 ch, (counts as 1 dc) * skip 2 ch, 1 shell into next tr, skip next 2 ch, 1 dc into next ch , rep from * to last rep, skip 2 ch, 1 shell into next tr, skip next 2 ch, ss to 1 ch at beg of round.

Round 24: 3 ch, (counts as 1 tr), 2 tr back into 1st st, * 1 dc in centre tr of shell, 1 shell into next dc, rep from * to last rep, 1 dc in centre tr of shell, 2 tr in base of first st, ss to 3rd of 3 ch at beg of round. Fasten off.

SMALL BASKET
Work as for the large basket using no 4 00 mm hook and a single strand of yarn only.

TO FINISH
Sew in all ends. Press according to ball band label. Starting at the marked stitch, thread the ribbon through holes, Tie into a bow and sew hems at ends of ribbon to neaten.

Body

Chapter 1
<u>Beautiful Bodies</u>

With the birth of each of my children there came that wonderful moment when he or she was placed into my arms and I was able to count tiny fingers and toes and begin to get to know this amazing little person who had been growing inside me for nine months. There in my arms was a perfectly formed human being: small, slimy, wrinkly, and even smelly, but absolutely perfect. Such a miracle!

A body is a very useful part of who I am and an essential part of my personality. Without a body I wouldn't be able to go shopping. Without a body my dream wardrobe full of beautiful clothes and designer shoes would be useless. Without a body it would be very difficult to read, or sing, or dance. There would be no great works of art, and no eyes to see them. No inspiring music and no ears to hear it. No days pottering in the garden, no watching the clouds go by, no splashing in muddy puddles, and no laughter. Hugging our children and loving our spouses would be difficult too.

Bodies are just such a good idea! And even though there are about seven billion of these bodies worldwide, incredibly they are all different. Different shapes, different sizes, different colours: but all wonderful. And all built from the same basic but incredible design—God's design. At the very beginning of man's story God had said, 'Let us make man in our image,'[11] and he did, and when he had made the man, he was pleased with his work.

As a child I used to like to play in the mud, building things. My children, too, brought home from school great works of art and I still have them on various shelves around the house and, of course, I think they are wonderful. But when God had finished creating his great work out of the dust of the earth he looked at it and said, 'Wow—that's *really* good!'

And it really was—and is—good. What's more, it wasn't just good, it was alive, it was eternal, it had a personality, and it had a purpose. It wasn't going to be left forgotten in some corner of the garden, waiting to dry out and blow away, or be trodden on by Tyrannosaurus Rex; it wasn't going to be left on some shelf to get dusty. This man was really special to God and he wanted to know him and relate to him forever.

---

[11] Gen 1:26, KJV

What a body can do

My body houses the real me and enables me to express all that I am as an individual. It is a physical creation that lives in and is limited by space and time. This absolutely amazing piece of biotechnology has:

- *Five senses:* with these it can communicate with the world and other bodies: Taste, Smell, Touch, Sight, and Hearing.
- *The capacity to move:* some parts of the body move automatically: for instance our heart beats without us thinking about it. But we can control the movement of other parts of our body so that we are able to move from one place to another, and we can express emotions.
- *A control centre:* the brain—which controls the processes that cause us to function. This enables us to think, to make choices, to store memories, to learn, and to feel emotions.

We function best and can fully achieve our goals and dreams only when all these parts are working properly.

Because we want the best for our children we need to know how to grow and maintain their bodies to be as healthy and whole as possible. To do this we have to understand what kind of raw material we are working with and where to find 'spare parts' when things go wrong. The famous children's rhyme has a go at answering this important question:

What are little girls made of?
'Sugar and spice and all that's nice,' that's what little girls are made of.
What are little boys made of?
'Slugs and snails, and puppy dogs tails,' that's what little boys are made of.[12]

Sweet! But the Bible says that little girls and little boys are actually both made out of the same stuff—mud! 'And the LORD God formed man of the dust of the ground, and breathed into his nostrils the breath of life; and man became a living soul.'[13]

So this incredible walking, talking, self-repairing, creative machine in which we live is made from the same basic components as the earth on which we live. And science backs this up.

---

[12] Traditional nursery rhyme.
[13] Gen. 2: 7, KJV.

About 80 per cent of a typical cell in a body is water and the rest is composed of elements such as carbon, hydrogen, nitrogen, calcium, and many others. The repair and maintenance of this incredible machine should merely require the correct application of replacement minerals which are plentiful in the earth. These minerals are so plentiful that is has been calculated that if you wanted to sell your body for its mineral value you would only get about £2.85 ($4.50)[14]—depending on the state of the stock market! But just look at what God made with these common raw materials:

- *The body:* consists of an outer casing made of about 14–18 square feet of skin which is several layers thick and has a variety of functions. First, it holds all the other stuff in: so that our insides are on the inside. It is the first line of defence against injury, it regulates body temperature, and it prevents nasty stuff from getting in—or out!
- *The heart:* is useful not just for falling in love, but also for pumping all the needed chemicals, body-building bits, and oxygen around the body. Amazingly the heart is capable of pumping all the body's blood around the body in just 10 seconds. And it can do this for around 80 years—or more.
- *The brain*: a top-of-the-range personal computer, it can process amazing amounts of information. It's capable of the long-term storage of data: over 100,000 words, 2,000 faces, the shopping list, what the children need to take to school every day, and how to make a roast dinner. The brain is connected to the rest of the body, sending and receiving messages from it, via 150,000 km (93,000 miles) of nerves. That's enough to stretch round the earth nearly four times. With all this complicated computer stuff it's amazing that the men in my life still can't hear anything when the 'game' is on TV.
- *The digestive system*: a long chemical sorting and processing plant built to provide the body with energy and replacement parts. The body will eat for about 3.5 years over the course of a lifetime. And every day this system processes around 10 litres (18 pints) of sloppy, half-digested food.
- *Sensor systems*: so that the human can interact with the rest of God's world: seeing, feeling, smelling, hearing, tasting.
- *Movement*: the body is supported on a frame of 206 bones to stop it flopping about. Over 600 muscles controlled by the central processing unit (brain) send signals via nerves to pull on the bones and create movement. The body can walk miles every day without its feet falling off or wearing out.[15]

And this amazing machine was created with the capacity to live for ever, without growing old or wearing out or needing glasses, hearing aids, and walking sticks. All the stuff needed for its

---

[14] http://www.coolquiz.com/trivia/explain/docs/worth.asp.
[15] Facts taken from Nick Arnold, *Bulging Brains* (Scholastic, 2000).

maintenance and repair was freely available in the environment that it inhabited. 'Placed in a special environment, in a real honest to goodness garden, planted with real honest to goodness trees bearing real honest to goodness edible fruits and edible leaves, he [Man] was so constituted that he could have lived forever.'[16]

Just one bite

The same environment that could have nourished them forever also contained something toxic. Adam and Eve were forbidden to eat from just one tree. But the fruit looked so nice and so juicy that eventually temptation got the better of them. They took a bite.

With just one bite the process of ageing began: they lost their ability to self-repair and to maintain their body's structural integrity. This one bite gave Adam and Eve, and all their descendants, wrinkles. Death had arrived on the scene, waiting as it were in the wings, before taking centre stage. But the ability to live eternally didn't totally evaporate: even then man could still have lived forever.

Then the Lord God said, "See, the man has become like one of us, knowing good and evil; and now, he might reach out his hand and take also from the tree of life, and eat, and live forever"— therefore the Lord God sent him forth from the garden of Eden, to till the ground from which he was taken. He drove out the man; and at the east of the garden of Eden he placed the cherubim, and a sword flaming and turning to guard the way to the tree of life.[17]

The earth still had all the raw materials to allow man physically to live forever because the tree of life had fruit that was capable of undoing the physical damage caused by the toxin. But the damage wasn't just physical. Disobedience had broken their relationship with God and now evil had entered the world. Because of his love, God could not allow man to live forever. Imagine a world like ours, with all its evil, all its corruption, subject to defeat, failure, and broken-heartedness—going on forever and gradually getting worse and worse. God placed an angel to stop us from accessing the one remedy that could sustain life in us permanently. But it was never his plan for us to die: he didn't make us mortal.

The Bible records tell us that Adam and Eve and their children lived for extended lengths of time. Adam lived until he was 930 years and he saw his great-great-great-great-great-great-grandchildren.

---

[16] Arthur C. Custance, *The Seed of the Woman*, available at http://custance.org/Library/SOTW/Index.html.
[17] Gen. 3: 22–4, NRSV.

Sadly, even with a limit on his lifespan, there was still time enough for humanity (now separated from God) to introduce corruption and evil onto the earth. By the time Noah was born 1,036 years after Adam, God's evaluation of the activities of the human race was not good: 'As far as God was concerned, the Earth had become a sewer; there was violence everywhere. God took one look and saw how bad it was, everyone corrupt and corrupting—life itself corrupt to the core.'[18]

And so God destroyed them and their world with a flood. To this day flood stories exist in the folklore of people-groups from every continent around the world. The Bible tells us that God sent this flood because of humanities evil and corruption. But Noah was considered to be righteous so he and his family were chosen to survive. But after the flood God reduced our lifespan even more: '. . . their days shall be one hundred twenty years.'[19]

Since then there have been times and places when people had an expected lifespan of only forty years or less. In medieval Britain the average man's lifespan was 30 years. This is so incredibly short it barely seems worth being born! Nowadays the lifespan for people in the Westernized world is over 80 years. In other parts of the world the average lifespan is still below 40 years but mainly because the high death rate among infants drastically affects the figures. You can imagine though that Adam and his grandchildren would have considered 80-year-olds to be mere teenagers.

Some people do still reach their God-given 120-year lifespan. But they usually live in parts of the earth where the environment and way of life still supports such longevity.

She puts her longevity down to hard work, simple food and clean mountain air. Perhaps it also helps that she prays five times a day. Whatever the secret, Zabani Khakimova was yesterday declared to be the world's oldest living person at 124. According to authorities in her native Chechnya, she remains in good health and continues to do housework and even a little babysitting for her huge extended family.[20]

Even though our average lifespan is now over 80 years it is usually accompanied by considerable loss of function as our knees start to creak, our eyesight fails, and our memory goes.

Dad was bed-bound in the living room for some years prior to his death. Always an active person, he loved gardening and had such green fingers that he could make almost anything grow. If only I could phone him up and ask how to propagate the honeysuckle that we have in

---

[18] Gen. 6: 11, THE MESSAGE.
[19] Gen. 6: 3, NRSV.
[20] *Daily Mail*, Friday, 1 August 2003.

our garden! How often I wish that I could remember some of that wisdom that he had stored up over his 86 full years. He was really frustrated as he watched his body wear out and his abilities become reduced to practically zero. One day when I visited him, he appeared to be looking on the floor for something: 'What are you looking for?' I asked. 'I think I've lost my sense of humour,' he replied, still sharp as a razor.

Our declining health

So why don't we all live, as Zabani has done, into late old age with little loss of function? The truth is that far from our lifespan being extended and our quality of life being improved by the amazing advances in the realm of science and medicine, it looks as though it may be being reduced.

> They were the first to enjoy free healthcare, and had the time of their lives in the Swinging Sixties. But the post-war 'baby boomers' are now paying the price. Today's 60-year-olds are the first modern generation to be less healthy than their immediate predecessors. Despite improvements in medicine and standards of living, they are more likely to be blighted by problems from aching knees and creaking hips to diabetes, asthma, and strokes. Today's 60-year-olds may face more health problems than previous generations despite a lifetime of free healthcare. Even simple tasks such as getting in and out of bed or climbing ten steps without a rest prove a challenge.[21]

And this decline in health is not limited to the baby-boomers. There has been a steady decline in the health of our children over these years. Statistics show us that childhood illnesses are on the increase.

- The International Study of Asthma and Allergies in Childhood surveyed more than 700,000 children in 56 countries since 1991. The latest numbers from ISAAC show a significant worldwide increase in allergy symptoms, particularly among younger children.[22]
- The number of children with autism has risen 12-fold in the past 30 years and may be 50 per cent higher than previously suspected, the most detailed study of the condition yet has found. Up to 250,000 children have autism or a related condition on the autistic spectrum, but have not been diagnosed, researchers say. They are in addition to the 500,000 children who are known to be affected.[23]

---

[21] Fiona Macrae, *Daily Mail*, 14 November 2009.
[22] Article at www.kidswithfoodallergies.org quoting M. I. Asher et al. (2006) 'Worldwide Time Trends in the Prevalence of Symptoms of Asthma, Allergic Rhinoconjunctivitis, and Eczema in Childhood: ISAAC Phases One and Three Repeat Multicountry Cross-sectional Surveys', *The Lancet* 368: 733–43.
[23] Jeremy Laurance, Health Editor ,*The Independent*, 29 May 2009.

- No one knows for sure whether the prevalence of ADHD per se has risen, but it is very clear that the number of children identified with the disorder and who obtain treatment has risen over the past decade.[24]
- In the opening years of the 21st century, there has been an astounding 80 per cent increase in the number of children who are being identified as having a specific disability which hinders learning.[25]
- In the UK, 22 per cent of boys and 28 per cent of girls aged 2–15 were either overweight or obese in 2002, according to Preventing Childhood Obesity, a report from the British Medical Association Board of Science. Doctors are now seeing in children and young people diseases and disorders once found only in the middle-aged and elderly, including Type 2 diabetes, problems with joints and raised blood pressure. Later in life obese children are at increased risk of heart disease and some cancers.[26]
- The number of under-5s in Europe with type 1 diabetes is set to double between 2005 and 2020, say experts. The researchers, from Ireland and Hungary, warn cases in older children will also rise substantially. Writing in *The Lancet*, they say genetics alone cannot account for the rapid rise, and suggest lifestyle factors are likely to play a role. The study is based on 29,311 cases of type 1 diabetes recorded in 20 European countries between 1989 and 2003.[27]
- Suicide is the third leading cause of death for 15–24 year olds (approximately 5,000 young people) and the sixth leading cause of death for 5–15-year-olds. The rate of suicide for 5–24 year olds has nearly tripled since 1960.[28]

As parents we don't want our children to be part of any of these statistics. Two of my children suffered with learning difficulties and I know how difficult and painful this can be both in their time at school and on into further education and work. Even though many people with disabilities are amazingly accomplished we don't want the heartbreak of seeing our children struggle with physical illnesses, emotional and learning disabilities, or mental illness and depressions. So what can we do?

We live at a time when ordinary people have access to more information than at any other time in our history. Because of this we can learn how this amazing piece of biotechnology, the body, works and we can find out how to keep it working. Now we can begin to take responsibility for our own health and well-being and the health and well-being of our children.

---

[24] www.emedicinehealth.com/attention_deficit_hyperactivity_disorder/page6_em.htm.
[25] Anne Keen, UK Health Minister 2001, cited in Christine Macintyre and Pamela Deponio, *Identifying and Supporting Children with Specific Learning Disabilities* (Routledge, 2003).
[26] Celia Hall, Medical Editor , *Daily Telegraph*, 23 June 2005, at www.telegraph.co.uk.
[27] From BBC News, 27 May 2009.
[28] American Academy of Child and Adolescent Psychiatry [AACAP], 1995, at www.nami.org.

The downside of having access to all this information is that it can be difficult to know what the truth is.

Pontius Pilate famously asked Jesus 'What is truth?' There is no recorded answer, but earlier in his life Jesus had announced 'I am the way, the truth, and the life.'[29]

Heresies

What we see Jesus model—how he lived his life, what he said, and what he says to us through the Holy Spirit—can and should guide us in the decisions and choices that we make about our own health and the health of our children.

As a mum I really want my children to be physically well. I want them to be able to run in the garden, to play football, to laugh as they spin round on the rope swing over the stream, to be able to read and write and learn without hindrances, to be free from irritating, debilitating, or life-threatening disorders. I want them to grow up to be whole adults, to form healthy relationships, to provide me with grandchildren, and to be able to follow Jesus passionately. I expect you want this for your children too.

But is that what God wants? What does he say about our bodies? Is he interested in them being healthy and functioning well? Or is he perhaps more interested in our souls and our spirits?

Many ideas that influence attitudes in the Church are little more than thinly disguised heresies. Heresies dressed up in nice Christian clothes, like the Sunday best we wear to church. Wolves in sheep's clothing. As believers our attitude to our bodies is often tainted with these false ideas and ways of behaving. Heresies break God's heart because they take us away from the best that he wants for us.

A heresy is a false teaching that may seem to be Godly, but is not. It may seem to be good but it is not. And like the thin end of a wedge, heresies gradually draw us away from God and his good purposes.

Gnosticism

Gnosticism is one of these. Whilst there are some people today who would describe themselves as Gnostics, the Gnostic belief system is more commonly found within other faiths and belief systems. Gnosticism promotes the idea that our bodies are not important—even evil—and that that they just house the spirit which is the important bit. Like the paper wrappers on fast food,

---

[29] John 14: 6, KJV.

Gnostics believe that our bodies are made only to be ripped off and trashed as soon as possible in order to get at what is really important. Gnosticism can be traced way back to the Garden of Eden when the Devil tempted Eve with the possibility of knowledge that would make her become like God. But it has grown up since that initial lie and can now be found at the root of many of the world's religions. It has also cleverly wrapped itself around the teachings of Christianity. We need to beware of taking on board these Gnostic teachings that do not represent God's heart or plan for us.

At the root of Gnosticism is the belief that the only way to know God is through 'gnosis'—the Greek word for knowledge. This knowledge is secret or hidden and can only be imparted by special people such as mystics, prophets, priests, or teachers. Within the priesthood itself there were even more levels where more knowledge was imparted to the extent that only those at he 'top' would really have a true understanding of 'salvation'.

Gnostics believe that Jesus gave special secret instructions to his closest disciples that were not meant for 'ordinary' believers. However, Jesus taught that salvation was through faith in him, not through some kind of knowledge, not even a special kind of knowledge. Salvation is available to all: 'For God so loved the world that he gave his only Son, so that everyone who believes in him may not perish but may have eternal life.'[30]

These ideas crept into the Church way back in its early days, but they continue to this day. We see them where church leaders and teachers who have studied at college or university or who have built a good reputation and work full-time in the 'profession' are elevated above those who are merely in the 'congregation' as 'pew-fillers'. Thus the traditional Church structure promotes the idea that a believer cannot be an active participant when the church meets, and that he should park his body down on a pew and listen. However, our goal as Christians is not to know *about* God, but to *know* God, to relate to him, and to communicate with him. This should involve our whole body—not just our bottoms! When believers come together for worship we should all have something to contribute: 'When you come together, each one has a hymn, a lesson, a revelation, a tongue, or an interpretation. Let all things be done for building up.'[31] For a Christian knowledge is not the end goal: 'Knowledge puffs up, but love builds up.'[32]

Gnostics also believe that the god who created the world was a god of low order who made a mistake. They believe that this lesser god is responsible for the sorry state of the world we see today and that he is in a constant fight with the supreme god. This is called dualism. Dualism

---

[30] John 3: 16, NRSV.
[31] 1 Cor. 14: 26, NRSV.
[32] 1 Cor. 8: 1, NRSV.

holds the concept that the dark and light are equal and that the fight between them is equal. This is simply not true, as there is only one creator God who far outweighs, and indeed is the creator of, all other forces and powers that would seek to fight against him.

Originating in the Garden of Eden Gnostic ideas promote the idea that we humans are really 'gods'. From this mindset we get our obsession with self. The theory of evolution is at its heart a Gnostic belief system because it promotes the idea of man ascending from chaos to god-hood through self-creation and selection. Man has now come so far in this process that he is able to be a knowledgeable participant and to consciously control and direct his own evolutionary process. The theory of Eugenics[33] was proposed and is still followed by Darwinists who believe that humans can influence their own evolution through selective breeding, genetic enhancement, sterilization, and even the 'eradication' of undesirables.

Science and Technology is seen as some kind of 'super-gnosis' through which we expect to be able to pursue these goals, to control matter, alter physical life, and even discover the secret to eternal life.

These Gnostic ideas are also promoted in popular culture: we are told in the *Matrix* movies that life as we know it is a fantasy, but that through 'enlightenment' our hero can escape this fantasy to become a 'god'.

The ascendancy of self in society does away with all absolute moral codes especially those attributed to an Almighty God and his words to mankind in the Bible. It seeks to replace this absolute moral code with a more fluid, politically correct code of ethics that changes as society changes. Society, culture, and self replace God as the object of worship and it is believed that all problems can be solved by man himself through enlightenment or gnosis.

The undermining of this absolute morality began in the very early days of the Church when the Christian faith was deliberately and wrongly separated from its Jewish roots. The Old Testament and in particular the books of the law were rubbished as Gnostics believed they were written by the lesser god. The Church has also been tainted with this self-obsession as the worship of God is sometimes overshadowed by our own needs and desire for self-gratification.

Gnostics believe that Jesus came in the body but really it was a sort of virtual body or hologram that was not subject to human feelings. They don't believe that Jesus was God in human form and some say that he didn't experience death on the cross but withdrew to his

---

[33] Eugenics: the study of or belief in the possibility of improving the qualities of the human species or a human population, especially by such means as discouraging reproduction by persons having genetic defects or presumed to have inheritable undesirable traits (negative eugenics) or encouraging reproduction by persons presumed to have inheritable desirable traits (positive eugenics). From dictionary .com.

'spiritual body' during the crucifixion. Christians reject this claim, as Jesus being fully human and fully divine is fundamental to Christian belief. The Bible teaches that Jesus' body that died was the same body that emerged alive from the tomb. After he went to heaven his body was changed into a 'glorified body' and he is now present in heaven at the right hand of God: 'the Lord Jesus, after he had spoken to them, was taken up into heaven and sat down at the right hand of God.'[34]

Without his humanity and his body Jesus could not have become the mediator between mankind and God: 'there is also one mediator between God and humankind, Christ Jesus, himself human.'[35]

We are told by the apostle John that one of the tests of a true believer is that they will confess that Jesus was fully human: 'By this you know the Spirit of God: every spirit that confesses that Jesus Christ has come in the flesh is from God.'[36]

Gnostics do not believe in a physical resurrection, but Christians believe that they too will be raised from the dead in their fully human body just as Jesus was. Job, who lived soon after the flood, uttered this famous and prophetic cry: 'For I know that my Redeemer lives, and that at the last he will stand upon the earth; and after my skin has been thus destroyed, then in my flesh I shall see God, whom I shall see on my side, and my eyes shall behold, and not another'[37]

Gnostics see this physical universe as hell and our bodies as the prisons that lock us into a hell of time and space. They seek to free themselves from the bondage of the material world through revelation or 'gnosis' so that they can be transformed and this world can become heaven. As a result Gnostics are hostile to the physical world, to matter and the human body, because they believe them to be evil. Gnostic salvation is only spiritual and does not involve the body or any matter. Their aim is to be reunited with the higher god at death or indeed to become 'god'.

As a result of this dismissal of the body Gnostics fell into two camps. The first were those who tried to disengage from anything earthly by rigorous self-denial, abstinence, isolation, and even the deliberate infliction of pain. There are many religions around the world that use pain in their rituals. The Shia Muslims whip themselves; in the Hindu ritual of Kavadi believers use meat hooks and skewers to pierce themselves; and in some Christian monastic orders self-denial comes in the form of wearing hair shirts and various other kinds of self-harm. These people

---

[34] Mark 16: 19 NRSV.
[35] 1 Tim. 2: 5, NRSV.
[36] 1 John 4: 2, NRSV.
[37] Job 19: 25–7, NRSV.

believe that pain purifies, atones for sin, and cleanses the soul; it is this belief that led parents to sacrifice their children in fire.

At the other extreme were the Gnostics who believed that whatever happened in the physical world was of no consequence and so they felt free to indulge in all kinds of immorality and excess. These people believed that because they had received divine knowledge and were enlightened, it didn't matter how they lived or what happened to the body. To them conduct was only good or evil in the eyes of man and there was no absolute law such as that given by God. Ethical relativism, which is endemic in our society, has its roots in Gnosticism. Ethical relativism is 'the belief that nothing is objectively right or wrong and that the definition of right or wrong depends on the prevailing view of a particular individual, culture, or historical period'.[38]

Both these extremes of Gnostic thought can be seen in the Church. Some believers feel that they must afflict or ignore the body and its needs in order to be truly spiritual, and other believers feel that physical experiences are irrelevant and unimportant so they can do what they like. These attitudes have had a dramatic effect on ordinary Christians, their beliefs, and their experiences. Sickness, disability, loss, emotional distress, and trauma are often seen as ways that God speaks to us, teaches us, guides us and disciplines us. We must 'bear' them, be brave, struggle through, and learn our lessons. Often we must suffer in silence or pretend that we are 'fine', maintaining the plastic smile, while 'God' showers us with random acts of supreme unkindness. Whilst it is true that believers are often persecuted, this does not come from a loving God but is the act of an enemy. The Bible also talks about judgement and discipline from God, but again these are not random but come on us when we have sinned and not lived according to God's plans and standards.

Jesus' example shows us that God wants to heal sicknesses, diseases, and distresses. He said: 'I came that they may have life, and have it abundantly.'[39] He lived his life as an example of this by 'doing good'[40] and demonstrating in his life God's desire to heal our physical and emotional sicknesses.

Because of Gnosticism, Church history is littered with attempts to split the human person into two distinct parts: the body with its needs and desires which is seen as inherently evil, and the soul and in particular the spirit which are seen as being good because they can communicate with God.

---

[38] http://dictionary.reference.com/browse/ethical+relativism.
[39] John 10:10, NRSV.
[40] Acts 10: 38, KJV.

The Early Church spent time trying to eradicate the teachings of Gnosticism, but they remain rife and we have just got used to them.

If we are truly to bring up our children in the way that God wants, then we need to realize that God is not against our bodies or our material needs. He is not waiting for us to die so that he can relate to us—he wants to relate to us now. He does care about what happens to our bodies. He cares if we are happy, he cares if we are sad, and he cares if we are sick or debilitated.

God cares about our bodies

In the Old Testament we can see just how much God cares about our physical well-being. The laws governing health and hygiene demonstrate that God is for us and not against us, and that he is for our bodies and not against them. God's laws place into society the rules and structures to keep us safe, healthy, wealthy, and happy.

> All these blessings shall come upon you and overtake you, if you obey the Lord your God: Blessed shall you be in the city, and blessed shall you be in the field. Blessed shall be the fruit of your womb, the fruit of your ground, and the fruit of your livestock, both the increase of your cattle and the issue of your flock. Blessed shall be your basket and your kneading bowl. Blessed shall you be when you come in, and blessed shall you be when you go out.[41]

Sadly our opinion of God is often that he's a boring old meanie out to spoil our fun. But nothing could be further from the truth.

---

[41] Deut. 28: 1–8, NRSV.

Chapter 2
<u>Jesus' Example</u>

In his life Jesus demonstrated how God wants to be involved with us and how he wants us to live. He said to his disciples: 'Whoever has seen me has seen the Father.'[42] So what can we learn about God from Jesus' life and teachings?

Jesus, it would seem, was a man in robust good health. There is no record of him struggling with illness, disability, or disease. During the course of his public ministry he walked many, many miles. According to Arthur Blessitt (who since 1968 has carried a cross around the world in every nation and is listed in the *Guinness World Records* for the world's longest walk, over 39,060 miles), during the three years of his public ministry Jesus walked 3,125 miles, or 5,029 km.[43] This is not the lifestyle of a sick man. If God didn't want his son to demonstrate a kind of 'how to live despite being ill' message then he does not want that for us either. The only afflictions that Jesus suffered were those that he chose: he fasted for forty days and afterwards he was hungry, and he suffered terribly on the cross when he took our punishment onto himself.

Jesus demonstrated God's desire to heal by healing those who came to him. He also taught and encouraged his disciples to do the same. The Bible records that every time someone asked Jesus for healing they received that healing. Never once did he tell them that their sickness was from God. If there is no sickness in heaven then God couldn't possibly send it onto the earth. The fact that we may well learn important lessons and get closer to God through our sicknesses, disabilities, or setbacks just demonstrates God's amazing ability to turn the Devil's plans upside down. Sickness was never in God's plan for us and in Jesus he showed that he wants to heal. This included healing the daughter of the woman from Syro-Phoenicia, to whom he said he was not called to minister; a soldier's servant who he didn't even visit; a woman who snuck up behind him and just touched his robe; and a man who didn't even ask.

There's no record of Jesus telling anyone to go away and learn some life lessons first. Nor did he require repentance as a prerequisite for healing. There were just no strings attached: healing was freely given to all who asked, no matter who they were or how they asked. It was an act of mercy, not something that could be earned. Not only this, but he positively wanted to heal the sick: 'a leper who came to him and knelt before him, saying, "Lord, if you choose, you

---

[42] John 14: 9, NRSV.
[43] www.blessitt.com.

can make me clean." He stretched out his hand and touched him, saying, "I do choose. Be made clean!" Immediately his leprosy was cleansed.[44]

In this way Jesus demonstrated what God is really like. He healed the sick, he cast out demons, and he raised the dead. He was setting people free from all the rubbish that the Devil had thrown at them. Rubbish that had affected people's bodies making them sick, debilitated, and worn out. His character hasn't changed—he still wants to heal and set people free.

God is for us, and wants us—our physical bodies—to be healthy, whole, and well provided for. In addition to this the Holy Spirit wants to move through us and through our children to touch a desperately needy world with this healing, wholeness, love, and new life. He can only do that through our bodies, and he can do it best if we are in good health. And, as we will see, God provided for our good health when he gave the law to Moses.

Jesus' obedience

Jesus was brought up with his brothers and sisters in a Jewish family in Israel, which was at the time under Roman occupation. Growing up in a tight-knit community, hardworking, and devoutly religious he would have been taught from the Old Testament by both Mary and Joseph and later the local rabbi. At age 10 he would have begun in-depth studies of the Jewish law so that by the age of 12 he would be ready to go through his bar mitzvah, which literally means 'son of the law'. At this point he would be ready to graduate into a life of walking with God.

After his bar mitzvah Jesus would have continued his studies until he was about 18 and at the same time would have been learning his father's trade of carpentry. Jesus learnt the law and could probably quote whole chunks of it off by heart. But he came to establish a new covenant with us based not on adherence to a set of laws but on the sacrifice that he would make.

A covenant (also called a testament) is a legally binding agreement between two people: we would call it a contract. The oldest form of covenant that we engage in today is that of marriage, but credit card agreements, political alliances, joining the golf club, and the 'Last Will and Testament' of a deceased person are all forms of a covenant. The covenant between God and man was set up after Adam sinned so that their relationship could continue. Under the old covenant, in order to continue in relationship with God a person had to keep the law.

The laws that Jesus would have learned and kept can be broadly divided into three main categories.

---

[44] Matt. 8: 2–3, NRSV.

• The Ceremonial Law

Ceremonial laws included rules about how to approach God: the sacrifices that had to be made, feast days, and all other religious duties. Before Jesus came, keeping these laws and duties was the only way to achieve right standing before God. But they were all temporary and prophetic. They pointed to Jesus and in picture language told how God was going to reconcile mankind to himself. Each of the feasts and each of the sacrifices point specifically to what Jesus did for us or what he will do at the close of this age. When Jesus came he kept all these laws and regulations, but in his role as the Lamb of God he became the sacrifice to end all sacrifices. Jesus entirely fulfilled these ceremonial laws, the feasts and the sacrifices, and when we believe in him we too become people who have fulfilled the requirements of these laws. Many people keep the feast days as a celebration of what Jesus did for us. But Jesus completely fulfilled the law, and when he cried out on the cross 'It is finished'[45] he put an end to the need to fulfil this ceremonial part of the law as the only way to achieve right standing with God.

• The Civil Law

These are the laws that governed how people live together in groups, such as villages, cities, and nations. The laws set out in the Old Testament demonstrate a remarkable understanding of how to live together and stay healthy, wealthy, harmonious, and happy. These laws include instructions about health and hygiene. They were way ahead of their time, they were different from the laws of other people-groups from the same era, and they separated the Israelites from other peoples by their practices and their robust health. Ancient peoples of this time had medicines and procedures for treating disease, but the biblical laws focused on preventing disease and promoting health.

Medical historian Ralph Major describes Moses as 'the greatest sanitary engineer that the world has ever seen' because 'Moses recognized the great principle that the prevention of disease is usually simpler and invariably more far reaching than the cure of disease . . . His doctrines [in the book of Leviticus] could be summed up by the objects of sanitation today—pure food, pure water, pure air, pure bodies and pure dwellings.'[46]

These civil laws also include laws about the use and the ownership of land, the lending of money and much more. As Christian believers we are not bound to keep these laws in order to gain or keep salvation, but because they are an expression of God's love for us and of his desire to keep us healthy we should allow them to be written on our hearts. The health of the Israelite

---

[45] John 19: 30, KJV.
[46] Ralph Major, *A History of Medicine* (Thomas, 1954), i. 62–4, quoted at
http://www.tomorrowsworld.org/magazines/2004/mar-apr/bible-health-laws.

people was conditional on these laws being kept at both an individual and a national level. It may well be true that out health depends on them too.

• The Moral Law

The moral law is enshrined in the Ten Commandments,[47] some of which form the basis for the laws of our Western nations.

These commandments often form an anomaly in our belief system. As Christians we believe that we are not bound by the law and so we eat pork, work seven days a week, and overwork our land, all without a qualm, while holding these ten laws to be inviolable and sacred. What a contrary bunch we are.

Because Jesus was a perfect man who had never sinned we know that he kept the whole law continually for thirty-three years. This means that as a human being it is possible to keep the law. However the traditions of the Jewish people had added layers of man-made rules on top of these laws. These extra laws had eclipsed the real heart of the law: to love god and to be just.

Jesus came to simplify the law and to write it on our hearts. Not to make it more complicated. His famous and sublime simplification sums up the whole law as a love command: 'You shall love the Lord your God with all your heart, and with all your soul, and with all your strength, and with all your mind; and your neighbor as yourself.'[48]

This is not one command but three. Three lots of loving: God, myself, and my neighbour—in that order. These three loves sum up all the ceremonial, civil, and moral laws.

Jesus was not bound by these laws but he chose to keep them all. He not only kept them but he used them as weapons in his encounter with Satan.

Jesus was led up by the Spirit into the wilderness to be tempted by the devil. He fasted forty days and forty nights, and afterwards he was famished. The tempter came and said to him, "If you are the Son of God, command these stones to become loaves of bread." But he answered, "It is written, One does not live by bread alone, but by every word that comes from the mouth of God."[49]

In this way he demonstrated that knowledge of the word of God, and the law in particular, are our defence against an enemy who would try to trip us up. If it was good enough for him it

---

[47] Exod. 20: 1–17.
[48] Luke 10: 27, NRSV.
[49] Matt.4: 1–4, NRSV

should be good enough for us. And in fact he actually tells his disciples that the law is still relevant:

> Do not think that I have come to abolish the law or the prophets; I have come not to abolish but to fulfill. For truly I tell you, until heaven and earth pass away, not one letter, not one stroke of a letter, will pass from the law until all is accomplished. Therefore, whoever breaks one of the least of these commandments, and teaches others to do the same, will be called least in the kingdom of heaven; but whoever does them and teaches them will be called great in the kingdom of heaven.[50]

And it will continue to be relevant right on into the millennial age when Jesus reigns on earth.

> In days to come the mountain of the Lord's house shall be established as the highest of the mountains, and shall be raised above the hills; all the nations shall stream to it. Many peoples shall come and say, "Come, let us go up to the mountain of the Lord, to the house of the God of Jacob; that he may teach us his ways and that we may walk in his paths." For out of Zion shall go forth instruction, and the word of the Lord from Jerusalem. He shall judge between the nations, and shall arbitrate for many peoples; they shall beat their swords into plowshares, and their spears into pruning hooks; nation shall not lift up sword against nation, neither shall they learn war any more.[51]

And yet as Christians we often believe that we don't need to follow any of the laws of Moses. For instance, one of the many laws that we don't even consider keeping is the prohibition against eating pork. But did the life and death of Jesus render all pigs and other unclean animals clean? Since that would have required a basic physiological change in these animals it seems unlikely. Although the Apostle Peter had a dream about eating all kinds of unclean foods the interpretation of it was that the good news of Jesus Christ was to be preached to non-Jews. It had nothing to do with eating food considered to be unclean.

If God 'advises' us not to eat certain things then we can be sure that it is still best not to eat them. In fact, the concept of clean and unclean animals was one that Noah understood and so it predates the law given by Moses to the Hebrew people.

Not under the law?

After Jesus' death and resurrection the apostles continued to observe many of the laws of Moses, meeting together on Saturday (the Sabbath),[52] observing the feasts such as the feast of Pentecost,[53] and avoiding unclean foods.[54] So when did all these practices get thrown out?

---

[50] Matt. 5: 17–20 NRSV.
[51] Isa. 2: 1–4, NRSV.
[52] Acts 13: 14

41

The early Christians continued to follow the law regarding clean and unclean foods for at least 200 years. Later, at the time of the council of Nicaea (AD 325) the Church—now the state religion—began to be openly anti-Semitic, distancing itself from the Jewish traditions and feast days. Feast days such as Easter (which is actually the spring festival to Ishtar or Semiramis) were scheduled so that they would hardly ever fall on the same day as Passover, and unclean foods were promoted as part of the Christian diet. In particular the Emperor Constantine, who reputedly had a love of pork, demanded that Christians should now eat it.

But did God's laws ever cease to be good practice? Did they ever stop being guidelines for good health? Should we consider the possibility that following them will be good for us and our children? God said: "If you will listen carefully to the voice of the Lord your God, and do what is right in his sight, and give heed to his commandments and keep all his statutes, I will not bring upon you any of the diseases that I brought upon the Egyptians."[55] The truth of these words was demonstrated during the black plague that swept round the world during the fourteenth century. Because of their hygiene laws the Jewish death rate from the plague was much lower. Sadly this led to persecution and many Jewish towns were burned because people thought the Jews were responsible for the plague.

It was also borne out by the rediscovery of the importance of hygiene in medical practice during the nineteenth century. This 'discovery' has been heralded as one of the greatest of medical breakthroughs. In the late eighteenth century hospitals were seen as places to go to die.

'Though 50 percent of all surgical patients died, both surgeons and society accepted this as being an unpleasant, but unavoidable, side effect. It's hard to imagine the conditions that existed, given today's strict adherence to sterile surgeries. Surgeons actually felt a sense of pride in wearing blood-covered surgical garments, seeing them as a status symbol. The never even considered washing their hands between surgeries, or before examining the next patient.'[56]

But things began to change and Joseph Lister in particular has been credited with that change: 'He also made surgeons wear clean gloves and wash their hands before and after operations with 5% carbolic acid solutions. Instruments were also washed in the same solution and assistants sprayed the solution in the operating theatre. One of his conclusions was to stop using porous natural materials in manufacturing the handles of medical instruments.'[57] When

---

[53] Acts 2: 1
[54] Acts 10: 14
[55] Exod. 15: 26, NRSV.
[56] http://www.scienceheroes.com/index.php?option=com_content&view=article&id=175&Itemid=173
[57] http://www.historicstockmarket.com/market/mobile_product_info.php?cPath=247&products_id=8946

Moses wrote down God's laws he had been first past the post with these same ideas for prevention rather than cure.

What are God's laws?

Jesus was angry with the Jewish leaders who made the law into a nitpicking exercise. He wanted them to see that the spirit of the law was what mattered. That is why he summed up all the law as a love command.

We are now increasingly able to understand the reasons behind many of these laws. In general the civil and moral laws were aimed at preventing bad stuff from getting into us and damaging us, either physically, emotionally, or spiritually. Thus the laws to do with health and hygiene were all about avoiding contact with toxins and pathogens. Toxins can land on us through any of the five senses. Seeing and hearing are the senses that affect our souls and spirits, but the things that we can taste, touch, or smell affect the body. The Law of Moses had something to say about the things we eat, the things we touch, and the things we smell or breathe in.

- ### The things we eat

One of the first recorded laws in the Bible was a food law. Later the law given to Moses was very detailed about what should or should not be eaten. It was also common practice to spend time not eating—fasting—and the health benefits of this cannot be overstated.

> If you want to add serious years to your life, you need to cut serious calories from your diet.
>
> Just how many? Dr. Michael Mosley, a presenter on BBC science show Horizon, says that people should consume as little as 600 calories per day. He'll present his findings next week [5 September 2012] in an episode devoted to fasting and lifespan.
> Why it works 'The bottom line is that it is the only thing that's ever really been shown to prolong life,' Mosley reportedly told *Radio Times*.[58]

Not only has the discipline of fasting mostly disappeared from Christian practice, but we have also thrown out the rule book and now eat many foods that were not considered fit to eat.

- *Types of meat:* Laws that were in operation way before the Law of Moses was written down distinguished between certain types of animals, some of which were clean and some were unclean. Only meat from clean animals was allowed to be eaten.

---

[58] http://articles.nydailynews.com/2012-08-01/news/32986083_1_calorie-restriction-study-claims-high-metabolic-rate.

Unclean animals can very loosely be described as those that consume unclean stuff. Vultures that eat rotting flesh, pigs that are scavengers, and shellfish or bottom-feeding fish that clean the water in seas and rivers, are all on the unclean list. Regarding pigs Dr Mercola has this to say:

> Pork is actually good meat from a biochemical perspective, but I believe there is more than enough scientific evidence to justify the reservations or outright prohibitions in many cultures against consuming it. Pigs are scavenger animals and will eat just about anything. Their appetite for less-than-wholesome foods makes pigs a breeding ground for potentially dangerous infections. Even cooking pork for long periods is not enough to kill many of the retroviruses and other parasites.[59]

But not all unclean animals are scavengers. Animals known for their high parasite infection such as rabbits and horses are also listed as unclean.

- *Blood:* The Bible is very clear about blood. Blood is the life force of the creature or person, and as long as the blood is flowing in their veins they are alive. Thus the soul is seen to be in the blood. The Law of Moses forbade the eating of blood because 'the life is in the blood'. This also has a sound scientific basis. Blood circulates through the body taking good stuff to cells and removing bad stuff. The bad stuff or toxins in the blood hasten the onset of decay in a dead body. If the blood is left in the animal we are more likely to eat meat that is decayed together with the toxic and infected blood. Meat that is slaughtered for consumption by Jews or Muslims is ritually slaughtered according to their laws so that as much blood as possible is drained from the animal. However, approved methods for slaughtering meat in the UK and the USA also involves the bleeding of the animal.

- *Food combinations:* Orthodox Jews do not eat meat and dairy products together. So that rules out cheeseburgers, lasagne, and Cornish pasties. Some go so far in separating their meat from dairy that they have separate kitchens, and separate pots and pans used in their preparation. All this is drawn from the verse in the book of Exodus that says 'You shall not boil a kid in its mother's milk.'[60] It's not known what this verse really means other than not boiling a kid in its own mother's milk so the assumption was made that meat and milk in general should not mix. From a scientific point of view it has been discovered that drinking milk with your meal inhibits the absorption of iron. The Hay Diet[61] also seems to support this view.

---

[59] Mercola, J. "Another Reason to Avoid Eating Pork Products" Retrieved Sep 20, 2013, from http://articles.mercola.com/sites/articles/archive/2002/09/25/pork-part-two.aspx.
[60] Exod. 23: 19, NRSV.
[61] A diet based on the proper combining of different kinds of food.

- *Types of plants:* Before Adam ate the wrong fruit, plants were intended to be the only source of food for man. Back in the Garden of Eden God had said: 'See, I have given you every plant yielding seed that is upon the face of all the earth, and every tree with seed in its fruit; you shall have them for food. And to every beast of the earth, and to every bird of the air, and to everything that creeps on the earth, everything that has the breath of life, I have given every green plant for food.'[62] Adam and Eve were forbidden to eat from the Tree-of-Knowledge-of-Good-and-Evil, because it had toxic properties. These properties were not just physically toxic, but also spiritually and emotionally toxic. Now we live in a world that bears plants: some good for us and some poisonous. The knowledge about which plants are poisonous has been passed down from generation to generation and we avoid them because we know that they will do us harm.

• The things we touch

The hygiene system given by God was written down by Moses, some 3,500 years before the germ concept of disease was even thought about. It is said that the biggest contribution to the health of mankind has been the quite recent discovery of hygiene systems that God had already given so long ago. No wonder King David said, 'Oh, how I love your law! It is my meditation all day long'[63]

It can be seen time and again that when man's laws and practices follow God's laws then there is blessing. Many lives would have been (and could still be) saved if we had read and practised God's laws. These laws have a lot to say about the various things we come into contact with through touch.

- *Human waste:* In Deut. 23: 12–13 God instructed the Israelites to bury human waste away from their living areas. Many diseases are spread through contact with human waste, the plague being one of them. Today cholera, amoebic dysentery, and E. coli enteritis still claim many lives in areas where this practice is not adhered to.
- *Contaminated waste:* Dressings that were contaminated with bodily discharges were to be burnt. Anything touched by an infected person had to be washed.
- *Personal hygiene:* anybody who touched an infected person—or anything that person had touched or sat on—was unclean for a length of time, and had to wash or be washed before touching anyone else (Lev. 15).
- *Hygiene and animals:* Anybody or anything that touched the body of a clean or unclean animal that had died was unclean and had to wash or be washed (Lev. 11).

---

[62] Gen. 1: 29–30, NRSV.
[63] Ps. 119: 97, NRSV.

- *Isolation of sick people:* People with potentially infectious diseases such as leprosy were to be isolated until a diagnosis could be made. If they were infected they had to live outside the camp or city until the infection cleared up. They had to warn people not to come near them by shouting 'Unclean!'
- *Burial:* Those who came into contact with a dead animal or person was unclean and had to wash himself and his garments. Any objects that had come into contact also had to be washed. If someone died in a tent, everyone who came in and everything inside—especially any open pots or jars, were also unclean and had to be washed or destroyed (Num.19: 11, 19, 22, and Lev. 11: 24–8, 40).
- *Drinking water supply:* If a dead animal was found in the water supply the water became unclean and could not be used. However if it was a spring—also called 'Living Water'—then the water could be used, as the water was constantly renewing itself (Lev. 11: 34–6).
- *Sexual hygiene:* The Israelites were forbidden to have any sexual relationships outside of marriage, with any close relative, or with any animal. (Lev. 18: 22, 20: 10–16 and Exod. 20: 14). The husband and wife were to make a closed unit, thus preventing the spread of sexually transmitted diseases (Gen. 1: 27, 2: 23–5; Matt. 19: 3–6).

• The things we smell

Breathing is a jolly useful function. It gets oxygen from the atmosphere around us into our bodies and it gets carbon dioxide—a waste product—out. Once there, it is oxygen that enables the cells in our body to release energy and thus to do what cells do: to keep our heart beating, our brain thinking, our hair growing, and our lungs working so that we can take in more oxygen. Without oxygen nothing works, and within a few minutes we die. So oxygen is pretty essential. But along with oxygen we also breathe in lots of other stuff. Some of this stuff is gaseous and some is made up of solid particles.

This flotsam and jetsam floating in the air can be sucked into our mouths or noses quite unintentionally when we breathe. That's why we have nose hair. Nose hairs are there to trap all that rubbish seeking entry. One thing I have learnt though, that no matter how long or effective these nose hairs they are no defence against Smarties.[64] When Christopher was young he successfully rammed a Smartie up each nostril. There was nothing for it: we just had to wait until they melted. He 'bled' turquoise from one nostril and red from the other for quite some time!

These nose hairs continue down into the lungs where they are called cilia. Here they catch bits of dust and trapped stuff and push them up towards our nose. As 'snot' this can be

---

[64] Multicoloured chocolate sweets.

removed from the body in an interesting variety of ways, your child will soon discover that this is what sleeves are for, his own and yours. Some people say that eating snot is good for you as it helps to boost the immune system. There are all sorts of other ways that the nose and mouth eliminate 'foreign bodies', such as swallowing, coughing, and choking.

But not all substances that accidentally get into our lungs are large or visible. We also breathe in germs, viruses, fungi, and gaseous toxins, all of which have the ability to cause us damage.

I shared a flat with my friend Anastasia. I was always really busy so when I took a bath it was a hurried affair. On a number of occasions I passed out afterwards, but assumed that this was down to the bath being too hot. Anastasia loved to take long, relaxing baths. One night I came home and there were police in the house. Our other flatmate had become concerned because the bathroom was in use for so long. Her long, relaxing bath had taken her on into eternity as carbon monoxide fumes from the boiler overwhelmed her.

Carbon monoxide is one of those invisible toxins that we breathe in. Once in our bodies in sufficient amounts it prevents the blood from being able to carry oxygen around the body. In severe cases death occurs. As I know only too well, in less severe but chronic cases a person can develop headaches, vertigo, flu-like symptoms, depression, memory loss, and confusion.

There are many other toxic gases, often man-made, including those that are used as weapons of mass destruction, and there are also many airborne diseases that we breathe in such as chicken pox, tuberculosis, and the flu.

The book of Leviticus also contains the first recorded instructions for the inspection and removal of mould. Mould can be breathed in causing symptoms that can in extreme cases prove fatal.

A more unlikely end to the Hollywood dream could not seem possible—but this week it was reported that the deaths of actress Brittany Murphy and her British screenwriter husband Simon Monjack might have been caused by mould growing in their luxury Los Angeles home. . . . It may seem extraordinary, but in fact mould in the home is a common health problem, affecting tens of thousands of people in the UK, explains Malcolm Richardson, Professor of medical mycology (the study of mould) at the University of Manchester.
'Britain is especially prone to moulds, due to it being damp and cold so often, and because a lot of the housing is old,' he says. 'Yet compared with countries such as America and Finland, there's not much awareness of mould or the health damage it can cause—it can be fatal.' There are hundreds of thousands of types of mould, he says, but only about ten

types cause health problems, commonly sinusitis, bronchitis and other respiratory conditions, as well as allergies.[65]

The hygiene laws already mentioned also have a direct effect on the prevention of airborne diseases, ensuring that people avoid contact with those diseases.

The use of perfumes and incense was also part of the ceremonial law given to Moses. These substances were burnt to create nice smells in the Temple and as anointing oil for the priests. With all the animal sacrifice that took place in the Temple some form of perfume would have made the whole place more pleasant to be in. But the spices used had benefits that far outweighed their fragrant properties.

Two of theses spices are frankincense and myrrh. Both of these have properties that help kill bacteria and disinfect. They are also natural insecticides and can be used to reduce the spread of airborne infection when people gather together, such as in temples. They help to heal wounds, promote cell renewal, and relieve rheumatism. They can also help with stress and act as an antidepressant. Myrrh is also used to embalm the dead. Modern medicine uses myrrh in mouthwashes and as an antiseptic.

Conclusion

You might ask how we as a family have observed these laws. While our children were young I had very little idea about the importance of what we eat and how it relates to our health. And I certainly had no understanding that the Biblical food laws might be relevant today. It's only more recently as I've struggled to understand health issues within the family that I have begun to understand just how crucial our diet is to our general health and wellbeing. The children were old enough by then to understand these new ideas and to be able to make their own decisions. But it's an ongoing process. Perhaps one of our greatest achievements is that we will all quite happily drink water and some of the children even prefer it to other drinks. Eating pork was never a real issue as I was brought up in a family that ate very little pork so it wasn't something that I ever introduced into family mealtimes. However, we are still in the process of phasing out pork products and if presented with pork when out to dinner we certainly don't throw up our hands in horror and run out screaming.

God promised to write his laws on our hearts and I would suggest that if we try to force ourselves to keep laws for which we have no heart understanding or vision then we may be in danger of becoming legalistic.

---

[65] http://www.dailymail.co.uk/health/article-1297862/Brittany-Murphy-Mould-home-kill-actresss-death-linked-fungus-LA-mansion.html#ixzz1PivhfcT7.

Chapter 3
Healthy Bodies

As we have seen, bodies are an amazing piece of biotechnology, but they are not independent or self-sufficient. Our bodies, our souls, and our spirits all require input from the outside in order to survive. The physical world around us has been set up as a support system to provide humankind with all that it needs to keep the body alive and well. Without these supplies the body will be seriously debilitated or die. Without oxygen we can survive for only a few minutes, without water we can survive for only a few days, and without food we can only survive for around thirty to fifty days.

Oxygen

When we breathe we take in air, which is a mixture of various gases including oxygen. As we have already seen, this oxygen passes from our lungs into the bloodstream and is transported to every cell in our body. Cells need oxygen for all their processes and it is these processes that keep us alive. The brain is the body's biggest consumer requiring about 20 percent of the available oxygen. After only a few minutes of oxygen starvation brain cells begin to die and the brain is irreparably damaged.

The air that we breathe contains about 20 per cent oxygen. In cities where there is high pollution this can reduce to as little as 12 per cent—anything less than 7 per cent is not able to support life. It has been suggested that low oxygen levels may be responsible for conditions ranging from mild fatigue to many of the life-threatening diseases that affect us. Pollution in some cities has caused severe problems not only with toxins but also with reduced oxygen levels: 'In Mexico City, home to 20 million people, the air pollution is so bad that the city has installed oxygen booths in the city centre.'[66] These oxygen booths can also be seen in Japan and India and oxygen bars are also becoming popular in cities around the world.

But lack of oxygen, pollution, and poor air quality are not just the problems of polluted cities, they can be problems in the home too. Moisture, insects, pets, appliances, radon gas, materials used in household products and furnishings, and smoke all reduce the air quality and potentially the oxygen levels in the air we breathe around the home.

Living with lower levels of oxygen is risky for adults, but for developing babies and children it is altogether more serious. Because cells need oxygen to divide and grow, low levels

---

[66] http://www.cpha.ca/en/programs/policy/environ.aspx.

of oxygen can disrupt foetal development especially in the early days and weeks after conception when the cells are dividing rapidly. Damage caused at this time is often not recoverable. Throughout their time in the womb and during their childhood, children, with their needs for growth and continued rapid cell division, are at risk if oxygen is in poor supply.

All of us could no doubt do with a better oxygen supply and this can be obtained in a number of ways:

- *Exercise:* Aerobic exercise such as running, swimming, and cycling, improve the capacity of the lungs. With a bigger capacity more air is taken in and more oxygen becomes available in the bloodstream. Exercise also increases the blood flow to all parts of the body, bringing with it more oxygen for the cells.
- *Music:* Apart from dancing, which can be a form of aerobic exercise, singing and playing a wind instrument such as the trumpet also help to increase the capacity of the lungs.
- *Deep breathing:* We all have the tendency to take fast shallow breaths, especially if we are busy and stressed. When we take shallow breaths we only fill the upper part of our lungs. Breathing deeply allows the whole of our lungs to be filled with air and so we get more oxygen. Deep breathing happens naturally when we take exercise, but for those with mobility problems it can be practised in an armchair.
- *Stop smoking:* Smoke inhibits your body's ability to absorb oxygen; mothers who smoke or who are 'passive smokers' reduce the levels of oxygen available for their unborn child.
- *Outdoor activity:* In places free from pollution being outside increases the availability of oxygen.
- *Opening the windows:* This is not rocket science, if you open all the windows the stale air will go out taking with it all manner of nasties, and clean air will come in. Not refreshing the indoor air often enough means that we keep on re-breathing the same air, which has less and less oxygen. This leads to all sorts of problems such as tiredness, brain fog, headaches, irritability, and so on. We live in a very old house, so although I regularly open all the windows fresh air is constantly leaking in round all the doors and windows. Newer houses that are designed to be well insulated are often less healthy as they trap the unhealthy gases released in our houses.
- *Green plants:* Plants absorb the carbon dioxide that we breathe out and give out the oxygen that we need to breathe in. It is thought that they absorb the harmful EMF[67] emissions from computers, televisions, and other electronic devices, and they are known to remove pollutants from the air.

---

[67] Electric and magnetic fields.

Plants remove toxins from air—up to 87 percent of volatile organic compounds (VOCs) every 24 hours, according to NASA research. VOCs include substances like formaldehyde (present in rugs, vinyl, cigarette smoke and grocery bags), benzene and trichloroethylene (both found in man-made fibers, inks, solvents and paint). Benzene is commonly found in high concentrations in study settings, where books and printed papers abound.

Modern climate-controlled, air-tight buildings trap VOCs inside. The NASA research discovered that plants purify that trapped air by pulling contaminants into soil, where root zone microorganisms convert VOCs into food for the plant.[68]

Water

Your cells are basically little bags of water, and from these cells all of life happens. The average adult is made up of 60 per cent water—or about 40 litres. We lose 3 or 4 litres of this water every day through breathing, pooing, peeing, and sweating. If we don't replenish this lost water the body struggles with overheating, raised heart beat, high blood pressure, cramping muscles, and tissue death in vital organs. Some doctors believe that dehydration is the root cause of chronic pain and many other diseases and that we don't correctly recognise or respond to the body's many signs of dehydration.

> There is no more important substance for good health than water. Your body cries out for it, your blood is made up of it, nerves, heart, lungs, bowels and brain do not function without it, yet we answer the body's thirst signals with tea, coffee, Fanta, Diet Coke, Budweiser and drugs! Hardly any wonder most western nations have a pub/bar culture to deal with the ravening thirst of their citizens. Many illnesses respond well to adequate hydration, according to the experts. Mental performance is enhanced. Limbs operate. Blood thinned. Pain banished. Bowels happy. Skin lustrous and clear. Toxins flushed away. Water, the stuff for life.[69]

Just as the air we breathe can become polluted and full of bad things so the water we drink can become polluted. Whether we take our water from a muddy swamp or a tap, this water may contain:

- Industrial waste from factories such as fuel oils, solvents, and even radioactive waste.
- Agricultural run-off—herbicides, insecticides, and nitrates.
- Chemical compounds from personal hygiene products and medicines such as antibiotics or hormones from oral contraceptives.

---

[68] http://www.bayeradvanced.com/articles/5-benefits-of-houseplants
[69] http://campaignfortruth.com/Eclub/250505/CTM%20-%20which%20water.htm.

- Various kinds of pathogens[70] including sewage-related bacteria.
- Parasitic worms and algae.
- Chemicals added to the water to clean it or to medicate us, such as chlorine and fluoride.

Unless we are able to filter our water adequately or have access to our own spring or clean well water we will be supplying our needs for water and poisoning ourselves at the same time. Whilst those of us who have water literally on tap are affected by pollutants that can cause illnesses such as rashes, earaches, liver and kidney damage, neurological problems, thyroid problems, cancers and more, there are millions who are dying because of the water they must drink to survive.

With so much money being sent to third world countries to provide food, drugs, and contraception it's a crime that there is still such an acute need for safe water sources. 'Globally, almost 1 billion people lack clean drinking water. 2.4 billion people have no access to hygienic sanitation facilities; 1.2 billion lack any sanitation facilities at all. Each day, an average of 5,000 children die due to water and sanitation related diseases, many easily preventable.'[71]

Food

Since our bodies are made from the very substances found in the earth they need these same substances to be constantly supplied as fuel, building blocks, and spare parts. Without them our children's growing bodies may not develop correctly and they may not grow up strong and healthy. Without them parts of our system begin to break down. So how do we access these vital substances?

God has cleverly designed plants and animals to be like living food factories. In order to grow, they draw nutrients out of the soil and process them in such a way that they each provide different but essential substances that we then eat. Eating and absorbing these nutrients maintains our bodies.

Isn't it amazing that cows can turn green grass into white milk, that a carrot pops up out of the earth, or that a tree can draw up nutrients that make an orange full of vitamin C—such a wealth of variety! All these different colours, textures, and tastes provide different but essential nutrients, along with immense variety and pleasure. God did not intend this eating business to be boring! Not only that, but these amazing living food factories also provide us with the raw materials for our clothing, protection from the elements, and endless enjoyment.

---

[70]Disease-causing organisms.

[71]http://www.undp.org/content/undp/en/home/ourwork/environmentandenergy/focus_areas/water_and_ocean_governance/water-supply-and-sanitation.html.

We all need to eat and, crucially, to absorb nutrients in order to be healthy. The food we parents feed our children will affect not only how strong and well they grow, but also their lifelong eating habits,which will affect the quality of their lives right through to old age, and also the health of their future children. So no pressure there then!

Not obtaining any one of the needed nutrients, especially in the early developmental stages of life, may produce symptoms that negatively affect our children's lives. If possible, we need to start thinking about our own health and nutrition way before our children are conceived to give them the best possible chance to grow up strong, whole, and healthy.

Eating for two

When we were thinking about having our first baby I was really worried that pregnancy would leave me fat and blobby. With my skinny jeans in mind I asked my Doctor for exercises that I could do pre-pregnancy so that afterwards my body would 'pop' right back into shape. Well, that didn't happen! Misunderstanding me completely, he put me in touch with a group called 'Foresight'.[72] This turned out to be one of those 'God accidents' and began my interest in the relationship between what we stuff into our mouths and our health.

> Originally founded in 1978, Foresight's programme is based on the premise that most unfavourable outcomes of pregnancy can be avoided if both parents make proper preparation, ideally beginning at least six months prior to a planned conception. Today's world of increasing environmental chemical pollution and commercial food processing, subtle chemical toxicities and nutritional deficiencies places many pregnancies at a disadvantage from their onsets. [73]

As a result of this contact we began to take multivitamin and mineral supplements—and continued this throughout our years of childbearing. Perhaps we should have done more. Looking back, it would have been good to have gone through the full Foresight programme. This analyses the health of both parents, their nutritional deficiencies and toxic overloads, and designs a programme specifically to restore their health to optimum level before conception— because the health of the sperm and the egg are of vital importance to the health of the resultant baby.

> In the past it has been wrongly assumed that the woman is responsible in the majority of infertile couples—yet up to 60 per cent of infertility is actually down to the man. Men also play a large part in causing birth defects—defective sperm may account for as much as 80

---

[72] http://www.foresight-preconception.org.uk.
[73] Ibid.

percent of genetic abnormalities. . . . Given that one in every sixteen babies has some level of defect, and one in six couples fails to conceive at all, it is not only advisable, but essential for you to take some simple steps to make sure you have super healthy sperm able to deliver the goods on time.[74]

Obviously the health of the mother and the egg are equally important:

Making healthy babies is like gardening. The best you can do is get the soil healthy, plant the seed, then feed and water it regularly. As you prepare to conceive, creating that perfect, nourishment-rich, and pollution-free womb is the best birthday present you could ever give your baby to be. The research is clear. A mothers' nutritional status at the time of conception and in the first few weeks that follow, is the single most important determinant of a baby's growth in those critical early stages . . . a mother's deficiency in any essential nutrient can cause birth defects and developmental problems in her growing baby.[75]

The good news is that during pregnancy we should be eating for two—and long before they become a twinkle in their father's eye. But this 'eating for two' should be more about good nutrition than double helpings.

Malnutrition

We've all seen the awful pictures of children and adults suffering from the effects of starvation. Starvation is the end result of extreme malnutrition, brought on by the more or less complete absence of food. This extreme state is usually caused by crop failure which in turn is often contributed to by war, political agendas, and man's inhumanity to man. Starvation is a preventable disaster: 'Somewhere in the world, a child dies of hunger every five seconds—even though the planet has more than enough food for all. UN Secretary-General Ban Ki-moon laid out this sobering statistic as he kicked off a three-day summit on world food security.'[76]

Starvation which occurs when there is not enough food is predominantly a third-world issue. But malnutrition—which happens when a body does not get enough nutrients, is a worldwide phenomenon affecting even the most prosperous of peoples: it is rampant in the Western world. According to experts, 'development has brought about a new global scourge—widespread malnourishment among overweight individuals eating calorie-rich, nutrient-poor diets. In fact, the world's population of 1.2 billion overfed and undernourished individuals now equals those starving from a lack of healthy food.'[77]

---

[74] Patrick Holford and Susannah Lawson, *Optimum Nutrition Before, During and After Pregnancy* (Piatkus, 2009).
[75] Holford and Lawson, *Optimum Nutrition*.
[76] http://www.cnn.com.
[77] http://web.archive.org/web/20080509132615/http://www.naturalhealingtoday.com/articles/global_malnutrition.html

Bodies that are crying out for nutrients display early warning signs in many forms such as: cold hands and feet, cracked fingernails, poor wound healing, obesity, bleeding gums, dry skin, loss of hair, and mental confusion. But the study of nutrition in medical school is woefully inadequate, leaving doctors poorly equipped to get to the root of these signs of deficiency. Instead their studies concentrate on pharmaceutical ways to treat sickness. And so we are prescribed drugs while the underlying causes are often not addressed.

Jesus' ministry displays a different approach, getting to the heart of the matter before addressing the symptoms.

When Jesus saw their faith, he said to the paralytic, "Son, your sins are forgiven." Now some of the scribes were sitting there, questioning in their hearts, "Why does this fellow speak in this way? It is blasphemy! Who can forgive sins but God alone?" At once Jesus perceived in his spirit that they were discussing these questions among themselves; and he said to them, "Why do you raise such questions in your hearts? Which is easier, to say to the paralytic, Your sins are forgiven, or to say, Stand up and take your mat and walk? But so that you may know that the Son of Man has authority on earth to forgive sins"—he said to the paralytic—"I say to you, stand up, take your mat and go to your home." And he stood up, and immediately took the mat and went out before all of them; so that they were all amazed and glorified God, saying, "We have never seen anything like this!"[78]

It is far better to deal with root issues in our lives, whether they are physical, emotional, or spiritual, than to concentrate on symptoms alone.

What we eat and what we don't eat can have a dramatic effect on our health. Lack of nutrients is the root cause of many major diseases from the past that are once again on the increase.

• Scurvy

James Lind, the English physician, discovered that vitamin C deficiency was causing scurvy in sailors. Eventually all British sailors were given a fruit ration—often of limes—from where we get the term 'limeys'.[79] As a result British sailing ships were able to make longer journeys. This contributed to the spread of the British Empire. The symptoms of scurvy are not nice: bleeding gums, loosened teeth, stiff or swollen joints, bleeding under the skin, convulsions, coma, and death. Far from being a thing of the past scurvy is once again on the increase:

Scurvy is making a comeback among England's children. Caused by a lack of vitamin C, the potentially fatal disease was a scourge of pirates and sailors in the heyday of the British

---

[78] Mark 2: 4–12, NRSV.
[79] 'Limey' is a slang word for a British person.

Empire, but was thought to be largely a thing of the past. However, newly released statistics show that the number of children admitted to hospital with scurvy soared by over 50 per cent in the past three years.[80]

More recently Nobel prize-winner Linus D. Pauling, researched the link between heart disease and vitamin C deficiency: 'Pauling believed that the heart dies from a silent form of scurvy. In effect, inadequate levels of vitamin C weaken collagen, which is not good news for coronary arteries as they face the greatest pressure when the heart beats. The end result is injured arteries and heart attack.'[81]

• Pellagra

The disease pellagra, which can produce symptoms like those of schizophrenia, is most commonly caused by a chronic lack of niacin (vitamin B_3) in the diet. It became endemic when people began to eat corn (maize) as part of their diet and also when flour began to be stripped of its nutrients in order to make white flour.

Always being firmly of the opinion that mental illnesses were mainly caused by emotional or spiritual pain and disorder I experienced a major paradigm shift in my thinking when I realized that how we 'feel' and our mental wellbeing can be massively affected by what we eat—or what we don't eat—such as too little of this essential vitamin.

The main symptoms of pellagra can be classified as the 'three Ds:' Dermatitis, Diarrhoea, and Dementia. These can result in a fourth 'D' which is Death.

• Rickets

Rickets, which is known to be caused by a lack of vitamin D, is a softening of bones in children which can lead to fractures and deformity. Once considered a disease of the poor living in the nineteenth century it is now making a comeback. Lack of vitamin D has also been linked to many other diseases from cancer to diabetes. Although vitamin D can—and in some cases should—be taken as a supplement, our main source of vitamin D is the sun. Recent scares regarding the sun and skin cancer have had a devastating effect on our vitamin D levels.

It's a tragedy that dermatologists and sunscreen manufacturers have done such a thorough job of scaring people out of the sun. Their widely dispersed message to avoid the sun as much as possible, combined with an overall cultural trend of spending more time indoors

---

[80] http://www.dailymail.co.uk (7 November 2009).
[81] http://www.canadafreepress.com/index.php/article/371.

during work and leisure time, has greatly contributed to the widespread vitamin D deficiency that's seen today.[82]

People at risk of vitamin D deficiencies are those who live furthest from the equator, who have dark skin, or who rarely go outside. This group includes many Muslim women who wear the hijab or full burqa.

> Muslim women who wear the hijab are at risk of serious illness because they do not get enough sun, doctors have warned. They said an alarming number of women who cover their skin are suffering bone deficiencies over a lack of vitamin D. Most of the body's vitamin D—which prevents rickets—is obtained through sunlight acting on the skin. Only a little comes from food. Doctors told a London conference today that people with dark pigment are at risk because of 'cultural reasons' and because they are less efficient at producing the vitamin. The bone disorder rickets has now broken out in young Muslim children as babies are not getting enough calcium from mothers' breast milk.[83]

• Beriberi

Beriberi is caused by a deficiency of thiamine (vitamin B_1). It affects many systems of the body, including the muscles, heart, nerves, and digestive system. Literally meaning 'I can't, I can't' in Singhalese, this reflects the devastating effect beriberi has on its victims. The symptoms of beriberi are very similar to that of Chronic Fatigue Syndrome. Beriberi is common in parts of South East Asia, where white rice is the main food. Alcoholics also suffer from beriberi because alcohol is known to inhibit the uptake of thiamine.

> Infants who are breastfed by a thiamine-deficient mother usually develop symptoms of deficiency between the second and fourth month of life. They are pale, restless, unable to sleep, prone to diarrhea, and have muscle wasting and edema in their arms and legs. They have a characteristic, sometimes silent, cry and develop heart failure and nerve damage.[84]

With such widespread malnourishment, many people may be silently suffering from the early stages of these diseases or even from the full-blown disease itself. With doctors poorly trained in nutrition, how many of these vitamin-deficient symptoms and diseases go unnoticed, undiagnosed, and unhealed? No wonder we in the West are so unhealthy. Treated with ever-increasing numbers of drugs that only attempt to mask the symptoms of a body crying out for nourishment, we often limp through life desperate for help and answers. We definitely don't want that for our children.

---

[82] Mercola, J. "Vitamin D is a Key Player in Your Overall Health" Retrieved Sep 20, 2013, from
   http://articles.mercola.com/sites/articles/archive/2008/11/01/Vitamin-D-is-a-Key-Player-in-Your-Overall-Health.aspx
[83] http://www.dailymail.co.uk/news/article-469196/Women-hijabs-need-sunlight-risk-illness.html.
[84] http://medical-dictionary.thefreedictionary.com/Thiamine+deficiency.

Food for fuel

As with a motor car, fuel is needed on a regular basis to provide energy for all the body processes, not just for running around but also for breathing, repairing, and thinking. The fuel that this energy comes from takes the form of:

- *Carbohydrates:* These are the providers of energy. They can be sugars such as those in sweets and fizzy drinks or starches such as bread and potatoes that turn into sugars during digestion. These sugars are broken down to release the energy we need.
- *Fats:* These are the richest source of energy and they are also used to store energy—as we know only too well by watching our waistlines. Fats are absolutely vital if we are to absorb many of the nutrients that we need, including vitamins A, D, E, and K and calcium. Fats are also vital for our brains, and many studies demonstrate that increased fat uptake produces increased intelligence. Your baby's brain needs fats to grow and develop and without these fats he may never reach his full potential. Of course not all fats are the same and we need to avoid the man-made trans-fats found in so many processed foods.
- *Proteins:* Proteins are the workers and building blocks in your cells. Your body's need for energy is normally supplied from carbohydrates and fats, but as a last resort it will also get energy from proteins.

When workers began to gather in the new industrial cities of the nineteenth century it was known that they needed fuel in the form of calories, but less was known about the other components of food. As a result food provided for these new industrial workers consisted mainly of cheap energy-giving foods—fat, sugar, and refined flour. They were made into bread, cakes, and biscuits, which are little more than empty calories providing energy and not a lot more. As a result of these empty calories people in the industrial cities became smaller and less healthy as they began to suffer from many vitamin deficiency diseases. It wasn't until the beginning of the twentieth century that 'special factors'—later called vitamins—began to be discovered.

The food industry

Until the 1950s, food was natural, often organic, and generally only eaten at meal times. There were no supermarkets and each shop was specialised: the baker sold the bread, the butcher sold the meat, the dairy sold the butter and milk, and so on. Often these foods were sourced locally. However all that changed and with that change our health and waistlines began to alter.

Now we shop in supermarkets and many of us have no clear idea what meals we are planning. We wander up and down the isles in a trancelike state, grabbing whatever is on offer. We also consume vast quantities of fast food that we eat 'on the hoof'—a concept that would have shocked and horrified our grandparents.

In the UK, during World War Two, the weekly ration for an adult was very limited. And yet we are told that the nation was never healthier. In an experiment where one family went back to a wartime diet, the Daily Mail reported that apart from weight loss there were other benefits:

The first shock was the weekly shop. My supermarket trolley is normally groaning with breakfast cereal, pizzas, pasta and snacks (including eight or nine packets of biscuits) but it now contained porridge oats, cornflakes, wholemeal bread, milk and rather grubby-looking root vegetables.

. . . But I think the real transformation was in the children: they slept better, had more energy and weren't as 'hyper'; there was markedly less fighting and whingeing.

. . . he normally spends a lot of time slumped in front of the TV and is quite lethargic, but he's been extremely active, careering around like a madman, which is totally out of character.

. . . Now that we've gone back to our old food, the tantrums and general irritability levels have started to rise.[85]

The mother in this experiment reported that the only downside was the time spent preparing meals. It was this need for fast food that sparked the food revolution that we have seen over the last fifty years.

In the1950s the American company C. A. Swanson and Sons produced the first ready meal—the 'Swanson's TV Dinner'. '
Gerald E. Thomas had one little idea that changed the sociology of the American family, encouraged the feminist movement, ignited the obesity epidemic and introduced countless Americans to something called Salisbury steak. And all for less than a dollar.

Thomas, who died this week at the age of 83, didn't invent the TV dinner (the U.S. Army and later an airline "food service" company had the same concept before), but he did invent the TV Dinner, C.A. Swanson & Sons' hugely popular meal-ready-to-heat. '[86]

---

[85] http://www.dailymail.co.uk/health/article-465769/Can-modern-family-survive-wartime-rations.html.
[86] http://www.washingtonpost.com/wp-dyn/content/article/2005/07/21/AR2005072102249.html. Paul Farhi

From here there was a veritable revolution not only in the way we ate but also in the appliances we needed to cook and store this food and the way we bought it. The modern kitchen gradually had to have fridges, freezers, and microwaves. Shopping was done at the newly emerging supermarkets and additives and preservatives were increasingly needed to keep the food fresh and tasty. All these inventions spawned even more ready meals and all manner of processed foods. There was money in all these TV Dinners and Fast Foods and the newly emerging global food companies and marketing boards began aggressively to promote their foods and beverages. These companies also began lobbying governments to make sure that legislation did not have an adverse effect on sales of their products. Today they spend millions on this lobbying process.

According to the website 'Open Secrets', millions of dollars were spent on lobbying in the USA: Coca Cola spent $5,890,000, the American Beverage Association spent $950,000, and the Sweetener User Association spent $200,000.[87] Lobbying is also big business in the UK and Europe.

> Food manufacturers have been pouring millions of pounds into a last-ditch attempt to block a European plan to put red warning labels on junk food. In one of the biggest lobbying efforts ever seen in Brussels, lobbyists for Europe's £800m-a-year food industry have been bombarding MEPs with thousands of emails, letters and phone calls and sponsored reports, lectures and conferences ahead of a vote in the European Parliament tomorrow.[88]

This powerful lobbying is considered to be the reason behind the demonization of fats and the over-consumption of sugars:

> But another health issue was on the radar: heart disease, and in the mid-70s, a fierce debate was raging behind the closed doors of academia over what was causing it. An American nutritionist called Ancel Keys blamed fat, while a British researcher at the University of London Professor John Yudkin, blamed sugar. But Yudkin's work was rubbished by what many believe, including Professor Robert Lustig, one of the world's leading endocrinologists, was a concerted campaign to discredit Yudkin. Much of the criticism came from fellow academics, whose research was aligning far more closely with the direction the food industry was intending to take. Yudkin's colleague at the time, Dr Richard Bruckdorfer at UCL says: 'There was a huge lobby from [the food] industry,

Washington Post Staff Writer Friday, July 22, 2005
[87] http://www.opensecrets.org/lobby.
[88] http://www.independent.co.uk/life-style/food-and-drink/news/food-companies-in-massive-lobby-to-block-colourcoded-warnings-2000523.html.

particularly from the sugar industry, and Yudkin complained bitterly that they were subverting some of his ideas.' Yudkin was, Lustig says simply, 'thrown under the bus', because there was a huge financial gain to be made by fingering fat, not sugar, as the culprit of heart disease.

The food industry had its eyes on the creation of a new genre of food, something they knew the public would embrace with huge enthusiasm, believing it to be better for their health – 'low fat'. It promised an immense business opportunity forged from the potential disaster of heart disease. But, says Lustig, there was a problem. 'When you take the fat out of a recipe, food tastes like cardboard, and you need to replace it with something—that something being sugar.'

Overnight, new products arrived on the shelves that seemed too good to be true. Low-fat yoghurts, spreads, even desserts and biscuits. All with the fat taken out, and replaced with sugar. Britain was one of the most enthusiastic adopters of what food writer Gary Taubes, author of *Why We Get Fat*, calls 'the low-fat dogma', with sales rocketing.'[89]

The same article from *The Guardian* newspaper also goes on to say that these sugars are not only bad for us, they also seem to be addictive. And the scientists looking into the obesity epidemic seem to be compromised:

The relationship between the food industry and the scientists conducting research into obesity is also complicated by the issue of funding. There is not a great deal of money set aside for this work and so the food industry has become a vital source of income. But this means that the very same science going into combating obesity could also be used to hone the products that are making us obese. Many of the scientists I spoke to are wary about going on the record because they fear their funding will be taken away if they speak out.[90]

In this way our diets were directed by powerful companies with vested interests. Many of us growing up during the last fifty years have been affected by the advertising and lobbying of men with making money as their only goal. Shunning fats that we desperately need for health we have been force-fed vast quantities of sugar that some people call the 'White Poison' along with a damaging cocktail of chemicals necessary to keep food fresh, tasty, and with a longer shelf life. As a result much of the food that we eat is little more than a chemical soup laced with minute amounts of real food that has often lost many of its vital and life-giving nutrients.

Sadly this also includes the foods and in particular the milk powder that we feed our babies. In an article that gives various recipes for homemade milk formula Dr Mercola also says;

---

[89] http://www.guardian.co.uk/business/2012/jun/11/why-our-food-is-making-us-fat.
[90] Ibid.

For most women, breastfeeding is clearly the best option for optimizing infant health, but if you are unable to breastfeed for any reason, making your own formula is the next best thing. Infant formulas have been found contaminated with all sorts of toxic chemicals. For example, the CDC found perchlorate, a chemical from rocket fuel, in 15 brands of infant formula, including two brands that accounted for 87 percent of the market share in 2000. The top offenders included Similar and Enfamil. Other contaminants discovered in some infant formulas include:

- Melamine (linked to kidney failure)
- Dioxin
- BPA
- AGEs (advanced glycoprotein end products)
- Genetically engineered ingredients

Commercial formulas often also contain extremely high levels of fructose—little better than feeding your baby a can of soda! Soy formulas should be avoided altogether, as they can have devastating health effects. I would add that you must be careful about the water you use to make up any infant formula. Some drinking water has been found to have high manganese, and children exposed to high level of manganese performed worse on cognitive tests than children with lower exposures. And the water you use should NOT be fluoridated.[91]

When preparing baby milk and foods in general it is also important to avoid the use of microwave ovens;

- Some studies show that food loses its nutritional value when micro-waved and can even become harmful as the molecular structure is changed. This seems to apply particularly to proteins.
- Food is heated unevenly and there may be hotspots that will burn your baby's mouth.
- When using plastic containers—especially those not designed for microwave use— toxic plastic molecules can leach into the food.
- Microwave ovens leak dangerous microwave radiation. You should not stand near to your microwave when in use, particularly if you are pregnant.

But food is more than just the stuff we shovel into our mouths to stop that hungry feeling and give us energy. If that were the case we could happily live on the empty energy units provided by a diet of TV dinners, fast food, and takeaways. But food should supply all the necessary

---

[91] http://articles.mercola.com/sites/articles/archive/2010/08/05/which-infant-formulas-contain-secret-toxic-chemicals.aspx

building blocks and raw materials for the endless growing, renewing, repairing, and essential living processes that go on in our bodies.

Food for nourishment

The body is constantly making new bits and transporting spare parts, fuel, waste products, and messages around itself. If the body is to stay healthy it is crucial that these processes are not hindered. Food should come packaged with more than just calories for energy: it should also be full of the building blocks for a healthy life. These building blocks come in the form of vitamins, minerals, and phytochemicals.

• Vitamins

There are thirteen vitamins needed for health but only four are produced in the body. These are Biotin, Vitamin B5 (Pantothenic Acid), Vitamin K, and Vitamin D. The remaining eleven need to be provided in the diet—or as a last resort as a supplement.

Some of these vitamins are water-soluble so they are carried and stored throughout the body by water. These vitamins need to be replaced continually because they are lost when body fluids are lost. Water-soluble vitamins include the B vitamins and vitamin C. Others, such as vitamins A, D, E, and K, are fat-soluble. They are carried by fats in the bloodstream and are stored in the body for longer periods. Deficiency can occur in those on very low-fat diets or with conditions, such as Crohn's disease, that affects their ability to absorb fats.

During pregnancy your baby will develop purely from the nutrients it can absorb. The right vitamins and minerals need to be present for each part of the body-building process. If there is serious deficiency in the required nutrient, a child may be permanently damaged or develop a deficiency disease. For instance it is recommended that the B vitamin folic acid should be taken in supplement form at least one month before conception and during the first trimester of pregnancy because it greatly reduces the risk of spina bifida and other neural tube defects.

Vitamins come packaged in the food that we eat for fuel. Although they are all different the various vitamins work together so that too much or too little of any one vitamin will affect the absorption of all the others. Governments have established recommended daily allowances (RDA) for vitamins and minerals. We often treat these guidelines as if they were a maximum dose that we should take. But actually these allowances are the *minimum* required to prevent disease and we often need more for optimum, or glowing, health. Much research has been done into the effect of vitamins and more is being discovered all the time.

One of the vitamins to come under the spotlight most recently is vitamin D. Vitamin D deficiency is thought to be very common especially for those of us who live further north. The initial symptoms of this deficiency are of general malaise, tiredness, and aches and pains. However the lack of this vitamin is now considered to be a risk factor for more serious diseases such as multiple sclerosis, stroke, heart disease, various psychiatric illnesses, and cancers. Dr Mercola says of vitamin D:

> Vitamin D, a steroid hormone that influences virtually every cell in your body, is one of nature's most potent cancer fighters. . . . I strongly recommend making sure your vitamin D level is 70 to 100ng/ml if you've received a cancer diagnosis. You can achieve this through direct, safe exposure to ultraviolet light, or if this is not possible, by taking an oral vitamin D3 supplement. Vitamin D works synergistically with every cancer treatment I am aware of, without adverse effects.[92]

For more information about the other vitamins and our often chronic deficiencies see page 270.

• Minerals

Vitamins are organic compounds made by plants and animals and they are found in all living things. Minerals, however, are inorganic: they come from elements in the earth and cannot be made by living organisms. Most of the minerals in our diet come directly from plants and water or indirectly from animal sources. The mineral content in our food depends on where it has come from as soil mineral content varies from place to place.

> Think of your body as a house. Vitamins are like tiny little maids and butlers, scurrying about to turn on the lights and make sure that the windows are closed to keep the heat from escaping. Minerals are more sturdy stuff, the mortar and bricks that strengthen the frame of the house and the current that keeps the lights running.[93]

Minerals have four main qualities;

- They are natural and not man-made.
- They are solid.
- They are inorganic: they are not carbon compounds that are found in living things.
- They are crystalline, having a distinct arrangement of atoms.

---

[92] Mercola, J. "This Popular Procedure Tripled the Cancer Risk of 1.65 Million People Last Year " Retrieved Sep 20, 2013, from http://articles.mercola.com/sites/articles/archive/2012/06/13/keep-young-girls-away-from-xrays-as-new-study-shows-them-to-increase-breast-cancer-risk.aspx?e_cid=20120613_DNL_art_1.

[93] From dummies.com at http://www.dummies.com/how-to/content/what-minerals-are-essential-to-a-healthy-diet.html.

There are thousands of different minerals, some with obscure names such as brianite, goslarite, heazlewoodite, and yttrocolumbite. Others have names that we all know as a 'girl's best friend' such as diamond, gold, ruby, and my favourite, aquamarine. There are some that are known to be very toxic to humans such as arsenic, lead, mercury, and uranium. These are becoming increasingly prevalent in our environment and in our consumer products. They accumulate in our bodies and once there they cannot be eliminated and so they are stored in places such as our bones, our hair, and our fatty cells. Accumulations of these toxic minerals have been linked to many illnesses from the seemingly minor feeling of 'brain fog' to various cancers and autism. They cause these serious health problems by interfering with normal biological function and by displacing other necessary minerals.

But minerals are also the building blocks of life that are found in every cell of the body. All the minerals found in the body and needed by the body originally came from the earth in the form of rock. These minerals exist in the earth and, unlike vitamins, cannot be made by living things—plants, animals, and us. However, with the exception of salt, we don't get our minerals by chewing on rocks! Minerals usually need to be processed by a plant in order to become useful to us. Plants absorb minerals from the earth through their roots and are designed to ingest and break them down, thus they are able to make their own food from these raw materials. We, however, as humans, and indeed most animals, are not in general able to make our own food—we have to eat it. Eating plants that have absorbed minerals makes these minerals available to us. A new supply of minerals must be constantly available to build strong bones, transmit nerve signals, maintain a normal heartbeat, and produce hormones. Without minerals we are dead.

Obviously then, the quality of soil on which plants are grown and animals are pastured is absolutely crucial to life. Minerals are constantly being renewed in good soil in which we can grow good, nutritionally rich food. This renewal of minerals in the soil happens when the massive number of living organisms in the soil break down dead organic matter, converting it into forms that can be taken up by plants. They are also renewed when streams and rivers flood, leaving a deposit of new nutrient-rich soil brought down from mountains and hills.

When agro-chemicals such as herbicides for weed control and pesticides for pest control are used, they affect these living organisms. Man in his great wisdom has also created chemical fertilizers that promote healthy growth of plants in soil that is nutritionally depleted. This all sounds great, but the chemicals used in these fertilizers typically only provide nitrogen, phosphorous, and potassium, which promote the growth of healthy plants rather than healthy people. Human beings need many more than three minerals to maintain optimum health. These fertilizers also have other negative side effects:

- They do not include trace minerals and as a result there has been a fall in the mineral content of our foods.
- Chemical fertilizers often contain trace amounts of the toxic minerals arsenic, cadmium, and uranium, which then accumulate in the soil and find their way into the food chain.
- Man-made fertilizers upset the delicate balance of minerals and organisms in humus-rich soil by killing off the beneficial bacteria needed for good soil.
- Chemical fertilizers can saturate plant roots with too much of one nutrient, making it difficult for crops to pick up and absorb the other minerals that they need.
- These chemicals run off the fields into the waterways and on into the sea causing the accelerated growth of algae, disrupting the normal functioning of water ecosystems, killing fish, and creating dead zones in the sea.
- They allow overuse of the land, which becomes increasingly mineral-deficient.

The law given to Moses provided for the soil by requiring that the land should be left uncultivated during every seventh year and every fiftieth year. Yet again we see that the law given to Moses has got the science right. The practice of letting the land lie fallow is one of the best ways of allowing the land to replenish its nutrients, and regain its fertility.

During the last century, over-farming and the use of agricultural chemicals has contributed to massive mineral depletion in our soils and in our crops, as this article in Time magazine reports;

> Thanks to the growing rise of chemical fertilizers and pesticides, modern crops are being harvested faster than ever before. But quick and early harvests mean the produce has less time to absorb nutrients either from synthesis or the soil, and minerals like potassium (the "K" in N-P-K fertilizers) often interfere with a plant's ability to take up nutrients. Monoculture farming practices—another hallmark of the Big Ag industry—have also led to soil-mineral depletion, which, in turn, affects the nutrient content of crops.[94]

Sir Albert Howard, the English botanist and organic farming pioneer said: 'The failure to maintain a healthy agriculture has largely cancelled out all the advantages we have gained from improvements in hygiene, in housing, and medical discoveries.'[95]

Vitamins, which are vital for health, cannot be assimilated without the aid of minerals. Since the body cannot manufacture a single mineral it is vital that the food we eat should regularly provide the essential and trace minerals that we need. Mineral deficiency causes all

---

[94] http://www.time.com/time/health/article/0,8599,1880145,00.html#ixzz2XUOIxbYn
[95] http://www.soilassociation.org/LinkClick.aspx?fileticket=cY8kfP3Q%2BgA%3D&tabid=388.

sorts of health issues such as anaemia—which is a lack of iron—and osteoporosis[96]—which is contributed to by a lack of calcium. We would do well to listen to our bodies when symptoms appear rather than just masking them with drugs and hoping they will disappear. A mild deficiency that displays itself as a minor and irritating symptom may well lead on to a life-threatening disease. This is particularly true for the elderly who are less likely to have a good nutritious diet and often less able to absorb the vitamins and minerals that they do consume. Some of the symptoms that we should pay attention to are:

- Hair loss and dry skin or nails can be a symptom of calcium deficiency.
- Dark circles under the eyes maybe caused by a lack of iron.
- Agitation, anxiety, irritability, nausea and vomiting, abnormal heart rhythms, confusion, muscle spasm and weakness, hyperventilation, insomnia, and poor nail growth can all be symptoms of magnesium deficiency
- Delayed wound healing and acne can be caused by a zinc deficiency.

Nutritional minerals that our bodies need to function, such as iron, zinc, and chromium, can also be toxic if consumed at high levels and we should be careful not to take random handfuls of either vitamins or minerals. The correct balance of nutrition is best achieved through a varied diet of good nutritional food rather than by popping all sorts of pills. And the absorption of minerals when taken in plant form is significantly more efficient than that from taking mineral supplements.

Another very efficient way of absorbing minerals is through the skin, such as in the widely used nicotine patches that help when giving up smoking or oestrogen patches for help with the menopause. These patches are similar to a plaster or band-aid, but they contain extra ingredients to be delivered into the body via the skin. These, either drugs or nutrients, can also be delivered through the skin via creams and sprays. The dose delivered in this way is absorbed straight into the bloodstream and there is evidence to suggest that bypassing the digestive system means that the drug or nutrient is delivered more effectively. Because skin absorbs the substances put on it we should beware of toiletries such as facial creams, make-up, shampoos, and baby lotions and not use any that we would not also be prepared to eat.

Throughout history people have used many different methods to absorb essential and healing nutrients through the skin, such as herbal poultices, therapeutic baths, clay and mud packs, sea swimming, and the wearing of precious metals or gemstones. Gold is thought to have anti-bacterial properties and help transport oxygen molecules into the skin. This helps

---

[96] Osteoporosis is a disease of bones that leads to an increased risk of fracture. In osteoporosis the bone mineral density (BMD) is reduced, bone microarchitecture deteriorates, and the amount and variety of proteins in bone is altered (Wikipedia).

with cell-renewal and is useful in the treatment of ulcers and inflammatory problems of the skin. Silver is a natural antibiotic, which is why gifts of silver were often given to babies specifically for use as teething rings. If you were 'born with a silver spoon in your mouth' you were more likely to survive through to adulthood. Copper bracelets are seen throughout history right up to the present day to help with arthritis and inflammation. Precious stones were also used for healing although in recent times this practice has mingled with new age ideas.

There are two types of mineral needed for nutrition—essential minerals and trace minerals. Trace minerals are not less important than essential minerals, we just need less of them, but they are the very minerals that are so often depleted from the soil by modern farming methods. There are also many other minerals that we may need but on which there has been very little research. It is thought that even some minerals that are known to be toxic, such as aluminium and cadmium, could in some forms or in very minute amounts also be needed for health.

For a more comprehensive look at minerals see page 274.

• Phytochemicals

Phytochemicals, also known as phytonutrients, are the new kid on the block. If you've heard of 'superfoods' then you've heard of phytochemicals. It's thought that they are chemicals that the plant produces to protect itself, but they have been found to have a beneficial effect on humans, helping to protect them against disease. Whilst they are not essential to life it is becoming apparent that they are essential to an increased *quality* of life. Currently there are thought to be in excess of a thousand phytochemicals and research is ongoing. The best known of these are: allicin found in garlic known for its antibacterial properties; lycopene, found in tomatoes, which is linked to the prevention of prostate cancer; and flavonoids, found in green tea, which are reputed to have many health benefits from weight loss to cancer prevention.

This recent understanding about phytochemicals is an example of how much more there is to understand about the amazing health-giving properties in the foods that God has provided for us.

Movement

Adam and Eve were placed in a special garden that God had made, and told to look after it. They weren't given two armchairs and room service. It would great to be a 'fly on the wall' and see what they did all day, but it seems sitting down wasn't a large part of it.

Along with eating the right foods to keep our bodies healthy, exercise also plays a key part. Most of us think that exercise is only for real sporty types and that we can take it or leave it. In some ways that's true. Adam and Eve didn't spend hours in the gym. But a healthy body will be drawn to movement, and an unhealthy body needs to move. As parents, the spare time to go in for any major exercise routine is going to be very hard to find, although we will be running on a treadmill of seemingly endless housework and childcare. Our children, however, are born with the desire to run around and play and we should do all we can to encourage this. When they are at school they will get exercise in the playground and in sports lessons. But when they leave school exercise of any sort can completely disappear from their lifestyle. It's important for them to start enjoying exercise while they are still at school so that there is a chance that they will keep it going after they leave.

Movement is important for all sorts of reasons that have got nothing to do with being an Olympic athlete or losing weight. Exercise is absolutely crucial to health.

- *It strengthens your heart:* Your heart is a muscle and like all muscles it will get bigger and stronger the more you use it. Any activity that gets it pumping harder—such as walking, swimming, dancing, digging, etc.— will make this happen. The stronger and bigger your heart is the slower it has to work to pump the blood around your body, and it pumps more blood around the body with each beat, this places less stress on it so that it lasts longer. The by-product of all this is lower blood pressure.

- *It improves your circulation:* The good stuff carried in the blood such as oxygen, nutrients, hormones, and antibodies, need to be delivered to every part of your body quickly and efficiently in order for it to function well. Blood is also a rubbish collector: it carries carbon dioxide and other waste products to the lungs, kidneys, and digestive system to be removed from the body. Our temperature is also determined by our blood supply. A stronger, more efficient heart obviously helps with this but activity does too. The movement of the muscles by activity or even massage stimulates the circulation of the blood so that it goes to and from the heart more efficiently. There is also a natural pump in the sole of your foot, consisting of a series of large veins called the Venous Plexus. These veins fill with blood, and when we walk, the blood is forced out and up the leg. Without movement the blood is likely to pool in the legs potentially causing swelling of the ankle, poor healing, varicose veins, ulcers, and even gangrene.

- *It boosts oxygen supply:* A healthy living person has healthy, living cells. Without oxygen, cells die. If oxygen-rich blood doesn't circulate as it should parts of the body affected will be unable to function, or in severe cases become gangrenous and die. Lack of oxygen affects the brain, causing a variety of symptoms that could be summed up as 'brain fog' and in extreme cases more severe forms of brain damage. It also causes generalised aches and pains and fatigue, and has been implicated as a cause of many diseases and in the formation of cancer cells. Exercise boosts the circulation and with improved circulation the cells receive more oxygen.

- *It increases energy levels:* The brain in particular thrives on oxygen. With exercise there is a greater blood flow to the brain supplying more oxygen. This results in greater mental alertness and feeling energetic. By exercising you could increase your IQ and—if you encourage your child to exercise—their IQ too. Exercise also causes the increased flow of blood to the capillaries. These are the very smallest of blood vessels that supply every cell in your body. When more of your body is oxygenated you feel more alive and full of energy.

- *It improves muscle tone:* Everyone has muscles. We have over six hundred of them and they cause movement by tightening up and then relaxing. With muscles it really is a case of 'use it or lose it'. We need our muscles for movement—both the kind we think about and the kind that carries on behind the scenes. Loss of muscle can come quite simply by lack of use. The elderly, people who are inactive, the bedridden and even astronauts can all suffer from muscle loss. Loss of muscles means that even simple day-to-day tasks become difficult and stressful. Muscles are particularly useful in pregnancy—after all, you've got to carry all that weight, and at the end of nine months push a baby out! Muscles also carry out the secondary task of helping with blood flow and the movement of lymph around the body.

- *It puts you in a good mood:* Exercise activates the neurotransmitters in our brain. These are used by our nerve cells to communicate with each other. It is thought that having low levels of these neurotransmitters contributes to depression, so by stimulating them our mood can lift. Exercise also stimulates the production of endorphins. These produce feelings of well-being, provide some natural pain relief, and help with relaxation.

- *It keeps you healthy:* Exercise helps with blood circulation and is the only means by which the lymph can circulate around the body. The lymph system delivers nutrients to cells and also has the important task of transporting white blood cells around the body; these are a major component of the immune system, they rush to areas of damage to repair and recycle cells, and they fight off bugs when they try to invade. Lymph also helps remove waste products from the body. The only way that the lymph system can move is by being squeezed by the muscles. Without this squeezing toxins gather at points around the body and white blood cells are not delivered to sites of damage.

If we get the food and exercise right our resistance to disease and ill-health will be greatly enhanced. But health may be about more than just healthy living. Surrounded by chemical toxins of all kinds we also need to avoid these often hazardous substances.

Chapter 4
<u>Unhealthy Bodies</u>

God's plan for man was for a life without death, health without sickness, and energy without weariness. He made man to reflect his glory and his radiance. But all this abundance relied on our continued relationship with God. When it all went wrong God gave us laws to follow. These laws, like the manual for a washing machine, give us guidance to keep our bodies working properly, guidance to promote health, and guidance about what will damage them. In addition to providing our bodies with good healthy nutrients, good healthy fresh air, and good healthy exercise, the laws that God gave tell us that there are things that we should avoid if we want to stay healthy.

Things that can damage us are called toxic or poisonous. A toxic substance is one that damages an organism, that is—your body. All substances—even the good ones—have the possibility of being toxic: even too much water can cause damage and even death. However, the amount of damage these toxins can do depends not only on the 'dose' of the toxin but also on the health of the organism, or body, it is affecting.

Germ theory

Louis Pasteur became famous for discovering the germ theory of disease and inventing pasteurization. Although he was primarily funded by the wine and textile industries he also found cures for chicken pox, cholera, anthrax, and rabies. He contributed to the practice of medicine by discovering that diseases are caused by germs, and that weak forms of a disease can be used as an immunisation agent. Thus he contributed to the development of vaccines. He also introduced the concept of viruses.

However, there are those that say that his work was not only copied but also that his germ theory was wrong. This affects you and me because Pasteur's theory appealed to the money men. Germs made money—they could become the enemy and the enemy could be attacked. Pasteur's germ theory says that specific organisms or germs can invade the body and cause a variety of separate, definable diseases. In order to get well, you need to identify and kill whatever germ made you sick. You do this with drugs, surgery, radiation, and chemotherapy. It is the job of science to discover the right drug, procedure, or vaccine to kill the bug without killing the patient. Often this is a delicate balancing act.

The attack on the 'germ' enemy that was initiated by Louis Pasteur continues to this day. We are taught Louis Pasteur's germ theory at our mother's knee when she tells us 'don't touch that, it's dirty'. We watch the adverts on TV where we see evil germs being 'zapped' by antibacterial products that we must buy in order to keep our children healthy. This germ theory is the foundation on which all allopathic—drug-and surgery-based—medicine rests. The message that germs make us ill has well and truly stuck. But what if this is wrong?

Contemporary with Pasteur were two scientists working in a similar field, Claude Bernard and Antoine Béchamp. Bernard was working on the theory that the body's ability to be healthy or to heal was dependent on its health or 'internal environment'. He believed that disease occurred only when the body's 'internal environment' became favourable for it to flourish. Béchamp, a medical doctor and a university professor with degrees in physics, chemistry, and biology, believed that our bodies are in effect mini-ecosystems or biological terrains in which nutritional status, level of toxicity, and acid/alkaline balance play key roles. Bernard and Béchamp believed that germs do not cause disease but accumulate where disease already exists. Bacteria, germs, fungi, and flies are all are attracted to dead stuff because they are the clean-up guys who get in there to break down dead matter and return it to the earth. Béchamp believed that germs do not attack a healthy body, but they show up to attack a body that is already compromised and diseased. This solves the riddle of why some people 'catch' an illness and others, though exposed to the same 'germs', do not. Because of his discoveries Béchamp argued against vaccines because he believed that 'The most serious disorders may be provoked by the injection of living organisms into the blood.'[97] He believed that disease is created when we are in a state of 'unhealth' and that to prevent disease we have to create health. On the other hand Pasteur believed that disease can strike anybody regardless of their state of health and that disease can only be prevented by building defences. While Béchamp's theories were swept under the carpet, Louis Pasteur went on to have a sparkling, well-funded career upon which our modern Westernized concepts of medicine are founded.

> The germ theory is still believed to be the central cause of disease because around it exists a colossal supportive infrastructure of commercial interests that built multi-billion-dollar industries based upon this theory. To the scientific satisfaction of many in the health field, it has long been disproven as the primary cause of disease. Germs are, rather, an effect of disease.[98]

Pasteur's work and legacy created better sanitation in hospitals and cleaner food via his pasteurisation techniques, thus enabling the sick and healthy alike to avoid contamination with biological toxins. But we should not forget the work of Bernard and Béchamp who brought us their understanding that it is not bugs that cause disease, but the health of the host. They believed that an imbalance in the body can allow bad bacteria to take over, resulting in disease. This imbalance can be caused by a number of different things, including: low immunity,

---

[97] http://thehealthadvantage.com/index.php/Site/BiologicalTerrainVsGermTheory, quote from Ethel D. Hume, *Béchamp or Pasteur? A Lost Chapter in the History of Biology* (CreateSpace, 2011) .
[98] Dr Bernard Jensen and Mark Anderson, *Empty Harvest* (Avery Trade, 1995).

acidity in the body, toxins, damage, and deficiencies in the tissues, stress, anger, and the whole range of negative emotions.

Health laws in the Bible confirm both these approaches: that we should avoid contact with external toxins, and that we should maintain our bodies well with good nutrition, good lifestyle, and good emotions.

Having already looked at ways to keep our bodies healthy we should now consider toxins so that we can work out a strategy to avoid them. Toxins that damage our bodies fall into two main categories: natural toxins and man-made toxins. In turn each of these two categories can be divided into three: physical toxins, biological toxins, and chemical toxins.

Naturally occurring toxins

• Physical toxins

These include things not usually thought of under the heading of 'toxic'. They are toxic in a very loose sense because they cause damage to the body. This damage can be caused by direct blows, concussion, heat and cold, fire, energy waves from natural sources such as sound and vibration, visible and invisible light sources, cosmic rays, radio waves, lightning, and radiation. One of the most common results from these types of toxins is sunburn, which we get from too much exposure to the sun's ultraviolet rays.

• Biological toxins

Naturally occurring biological toxins include poisons from animal sources such as the sting of a bee or the venom from a snake bite, and are usually part of the animal's defence system. We know that we should avoid such animals: it is written into our social code and taught to us from birth.

However, animals can also be toxic because of how they live or what they eat. For instance, shellfish live by filtering huge volumes of water and removing particles from this water: 'One mussel alone can cleanse as much as a gallon of water per hour. Add up the work of a whole mussel community, and you get a virtual water treatment plant.'[99] If we then eat these creatures we will eat the toxins that they have filtered out. The most toxic of these is saxitoxin. When people eat shellfish contaminated with saxitoxin, a deadly syndrome known as paralytic shellfish poisoning results. God's law prohibits eating these kinds of creatures: 'Everything in the waters that does not have fins and scales is detestable to you.'[100]

---

[99] http://newswatch.nationalgeographic.com/2010/03/22/this-world-water-day-a-salute-to-the-unsung-heroes-of-clean-water/
[100] Lev. 11: 12 NRSV.

Moulds and fungi are also sources of biological contamination. Mould and fungal spores are one of the factors that may contribute to what is called 'Sick Building Syndrome'. Sick Building Syndrome can produce ailments such as headaches, nausea, aches and pains, fatigue, loss of concentration, shortness of breath, and skin irritations. They typically affect groups of people who work or live in the same building.

Candida albicans is a fungal condition that can cause major health concerns. It's a naturally occurring fungus that lives in and on each and every one of us. However if we have an impaired immune system, take antibiotics, suffer from stress, or overindulge our love of chocolate (or other carbohydrates) it can begin to take over, growing in all sorts of places where you don't want it. This leads to the itchiness of thrush or athlete's foot or symptoms such as unexplained allergies, chronic inflammation, digestive disorders, loss of energy, and the inability to concentrate.

Human beings also play host to a variety of other parasites, from head lice to all kinds of worms. Parasitic worm infestation is far more common than we would like to think—and not only in children. Parasites are not nice and we don't like to think that we in the West might be playing host to such creatures. But ignorance is not bliss. We pick these critters up from our pets, unwashed fruit and veg and poorly cooked meat, and by drinking contaminated water. They can range in size from microscopic to several metres in length and can live in almost any organ of the body. They live off our food, often leaving us severely depleted and undernourished. Symptoms can range from bloating, itchiness, and allergies to diarrhoea and weight loss. Some believe that cancer and heart disease are linked to parasite infection. There are a number of herbs believed to eliminate worms, including garlic, pumpkin seeds, and black walnuts. Hyssop can also be used to kill and eliminate parasites in the gut. King David mentions hyssop when he is asking God to cleanse him from the inside out: 'Behold, thou desirest truth in the inward parts: and in the hidden part thou shalt make me to know wisdom. Purge me with hyssop, and I shall be clean : wash me, and I shall be whiter than snow.'[101]

• Chemical toxins

God gave all the seed and fruit bearing plants and trees for food. And we also know that the Garden of Eden contained at least one toxic plant because God said to Adam and Eve: 'but of the tree of the knowledge of good and evil you shall not eat, for in the day that you eat of it you shall die.'[102] Adam and Eve's wrong decision upset the balance of the world's ecosystem, thorns and thistles emerged, and predatory plants that we now call weeds took over.

---

[101] Ps. 51: 5–7, KJV.
[102] Gen. 2: 17, NRSV.

Chemical toxins are found in plants such as deadly nightshade, certain fungi, the beautiful laburnum tree, and even potato plants. Often, these toxins form part of a plant's natural defence system, protecting them from other plants or animals that prey on them or compete with them. The knowledge about these poisonous plants used to be passed down from generation to generation, but much of this folklore died out as families have become less connected to the land.

Our environment can also contain chemicals that are toxic to us. Minerals such as arsenic, mercury, lead, and cadmium are toxic in various concentrations to both plants and animals. Where these occur naturally in large concentrations the people living on the land may become sick.

More recently, exposure to arsenic from natural sources in the environment has become a concern. In the early 1990s, an unprecedented arsenic poisoning in Bangladesh brought international attention to the toxic effects of naturally occurring arsenic in drinking water. . . Drinking-water arsenic at these levels is also associated with an increased risk of diabetes mellitis (type 2 or adult-onset diabetes), with damage to heart and blood vessels and, in some areas of the world, a condition called blackfoot disease. This causes the feet or sometimes hands to lose circulation and to turn "black." There is also a strong association between arsenic in drinking water and an increased risk of lung, skin, bladder and other cancers.[103]

Another naturally occurring poison is radon. Radon is prevalent in the UK, and nearly everyone there is exposed to this gas. Radon is:

a naturally occurring radioactive gas caused by tiny particles of uranium present in all rocks, soils, brick and concrete. Radon is a colourless and odourless gas, and therefore not detectable by human senses alone. Radon gas from natural sources can accumulate in buildings, especially in confined areas such as attics and basements. In small amounts, radon gas does not present a significant health risk, however, in higher concentrations there is a significant risk of lung cancer. In the UK between 1000 and 2000 deaths each year are estimated to be caused by exposure to radon. In fact, radon is the second leading cause of lung cancer, after smoking in the UK.[104]

If you live in the UK you might want to check radon levels in your area.[105]

[103] http://www.dartmouth.edu/~toxmetal/arsenic/facts-on-arsenic.html.
[104] http://radonkit.co.uk/blog/uk-radon-maps/.
[105] www.homecheck.co.uk/EnvSummary.do.

Man-made toxins

• Physical toxins

The human race has devised a number of ways to get round the planet as fast as possible. However if you're in the wrong place at the wrong time these forms of transportation can also be lethal. The *Daily Mirror* carried out a survey which included the unlikely statistic that you've more chance of being killed in a plane crash than by a falling coconut. But you're more likely to be killed by that falling coconut than by a runaway rollercoaster. The article also goes on to say that, worldwide, three thousand people are killed in road crashes daily, and that the safest way to travel is by bus—the odds of being killed by a bus are 13 million to one.[106]

Apart from modes of transport, other dangers that we have created for ourselves include falling off things like ladders and high buildings, chainsaw accidents, gunshot wounds, and war. War is one of the most dangerous things on the planet, causing an estimated 160 million[107] deaths during the twentieth century. However our own governments pose our greatest threat as, 'more people have been killed in the 20th century by their own governments than by all wars combined.'[108]

• Biological toxins

The official definition of biological toxins is that they are toxic substances of natural origin produced by an animal, plant, or microbe, and that they are not man-made. But in his 'evolution' towards becoming a god, man has been practising! Even as long ago as the ancient Romans man discovered how to use biological agents as weapons. These weapons release viruses, bacteria, or other germs to cause illness or death. Recent use of such bio-weapons includes:

> The Japanese Military Unit 731 at Ping Fan, Manchuria, experimented extensively with bioweapons, killing thousands of prisoners of war with anthrax, cholera, plague, dysentery and other infectious agents. They also released plague on the Chinese civilian population of Chekiang Province on several occasions by dropping from airplanes laboratory-grown fleas fed on infected rats.[109]

However, advances in molecular biology have unleashed a new threat to mankind, in the form of genetically engineered pathogens. This biotechnology that promised to save lives by the treatment of many human diseases also has the potential for the development of deadly bio-

---

[106] http://www.mirror.co.uk/news/weird-news/scientists-calculate-odd-ways-to-die-282884.
[107] http://www.scaruffi.com/politics/massacre.html.
[108] http://www.developmenteducation.ie/5-50-500/_files/067-murderous-governments.pdf
[109] http://www.americanscientist.org/issues/feature/the-growing-threat-of-biological-weapons/3.

weapons. 'Both bacteria and viruses may now be engineered to be qualitatively different from conventional bioweapon agents. In terms of bioweaponry, this includes imbuing them with such "desirable" attributes as safer handling, increased virulence, improved ability to target the host, greater difficulty of detection and easier distribution.'[110]

• Chemical toxins

All of life is a series of chemical reactions, and we are surrounded by chemicals all day long. These chemicals, whether natural or synthetic, can be either good or bad. Natural chemicals occur naturally, and synthetic chemicals are those that a chemist has created in laboratory conditions. Sometimes these synthetic chemicals are similar to those found in nature and some are not found in nature at all. Many of these totally man-made chemical compounds, such as PBDEs,[111] are toxic:

> PBDEs—are everywhere: in your TV, your computer, your toaster and your sofa. They've been in use since the 1970s. The global demand for PBDEs was 200,000 tons in 2003 alone. But PBDEs don't stay put. Sit down on a foam cushion and you're releasing countless, invisible PBDE particles. When the TV gets hot, still more escape. Scientists find PBDEs in house and office dust. They rinse off our clothes in the laundry and run down the shower drain, winding up in sewage that's applied to farm fields as fertilizer. The flame retardants bioaccumulate, or build up, in fish and cats and orcas and foxes. They also build up in people. We eat PBDEs when they contaminate our food, particularly meat and dairy products. They latch on to dust and other particles, so we breathe them in, or ingest them when dust settles on food or when children stuff their fingers into their mouths. Scientists look for PBDEs in breast milk because the chemicals stick to fat.[112]

In the last century synthetic chemical production increased so much that it has now become virtually impossible to avoid pollution.

> There is not one animal or person on Earth—from a polar bear in the Arctic, a tree-frog in the tropical rainforest, to a newborn child anywhere on this planet—that has not been exposed to a cocktail of man-made chemicals. Almost all of them have been developed over the last several decades: chemicals to control disease, to increase food production, or to simply provide convenience for man's day-to-day living. But ironically, many of these well-intentioned chemicals are now threatening wildlife and people with the very qualities that make them useful: toxicity and stability. Today there is unequivocal evidence that a

---

[110] http://www.americanscientist.org/issues/feature/the-growing-threat-of-biological-weapons/8.
[111] Polybrominated diphenyl ether.
[112] http://www.seattlepi.com/local/309169_pbde28.html.

number of man-made chemicals have already caused serious damage to the health of humans and wildlife all over the globe.[113]

A recent report by the Royal College of Obstetricians and Gynaecologists[114] has highlighted the risks of all this chemical exposure to our unborn babies.

> The mother is the guardian of her baby's development and future health; any external influences on the baby predominantly come from the mother. . . It is being increasingly recognised that predisposition to some adult health disorders is determined by the quality of the baby's development in the womb and soon after birth.
>
> . . . In recent years there has been increasing concern over the potential for exposure of environmental chemicals to the mother and baby to cause adverse health effects in the child. Epidemiological research has linked exposure to some of these chemicals in pregnancy with adverse birth outcomes; pregnancy loss, preterm birth, low birth weight, congenital defects, childhood morbidity, obesity, cognitive dysfunction, impaired immune system development, asthma, early puberty, adult disease and mortality (cardiovascular effects and cancer).

Whilst the report recognises that it is impossible to assess the risk posed by exposure to these chemicals, it does suggest some ways in which we can limit this exposure;

- use fresh food rather than processed foods wherever possible
- reduce use of foods/beverages in cans/plastic containers, including their use for food storage
- minimise the use of personal care products such as moisturisers, cosmetics, shower gels and fragrances
- minimise the purchase of newly produced household furniture, fabrics, non-stick frying pans and cars whilst pregnant/nursing
- avoid the use of garden/household/pet pesticides or fungicides(such as fly sprays or strips, rose sprays, flea powders)
- avoid paint fumes
- only take over-the-counter analgesics or painkillers when necessary
- do not assume safety of products based on the absence of 'harmful' chemicals in their ingredients list, or the tag 'natural'(herbal or otherwise)

All this chemical pollution started when man began to play about with natural substances so that he could make metal and glass, dyes for cloth, fermenting processes, wines and beers,

---

[113] http://www.panda.org/wwf_news/multimedia/photogallery/gallery.cfm?uGalleryID=580.
[114] Report at: http://www.rcog.org.uk/files/rcog-corp/5.6.13ChemicalExposures.pdf

medicines, perfumes and all the consumer items that he increasingly wanted and needed. The act of war was also responsible for great leaps in our understanding of chemicals. Over time these processes were further refined and they were also combined with philosophy and magic. Early 'chemists' wanted to understand life, to change metals into gold, and to find the 'elixir of life'—a potion that would bring eternal life. These alchemists, as they were known (with their procedures, equipment, and their identification and use of different substances), together with the apothecaries (and their use and understanding of medicines), laid the foundation for modern chemistry. As new consumer items were discovered so the chemical industry grew. Today it is a huge global industry responsible for many of the toxic chemicals that are now being dispersed into the environment. Some of these chemicals are naturally occurring, such as sulphur dioxide, hydrocarbons, and metals. However, we also produce and release into the environment large quantities of synthetic chemicals, which include thousands of different pesticides, medicines, and various kinds of industrial chemicals. Man-made chemicals that surround us in our consumer products and our environment are implicated in most of the major illnesses that afflict us in our modern civilized world. These diseases such as cancers, heart disease, diabetes, and allergies do not afflict those who have managed to avoid the onward march of Western civilization.

This onward march of civilization has been fuelled by the huge size of the chemical industries and their aggressive pursuit of new markets for their products.

Chemistry has spawned industries with vast global empires and revenues greater than the GDP[115] of many countries. According to the Forbes 'Rich List', four out of the top five richest companies are global oil businesses with Royal Dutch Shell being at the top which in 2009 had revenues of 458,361 million US dollars.[116] To put this in perspective this is similar to the GDP of Norway which is 24th on the IMF richest countries list with a GDP of 451,830 US dollars.[117]

These huge companies wield tremendous power in our governments. They are one of the main reasons that efforts to find new fuel sources and clean up the old ones have been so unsuccessful. 'Oil and utility companies such as Exxon Mobil Corp. and Southern Co. spent $367 million over the last two years pushing the U.S. Congress to pass energy legislation.'[118]

But their pollution goes beyond the physical: they have also been implicated in wars, human rights violations, and genocide.

---

[115] GDP represents the value of goods and services produced in the country from all sections of the economy; agriculture, manufacturing, energy, construction, the service sector, and government (http://news.bbc.co.uk/1/hi/88618.stm.

[116] http://money.cnn.com/magazines/fortune/global500/2009/full_list/.

[117] http://en.wikipedia.org/wiki/List_of_countries_by_GDP(nominal).

[118] http://www.bloomberg.com/apps/news?pid=10000103&sid=agbeVimf04Ec&refer=us.

Multinational Corporations (MNCs) have played a significant role in some of the most destructive civil wars of the developing world. From Colombia, Sierra Leone, Angola, the Democratic Republic of Congo, Azerbaijan, to Myanmar, MNC engagement has aggravated conflict and fed pervasive corruption through the extraction of lucrative natural resources, such as oil and natural gas, timber, diamonds, and other precious minerals.[119]

And:

Canada's largest oil company, Talisman, is now in court for allegedly aiding Sudan government forces in blowing up a church and killing church leaders, in order to clear the land for pipelines and drilling. Under public pressure in Canada, Talisman has sold its holdings in Sudan. Lundin Oil AB, a Swedish company, withdrew under similar pressure from human rights groups.[120]

But oil companies are not the only polluters. Another major offender is the agrochemical industry. In the second half of the twentieth century this industry grew as farmers and gardeners began to use synthetic fertilisers.

But such benefits haven't come without environmental costs—namely the wholesale pollution of most of our streams, rivers, ponds, lakes and even coastal areas, as these synthetic chemicals run off into the nearby waterways. When the excess nutrients from all the fertilizer we use runs off into our waterways, they cause algae blooms sometimes big enough to make waterways impassable. When the algae die, they sink to the bottom and decompose in a process that removes oxygen from the water. Fish and other aquatic species can't survive in these so-called 'dead zones' and so they die or move on to greener underwater pastures.[121]

Not content with their profits from this new global business, these vast agrochemical companies began to develop biotechnology and in the 1990s the first genetically modified foods appeared.

Genetic modification is a technology which allows scientists to take 'genes' from one organism and put them into another. This changes the way the organism develops, making new types of plants and animals. It is often claimed that genetic modification is just an extension of the plant and animal breeding that has been going on for hundreds of years. This is *not* true. Traditional breeders are restricted by natural barriers that stop unrelated organisms (such as a rat and a cotton plant) from breeding with each other. Genetic modification is

[119] http://www.sudantribune.com/spip.php?article22901.
[120] http://www.commondreams.org/views05/0819-26.htm.
[121] http://www.thegoodhuman.com/2009/07/12/pesticides-fertilizers-herbicides-and-water-pollution/.

entirely different. It allows genes to be crossed between organisms that could never breed naturally. A gene from a fish, for example, has been put into a sweetcorn.[122]

One of the first laws to be seen in Genesis states that vegetation, animals, and man were limited to producing fruit only after their own 'kind'—or species. Genetic modification rides roughshod over this law. It is often claimed (by those involved in GM technology) that genetically modified crops will help with the problem of world hunger. But Friends of the Earth point out: 'There is more than enough food to feed everyone very well at the moment, yet hundreds of millions of people go hungry and nearly two billion are malnourished. The real roots of world hunger are economic and political.'[123] As for whether foods that have been genetically modified are a health risk, nobody really knows. This new technology has been the subject of hardly any long-term testing. Early signs point to an increased chance of allergies and the potential for resistance to antibiotics. It is possible that GM crops could adversely affect other plants and animals such as bees, which in turn would catastrophically affect the food chain and our health.

So why bother with GM foods when we already have enough food? The fact is that the mega companies involved in this research know that they cannot make a penny out of ordinary crops, but the technology involved in the creation of GM crops can be patented. Indeed the very elements of life—the genes—can now be patented. These greedy companies want to control the world's food supply. Is it possible that they also want to control the peoples of the world, who will have to beg at their door for bread?

Genetic modification of food crops is coming under the control of big companies that started out selling chemicals. Companies such as Monsanto are buying up genetic modification companies, seed suppliers and grain merchants. They use patent laws to 'own' every GM plant grown from their seed. Some companies even produce contracts for farmers which force them to pay a 'technology' fee, require the farmer to use the company's own chemicals, prevent them from saving seed and even allow the company to inspect the farm. Tight controls like these enable the companies to make profits all along the food chain.

Genetic engineers have recently found a way to stop seed saved from one harvest from growing the next year. This 'terminator technology' directly threatens the ancient farming practice of saving a part of the harvest to grow as next year's crop. Over 1 billion of the world's poorest people rely on farm-saved seed for their food. Terminator seeds would end this practice. This will reduce the self-reliance of farmers and force them to spend money each year on new seeds from the genetic modification companies. As this process goes on,

---

[122] http://www.foe.co.uk/resource/briefings/gm_crops_animal_feed.html.
[123] Friends of the Earth briefing on GM food: www.foe.co.uk/resource/briefings/gm_food.html.

farmers will have less say over what they grow and consumers will have less power to choose what they want to eat.[124]

This is theft on a grand scale. A new kind of theft with a new word specially coined for it— Biopiracy: "'Biopiracy' is the term used to describe the patenting of genes, by private companies, that were originally selected for by indigenous people, using traditional breeding methods. Many developing countries regard this as the theft of their genetic resources, and biopiracy has become an extremely contentious issue in recent years. Greenpeace has accused DuPont of using 'tricky patents' (i.e. passing off items as their 'inventions' when they quite clearly aren't) in an attempt to gain control over the most important food crops.'[125]

These chemical industries have produced three ugly sisters: the petrochemical industry, the agrochemical industry, and perhaps the biggest of the three, the pharmaceutical industry.

Medicines

Medicines have been with us for as long as illness has. Early man used sophisticated forms of diagnosis and plants for healing, as seen in the mummified remains of a man who lived 5,300 years ago. This man, who was found in the Italian Alps, was carrying a dried fungus that he would have used as medicine for his parasitic state. 'This discovery ranks as the world's oldest documented example of the practice of medicine, and it suggests that prehistoric humanity was more medically sophisticated than previously believed. After all, the Iceman or someone else had diagnosed his malady correctly and had recommended a reasonably appropriate treatment—an herbal treatment—around 3300 BC' [126]

Since very early in human history, people relied on medicinal plants to cure them of their illnesses. Some of the better-known healing plants are:

* *Aloe*: Aloe has been used for thousands of years, there are pictures of aloes on Egyptian temples, and the Greek physician Dioscorides wrote of its benefits to heal wounds and treat haemorrhoids. It is useful for all skin wounds including acne, sunburn, and insect stings. Taken orally, aloe also appears to work on heartburn, arthritis and rheumatism pain, asthma, intestinal worms, indigestion, stomach ulcers, colitis, haemorrhoids, liver problems such as cirrhosis and hepatitis, kidney infections, urinary tract infections, prostate problems, and as a general detoxifier. Studies have shown that it has an effect on lowering blood sugar levels in diabetics. 'In 1994, the US Food and Drug Administration approved Aloe Vera for the treatment of HIV. Ongoing studies

---

[124] ibid.
[125] Dupont: Corporate crimes http://www.corporatewatch.org/?lid=173
[126] http://www.enotalone.com/article/9469.html.

worldwide show that Aloe taken in highly concentrated doses can stimulate the production of white blood cells that may help fight viruses and also tumours.'[127]

- *Echinacea:* 'The purple coneflower is the best known and researched herb for stimulating the immune system. Thousands of Europeans and Americans use Echinacea preparations against colds and flu, minor infections, and a host of other major and minor ailments. This Native American herb has an impressive record of laboratory and clinical research. Thousands of doctors currently use Echinacea for treating infectious diseases.' [128]

- *St John's Wort:* 'is one of the most frequently used treatments for mild-to-moderate depression in Germany, and it seems destined to become just as popular in the US. The plant has also generated intense scientific interest because of its potential as an antiviral agent.'[129]

- *Garlic:* 'Perhaps the world's best example of a medicinal food, garlic is one of the most intensively studied herbs in natural medicine today. An impressive collection of results from both clinical and laboratory studies point out the protective value of garlic against the leading diseases of the modern world, including heart disease, cancer, and infectious diseases. While it is still unclear exactly how garlic works, researchers agree that few herbs—or foods—fit so well into an overall strategy for health promotion.'[130]

Hippocrates—known as the father of modern medicine—was right when he said; 'Let food be thy medicine and medicine be thy food.'

During the nineteenth century chemists began to look at these healing herbs and isolate the chemicals that made them work. Hippocrates had left records of pain relief treatments, including the use of powder made from the bark and leaves of the willow tree to help heal headaches, pains, and fevers. In 1828, Johann Buchner, professor of pharmacy at the University of Munich, isolated crystals from the willow bark which he called salicin. It was the German company Bayer who went on to patent the substance called aspirin, which is a combination of this salicin and other chemicals that make it less rough on the stomach.

Whilst herbs can be dangerous if used incorrectly (for instance aspirin and willow bark should not be used by children under sixteen) they generally have fewer side effects and have been tested over thousands of years as to their effectiveness. In addition to this, the mix of ingredients in each herb may balance each other, buffer each other, and act together to make it work better than an isolated chemical. For instance, natural willow bark contains large

---

[127] http://www.herbwisdom.com/herb-aloe-vera.html.
[128] http://www.herbs.org/greenpapers/echinacea.html.
[129] http://www.herbs.org/greenpapers/stjohnswort.htm.
[130] http://www.herbs.org/greenpapers/garlic.htm.

amounts of tannin known to protect the stomach. It also has antioxidant, fever-reducing, antiseptic, and immune-boosting properties. But pharmaceutical companies cannot patent plants or herbs.

So what happened to modern medicine, how did it stray so far from its herbal roots? Perhaps the story begins with John D. Rockefeller whose father was a travelling medicine man selling cures for cancer. But his cure called 'Nujol' was nothing more than crude oil in a bottle. John D. Rockefeller owned the standard oil company, which by aggressive dealings went onto become the largest oil company in America. A subsidiary of Standard Oil reinvented Nujol, marketing it as a laxative. This brought in breathtaking profits, and so began John D. Rockefeller's interest in the drugs industry. In 1913 John D. Rockefeller set up the Rockefeller Foundation.

At the same time Andrew Carnegie, who had amassed a fortune from the coal industry, was struggling with the problem of his increasing bi-products. His breathtakingly simple answer was to use these bi-products to create a range of medicines—much like Rockefellers' Nujol—and turn his waste into profit. In order to increase these profits he set up the Carnegie foundation.

Both of these seemingly charitable foundations were set up to provide huge amounts of funding for selected good works and education. These included the organizing and funding of medical schools across America and later in many countries around the world. These medical schools only received funding if they taught and emphasized the 'allopathic'[131] way of treating disease. Pasteur's Germ Theory fitted well with this new drug-based medicine and so the myth was born that the only way to deal with all the bad germs was to find new wonder drugs to kill them. It was a marriage made in Wall Street. This marriage was further confirmed by the discovery in the 1930s—by the British scientist Dr Alexander Fleming—of penicillin. This brought more credibility to allopathic medicine than probably anything else in its history. Penicillin was truly a wonder drug able to control infections that had caused millions of deaths down through the ages.

And so penicillin began to work miracles in the lives of ordinary people. However the bacteria that penicillin kills are cunning little monsters and they are able to mutate so that eventually the penicillin does not work. Just a few decades later the true legacy of this wonder drug is making itself heard:

When the first antibiotics were introduced in the 1940s, they were hailed as 'wonder drugs', the miracles of modern medicine. And rightly so. Widespread infections that killed

---

[131] Allopathic medicine is a system in which symptoms and diseases are treated using drugs, radiation, or surgery.

many millions of people every year could now be cured. Major diseases, like syphilis, gonorrhoea, leprosy, and tuberculosis, lost much of their sting. The risk of death from something so common as strep throat or a child's scratched knee virtually vanished. . . . The emergence and spread of drug-resistant pathogens has accelerated. More and more essential medicines are failing. The therapeutic arsenal is shrinking. The speed with which these drugs are being lost far outpaces the development of replacement drugs. In fact, the R&D [research and development] pipeline for new antimicrobials has practically run dry. The implications are equally clear. In the absence of urgent corrective and protective actions, the world is heading towards a post-antibiotic era, in which many common infections will no longer have a cure and, once again, kill unabated.[132]

Rockefeller, who by now also controlled many newspapers, pursued an aggressive campaign promoting the idea that illnesses could only be treated by the use of drugs and that any non-drug cure was the result of quackery. That aggressive campaigning still takes place and ever more ailments are being 'discovered' for which drugs can be prescribed. 'Disease mongering is the selling of sickness that widens the boundaries of illness in order to grow markets for those who sell and deliver treatments. It is a process that turns healthy people into patients, causes iatrogenic [illness caused by medical treatment] harm, and wastes precious resources.'[133]

Despite the failure of many drugs to deliver much more than debilitating side-effects, laws were passed in both the USA and the UK outlawing various herbs, remedies, and practices that claim to bring effective healing without the use of conventional drugs. It is now against the law in the USA and the UK to advertise any natural or herbal cure for cancer and many of these natural therapies have been removed from sale or outlawed. 'A self-proclaimed healer is being prosecuted over testimonials on his website claiming he can cure cancer. . . . But he is being taken to court by trading standards officers under the Cancer Act of 1939, which bans advertising offers to treat cancer and carries the threat of a three-month jail sentence.'[134]

We have also recently seen the appearance of the EU food directive that seeks to ban many health foods, vitamins, minerals, and other health products. This law seeks to ban supplements that have been widely available for centuries with no side-effects. It is the result of energetic lobbying by the big pharmaceutical companies who want to take over the alternative health industry or see it sidelined and eliminated.

---

[132] Statement by WHO Director-General, Dr Margaret Chan, 6 April 2011, http://www.who.int/mediacentre/news/statements/2011/whd_20110407/en/.
[133] http://www.plosmedicine.org/article/info%3Adoi%2F10.1371%2Fjournal.pmed.0050106.
[134] http://www.dailymail.co.uk/news/article-1254389/Distance-healer-faces-court-internet-claim-hes-miracle-worker-cure-cancer.html.

The Alliance of Natural Health (ANH) is set to legally challenge the contentious EU Directive on Food Supplements (FSD). The FSD passed into European law in July 2002 and effectively brings about a ban on 300 nutrients included in 5000 health products, most of which are in dietary supplements closest to food forms. In July this year, the House of Commons Standing Committee for FSD Regulations met and voted the Food Supplement Directive through into English, Scottish and Welsh law. Dr Robert Verkerk, executive director of London-based ANH hopes a successful challenge would result in the FSD being overturned by all EU states.

Two Labour MPs have voiced concerns about the way the Regulations were voted through by the Standing Committee. Kate Hoey MP (Vauxhall) revealed what happened: 'I was a member of this committee until I said, very honestly, that I would vote against the regulations.' She was, together with five other MPs, 'unceremoniously removed' from the committee the night before the vote took place and replaced with MPs who voted in favour of the FSD. According to Kate Hoey, this gives a clear message that the government cares more for the pharmaceutical industry that it does about ordinary people. Her views are shared by Jeremy Corbyn MP (Islington); he said: 'The FSD is a product of ruthless lobbying tactics by the pharmaceutical industry which is not keen on the diversity of supply of vitamin supplements available in health food shops.' He backs the ANH move to legally challenge the Directive.

Legal challenges are seldom made to the 40 000 EU Directives implemented since the UK joined the Common Market in 1972, ostensibly to share in the Common Agricultural Policy (CAP). But Conservative MP Daniel Hannan complained to the Daily Telegraph last September 3, that, 'whenever you see an apparently insane Brussels Directive, someone, somewhere stands to gain.' And in his view, the Directives affecting natural remedies resulted because of lobbying by the large pharmaceutical companies.[135]

The imminent implementation of this directive could have a negative effect on the health of many in the Western world who are lacking in essential nutrients, and could be classified as malnourished.

Despite being a deeply religious man, John D. Rockefeller was heavily involved in the eugenics[136] movement and a Nazi sympathizer. In 1939 the Rockefeller empire formed an alliance with I. G. Farben of Germany. This alliance was known as the Drug Trust. I. G. Farben were the patent holders for Zyklon B, the gas used in the extermination camps during World War Two, and the camp at Auschwitz was owned and managed by I. G. Farben as an industrial complex run by prisoners. Funded from America, they also used prisoners as guinea

---

[135] http://www.i-sis.org.uk/vitamins2.php.
[136] Eugenics is the study of methods to improve the human race by controlling reproduction.

pigs for experimental medications and vaccinations. 'The factory of death in Auschwitz—largely financed by the world's largest drug companies at that time—was the cradle for the multibillion dollar market of toxic "chemo" drugs promoted by the very same companies to tens of millions of cancer and AIDS patients.'[137]

Currently the Rockefeller's interest in the drugs business is huge: 'The Rockefellers own the largest drug manufacturing combine in the world, and use all of their other interests to bring pressure to continue and increase the sale of drugs. The fact that most of the 12,000 separate drug items on the market are harmful is of no concern to the Drug Trust.'[138]

But their interests do not stop there. Nominally distributed among various family members, trustees who act for the family and trust funds, the Rockefellers control many of the largest companies in the world. This family fortune is controlled from a central family headquarters on the 56th floor of 30 Rockefeller Plaza, New York City.[139] The value of these holdings disclosed at a hearing in congress in 1974 was even then estimated at 70 billion. The Rockefeller family is known to have total or partial control of the Exxon, Esso and Mobil oil companies, Pfizer, Bayer and Eli Lilly pharmaceutical companies, along with General Motors, General Electric, Chrysler, RCA, Eastman Kodak, Honeywell, Colgate-Palmolive, Hewlett Packard, JP Morgan Chase bank, Prudential, American Express, and Citibank. They also exercise control over much of the media. According to John Francis Hylan mayor of New York City from 1918 to 1925; 'These international bankers and Rockefeller-Standard Oil interests control the majority of the newspapers and magazines in this country. They use the columns of these papers to club into submission or drive out of office public officials who refuse to do the bidding of the powerful corrupt cliques which compose the invisible government.'[140]

But the highest money-earning companies in the Rockefeller portfolio are the pharmaceutical companies.

Although the pharmaceutical industry claims to be a high-risk business, year after year drug companies enjoy higher profits than any other industry. In 2002, for example, the top 10 drug companies in the United States had a median profit margin of 17%, compared with only 3.1% for all the other industries on the Fortune 500 list. Indeed, subtracting losses from gains, those 10 companies made more in profits that year than the other 490

[137] http://www4.dr-rath-foundation.org/THE_FOUNDATION/rolduc_09arp04.html.
[138] Morris A Bealle, *The Drug Story* (Columbia Publishing, 1949). Online at http://www.whale.to/a/bealle.htm.
[139] http://socrates.berkeley.edu/~schwrtz/Rockefeller.html, transcript from hearings in congress, November 1974.
[140] http://www.economania.co.uk/quotes.htm

companies put together. Pfizer, the world's number-one drug company, had a profit margin of 26% of sales.[141]

You would expect that companies who derive their wealth from our illnesses would be on our side and that they would want to make us healthy—but do they? These companies with enormous profits at stake are not known for their altruism. It seems that they are driven only by the need to create more profits for their shareholders. All the research they do and all the products they market are aimed at this one thing—more profit.

> There was a time not long ago when the corporate giants that PhRMA represents were merely the size of nations. Now, after a frenzied two-year period of pharmaceutical mega-mergers, they are behemoths which outweigh entire continents.
>
> The combined worth of the world's top five drug companies is twice the combined GDP of all sub-Saharan Africa and their influence on the rules of world trade is many times stronger because they can bring their wealth to bear directly on the levers of western power. [142]

Despite the squeaky clean image that they like to put over, the products that the pharmaceutical industry markets are more about profit than they are about caring for people. The profits of these huge drug companies may well be tied into increasing your ill health rather than in promoting your good health. For instance, huge amounts of money are raised every year—much of it through charity donations—in the attempt to find a cure for cancer. So why hasn't the cure for cancer been found? And why are the only 'cures' being investigated drug-based cures? A key to this mystery may lie in the fact that if a cure were found all those cancer organisations would cease to have a purpose, huge numbers of people would be out of work, and drug company profits would plummet.

---

[141] Article on the Canadian Medical Association website, www.cmaj.ca/content/171/12/1451.full.
[142] Article in the Guardian: Industry that stalks the US corridors of power:
http://www.guardian.co.uk/world/2001/feb/13/usa.julianborger

Chapter 5
The Pharmaceutical Industry

The claim of the drug companies is that their drugs will do 'wonders for us', making us healthy, happy, fulfilled, and prosperous. The Eli Lilly website states: 'Lilly makes medicines that help people live longer, healthier, more active lives.'[143] The claim made by Bayer is equally lovely: 'Our aim is to discover and manufacture innovative products that will improve human and animal health worldwide. Our products enhance well-being and quality of life by diagnosing, preventing and treating disease.'[144] GlaxoSmithKline have an all-embracing tag line obviously dreamed up by a very highly paid advertising agency: 'We are dedicated to improving the quality of human life by enabling people to do more, feel better, and live longer'.[145]

So are these claims true? How many of our friends who seem to be healthy take prescription drugs to produce or enhance that health? We are taking more drugs than ever and yet according to Dr Mercola we are getting sicker.

The average American, aged 19 to 64, now takes close to 12 prescription drugs every year! The average senior typically fills over 31 prescriptions every year, and even children, between the ages of 0–18, are taking an average of close to 4 prescriptions annually. But with all of these drugs, Americans are not walking around with stellar health. Instead, chronic disease rates are rising and the latest study published in Health Affairs revealed that the United States now ranks 49th for male and female life expectancy worldwide, a ranking that has *fallen* sharply from fifth place in 1950. At the same time that life expectancy has been declining at faster rates than many other industrialized nations, per capita health spending has been on the rise.[146]

The evidence all around us, and seen in our friends and relatives, seems to point to a conclusion rather different to the rosy view put out by the slick advertising of the pharmaceutical companies. The evidence suggests that our quality of life reduces as we take more pharmaceutical drugs.

---

[143] http://www.lilly.com/about/Pages/about.aspx.
[144] http://www.bayerhealthcare.com/scripts/pages/en/company/corporate_profile/index.php.
[145] http://www.gsk.com/.
[146] Mercola, J. "More Drugs Do Not Mean Better Care" Retrieved Sep 20, 2013, from
   http://articles.mercola.com/sites/articles/archive/2010/12/11/more-drugs-do-not-mean-better-care.aspx.

What are pharmaceutical drugs?

Drugs are developed to target one particular symptom—such as high cholesterol—which may only be a small part of a bigger health picture. If clinical trials demonstrate that the isolated symptom can be altered for the better, then the drug is deemed to be safe and effective and will go on sale. Drug companies invest vast sums of money in these clinical trials and there are many documented cases of falsified outcomes. 'A prominent Massachusetts anaesthesiologist allegedly fabricated 21 medical studies that claimed to show benefits from painkillers like Vioxx and Celebrex, according to the hospital where he worked.'[147]

There is also an alarming new trend for the pharmaceutical companies to outsource their clinical trials to poor regions around the world which may render the reliance on these trials even more unjustified. 'Prescription drugs kill some 200,000 Americans every year. Will that number go up, now that most clinical trials are conducted overseas—on sick Russians, homeless Poles, and slum-dwelling Chinese—in places where regulation is virtually nonexistent, the F.D.A. doesn't reach, and "mistakes" can end up in pauper's graves?'[148]

Drugs do alter symptoms, often positively, but all drugs have other effects—side-effects. In clinical trials if these side-effects are deemed to be worse or more life-threatening than the symptom being targeted then the drug will not be licensed. But not all side-effects are discovered in clinical trials and not all side-effects are considered to be a problem.

For instance, statins are prescribed to lower cholesterol which is thought to contribute to heart disease. They do lower cholesterol, but at the same time compromise the ability of the liver to create *all* types of cholesterol, including the 'good' cholesterol and important hormones that the body manufactures from cholesterol. Statins may work to lower cholesterol but they also alter the body's healthy physiology in many other ways.

One in three people over the age of 45 in the UK currently takes statins—that's a staggering 7 million people. It costs the National Health Service £450 million per year to fulfill these prescriptions . . . which goes straight into the pockets of the drug companies and their consultants in the medical establishment.
But all these people—and you may be one of them—are putting themselves at risk. Pharmaceutical companies also don't want you to know that statins seriously deplete your body of Coenzyme-Q10 (CoQ10)—the vital heart nutrient that naturally <u>PREVENTS</u> heart attacks and strokes.

---

[147] *Wall Street Journal*, http://online.wsj.com/article/SB123672510903888207.html.
[148] Donald L. Barlett and James B. Steele, 'Deadly Medicine', *Vanity Fair*,
http://www.vanityfair.com/politics/features/2011/01/deadly-medicine-201101

CoQ10 stops cholesterol from blocking arteries, it helps lower blood pressure and rejuvenates heart cells . . . Yet statins destroy this essential 'life spark' . . . diminishing it to such an extent that it reaches dangerously low levels. This increases your risk of serious side-effects like muscle wastage and pain, confusion, forgetfulness, disorientation, fatigue, liver damage, migraines, nausea and diarrhoea, to name but a few . . . One simply needs to look at all the known side-effects of statins to realise that any possible benefit from taking these drugs comes at a massive price to your health.[149]

And evidence points to the fact that using one drug quite easily leads to needing another:

[S]tatins are now being pushed onto perfectly healthy people who have cholesterol levels of 115, for example. They're supposed to start taking statins as a preventative measure, even though there's nothing wrong with them. With a similar lack of wisdom, the American Diabetes Association has recommended that all diabetics start taking statin drugs *even though there is no scientifically proven benefit to doing so* just in case some benefits are someday discovered!

And statin drugs are already known to cause an alarming number of dangerous side effects. After being consumed for just a few days, statin drugs start interfering with normal liver function. Within a matter of weeks or months, the patient often shows new symptoms or disorders. Upon visiting a western medical doctor, they are diagnosed with another disease or condition and—guess what?—given another prescription drug to take in combination with the statins. In the business world, this is called 'upselling the customer'—getting the same customers to buy more stuff, thereby greatly increasing your profit margin.

And so it goes: one prescription after another, like boxcars on a train, until the patient is: 1) financially depleted, and 2) suffering the ravages of extreme chemical toxicity from prescription drugs. By the time a typical patient finally dies from complications caused by the prescription drugs, they may have spent $100,000 or more on drugs alone. And that number can be multiplied even further if 'heroic drugs' are prescribed during the patient's last surviving days.[150]

It's a fact that as we get older we will typically take more and more drugs, but these drugs are rarely tested together, and even more rarely tested in older people who have an altered physiology and reduced ability to eliminate toxins. Taking a cocktail of drugs can lead to multiple side-effects that together may reduce your quality of life and quite often your length of life.

---

[149] http://www.thecholesteroltruth.com/pages/about-the-cholesterol-truth?gclid=CPmHv7z__qsCFUtB4Qod31B1kQ.
[150] http://www.naturalnews.com/001352.html.

While drugs can be useful in the short term, to consider taking them in the long term without looking to some more natural and holistic cure could be very short-sighted. I have seen time and again amongst my friends, work colleagues, and acquaintances the utter reliance that we have on health professionals, conferring on them almost godlike status and never questioning their pronouncements and cures. It seems to me that we should not hand over responsibility for our own health so easily.

Before we reach old age, and certainly before our children reach old age, we should be investing our time, our intellect, and our faith into a healthy living lifestyle that emphasises prevention and does not always seek the quick fix of prescription drugs.

The desire to solve problems by taking drugs is a product of our culture, perpetuated by everyone, from drug manufacturers, to doctors, to government health officials, to you. When you teach your child that the appropriate response to pain or discomfort is to take a pill, the obvious result is that he will seek comfort by taking drugs when faced with the challenges of adolescence and, later, as an adult.[151]

Another side-effect of taking pharmaceutical drugs is that of acid build-up. Just as our bodies have a small temperature range in which they function best, research also shows that the body has a right ph level at which it functions best. 'Ph' is a unit of measurement of the acidity or alkalinity of liquid: pure water is said to be neutral, with a ph close to 7.0; solutions with a ph less than 7.0 are said to be acidic; and solutions with a ph greater than 7 are alkaline. Healthy cells in the body have a ph level that is slightly alkaline—just over 7.3. When the body becomes too acidic it cannot heal itself efficiently or neutralize waste products and flush them out. Acids are created when we make energy or renew our cells—which is all the time. When our body is acidic, it creates a welcoming environment for viruses and bacteria to come in and begin to flourish. As a result we experience lack of energy, frequent illnesses, and pains. This is the perfect terrain for chronic, degenerative, and auto-immune symptoms, including cancer, high cholesterol, high blood pressure, and heart disease. Ageing occurs because of acidic build-up caused by the foods we eat, the toxic burden of heavy metals, environmental pollution, food additives, chemicals, bacteria, viruses, plastics, and pesticides. Stresses and negative emotions are also known to create biological responses that make us more acidic.

Instead of bringing healing the drugs we take may be making us ill. And according to Patrick Holford: 'Many common medicines are also anti-nutrients.' By this he means that: 'they stop nutrients being absorbed and used, or promote their excretion'.[152]

---

[151] Mercola, J. "More Drugs Do Not Mean Better Care" Retrieved Sep 20, 2013, from
   http://articles.mercola.com/sites/articles/archive/2010/12/11/more-drugs-do-not-mean-better-care.aspx.
[152] Patrick Holford, *The Optimum Nutrition Bible* (Piatkus, 2004).

For more information about drugs and their various side-effects the website at www.drugwatch.com gives masses of information.

We hope that our children will not need to take many or any prescription drugs but one area of the pharmaceutical industry that will affect them is vaccination.

Vaccination

Vaccination is just one of those things that we do. We are born, we are vaccinated, we go to school, we go to college and possibly university, we get a job, we get a car, we buy a house, we find a partner or spouse, we have babies and we vaccinate them. It's a no-brainer.

I felt very uneasy about having my babies vaccinated but I still did it. We have been taught from the cradle that vaccination is not only good for us but it is also the saviour of mankind, the best thing since sliced bread, the sacred cow.

And so I went through these processes and when it came time to vaccinate my babies I squashed all feelings of doubt and submitted them up to this rite of passage. But was that inner feeling of doubt the voice of the Holy Spirit trying to shout through the pressures that would ensure I took part in this ritual?

The pressures and wisdom of society so often crowd out the voice of the Holy Spirit, but as Christians we must make our decisions based on what he says and not on what we are pressurised into believing. We are called to be a group of people who are different, set apart, and holy.

Given my time again I would definitely delay the vaccination schedule for my babies and probably abandon it altogether. The more I learn about this procedure the more I am concerned about the side effects and question the benefits.

History of vaccination

Vaccination is no new science. It has been with us ever since man first observed that people who had recovered from a major infectious disease never caught it again. This gave rise to various localised attempts to prevent disease by infecting a healthy person with a mild form of the disease so that they would not get the full-blown version. Earliest accounts say that the practice of inoculation started in India around 1500 BC or possibly even earlier.

The Chinese also practised inoculation: they would take the scab from an infected person, grind it up and sniff it through the nose.

This practice of curing a disease with its own products (isopathy—which is similar to the theory of 'like cures like' that is the basis of homeopathy) officially reached the West in the

1500s when Paracelsus, genius of the Renaissance, studied the secret teachings of ancient folklore, sympathy healing, and magic dating back to the Druids and seers of ancient Britain and Germany. Through his studies of these ancient healing arts he introduced the idea of vaccination to the West.

One of his sources may have been Turkey. It was in Turkey that a woman received a vision from the 'Virgin Mary' outlining inoculation as a method for the prevention of smallpox. The practise of making a cross-shaped cut and applying smallpox pus or scabs into it spread across Turkey, and was brought to the UK by the wife of the British Ambassador, Lady Mary Wortley Montagu.

A young Edward Jenner was inoculated in this way, and while he didn't get smallpox he never really regained his health.[153] He later studied medicine, and became particularly fascinated with smallpox. On realizing that milkmaids who caught cowpox never caught smallpox he began his experimenting. His first subject was the son of a local farmer. James Phipps was infected with cowpox, and later, on recovery, was reinfected with smallpox, which he did not catch. Jenner reinfected the boy several times. Phipps died from tuberculosis at the age of 20; Jenner vaccinated his own son and he too died of tuberculosis at the age of 21.

Although initially the medical professions were sceptical of this new vaccination with cowpox, it was soon widely accepted. In 1840 older forms of inoculation with smallpox were outlawed and in 1853 Jenner's 'vaccination' became compulsory. Riots began immediately as some people believed that vaccination caused smallpox. In 1869 William Johnson of Leicester became the first person to be imprisoned for two weeks because of his refusal to allow his child to be vaccinated. Eventually in 1898 a conscience clause was added to the act.

Vaccination continues to create controversy although the medical profession and of the course the pharmaceutical companies are very keen to defend it.

Does vaccination work?

In May 1980, after an intense eradication programme that included the use of vaccination, the Thirty-Third World Health Assembly declared that smallpox had been eradicated globally. But was it Edward Jenner's vaccination that saved the world?

Initially the vaccination was dirty and unsafe and often the person being vaccinated also received doses of other infections, such as syphilis which was spread through Europe by vaccination. Even the use of safer, cleaner vaccines did not halt the problems with various side-effects being reported, the most serious of these being encephalitis. Evidence began to mount

---

[153] http://www.jenner.ac.uk/edwardjenner.

that far from eradicating smallpox the epidemics had increased dramatically after 1854, the year that vaccination was made compulsory. Before compulsory vaccination the incidence of smallpox had been declining, possibly due to better sanitation and nutrition. However, even though 97 per cent of the population were vaccinated, there was a smallpox epidemic in London between 1857 and 1859. This accounted for more than 14,000 deaths. There was a similar outbreak between 1863 and 1865 accounting for 20,000 deaths. Between 1871 and 1873 the whole of Europe was swept by the worst smallpox epidemic in recorded history. People began to wonder if in fact the smallpox vaccination had caused these outbreaks. As other countries introduced compulsory vaccination they too saw an increase in deaths from smallpox.

> In the Philippines, prior to U.S. takeover in 1905, case mortality from smallpox was about 10%. In 1905, following the commencement of systematic vaccination enforced by the U.S. government, an epidemic occurred where the case mortality ranged from 25% to 50% in different parts of the islands. In 1918–1919 with over 95 percent of the population vaccinated, the worst epidemic in the Philippines' history occurred resulting in a case mortality of 65 percent. The highest percentage occurred in the capital, Manila, the most thoroughly vaccinated place. The lowest percentage occurred in Mindanao, the least vaccinated place, owing to religious prejudices.[154]

The last and ultimately successful attempt to eradicate smallpox was found to be more effective when mass vaccination was not practised, but containment and isolation were used as the primary ways to treat an outbreak. And it seems that smallpox was on the wane anyway.

> Variola had already stopped infecting people in more than 8 out of 10 countries throughout the world when WHO launched a worldwide vaccination campaign against smallpox in 1967.(25) At that time, only 131,000 cases were reported.(26) Yet, authorities credit their global initiative with eliminating the disease. Some medical historians question the validity of this claim. Scarlet fever and the plague also infected millions of people. Vaccines were never developed for these diseases yet they disappeared as well.[155]

But smallpox is not a vaccination your child will be offered. He will though be offered many, many more. In some European countries and in the USA vaccination is mandatory for children entering school. Parents not wanting to vaccinate their children often come under the harsh spotlight of the welfare agencies, and usually have to home-school their children.

---

[154] http://www.naturodoc.com/library/public_health/truth_re_smallpox_vaccine.htm.
[155] http://thinktwice.com/smallpox.htm

The present generation of children is the most vaccinated in human history. Both the number of vaccines and their combinations have increased considerably from those given to their parents and grandparents. These vaccinations are not small local affairs, but part of a one-size-fits-all global campaign. Not only are there more actual visits to the doctor, but more of the vaccinations involve the use of combination vaccines, such as the 5-in-1 single jab. If he has only a mild reaction to these jabs your baby will be ill for a number of weeks throughout his first year.

According to the NHS[156] your child will be vaccinated against five diseases during his first year: at 2, 3, and 4 months. At 12 months he will be given more boosters for the same diseases along with his first MMR shot. At just over 3 years he will receive his next MMR together with diphtheria, tetanus, pertussis (whooping cough), and polio (DtaP/IPV), given as a 4-in-1 pre-school booster. Girls of around 12 years will then receive the cervical cancer (HPV) vaccine, and at 13–18 years they will all have the diphtheria, tetanus, and polio booster (Td/IPV), given as a single jab. In addition to these you can opt for more, such as the chickenpox and the BCG (tuberculosis) vaccination, both of which are offered to babies and children considered to be in high-risk groups.

The smallpox vaccination seems to have been vastly overrated, but what of these newer vaccines?

As a mother who has for nine months nurtured this precious human being in your womb, trying to eat all the right things, avoiding alcohol, smoke, fumes, and other toxins, you are now told that he must be injected with an array of different viruses and bacteria all washed down with a cocktail of chemicals that are supposed to protect him and ensure his health. By the time he is 13 months old he will have been exposed to an increasing number of different vaccines and many different lethal diseases. But are the vaccines safe?

How do vaccinations affect us?

Vaccination is based on the correct observation that when a person recovers from a disease he or she then usually become immune to that disease for life. Not so long ago it was common for mothers to hold chickenpox 'parties' so that their children could catch chickenpox and get it over and done with while they were young when the disease would be less serious. Vaccination is considered to be very similar, but is it?

The science behind the concept of vaccination says that if your child is exposed to a weakened version of the disease he will develop antibodies and become immune. It is believed

[156] http://www.nhs.uk/Planners/vaccinations/Pages/Vaccinationchecklist.aspx.

that this will work in the same way that catching the disease does. But a little knowledge can be a very dangerous thing.

When a person catches a disease those 'bugs' have often had to fight their way through the body's multilayered defence system consisting of the skin, mucus in the nose and throat, nasal hairs, saliva, the actions of the spleen and the digestive system, the thymus gland, the tonsils, and the operation of the pituitary gland that directs all these systems. When any of these functions in the body encounter disease it triggers the body's natural response, which is to produce extra antibodies, so that when the disease begins to take hold the white blood cells are all ready to do their job of neutralising the infection. Vaccination bypasses all these functions by injecting foreign matter directly into the blood stream. Some children seem to be particularly at risk from this process. According to the Vaccine Risk Awareness website:

Injection of vaccine via this unnatural route can use up 70% of the immune system's resources, instead of the usual 3 to 4% with a wild occurring disease (according to Cynthia Cournoyer, 'What About Immunizations?', Dennis Nelson Publishers, 1991).

Because the body has no extra antibodies waiting to counter the vaccine, it can go into overdrive in an attempt to deal with the situation, taking much-needed vitamins away from bones and other organs, to use for the production of more antibodies. This means that the other vital systems go short on vitamins, in extreme cases leading to bone fractures caused by the immune response leaching vitamins to cope with the vaccine. This lack of vitamins can also cause bruising and retinal bleeding and haemorrhaging, which is why some vaccine-damaged babies have been falsely labelled as 'shaken baby syndrome' cases. These type of vaccine injuries are similar to those caused by trauma.

The massive surge of antibodies created by the vaccine can also cause the body to become hypersensitive and this is responsible for the increase in allergies and auto-immune diseases. Allergies are an over-exposure to toxic elements that the body is unable to cleanse itself of.

If the adrenals, which include the pancreas, the pituitary gland and the spleen, become over-stimulated, for instance by vaccination, this can cause the body to become toxic and unable to regulate itself. This has been linked to heart disease, diabetes, asthma and bronchitis, to name a few. Over-stimulating the adrenals also causes a decrease in circulation of blood round the body, and atrophying of vascular vessels.

. . . In the time immediately following vaccination, when extra vitamins are being used up to fight the vaccine, this may actually make the person more susceptible to the disease. For instance, in the Merck, Sharp and Dohme LTD product information for HIB vaccine, it states: 'Cases of Haemophilus B disease may occur in the weeks after vaccination', and in Lederle Hibtiter information sheet, 'Cases of HIB disease, although rare, may occur after vaccination.' This is known as 'provocation disease', i.e. disease caused by vaccine.

. . . Large numbers of chronic diseases have evolved in the place of infectious disease since the introduction of mass vaccination, including ME, Lupus, Guillain-Barre Syndrome,

Autism (previously known as Kanner Syndrome, discovered by Dr. Kanner in the 1940's), MS, Ebola virus, AIDS, Lichen Planus, Vulvodynia and other hypersensitivity conditions, not to mention the rife and uncontrollable rates of cancer, heart disease, asthma, eczema and other allergies. Even meningitis was extremely rare before the 20th century.[157]

Herd immunity

One of the aims of vaccination is to create 'herd immunity':

> Herd immunity theory proposes that, in contagious diseases that are transmitted from individual to individual, chains of infection are likely to be disrupted when large numbers of a population are immune or less susceptible to the disease. The greater the proportion of individuals who are resistant, the smaller the probability that a susceptible individual will come into contact with an infectious individual.[158]

The term 'herd immunity' was first coined in 1933 by a researcher looking at patterns of measles outbreaks in the USA between 1900 and 1931—before the measles vaccine was created. He observed that when 68 per cent of children had a naturally acquired immunity to measles then there were no epidemics. This phrase and the theory behind it was borrowed by the vaccine promoters to encourage uptake of vaccination based on the idea that if a large number of people were vaccinated then a 'firebreak' would be created and that this would prevent, or slow down, the spread of the disease. There are some problems with this:

- Vaccination-acquired immunity does not last for very long, and the age at which epidemics of the disease are likely is thus raised to an age at which it will be more severe. Vaccination creates a population vulnerable to epidemics at a later stage in life. According to Barbara Loe Fisher, co-founder and president of the National Vaccine Information Center:

> The vaccinologists have adopted this idea of vaccine induced herd immunity. The problem with it is that all vaccines only confer temporary protection . . . Pertussis vaccine is one the best examples . . . Pertussis vaccines have been used for about 50 to 60 years, and the organism has started to evolve to become vaccine resistant. I think this is not something that's really understood generally by the public: Vaccines do not confer the same type of immunity that natural exposure to the disease does.[159]

---

[157] http://www.vaccineriskawareness.com/Your-Immune-System-How-It-Works-And-How-Vaccines-Damage-It.
[158] http://en.wikipedia.org/wiki/Herd_immunity.
[159] Mercola, J. "Mounting Evidence Shows Many Vaccines are Ineffective and Contribute to Rise of Outbreaks Caused by Mutated Viruses" Retrieved Sep 20, 2013, from http://articles.mercola.com/sites/articles/archive/2012/07/30/whooping-cough-vaccine.aspx?e_cid=20120805_SNLNew_MS_1.

- Vaccinated people are just as likely to develop the disease they have been vaccinated for. According to Dr Mercola:

  > Of the children who contracted chickenpox in an outbreak in Maryland in 2001, 75 percent of the affected had been vaccinated against the disease. Similarly, last year the US experienced the largest outbreak of mumps since 2006. More than 1,000 people in New Jersey and New York fell ill, yet 77 percent of those sickened were vaccinated against mumps.[160]

- It has been said that those who are unvaccinated pose a risk to society. However, far from catching a disease from the 'unvaccinated' you are actually much more likely to catch it from the recently vaccinated. Recently vaccinated people carry the disease and are capable of passing it on to others.

  > Some vaccines are live and can shed in the child's urine, excrement and saliva. Vaccine viruses can end up in our water supply by entering the sewage system and infect unvaccinated children, as reported in the 'diseases in the vaccinated' pages and http://www.vaccineriskawareness.com/Vaccine-Shedding. Killed virus vaccines have also been known to mutate and spread disease. For instance, a 16 year old girl died of meningitis B after kissing her boyfriend who'd just had the meningitis C vaccine. Scientists proved the bug was a mutated version of the vaccine virus, *New England Journal of Medicine*, Volume 342:219-220, January 20, 2000, number 3.[161]

- New reports say that vaccines are now creating dangerous mutations of the very infections they are supposed to protect against.

  > In 2007, US health officials admitted that the pneumococcal vaccine had created superbugs that caused severe ear infections in children. Similarly bad news emerged about the hepatitis vaccine that same year, when immunologists discovered mutated vaccine-resistant viruses were causing disease. And in developing countries, even to this day, health officials are concerned that polio viruses in the vaccine may not only be mutating, but may be causing the very disease they are supposed to prevent.[162]

---

[161] Mercola, J. "This Devastating Mistake Can Wreck Your Immune System..."Retrieved Sep 20, 2013, from http://articles.mercola.com/sites/articles/archive/2011/04/29/the-emergence-of-vaccine-induced-diseases.aspx.

[161] http://www.vaccineriskawareness.com/The-Herd-Immunity-Theory-Treating-Our-Children-Like-Cattle.

[162] Mercola, J. "Mounting Evidence Shows Many Vaccines are Ineffective and Contribute to Rise of Outbreaks Caused by Mutated Viruses" Retrieved Sep 20, 2013, from http://articles.mercola.com/sites/articles/archive/2012/07/30/whooping-cough-vaccine.aspx?e_cid=20120805_SNLNew_MS_1

What else is in the vaccine and why?

The original and often primitive forms of immunisation contained the bacteria or viruses and nothing else. Nowadays vaccines contain not only the vaccine itself but also a mix of toxic chemicals, metals, blood, and animal or human tissue.

Vaccines are now made in huge quantities so obviously huge quantities of the bacteria or virus need to be created. The bacteria and viruses used in vaccines have to be grown in laboratory conditions on animal or human tissue, eggs, and yeast. 'Scientists have "cell lines"— immortal cells that can keep on dividing indefinitely, derived originally from a variety of sources, including monkeys, hamsters, or from human foetuses.'[163] In addition to these cell lines the germs have to be fed and this is often done with blood products such as bovine serum. Mercury is sometimes used at this stage to prevent unwanted microbial growth. Once grown the active germs have to be separated from the cells on which they were grown and then if necessary deactivated. Formaldehyde—a known carcinogen—is often used in this process. Some of these unwanted substances can remain in the vaccines:

> Residual substances are those substances used in the course of manufacture of the vaccine but which are not included in the finished vaccine product. There may be residues of these substances in miniscule amounts. They often come from the manufacturing processes of either culturing the organism or of inactivating the live organism or toxin, ready for use in the vaccine.[164]

Chemicals are also added to help with the effectiveness of the vaccines. Some of these additives are just 'not nice', such as aluminium, which has been implicated in the rise of Alzheimer's disease and childhood learning difficulties, and squalene which some believe is the cause of Gulf War Syndrome and also causes reduced fertility. For more information about the individual vaccinations and additives, see page 282.

Who benefits from the vaccination programme?

Since the avian flu epidemic, when governments started clamouring for vaccines, the vaccine market has become big business.

> In a year that will be remembered for widespread public worry about the H1N1 virus, or swine flu, vaccines have become a $24-billion business. Analysts predict the global vaccine industry will top $40-billion by 2012. For companies like Glaxo, Sanofi-Aventis, Merck & Co., Novartis AG and Pfizer Inc., the fear of a pandemic has translated into a financial

---

[163] http://news.bbc.co.uk/1/hi/health/981452.stm.
[164] http://www.immune.org.nz/?t=920.

windfall that has been years in the making. Worldwide, nearly 1 billion doses of H1N1 vaccine have been ordered in 2009.

. . . Soaring vaccine sales are also pushing companies to chase profit in other types of shots. The race is now on to develop blockbuster vaccines, defined as those that bring in more than $1-billion annually. Two recently developed vaccines—Prevnar for pneumonia and Gardasil for cervical cancer—have become blockbusters, selling close to $2-billion a year.[165]

With such huge profits at stake it's unlikely that we will see a reduction in the vaccination programme any time soon. In reality we are more likely to see an increase in fear-mongering and tales of new pandemics that may be just around the corner. This will almost certainly lead to a mandatory schedule of childhood vaccination across the globe.

Other agendas of the vaccination programme

Huge profits may not be the only agenda raising the vaccination profile. The eugenics movement (which is aimed at improving the genetic composition of the population) of the late nineteenth and early twentieth century has not gone away. The outworking of this is that only the 'healthy', 'nice', or 'approved' people should be allowed to procreate. Coupled with the green movement that sees mankind as being 'bad' for the earth, causing pollution and increasing carbon gases, the 'need' for a reduction in world population has become a major influence on global policy. Many of our leaders now believe that the world population figures, which have reached seven billion, should be reduced possibly to as little as five million or even less. For instance Mikhail Gorbachev said 'We must speak more clearly about sexuality, contraception, about abortion, about values that control population, because the ecological crisis, in short, is the population crisis. Cut the population by 90% and there aren't enough people left to do a great deal of ecological damage.'[166]

However, the proponents of this drastic reduction are aware that enforced population control and all the ghastly methods it would use would not be tolerated and they need to come up with other less confrontational methods of population control. Vaccination is a great way to achieve this goal by stealth. Sadly this is no new idea—it has already been tried.

During the early 1990s, the World Health Organization (WHO) had been overseeing massive vaccination campaigns against tetanus in a number of countries, among them Nicaragua, Mexico, and the Philippines. In October 1994, HLI received a communication from its Mexican affiliate, the Comité Pro Vida de Mexico, regarding that country's anti-

[165] http://www.theglobeandmail.com/life/health/new-health/conditions/cold-and-flu/h1n1-swine-flu/how-vaccines-became-big-business/article1414474/page6/.

[166] http://www.infowars.com/from-7-billion-people-to-500-million-people-%E2%80%93-the-sick-population-control-agenda-of-the-global-elite/.

tetanus campaign. Suspicious of the campaign protocols, the Comité obtained several vials of the vaccine and had them analyzed by chemists. Some of the vials were found to contain human chorionic gonadotrophin (hCG), a naturally occurring hormone essential for maintaining a pregnancy.

hCG and Anti-hCG Antibodies

In nature the hCG hormone alerts the woman's body that she is pregnant and causes the release of other hormones to prepare the uterine lining for the implantation of the fertilized egg. The rapid rise in hCG levels after conception makes it an excellent marker for confirmation of pregnancy: when a woman takes a pregnancy test she is not tested for the pregnancy itself, but for the elevated presence of hCG.

However, when introduced into the body coupled with a tetanus toxoid carrier, antibodies will be formed not only against tetanus *but also against hCG*. In this case the body fails to recognize hCG as a friend and will produce anti-hCG antibodies. The antibodies will attack subsequent pregnancies by killing the hCG which naturally sustains a pregnancy; when a woman has sufficient anti-hCG antibodies in her system, she is rendered incapable of maintaining a pregnancy.

HLI reported the sketchy facts regarding the Mexican tetanus vaccines to its World Council members and affiliates in more than 60 countries. Soon additional reports of vaccines laced with hCG hormones began to drift in from the Philippines, where more than 3.4 million women were recently vaccinated. Similar reports came from Nicaragua, which had conducted its own vaccination campaign in 1993.[167]

Vaccines can and do severely damage some children. However, for every severely vaccine-damaged human being such as those who die or end up with severe brain damage or autism, there will be many more chronic reactions that cause general malaise, ill-health, and the 'unhealth' of metabolic disorders such as diabetes, or brain disorders such as dyslexia and ADHD. All these can wreak havoc on young lives, on their families, and on those who find that being a parent turns from a joy to a life sentence.

As parents we must each make our decision whether and when to vaccinate, based not on the blind faith and the bully-boy tactics that are used by medical and pharmaceutical professionals, but on our own individual circumstances, our understanding of the issues, and the prompting of the Holy Spirit.

Conclusion

By far the greatest pollutants to our bodies, our lifestyles, and our planet are these great chemical industries. Translating the Greek word pharmakia—from where we get our word

---

[167] http://www.thinktwice.com/birthcon.htm.

pharmaceuticals—as 'black magic arts', The Message translation of the Bible records God's judgement on the world system at the close of this era: 'Heaved and sunk, the great city of Babylon, sunk in the sea, not a sign of her ever again . . . Her traders robbed the whole earth blind, and by black-magic arts deceived the nations.'[168]

---

[168] Rev. 18: 21, 23, THE MESSAGE.

The Patter of Tiny Feet

SIZES

To fit age: 0-3[3-6:6-9: 9-12] months

Length of foot: 7[9:11:13] cm / 2.75[3.5:4.5:5.25] in

MATERIALS

1 x 50g ball of Debbie Bliss Cashmerino DK (121yd/110m per ball).

Set of four 4 mm bamboo double pointed needles 20 cm (8 in) long. (UK6/US8)

2 Buttons or Toggles

The Patter of Tiny Feet

TENSION
22 sts and 28 rows to 10 cm over stocking stitch using no 4 mm needles, (UK/Canada/Australia no.8/US6) Use larger or smaller needles if necessary to obtain correct tension.

ABBREVIATIONS
See page 305.

LEFT BOOT
Using two from the set of four dpn's cast on 36[40:44:48] sts and work 4[6:6:8] *rows* in garter stitch.
Next row: k2, k2tog, yo, knit to end. Now knit 5[7:7:9] *rows* in garter stitch (Ending at same end as buttonhole.) Cast off/bind off eight sts *knit wise,* knit to end of row. (This is a WS row) Break Yarn.
**

Now with RS facing slip first 5[6:7:8] sts from beg of the needle onto a separate needle, (Needle 1). Slip next 9[10:11:12] sts onto another needle, (Needle 2). Leave next 9[10:11:12] sts on needle, (Needle 3), and place last 5[6:7:8] sts from end of this needle onto end of needle 1. The work now forms a ring with 10[12:14:16] sts on needle 1 and 9[10:11:12] sts on each of needles 2 & 3.

With RS facing rejoin yarn to needle one and work as follows;

Next row: dec 1[1:0:1] st, knit across rem sts from needle 1 only, turn and work in *rows* of garter stitch on these 9[11:14:15] sts for 15[17:19:21] more *rows*. (End with a WS row)

1st 3 sizes only
Next round: k2tog, knit to last 2 sts, k2tog.
Rep this row once more, then knit one row on these rem 5[7:10] sts.

Last size only
Next round: knit
Next round: k2tog, k to last 2 sts, k2tog.
Knit one row on these rem 13 sts.

All Sizes
With the spare needle and working from the RS, pick up and knit 8[9:11:13] sts along the edge of these 15[17:19:21] rows, then knit the 9[10:11:12] sts from needle 2. (There are now 17[19:22:25] sts on needle 2) With spare needle knit the 9[10:11:12] sts from needle 3, then pick up and knit 8[9:11:13] sts, along the other side of the 15[17:19:21] rows. (There are now 17[19:22:25] sts on needle 3) Break yarn. Re-arrange the stitches by

placing 4 sts from the end of needles 2 and 3 onto each end of needle 1. There are now 13[15:18:21] sts on each needle.

With RS facing rejoin yarn to the beg of needle 1 and work in *rounds* as follows;

1st **round**: purl.

2nd **round**: knit.

These 2 rounds form garter stitch, rep these 2 rounds 3[3:4:4] more times, then work the first of these 2 rounds once more.

Next round: from needle 1; k4[5:6:7], k2tog, k1[1:2:3], k2tog, k4[5:6:7], from needle 2; k10[12:15:18] sts k2tog, k1, from needle 3; k1, k2tog, k10[12:15:18] sts.

Next round: purl.

Next round: from needle 1; k3[4:5:6], k2tog, k1[1:2:3], k2tog, k3[4:5:6] from needle 2; k9[11:14:17] sts k2tog, k1, from needle 3; k1, k2tog, k9[11:14:17] sts.

Next round: purl.

Next round: from needle 1; k2[3:4:5], k2tog, k1[1:2:3], k2tog, k2[3:4:5], from needle 2; k8[10:13:16], k2tog, k1, from needle 3; k1, k2tog, k8[10:13:16].

Next round: purl.

Next round: from needle 1; k1[2:3:4], k2tog, k1[1:2:3], k2tog, k1[2:3:4], from needle 2; k7[9:12:15], k2tog, k1, from needle 3; k1, k2tog, k7[9:12:15], Cast off/Bind off *purl wise*.

RIGHT BOOT

Using two from the set of four dpn's cast on 36[40:44:48] sts and work 4[6:6:8] *rows* in garter stitch.

Next row: knit to last 4 sts, yo, k2tog, k2.

Now knit 5[7:7:9] *rows* in garter stitch (Ending at opposite end to buttonhole.)

Next row: knit to last 8 sts, cast off/bind off these rem 8 sts *knit wise*. (This is a WS row) Break yarn.

Now work the same as the left boot as given from **.

TO MAKE UP

Sew cast off edges together from WS using over sew stitch so that the seams lays flat when opened out. Sew in all ends. Sew button into place to correspond with buttonhole on overlap and so that the overlap drops slightly at the side.

Soul

Chapter 1
<u>What is a soul?</u>

Christians believe that God is a 'Trinity'. By this we mean that God exists as a unity of three distinct persons: Father, Son, and Holy Spirit. Each of these three persons is fully divine but distinct from the other, each has a will and emotions, and says 'I' and 'you' when speaking. The Father is not the same person as the Son, who is not the same person as the Holy Spirit, who is not the same person as the Father. And yet there are not three gods, there is only one God.

Since God lives in the spiritual world and we live in the natural world we find this difficult to understand. Paul put it really well when he said; 'We don't yet see things clearly. We're squinting in a fog, peering through a mist. But it won't be long before the weather clears and the sun shines bright! We'll see it all then, see it all as clearly as God sees us, knowing him directly just as he knows us!'[169]

Because our understanding of the spiritual world is limited it's not surprising that many of the things to do with God are a complete mystery to us. But even so we know that we are made in the image of this God who is a trinity. The trinity has an organisation: God the Father is the first part, the Son is the second part (because he is 'begotten'[170] and sent by the Father[171]), and the Holy Spirit is the third part (because he is sent by the Father and the Son[172]). We too have three parts to our personality usually referred to as the body, the soul, and the spirit.

Our soul can be likened to God the Father: it is our very essence, the 'I' part of me, the place where 'I' think, the organisational hub, the decision-making part of me, the feeler of emotions and the creator of creations. We do not *have* a soul, we *are* a soul, and this soul directs our bodies and often our spirits. Jesus lived his life as a soul totally submitted to his Father's will. He had unbroken communication with him and could clearly see and hear what the Father was saying and doing: 'I tell you, the Son can do nothing on his own, but only what he sees the Father doing; for whatever the Father does, the Son does likewise'[173]

The soul is not some separate part of man that is contained within a body, like the coffee inside a mug: I don't have a soul, I am a soul. If my body is damaged the ability of my soul to

---

[169] 1 Cor. 13: 12, THE MESSAGE.
[170] John 3: 16.
[171] 1 John 4: 10.
[172] John 14: 26, 15: 26.
[173] John 5: 19, NRSV.

express itself is damaged. The Bible says that Adam *became* a living soul when God breathed into the body that he had formed from the dust: 'then the Lord God formed man from the dust of the ground, and breathed into his nostrils the breath of life; and the man became a living being'[174]

In this verse the word translated 'breath' is the Hebrew word *nephesh*, which we translate as soul, as in the 'soul' part of 'living soul' in the same verse. This same word is also used to describe animals in Genesis 1: 30 where it is translated 'breathes': '"To all animals and all birds, everything that moves and breathes, I give whatever grows out of the ground for food." And there it was.'[175]

There seems to be a definite order to the created world. Plants have a body that has life but not breath. This life originated in God, and some people believe that plants have a form of primitive communication with each other. Animals have a body, they breathe and we know that they have intelligence and the ability to communicate. I believe that they have a soul, but whether they have any form of spirit is unclear. Only man has a body, a soul, and a spirit that are capable of communicating with each other *and* with God. Perhaps this is because, as the Bible records, God personally breathed into Adam to give him his life and soul—man was made in God's image or likeness. It was personal to God and has been ever since.

Maisie, the best dog in the world, lived with us for only ten and half years. Years full of doggy mayhem, muddy feet, dribble and slobber, drifts of hair all over the carpets, and the naughty habit of chasing the neighbour's cat. But she had big brown eyes that could melt your soul, and she always brought me both my slippers every time I came through the front door. Not until she died did we realize how much her personality had imprinted itself on our hearts. Whilst it is clear that there are animals in heaven I really don't know if she will be waiting to greet us when we get there. But when she was with us she demonstrated God's heart through her faithfulness, trust, and unconditional love.

So, like God, we humans have three parts but each part is equally important and inseparable from the others. My soul is the union of my human spirit and my body and thus to have both a human spirit and a body are absolutely vital parts of being a soul.

When Adam sinned he lost his contact and relationship with God. By following Satan rather than God he placed himself, all his descendants, and all that he had dominion over, under the authority of Satan. He became a slave in another kingdom, where evil ruled. Satan— a legalist—would not now release him or his descendants from this kingdom without a price

---

[174] Gen. 2: 7, NRSV.
[175] Gen. 1: 30, THE MESSAGE.

being paid. That payment had to be made in blood. And that blood was the life or soul—*nephesh*—of Jesus: 'For the life of the flesh is in the blood; and I have given it to you for making atonement [*amends*] for your lives on the altar; for, as life, it is the blood that makes atonement.'[176]

When God slaughtered an animal and made clothing for Adam and Eve it was the first sacrifice of a sacrificial system set up to cover over our sin. This enabled man to remain in contact with God—who is holy—until a final 'once for all' sacrifice would be made by his son—Jesus.

This sacrificial system that God patterned is found in all religions on all continents to this day. It also passed down through the Hebrew people and because of this Judaism was a very bloody religion. Over the centuries millions of animals were slaughtered and rivers of blood were shed in the Temple. And yet even though this blood represented a 'life for a life'[177]—a soul for a soul—none of this blood was truly effective. The sacrifices had to be continually repeated, and man was not truly able to transfer from Satan's kingdom into God's Kingdom.

But these sacrifices had a purpose. They were a constant reminder of the sinfulness of man and his need for reconciliation with God. In picture language they looked forward to a time when the perfect and complete sacrifice would be made. They made a covenant between God and Man. The sacrifice provided an exchange—albeit temporary—whereby a man's sin could be transferred onto an innocent animal who then took the man's due punishment—death. This kept the way open for God and man to have contact. Because of these sacrifices the Jews who lived before Jesus were saved by faith in the same way that we are.

The perfect and complete sacrifice was made when Jesus died. He died as a perfect man who had never lived as part of Satan's kingdom. When Satan orchestrated the death of Jesus he became guilty of the murder of an innocent man. Not only that but, without cause, Jesus was subjected to many of the awful things that can happen to us such as shame, pain, poverty, captivity, and ultimately death so that we could be released from all these things.

He was despised and rejected by others; a man of suffering and acquainted with infirmity; and as one from whom others hide their faces he was despised, and we held him of no account. Surely he has borne our infirmities and carried our diseases; yet we accounted him stricken, struck down by God, and afflicted. But he was wounded for our transgressions, crushed for our iniquities; upon him was the punishment that made us whole, and by his

---

[176] Lev. 17: 11, NRSV (italics mine).
[177] Deut.19: 21. NRSV

bruises we are healed. All we like sheep have gone astray; we have all turned to our own way, and the Lord has laid on him the iniquity of us all.[178]

When we have faith in Jesus we are able to move from Satan's kingdom and rule to God's kingdom and rule.

One of our main roles as parents must be to bring our children to the place where they can personally accept the sacrifice of Jesus, and be freed from the tyranny of Satan's kingdom of death, pain, and futility.

When does our soul arrive?

The Bible states very clearly that the life—and this word 'life' is the same word as 'soul' in the original Hebrew—is in the blood: 'For the life of every creature—its blood is its life.'[179]

A foetus doesn't breathe like you and me. It takes oxygen and other nutrients from the mother's blood. But even as early as ten days after conception a primitive form of blood begins to circulate. This blood is not produced by the mother: it is unique to the growing baby. The heart starts pumping at around twenty days. Since the Bible states that the life—or soul—is in the blood then it seems likely the new baby has a soul if not from conception then at least from the beginning of this blood circulation. The Bible speaks of the unborn child as an unborn personality with all the attributes of a soul: emotions, will, destiny, and in the case of Jesus— Lordship. When the heavily pregnant Elizabeth greeted the newly pregnant Mary she exclaimed: '"And why has this happened to me, that the mother of my Lord comes to me? For as soon as I heard the sound of your greeting, the child in my womb leaped for joy."'[180] Clearly the babe in her womb—John the Baptist—was operating in the gift of discernment even before birth.

Adam was created a living soul when God breathed into him, so breath plus body equals soul. No other humans (including Eve) were said to have been made into living souls by the direct action of God breathing into them. It seems that God invested Adam and his offspring with the capacity to create human souls. In fact God's first command to Adam was to 'Be fruitful and multiply, and fill the earth and subdue it.'[181]

---

[178] Isa. 53: 3–6, NRSV.
[179] Lev. 17:14, NRSV
[180] Luke 1: 43–4, NRSV
[181] Gen. 1: 28, NRSV.

Where does our soul go at death?

'From the moment of birth, death is our only certainty.'[182] But like the elephant in the room we usually avoid thinking or talking about it. So whilst we may make detailed plans for our lives and for the lives of our children we rarely pay much attention to our ongoing journey into eternity. But death cannot be kept at bay. The death of close family or friends and an increasing awareness of our own frailty constantly bring it to the fore. So what happens at death?

From a medical point of view death happens when all the vital organs stop working. The body is then buried and decays and the soul and spirit depart: the Bible refers to this as 'sleep'. Some people believe that when the body dies there is a complete end to consciousness and existence: the person is gone. Others believe in reincarnation: that their souls are 'recycled' into another body whether human or animal. Others would say that they just don't know. Jesus taught that there is life after death and he came back from death to prove it.

> Mohammed died and we have not heard from him since – he has never been back to say, 'I told you I was right'. There is just an eerie silence. Buddha has not come back. None of the others have come back. They are still in their tombs.
> But Jesus' tomb is empty. He embraced death and, having embraced it, then showed that he had mastery over it.[183]

The Bible consistently teaches that there is life after death: that when the body dies—or goes to sleep—the soul separates from it and goes off to wait for judgement. At this judgement the body and soul are reunited.

> I saw a Great White Throne and the One Enthroned. Nothing could stand before or against the Presence, nothing in Heaven, nothing on earth. And then I saw all the dead, great and small, standing there—before the Throne! And books were opened. Then another book was opened: the Book of Life. The dead were judged by what was written in the books, by the way they had lived. Sea released its dead, Death and Hell turned in their dead. Each man and woman was judged by the way he or she had lived.[184]

Furthermore Jesus says that not everyone will go to the same place after death. There will be a separation. 'Don't act so surprised at all this. The time is coming when everyone dead and buried will hear his voice. Those who have lived the right way will walk out into a resurrection Life; those who have lived the wrong way, into a resurrection Judgment.'[185]

---

[182] Except for those Christians who are alive when Jesus returns.
[183] Roger Price, *Explaining What Happens after Death* (Sovereign World, 1992).
[184] Rev. 20: 11–13, THE MESSAGE.
[185] John 5: 28–9, THE MESSAGE.

He also tells the story of a rich man who died and went to a place where he was in torment. A man who had begged at his gate also died, but he went to be with Abraham: a different part of the same place. All three of these men went to the same place at death, they all had consciousness after death, and the rich man could certainly see the beggar with Abraham and know him by name. Whether the beggar could see the rich man is not stated.

So where is this place? In English we call it 'hell', but in Hebrew it is 'sheol' and in Greek, 'hades'. These words all mean 'the unseen world of departed spirits', and differ from the word 'grave' which is where the body is put at death. According to Jesus' story there were—at least—two parts to hell: one place for the unrighteous and one for the righteous, which is also known as 'paradise' or 'Abraham's bosom'. The righteous souls in this place were taken up with Jesus when he ascended into heaven: since then, 'up' is where all Christians go when they die. At the return of Jesus, his followers will come back into their bodies and have eternal life with Him.

> The Master himself will give the command. Archangel thunder! God's trumpet blast! He'll come down from heaven and the dead in Christ will rise—they'll go first. Then the rest of us who are still alive at the time will be caught up with them into the clouds to meet the Master. Oh, we'll be walking on air! And then there will be one huge family reunion with the Master. So reassure one another with these words.[186]

Jesus will then take his rightful place as King on the earth and will reign for a thousand years. It is not until the end of this period of time that the rest of the dead, who are located in Hell, will come back into their bodies for the judgement.

When Nathan—our second son—died I was consumed with the question of where he had gone. I could find very little in books or even the Bible to answer my question. He was not of an age to understand and make any kind of decision to follow Jesus, so what had happened to him?

Nathan died of meningitis two weeks before Christmas 1989. I tried to get the doctor to visit, but he was too busy: 'give him Calpol', he said. At the hospital I was told to stop fussing so much: 'give him steam inhalations', they said.

I was back in Accident and Emergency when he seemed to stop breathing, the nurse rushed off with him, and I was shooed out of the room.

---

[186] 1 Thess. 4: 16–18, THE MESSAGE.

We were ushered into a side room: I was peeling oranges for David—our firstborn. He liked oranges. The doctor came in and sat down: 'I'm sorry' he said 'but we were unable to resuscitate him.'

I carried on peeling oranges, there was silence. The words didn't seem to be making any sense. Like the washing in a tumble drier they were just going round and round in my head, but not making any sense. Eventually they penetrated my consciousness: 'Do you mean he's dead?' I said. 'Yes' said the doctor.

Nathan's body was stiff and cold when we kissed him goodbye and left him there. We drove home with an empty car seat to an empty house, and a solid wall of pain. Life had to go on, David was 2½: he needed feeding and playing with—trips to feed the ducks and cereal packets to turn into angels. The tree that Nathan had helped to decorate was twinkling in the corner of the lounge. A funeral had to be arranged and Christmas celebrated.

It was more than a month before the shock began to dissipate and the grief set in. Then there were the questions: 'How could you let this happen, God?' And 'Where were you?'

There were people's words of comfort: some wise and lovely, but some just had to be endured. 'God will use this sacrifice . . .', 'God chose this path for you . . .' And the most misunderstood phrase of all, 'God is sovereign'.

I thought everybody must have heard the news, surely it thundered in the heavens as God threw the furniture around in anger at what had happened! But I frequently bumped into people who didn't know, and I would have to say those words again 'Nathan's dead—meningitis.'

People were so very kind and well-meaning. I think we would have starved if it hadn't been for the meals that arrived on a daily basis. If I had been eating I would have got very fat, but the weight was dropping off me. It's funny the things you think when you've buried your baby. On days when it was cold I was worried that I hadn't wrapped him up enough. And who would change his nappies? And when I laid the table for tea it seemed that all I had to do was lay his place and put his high chair there and he would come back, bringing normality with him. But the nightmare went on.

So where was God? Amongst all the stuff people were saying what was *he* saying? I called and called but to begin with I couldn't hear him through the crashing cymbals of my own emotions. But I knew that he was there. My experience of him thus far had proved to me that no matter how dark the tunnel I was crawling through he was there with me and he would bring me out of it, stronger, richer, fuller. And he did.

But where did Nathan go? We know that God is just and loving but we also know that he works according to a strict legal system and that he cannot dwell with sin. As we know only too well, babies are born with the predisposition to sin—to fall short of God's standards—and their natural tendency is to start sinning as soon as possible. However the Bible refers to babies, children, and those who are mentally impaired as 'innocent'[187] and as those who 'do not yet know right from wrong'.[188]

Although not stated in black and white, biblical logic indicates that only those who can be held accountable will stand before that Great White Throne to be judged. All others are saved by the blood of Jesus just as believers are. Because they are saved they do not appear before God on this great day of judgement.

The Bible also appears to teach that the children of believers go to heaven because of their parents' faith. As the seed of their parents they are part of the covenant that their parents have made with God. Only if and when these children come of an age and ability to deliberately step out of this covenant do they cease to be part of it.

King David considered that his child who died had gone on to the same place that he too would go at death: 'I shall go to him, but he will not return to me.'[189]

God is a loving Father who wants the best for us in this life. However, for all sorts of reasons we can lose our way or an enemy attack may get through our defences and cause us untold pain. But I know that when Jesus comes back for his people our family will once again be complete as Nathan joins us in the great celebrations on that day.

How does the soul function?

The soul is the essence of 'me' expressed through my thoughts, my will, and my emotions, all working through my mind, which is the central processing unit for all conscious and unconscious thought processes. My soul is the receiver of all information that comes from my body—the five senses of seeing, hearing, smelling, tasting and touching—and from my spirit. Once it has received all this information it is my soul that makes decisions and may form a plan of action.

The processes of the mind all take place in the brain, which is a physical organ. As we have seen, this organ can be affected physically by good or bad nutrition, the amount of oxygen it receives, and many other factors. The physical health of the brain is of vital importance as it

---

[187] Jer. 19: 4–5, NRSV.
[188] Deut. 1: 39, NRSV.
[189] 2 Sam. 12: 23, NRSV.

affects the health of our mind which can in turn affect our soul. Likewise the health of the soul can affect the health of the body and the health of the spirit.

The mind can also be affected positively or negatively—and usually a combination of both—by our upbringing: the actions of our parents, society, and circumstances. These can all colour our future life, our behaviour patterns, and our ability to function. The fall of Adam and the subsequent shortcomings of his offspring created echoes in the soul of every child born in the future. As Christians we may need to find release through prayer from these generational echoes, not only for our own lives but also for the lives of our children.

It is important to have healthy minds—both physically and emotionally—because it is through the mind that the soul and the spirit express themselves. Like the filter on a camera, unhealthiness in our minds will colour all expressions from our soul and spirit and, like a virus, will also reach out to affect others. For instance: the writer to the Hebrews says that bitterness can spread from person to person: 'See to it that no one fails to obtain the grace of God; that no root of bitterness springs up and causes trouble, and through it many become defiled.'[190]

The functions of the mind include all conscious and unconscious processes. The unconscious processes include breathing, the beating of our hearts, all the other fine tuning mechanisms that a healthy body needs, the storage of memories, our learning, and our dreams. The conscious processes include thought and intellect, memory, perception, emotion, imagination, and will. The conscious mind receives messages from the sensors in the body so that it can see, hear, feel, taste, smell, and touch, and process all these messages. It also gives directions to the body and affects the working of our unconscious minds.

As parents we have an incredible amount of influence on our growing children. For nine months they are nourished in a near perfect environment where, it is hoped, they lack for nothing. When they are born this process of growing and learning continues for many more years. I recently watched on TV a giraffe giving birth. The baby plopped onto the ground from a great height and then very quickly had to struggle to its feet, find its source of food, and be ready to run. Mum stood by trying to help as much as her instincts allowed. But baby humans are born completely helpless and have to be nurtured as they begin to acquire all the life skills that they will need. We are the 'animal' that cares for its young for the longest time.

The family unit should be the safe place provided for them as they embark on this growing and learning process: 'A strong, loving and supportive family is the best environment for raising children and the best start for ensuring that the rights of children are fulfilled.'[191]

---

[190] Heb. 12:15, NRSV.
[191] UNICEF Executive Director Carol Bellamy, http://www.unicef.org/childfamily/index_22357.html.

In the West this environment has begun to break down: first with the loss of the extended family and the emergence of the nuclear family, and more recently with many alternative forms of family units becoming the norm. Whilst these may provide for many of the needs of a growing child they will never be able to outdo the family unit that God intended, where there is one mother, one father, and a host of other close relatives who all have love and care for the new child.

> . . .positive outcomes for children raised in two-parent families such as higher education, higher income, and better health and longevity as adults, and negative outcomes for lone-parent children such as alcohol and drug abuse and early sexual encounters are 'consistent across the board'. The same is true in countries such as the U.K. and the U.S.[192]

---

[192] http://en.epochtimes.com/news/7-9-21/59992.html quoting Dave Quist from the Institute of Marriage and Family Canada.

Chapter 2
<u>The Mind</u>

Thought is the mental process by which we as humans understand the world. However in order to grasp new information we need old information through which to understand it. This old information acts as a frame of reference for the new information. We see this when we are trying to describe a new experience; for instance, we might say 'he was as tough as nails' or 'her eyes twinkled like the stars'.

The prophet Ezekiel had a real struggle when he was trying to describe his visions of God in Heaven, so he used the things he knew about to describe the things he didn't know about:

> . . . the sky opened up and I saw visions of God . . . I looked: I saw an immense dust storm come from the north, an immense cloud with lightning flashing from it, a huge ball of fire glowing like bronze. Within the fire were what looked like four creatures vibrant with life. Each had the form of a human being, but each also had four faces and four wings. Their legs were as sturdy and straight as columns, but their feet were hoofed like those of a calf and sparkled from the fire like burnished bronze.[193]

Jesus often made his teaching clearer by using picture language with images of things with which his listeners were familiar, and with humour, so that people could understand what he was saying. 'Everyone who hears these words of mine and does not act on them will be like a foolish man who built his house on sand. The rain fell, and the floods came, and the winds blew and beat against that house, and it fell—and great was its fall!'[194]

As humans who are growing, our children will make sense of the world by using what they already know to understand what they are learning. If their early experiences and understandings of life are imperfect—and they always are—then they will make sense of life through an imperfect filter. In extreme cases some may grow into adults who cannot make much sense of life at all.

Software programs such as Microsoft Office or Apple Snow Leopard are needed in order to interpret messages on the computer. It can be very frustrating to receive a message that can't be opened because we don't have the right software. Fortunately computers and software programs are a lot better now and unreadable messages are very few and far between. The same

---

[193] Ezek. 1: 1–7, THE MESSAGE.
[194] Matt. 7: 27, NRSV.

cannot be said for human beings. As we have moved more and more into the technological age with its instant messaging, fast communication, twenty-four hour TV, and subsequent loss of family life, we have witnessed a decline in many of the skills children need for life: not only those that encompass reading, writing, and maths, but also the transferable skills such as the ability to think through a problem and resolve it, to research a subject and write an essay, and to take risks, and emotional skills that are absolutely vital for our ongoing relationships within a family group and in the workplace.

> Increasingly, children in general have problems focusing their concentration, exercising self restraint and taking account of other people's needs and interests. . . .
> Everywhere I went it was the same story: four and five year olds were coming to school with poorer language skills than ever before; they weren't arriving with the repertoire of nursery rhymes and songs little ones always used to know, and children of all ages found it increasingly difficult to sit down and listen to their teacher or to express complex ideas in speech or writing.[195]

Because we all have different experiences of life we all have different 'software programmes' so we all see, perceive, or filter things differently. Some people are constantly optimistic and cheery, such as the person who always sees things through rose-coloured spectacles. Some are negative or pessimistic such as the man who sees the glass as being half empty. Through humour we can put ourselves in other people's shoes:

- The economist would say that, the glass is 25% fuller than at the same time last year.
- The banker would say that the glass has just under 50% of its net worth in liquid assets.
- The psychiatrist would ask, 'What did your mother say about the glass?'
- The physicist would say that the volume of this cylinder is divided into two equal parts; one a colorless, odorless liquid, the other a colorless, odorless gas. The cylinder is neither full nor empty. Rather, each half of the cylinder is full, one with a gas, one with a liquid.
- The seasoned drinker would say that the glass doesn't have enough ice in it.[196]

So the brain is wired in such a way that what goes into it—especially in our early years—will be the filter by which we see and understand the rest of our lives. Many of the experiences we have as children are common to us all so we do, fortunately, have common points of reference and can make meaning of the world around us and interact with others.

---

[195] Sue Palmer, *Toxic Childhood* (Orion, 2006).
[196] Jokes from: http://www.slinkycity.com/half-full-or-half-empty.html.

The bonding of the parent and child is the foundation, or operating software, from which all human experiences will grow and be understood. Within this parent–child bond the child will experience to a greater or lesser extent:

- love and care
- touch and feeling
- safety and security
- stimulation and freedom of expression
- health and wellbeing
- the provision of needs
- the development of trust
- spiritual communication.

So what happens when we receive too little—or even too much—fulfilment of these early needs?

• Love and care

The love and care that children receive from their parents find their source in the bond that is formed during pregnancy and immediately after birth. Without this bond of love parents will find it difficult to maintain the high level of care and commitment that the child needs.

In an ideal situation both parents will be drawn to their baby: they will feel a longing to smell, touch, cuddle, rock, talk, sing to him and gaze at him. He will respond in a similar way by touching, smelling, sucking, clinging, snuggling, babbling, and gazing. This all creates a positive feedback loop where the parents' behaviour brings pleasure and nourishment to their baby, and their baby's behaviour brings pleasure to them. In turn this creates and reinforces a bond between the parents and the child.

For all sorts of reasons some children experience impaired, damaged, or even non-existent bonding, and this can go on to affect them throughout life.

The impact of impaired bonding in early childhood varies. With severe emotional neglect in early childhood the impact can be devastating. Children without touch, stimulation, and nurturing can literally lose the capacity to form any meaningful relationships for the rest of their lives. Fortunately, most children do not suffer this degree of severe neglect.[197]

As ever, doctors and therapists like to create labels to describe mental disorders. The label Reactive Attachment Disorder is one such label.

---

[197] Bruce D. Perry, MD, Ph.D., at http://teacher.scholastic.com/professional/bruceperry/bonding.htm.

Reactive Attachment Disorder (RAD) is the result of several interruptions that occur during the formative period of a child's development. Their ability to 'attach', trust others and relate to primary caregivers is negatively affected.

A child's ability to bond with or 'attach to' others is greatly determined by what happens between the infant and caregiver during the first few months, when the brain is rapidly developing.

Relating to an inconsistent caretaker or having the lack of a nurturing and loving relationship can physically change the 'wiring' of the brain and lead to difficulty regulating emotions and behaviour. This may result in poor impulse control, a sense of separation and mistrust. There may be expressions of anger or controlling and attention-seeking hyperactive behaviour. These can be confused with other conduct disorders such as ADHD and OCD, which may sometimes coexist, making management more difficult. These children can have difficulty accepting comfort and may be either overly affectionate or unable to express affection. One of the most difficult situations for parents to deal with is the disbelief of others outside the family who are exposed only to the child's endearing qualities which seem to contradict the behaviours encountered in the home.[198]

Being an adopted child I experienced interruptions in my care at an early age. Although my adoption took place at eight weeks, I had spent these first eight weeks in a mother and baby home, initially cared for by my birth mother, and then by the staff. The bonds with my primary and secondary caregivers were thus broken. I was adopted into a loving family with a mother, father, and one sister who had been adopted previously. Throughout my life I was and still am a person who likes to be alone. This caused me to be very late developing speech and, as an adult, I still struggle with stringing a sentence together. As a child I was aware that my lack of giving back love and affection deeply troubled my father and he made strenuous efforts to form an attachment. These efforts made me squirm and I found them very difficult. His desire to bond with me only highlighted my inability to bond and created a sense of frustration in me. Conversely my mother made no such demands and seemed innately to understand me. I loved her deeply even though I lacked the skills to express it. I have been, and am still on, a long road to healing that has only been made possible by Jesus.

For children who have been neglected from birth, especially those who have been in third world orphanages, a loving adoptive family is sadly just not enough. Lack of love and stimulation from birth means that the brain never gets wired up right: the software programme just isn't there. This lack of love can also have devastating physical effects.

---

[198] http://www.internationaladoptionstories.com/rad.htm.

But how could simply being in an orphanage kill a baby? Basically, they die from lack of love. When an infant falls below the threshold of physical affection needed to stimulate the production of growth hormone and the immune system, his body starts shutting down. . . . In humans, the immune system seems to be profoundly affected, making these children especially vulnerable to all types of disease—probably because not being nurtured is extremely stressful and high levels of stress hormones can turn off the immune system. (That's why corticosteroids—essentially stress hormones—are often used to treat auto-immune diseases where too much immune response is the problem.)

In fact, 'failure to thrive' in human infants has been shown to result from lack of individualized, nurturing, physically affectionate parental care, whether in an orphanage or due to extreme parental neglect. Babies' brains expect that they will experience nearly constant physical touch, rocking and cuddling: without it, they just don't grow. And without receiving kind empathetic care, they are less likely to behave that way towards others as they get older.[199]

Children with any level of deprivation in their early years will need far more than emotional healing. They will need a creative miracle in order to fully reach their potential. Jesus is the only source of such creative miracles: 'Jesus told them, "Go back and tell John what's going on: 'The blind see, the lame walk, lepers are cleansed, the deaf hear, the dead are raised, the wretched of the earth learn that God is on their side'"'[200]

But is it possible to love our children too much? In the Bible we find a wonderful definition of love;

. . . no matter what I say, what I believe, and what I do, I'm bankrupt without love.
Love never gives up.
Love cares more for others than for self.
Love doesn't want what it doesn't have.
Love doesn't strut,
Doesn't have a swelled head,
Doesn't force itself on others,
Isn't always 'me first,'
Doesn't fly off the handle,
Doesn't keep score of the sins of others,
Doesn't revel when others grovel,
Takes pleasure in the flowering of truth,
Puts up with anything,

---

[199] http://www.huffingtonpost.com/maia-szalavitz/how-orphanages-kill-babie_b_549608.html.
[200] Matt. 11: 4–5, THE MESSAGE.

Trusts God always,
Always looks for the best,
Never looks back,
But keeps going to the end.
Love never dies.[201]

Love involves being consistently concerned to promote the welfare of another person. The sad experiences of children raised in institutions show us that love is something that has first to be modelled to us before we can give it. This is confirmed in the Bible: 'First we were loved, now we love.'[202] It is impossible to love our children (properly) too much, but sadly we can model imperfect forms of love.

As parents we were all parented by imperfect and often broken people and the love we received was faulty. What was modelled to us affects how we will parent our own children. How many of us can hear the words of our parents echoing through the things we say to our children? Things we thought we would never say:

* 'Wait and see'
* 'Ask your mother'
* 'Wait until your father gets home'
* 'Because I said so'

Parents who themselves have an overwhelming emotional need to be loved will find it difficult to love their own child unconditionally. They will be constantly looking for affirmation and a return of love from the child. This kind of parent may well shower love, hugs, kisses, and presents on the child, all with the underlying aim of receiving love rather than giving it. They may also lack the ability to bring the other sides of love—discipline, guidance, and correction. Often they will find it difficult to be consistent in their love: like a faulty tap running hot and then cold they love their children only when it suits them.

Parenting is not just about showering love on our children. It is our responsibility to train them and guide them so that they will grow up to be whole, responsible members of a community. This may not win us any popularity contests, but they need us to say 'No!' sometimes. We are their parents not their best mates.

Perhaps the most important thing both mothers and fathers can do for their child is to find their own healing so that they can truly love their child. 'The major reason I have found

---

[201] 1 Cor. 13: 3–8, THE MESSAGE.
[202] 1 John 4: 19, THE MESSAGE.

that children become neurotic is that their parents are too busy struggling with unmet infantile needs of their own.'[203]

• Touch and feeling

Skin is the largest organ in the body. It covers your entire body and if laid flat would cover an area of two square meters. It varies in thickness from half a millimetre to four millimetres and it accounts for about 16 per cent of your body weight. The top layer of your skin is being replaced all the time and every thirty days you get an entirely new outer covering. Apart from keeping the insides in, the skin has a number of other important functions.

- It protects us from injury to internal organs: it is a barrier to bacteria, it produces melanin which protects against UV light and it is waterproof—preventing loss of body fluids.
- By constricting or dilating small blood vessels within it, and by the production of sweat, skin controls body temperature, preventing both loss of body heat and overheating.
- The UV rays in sunlight convert molecules within the skin into vitamin D. This is absorbed into the blood vessels and used by the body for the maintenance of bones and for the absorption of calcium and phosphorus.
- Skin is also a sensory organ. Nerve endings in the skin are stimulated by things such as pressure, pain, heat, and cold. They send messages to the brain for interpretation and action. Some messages are acted upon before being interpreted by the brain. These are the reflex actions that we have when, for instance, we feel pain.

From the cradle to the grave, human beings have an innate need to be touched. Touch is the first and often the last sensation that we experience on this earth.

It is primarily through the skin that the baby learns about the world. In the womb touch is the first sense to develop and the process of birth develops it further. A baby has over five million sensory cells in its skin. For most parents touching their baby is something that is done instinctively. We can't get enough of all that skin-on-skin cuddling and touching and neither can our babies. Babies that are touched a lot are calmer, they cry less and they sleep better. This in turn leads to better brain development. They also have better immune systems. Touch helps to develop their motor skills and their understanding of the world around.

In the Western world we have been very affected by so called 'child experts'—often the mothers and grandmothers in our own families—who have said that we mustn't touch and hold our children too much because it will spoil them. It is thought now that this lack of touch

---

[203] From the article Neurosis: by Dr Arthur Janov, http://www.continuum-concept.org/reading/neurosis.html

has contributed to the current explosion of violent behaviour in our young people. In an article by Dr Tiffany Field titled '*Violence and Touch Deprivation in Adolescents*', she says, 'the cultures that exhibited minimal physical affection toward their young children had significantly higher rates of adult violence, and, vice versa, those cultures that showed significant amounts of physical affection toward their young children had virtually no adult violence.'[204] As we have already seen, babies that are not touched don't do so well at all:

> In the thirteenth century, Holy Roman Emperor Fredrick II removed a group of infants from their families and put them in the care of nurses who were instructed to attend only to the infants' most basic needs—the infants could be fed and bathed but not held, hugged or spoken to. It was Fredrick's intent to see what language the babies would speak if they were raised generically, without benefit of touch or adult verbal stimulation. Unfortunately, Fredrick did not find his answer. All of the infants died before they were old enough to speak.[205]

In fact touch is a very important form of communication. We can often sense the emotion behind a touch, whether it is friendly, sexual, compassionate, threatening, or parental. 'A 2006 study by Matthew Hertenstein demonstrated that strangers could accurately communicate the "universal" emotions of anger, fear, disgust, love, gratitude, and sympathy, purely through touches to the forearm, but not the "prosocial" emotions of surprise, happiness and sadness, nor the "self-focused" emotions of embarrassment, envy and pride.'[206]

I recall as a pre-teen being somewhat disturbed by the touch of a friend's father. He would often play tickling games with us and I was concerned about this without knowing why. In fact I beat myself up about it because I had been brought up to believe that adults were always right. When this man did step over the line and abuse me I realised that my sense of disquiet had been a right response.

We need to teach our children to recognise, believe, and act on their inner promptings, which involves giving them permission and space to talk about their feelings and the freedom to get it wrong. Too often these inner 'knowings' or promptings have been shut down and we become adults who cannot respond to them. Good forms of touch are good and, indeed, necessary for survival. Sadly the prevalence of those with other agendas in our society means that there is little touch between non-family members. And in schools, teachers no longer have any physical contact with their pupils, either to discipline or to comfort.

---

[204] http://findarticles.com/p/articles/mi_m2248/is_148_37/ai_97723210/.
[205] http://www.intuitivebodywork.net/Importance_of_Touch.
[206] http://bps-research-digest.blogspot.co.uk/2011/02/how-well-can-we-communicate-emotions.html.

Picture the scenario: a six-year-old girl is playing a game with her school friends, she runs across the playground, falls and cuts her knee and cries. What's your reaction?

Well it's obvious—to help her and comfort her, perhaps put a reassuring arm around her shoulders and wipe her tears away.

But if you're her teacher, would you do the same thing? It's something I've frequently asked teachers, and their response to that scenario is always the same—a firm 'no.'

It sounds at best, steely and cold—at worst, heartless, but teachers and indeed all those who work with children are increasingly aware that what seems to be the most normal and natural response to a distressed child could have serious implications for their career and their reputation.[207]

Touching was more prevalent in the Middle East during the time of Jesus where it was common practice to anoint the sick with oil. In both cases all or part of the body was smeared or rubbed with the oil. This is the kind of anointing talked about in the book of James: 'Are you sick? Call the church leaders together to pray and anoint you with oil in the name of the Master. Believing-prayer will heal you, and Jesus will put you on your feet. And if you've sinned, you'll be forgiven—healed inside and out.'[208]

Nowadays the Christian practice of anointing the sick with oil—if practised at all—has been reduced to the ritual of a quick, rather sanitised dab with oil on the forehead during a healing service, but it seems that in reality the anointing with oil was part of the healing process, not just a ceremonial action. Perhaps when we are sick, we should ask the 'elders' not only to pray for us but also to come and give us a massage with oil! 'Peer-reviewed medical research has shown that the benefits of massage include pain relief, reduced anxiety and depression, reduced blood pressure & heart rate. The release of endorphins and serotonin, preventing fibrosis or scar tissue, increasing the flow of lymph, and improving sleep.'[209]

Touching and hugs are important throughout our lives, but as we get older they can become few and far between. 'Many elderly miss out on touching and particularly hugging so if you want to live to 100, find someone to hug. Even just hugging your pet will help, but regular hugs are important. The recommended daily allowance is as many as you can get, but a minimum of 4 hugs per day.'[210]

The truth is we all need hugs:

---

[207] http://news.bbc.co.uk/1/hi/wales/8073905.stm.
[208] James 5:14–15, THE MESSAGE.
[209] http://www.osteopath.co.uk/massage.htm.
[210] http://healthmad.com/health/four-secrets-to-living-well-to-100-dogs-hugs-drinking-and-cell-phones/.

The hug! There's just no doubt about it,
We scarcely could survive without it.
A hug delights and warms and charms,
It must be why God gave us arms. . .[211]

• Safety and security

One of the by-products of all the touchy-feely love and hugs, singing, rocking, feeding, and caring that we give our babies and children is that they will feel safe and secure. Safety and security is one of our primal needs, and it is one of the blessings that God wants for us. 'Observe my statutes and faithfully keep my ordinances, so that you may live on the land securely. The land will yield its fruit, and you will eat your fill and live on it securely.'[212]

The safety and security that a baby feels from the point of conception onwards is the rock on which he will stand throughout life as he reaches out into the wider world and makes his mark on society. Jesus said that hearing his words and not acting on them was like building on sand:

> These words I speak to you are not incidental additions to your life, homeowner improvements to your standard of living. They are foundational words, words to build a life on. If you work these words into your life, you are like a smart carpenter who built his house on solid rock. Rain poured down, the river flooded, a tornado hit—but nothing moved that house. It was fixed to the rock. 'But if you just use my words in Bible studies and don't work them into your life, you are like a stupid carpenter who built his house on the sandy beach. When a storm rolled in and the waves came up, it collapsed like a house of cards.[213]

This truth can also be applied to the basic foundations of our lives. The principle holds true, that we need to build our lives on a stable foundation. One of these stable foundations is this strong feeling of being safe and secure. This is built into our lives from way back before birth. As our children grow and reach out into the world they need to be standing on a strong rock of safety and security so that they will be able to build lives that do not keep collapsing.

I was in my twenties and struggling to make a way in life. It seemed as if everything I did came to nothing or collapsed. I felt that what I was building was God's will so why wasn't any of it working? One night I had a dream. In the dream I was building a house, it was a really lovely house and it was nearly finished. Suddenly it collapsed and was swept away. I looked at

---

[211] Author unknown.
[212] Lev. 25: 18–19, NRSV.
[213] Matt. 7: 24–7, THE MESSAGE.

the place where it had stood. There was nothing but shingle and stones. I looked around and I realised that I had been building my lovely house on the scree covered side of a mountain. [214] God spoke to me and said that the house that I was building was good, the rock that I was building on was also good, but the foundations were being built onto debris in my life. They were not secure, and could not hold the weight of the building. I was to clear the debris and get the foundations right and then the building would stand. As I have found healing for my inner needs this has set my life on a far more stable foundation.

So how do we build this safety and security into our children's lives? Right from the start, how we feel about the pregnancy and what happens to us as parents will affect our unborn babies. 'Chronic anxiety or wrenching ambivalence about motherhood can leave a deep scar on an unborn child's personality . . . how a man feels about his wife and unborn child is one of the single most important factors in determining the success of a pregnancy.'[215]

It's not just how we feel about the baby—a whole host of other stresses can affect him. Things that we can do something about, like our busy lifestyles, and also things that are not under our control, such as illness or death in the family, financial concerns, or, on a wider scale, recession, war, and natural disasters. These are all potential stressors for a mum to be. 'For one thing, a growing number of studies are confirming what used to be considered just an old wives' tale—that stress really isn't good for pregnant women. It not only increases the risk of pre-term labor, but possibly a host of other problems for babies after birth.'[216]

And then there is the whole subject of what we eat and the toxins around us, which I covered in the previous section.

Dr Michael Lieberman showed that an unborn child grows emotionally agitated (as measured by the quickening of his heartbeat) each time his mother thinks of having a cigarette. She doesn't even have to put it to her lips or light a match; just her idea of having a cigarette is enough to upset him. Naturally the fetus has no way of knowing his mother is smoking—or thinking about it—but he is intellectually sophisticated enough to associate the experience of her smoking with the unpleasant sensation it produces in him. This is caused by the drop in his oxygen supply . . .'[217]

Obviously, as pregnant mums, we can't spend all day thinking happy thoughts and knitting bootees, but we should be more aware of the effect that our complicated and sometimes

---

[214] 'Scree' is a term given to an accumulation of broken rock fragments at the base of crags, mountain cliffs, or valley shoulders.
[215] Dr Thomas R Verney with John Kelly, *The Secret Life of the Unborn Child* (Dell, 1982).
[216] http://www.medicinenet.com/script/main/art.asp?articlekey=51730.
[217] Verney, *Secret Life*.

frenetic lifestyles will have on the baby. And if baby feels safe and secure in the womb the chances are that he will be easier to look after once he has popped out.

Once this momentous event has happened and changed life forever, your baby's need for safety and security continues. All that love and care, touch and feeling can and should now be lavished on baby to keep strengthening these foundations. As a newborn, he doesn't understand words, just the way they are spoken; he doesn't understand touch, he just knows if it is soft or harsh, nasty or nice. Like a sponge he is soaking up emotions and storing them for his onward journey.

Eventually he will begin to reach out and become his own little person, taking part in the world and society. This is when safety and security take on a whole new meaning. Keeping him in that safe, secure environment—without stifling his need to explore, experiment, and have a variety of different experiences—can seem like an impossible task. But it is his foundational sense of safety and security that will give him the wings to fly.

- ## Stimulation and freedom of expression

Even before your baby is born his brain is wired up and ready to make connections and learn stuff. From about the fifth month of pregnancy he will be aware of things going on in the world outside—such as light and dark, heat and cold, noisy and quiet times, and the various voices of his family. Some people believe that playing music to your 'bump' will enhance his intellectual development.

But this learning and making connections explodes into activity when he is born. The birth experience itself is a major inrush of stimulation, and then he is thrust into a whole new world of seeing, hearing, touching, and being separate from mum.

Most of the brain's cells are formed before birth. But the cells actually make most of their connections with other cells during the first 3 years of life. . . . Early experience is very important in brain development. The baby's day-to-day experiences help decide how her brain cells will connect to each other. And if the baby does not have certain kinds of experiences, some areas of the brain will not make the necessary connections.[218]

The serious business of playing is one of the main ways that these connections are made. It's amazing that we understand that a baby will learn through play, but as soon as he gets to school we expect him to sit down, be quiet, and learn boring stuff that he's not interested in. Undoubtedly the discipline of learning is also a skill that needs to be acquired—but at 3, 4, or 5 years old? I think not. It seems likely that all he will learn is that learning is boring. But

---

[218] http://www.fcs.uga.edu/pubs/current/FACS01-2.html.

children are wired up to find learning exciting and we should play to these strengths and not squash them. So what brain connections does he need to make?

- *Seeing:* Unlike animals, that are often born blind, your baby is able to see from birth. However, his brain has not yet made all the right connections for him to process this information, so to begin with everything he sees is fuzzy. Initially baby is able to see you while feeding and he loves to look at your face and the faces of family members. But all activities that stimulate a baby's sight will ensure good visual development. His sight will gradually develop over the course of the first few months of his life and he will increasingly be able to make meaning of his environment. Shapes and colours and bold pictures will all help him get the connections necessary to see and focus, follow movement, find lost toys and eventually to recognise fine detail and things at a distance.
- *Hearing:* The brain needs to learn to make sense of the sounds that it hears. It needs to learn the difference between loud and soft sounds, their distance away, their direction, and of course what they mean. This process all begins before baby is even born. The womb is a very noisy place, and some months before birth baby can hear his mother's heartbeats, the grumbling of her stomach, sudden loud noises like a door slamming in the wind, and loud music. Loud sounds may cause baby to react by moving suddenly, soft sounds such as music may calm him. Because of these sounds, when baby is born he will have a sense of hearing that is well established. Many fathers—and my husband Mark was no exception—like to talk to their babies while they are still bumps. As Christians we can also speak to their spirits, declaring good things over them, singing psalms and songs, praying for them, and reading Bible stories to them. Almost certainly the first sound that baby will understand will be his mother's voice, followed soon after by that of his father and other members of the family. This ability to hear and distinguish sound is vital to the formation of language skills.
- *Language:* It is thought that babies are learning words from way before they begin to speak them, and that in particular they are learning the words for things that interest them—rather than the boring stuff that grown-ups are interested in. Reading stories and talking to baby forms the basis for his language skills, which are likely to begin at around 10 months. Singing nursery rhymes and songs will help with this learning by giving him a feel for the language long before he understands the words. Eventually when he begins to put words together into sentences we as parents and caregivers really will have to stop talking and start listening so that he can learn to use these new language skills to communicate thoughts and feelings. All too often though, as soon as our children start to talk we tell them to 'shut up'.
- *Feeling:* Babies become familiar with their world by touching and feeling it. They will experience many new sensations, such as rough, smooth, furry, shiny, or prickly.

Providing them with a variety of these surfaces to touch and feel will help build the connections for this sense. Most babies go through the stage of putting everything in their mouths. They do this because the tongue is very sensitive and they are learning more about the world around them through this sensitivity. I remember the 'everything in the mouth' stage as a time when every last small Lego piece had to be picked up off the floor. If I did any sewing I would count the pins and needles that I was using, making sure that I put the same number away, and none were left on the carpet!

- *Smelling:* The sense of smell is well developed at birth. It has been shown that babies can smell the amniotic fluid in the womb. Because the baby's sight develops slowly, the sense of smell is one of the main ways the newborn will know when his mother is near. He will also be able to distinguish other members of the family by their smell and the smell of his mother will usually calm him. (When David was first born, he was very sensitive to smell, and I would make up his cot using my nightdress—used and nice and smelly—as the sheet. He slept like a log!) This sense of smell will develop as he is exposed to a variety of different smells. These need to be good wholesome smells rather than chemical smells such as air fresheners, or pollution such as cigarette smoke. Seventy five per cent of our sense of taste comes from the sense of smell, so developing it is vital if the baby is to be interested in foods as he is weaned.

- *Taste:* At birth, babies are capable of detecting only three of the four main tastes: sweet, sour, and bitter. But they prefer sweet things, probably because breast milk is sweet. It seems that they cannot detect salty taste so if you were to give a newborn salty water, he would drink as much as he would plain water. The ability to taste salt comes at about 4 months. As with all the senses, taste will develop over time as the baby is exposed to variety. A breastfed baby will be exposed to a greater variety of taste because the flavours of the various foods that mum eats affect the taste of the breast milk. It is thought that experiencing a wide range of flavours in this way will encourage lifelong healthy eating habits, and in particular stop babies being fussy eaters when they are weaned. Bottle-fed babies will not, of course, have this variety. 'Researchers at the University of Copenhagen conducted tests on breast milk to see how the flavour changed with the mother's diet. They found that different foods caused subtle shifts in the flavour of breast milk, which appear to prime babies for the wide range of foods they are likely to encounter once they are weaned.'[219]

- *Movement:* Every time your baby moves he is strengthening the connections that are being made in his brain and the signals that go from the brain to move the muscles. Eventually you will notice that he begins to control these movements, reaching out to

---

[219] http://www.howbreastfeedingworks.com/?p=241

touch your face or bash a toy. It's a miracle that he goes from helpless newborn to walking in such a short space of time. He refines his fine motor skills and his hand–eye coordination in the same way. All these skills develop in our babies because of stimulation.

• Health and wellbeing

It goes without saying that anybody with a sickness has a poorer quality of life, and if the sickness is serious, chronic, or prolonged it is likely to affect the whole family. Children who are sick will often miss out on important stages of development and growth. They may be less curious and less stimulated to learn. They may miss out on cuddles and kisses. They may miss out on school and making friends. They may feel insecure and afraid. There are a whole host of things they may miss out on depending on when they are sick, what the sickness is, and how long it lasts.

We want our children to be well and we want to do everything in our power to raise our children to be healthy. One of my motivating factors for writing this book is to point the way to understanding how to raise our children to be healthy, and if they are sick to provide for them and lessen the effect of that sickness. As Christians we will pray for our children to be made whole and well but my experience of God has led me to believe that sometimes he does that by providing wisdom about the way forward. We may need to address a faulty way of living and change our lifestyle. The promises of blessing always came with a condition: God said, 'If you will listen carefully to the voice of the Lord your God, and do what is right in his sight, and give heed to his commandments and keep all his statutes, I will not bring upon you any of the diseases that I brought upon the Egyptians; for I am the Lord who heals you.'[220] Sometimes we just need to know what to do practically, and how to pray.

Our eldest son was an adorable baby. But he became a very difficult child. He was unpredictable, wild, sometimes violent; restless, always running, and never playing with anything for very long. Our house constantly looked like a bomb had hit it as he ran from one activity to the next. We would go to see a friend or do an activity but as soon as it ended he would want to do something else. I would take him to the park to feed the ducks, but he wouldn't stop long enough to feed them, we would go to the swings but he wouldn't swing. On and on he just kept on running. Life was lived on the run. Into that running race were born our other children. We were never able to play games with them—the snakes and ladders would be thrown across the room—Lego towers were demolished, precious drawings were torn up or scribbled on. Like full-time referees we had to somehow minimise the negative effects of all this running and chaos on their developing lives. I began to believe that I was a bad parent

---

[220] Ex. 15: 26, NRSV.

doing everything wrong. He was about 10 when I saw an article in a newspaper talking about 'hyperactive' children and ADHD. This was before the days of the internet, so I immediately went to the library and found a book about ADHD. I wept as I read it because it was describing my boy and the chaos of life in our household.

I didn't rush to the doctors for a diagnosis and medication: instead we began to pray. And we were praying now with an understanding of *how* to pray. Things began to change almost straight away. I didn't realise how important it was at the time, but within days of our starting to pray in this new way, he joined a swimming club, and eventually began competitive swimming. I have subsequently discovered that exercise—and especially swimming—helps build new brain cells, and is also really good for boys with ADHD as it helps them to burn off energy and to focus. God had stepped in with a totally unexpected solution.

> 'Across the board, exercise increases brain function, memory retention and other key areas of cognition up to 20 percent,' [Kramer] says. Although Kramer and his colleagues don't understand precisely how working out bolsters brain health, they have a few theories . . . exercise may actually encourage the brain to make new connections between neurons and to build new vascular structures.[221]

> Exercise turns on the attention system, the so called executive-functions-sequencing, working memory, prioritizing, inhibiting and sustaining attention . . . On a practical level, it causes kids to be less impulsive, which makes them more primed to learn.[222]

As David began to swim he also began to pick up—what had been for him—the really difficult task of reading. By the time he was 13, when he changed schools, he was put in the top sets for all his subjects and amazingly managed to keep up and pass all his GCSEs. Still extremely active, he is now an officer in the British Army and we are enormously proud of him.

• Provision of needs

Dr Arthur Janov, who developed a form of therapy called 'Primal Therapy', states:

> We are born needing, and the vast majority of us die after a lifetime of struggle with many of our needs unfulfilled. These needs are not excessive—to be fed, kept warm and dry, to grow and develop at our own pace, to be held and caressed, and to be stimulated. These Primal needs are the central reality of the infant. The neurotic process begins when these needs go unmet for any length of time. A newborn does not know that he should be

---

[221] Sandra Kettle, 'Build a Better Brain' (experiencelife.com/article/build-a-better-brain/).
[222] Dr John Ratey (www.johnratey.com). quote at: www.additudemag.com/adhd/article/3142.html

picked up when he cries or that he should not be weaned too early, but when his needs go unattended, he hurts.[223]

Most mothers will supply the needs of their baby instinctively. When told not to cuddle the baby too much, or not to pick up the baby when he cries, everything inside her will scream 'but I must'. For those of us who have missed out on the provision of these needs God is able to rewire our brains with a creative miracle as we come to understand the completeness of his provision for us.

• Development of trust

Trust is: reliance on the integrity, strength, ability, surety, etc., of a person or thing; confidence. Confident expectation of something; hope.[224]

When a baby is born he is totally helpless and dependent on his parents. As his parents supply his needs he builds up trust in them. All that cuddling, kissing, feeding, and stimulation that I have already talked about creates trust.

As the baby begins to build up trust in his parents so he also builds up trust in God. To the newborn his parents are God, they understand him and provide all his needs. And it is a while before he becomes aware that he is separate from them. This trust forms the foundation on which he will stand for the rest of his life. It is from this foundation that he will reach out, become independent, and fulfil the calling on his life. He will make friends and trust them, he will find a life partner whom he trusts, and he will begin to trust God. A child that has not learned to trust, or has had the trust betrayed, will live a life characterised by fear and anxiety. He will find it hard to make and keep friends, he will find it hard to create a marriage, and he could well find it hard to relate to God. Trust is like a mirror—once broken you never see things the same way again. And like a mirror the reflection you see of yourself will be distorted.

• Spiritual communication

The bond between a parent and a child is a spiritual bond that we would call a soul tie. Soul ties are formed when we have a strong bond with another person such as:

- A parent or child
- A friend
- A marriage partner
- Church members

---

[223] http://www.primaltherapy.com/FRAMESbasic/aptFrame.htm.
[224] http://dictionary.reference.com.

136

Good soul ties are a channel of love that flows between the people who have bonded together. But soul ties can have a negative effect and the channel can become a route for bad stuff to pass from one person to another. Bad soul ties need to be prayerfully undone, as do soul ties that have run their course. The soul tie between parent and child should be undone when he or she gets married: so, for instance, the father 'gives the bride away'.

Conclusion

Thus the foundation that we need for life begins at conception and continues throughout our childhood. If our own foundation is somewhat slippery then our ability to be good parents will be affected. In this way issues that affect our body, our soul, or our spirit may be passed down a family line. We may also find that in those areas where we have lacked the correct nurture—love, trust etc.,—that we also have problems relating to God and receiving those same things from him. Only as we seek healing from Jesus for our own inner needs and pains can we parent our children in the way that they need and prevent negative family traits from being passed on to succeeding generations.

Chapter 3
<u>The Intellect</u>

Intelligence is a very difficult concept to define. Intellect is described as 'the power of the mind to think in a logical manner and acquire knowledge'. Even psychology experts have not agreed upon what this actually means. Intelligence can be divided into various subcategories such as reasoning, problem solving, and memory, and so creating a consistent scale by which one can measure intelligence is quite difficult.[225]

There is a difference between knowledge and intellect. Knowledge is a series of facts: our children are learning these facts from the moment of conception—what things feel like, what they look like, what they taste like, and so on. As time goes by the newborn begins to put language to these things–mummy, daddy, cat, red, blue, banana, and so on. To this they add reading skills, and on this they build knowledge about the world: simple science, how things work, skills such as drawing, various sports, playing musical instruments, and how to turn the TV on.

But these things are not intellect. Intellect is the ability to learn, and the ability to then sift and sort that learning—or knowledge—into concepts, thoughts, ideas, memories, and words. Intellect gives rise to the concepts of right and wrong, good and evil. Intellect is the receiving ground for knowledge. This ability to sift facts in order to reason and solve problems is one of the core skills that our TV- and computer-age children have begun to lose.

Intellect can be impaired by negative influences and circumstances such as ill health, lack of oxygen to the brain, poor nutrition, premature birth, toxic substances such as mercury, lack of stimulation, stress, negative emotions, and evil spirits.

Intellect is also affected by genes—so if you are superintelligent then your children are likely to be superintelligent too. Studies of twins separated at birth show that despite growing up in different environments they end up with the same intellectual abilities and often incredibly similar life histories and preferences.

This doesn't just apply to twins. My own history is pretty bizarre. I started looking for my birth mother when the law was changed to allow this. At that time I had a preference for writing letters on airmail paper and using green ink in a fountain pen. It was quite hard

---

[225] http://www.scq.ubc.ca/the-genetic-basis-of-intelligence/

obtaining this green ink and I had to travel to London to buy it. This was not something that would have been encouraged by my parents as my father didn't believe in spending money on 'fripperies'.[226]

Eventually I had an appointment with the mother and baby home where I was born. I was shown the notes that had been made at the time and there was a letter with these notes, written by my mother, to arrange her arrival at the home. The letter was written with a fountain pen using green ink. She tells me that it was a deliberate choice to buy green ink as green was her favourite colour. Later, after finding her and doing research into her birth parents (she too was adopted) I discovered that we come from a French Huguenot background. The Huguenots were Protestant believers who fled persecution in France and settled in the UK, predominately in the East End of London—now known for its fashion industry. They brought with them their hard-working ethic and their trades, amongst which were the clothing trades of silk weaving, dressmaking, and millinery. And in these footsteps I followed as a fashion designer and my daughters too. Rosannagh after obtaining a first class honours BA in Fashion is now studying the History of Design at the Royal College of Art, and Elisia is studying surface pattern design. Whilst the discussion about the effect of nature versus nurture rages on I would like to suggest from my own experience that both are equally influential.

There have been a number of programmes aimed at increasing a baby's intellect, some of them starting before birth and some of them claiming to have the newborn speaking at 3 months or so. In reality the average healthy baby who is loved, stimulated, fed with good nutritious food, kept away from toxins and stress, and prayed for, will be intelligent.

To this intelligence we then add knowledge. Throughout the world in all different cultures children are put through some sort of learning programme. In the developed countries that learning usually takes place in schools. But indigenous peoples teach their children how to survive in their environment, how to hunt and fish, and which plants are useful as medicines or food.

In the UK we pop our wee babies off to school at the tender age of 5, or even earlier if they happen to be born later in the year. This is truly bonkers: consider the difference in ability of the child born on 31 August in one year with the child born on 1 September a whole year earlier. Children who are younger in their year group perform less well than the older ones.

. . . children born between June and August struggle for years to catch up with their older classmates, are more likely to truant, less likely to excel at sport, and are at a 'clear and

---

[226] Definition: Pretentious, showy finery; pretentious elegance; ostentation. Something trivial or non-essential.

139

long-term disadvantage in the education system'. September-born pupils are 20% more likely to go to university than those born in August.[227]

For many parents sending their children off to school as soon as possible is an economic necessity, releasing mum to go off to work while the school provides free childcare—and, it is hoped, some education—during the day. In our local town one school is now offering thirty hours a week to all 3-year-olds—all paid for by the government.

Because of the breakdown of the wider family most mums are ready for a break by the time this provision starts. Although there are some 'supermums' who find it hard to part with their 5-year-olds I wasn't one of them! I was really ready for my children to go off to school.

Edgar W. Howe, the novelist and magazine editor known for his sharp wit, wrote: 'If there were no schools to take the children away from home part of the time, the insane asylums would be filled with mothers.'[228]

But rigid school starting ages that don't take account of the child's emotional and developmental needs mean that many children are just not ready for full-time school by the time they are waved off on the school bus. Perhaps this is particularly true of boys.

My three-year-old son and I went shopping for his school uniform over the summer holiday. As he stood in the changing room, swamped by even the smallest trousers, several people commented that he looked too young to start school. I couldn't agree more. Scarcely will he have blown out the candles on his fourth birthday cake than I'll be waving him off at the school gates. The poor little man still puts his pants on back to front, needs a nap after lunch and thinks baby pigs come out of eggs. How is he going to cope with literacy and numeracy hours and SATs, let alone the horrors of school toilets?[229]

Children in the UK start school at 5 years old and some schools in Europe have a school starting age of 7. However, around the world (including the USA) 6 years old is the normal school starting age.

Studies carried out by the International Association for the Evaluation of Educational Achievement (IEA) support this view. Looking at the relationship between the age of starting school and reading performance at the ages of 9 and 14, they assessed children from 32 different countries, in most of which children started school at 5, 6 and 7, and found the top-achieving countries had a later starting age.[230]

---

[227] http://www.guardian.co.uk/education/2009/feb/14/starting-age-four-school.
[228] http://www.brainyquote.com/quotes/quotes/e/edwardwho104547.html.
[229] Catherine Bruton, 'Do we send our children to school too young?', *The Times* online. 06/09/2007
[230] Ibid.

So having decided what age your baby is going to start school, what sort of school should he go to? Or should he go to school at all? There are really only four options when it comes to schooling:

- Home schooling
- Private Christian schools
- Independent or public schools
- State schools, also known rather confusingly in the USA as public schools.

• Home schools

If we as Christians want our children to be brought up in line with our Christian principles then home schooling is one of the options. Many people are choosing to take their children out of the school system and home schooling is on the rise.

> A freedom of information request uncovers evidence that more and more parents are giving up on state education.
>
> It's Monday afternoon in Bromley, Kent—it's term time but not for Samuel, 10, Joshua, nearly 12, and 5-year-old William. All are educated at home by their parents—cooking, blogging and drawing all on their curriculum.
>
> Two years ago, Samuel who has Aspergers was taken out of school after he was bullied and began to self harm. His brother was given the option and just a day after Samuel left, decided he'd quit too. William—also on the autistic spectrum—hasn't been enrolled. Schooling isn't compulsory—ensuring your child gets an education is. In the Newsteads' case, that includes regular trips to the library and museums—and meeting up with other home educated children. There is no reliable data on how many of these children there are—estimates say up to 50,000—but the exclusive data obtained by Channel 4 News Online shows it's rising.
>
> . . . 134 local education authorities in England, Scotland and Wales replied to our freedom of information request.
>
> . . . And in those authorities with figures for the last five years, there's been an average increase of 61 per cent in the number of children being educated at home. In some areas it's far higher—Lancashire for example has seen an 829 per cent increase in home schooling since 2002.[231]

People who home school their children do so for a variety of reasons. Some do it because they believe that the education they can give their own children will be better and more appropriate for their child at his stage of development and for his interests. As happened to Beatrix Potter,

---

[231] Katie Razzall and Lewis Hannam, 'UK home-school cases soar' (www.channel4.com).

who said: 'Thank goodness I was never sent to school; it would have rubbed off some of the originality.'[232]

Some do so because it gives the family freedom to travel wherever they want or need to go, and others have children with special needs that are not being met. A large number of gifted children are home schooled because of the state system's 'one size fits all' approach to education. Children who are home schooled will not be subject to the peer pressure, bullying, violence, and disruption of lessons by other students, nor will they have to cope with long days and hours of travelling, and the boredom of enduring lessons not pitched at the right level.

Faith is another major reason for home schooling. Schools in the USA are secular and do not teach faith at all. UK schools are required by law to have a daily act of worship which is wholly or mainly Christian, although parents are able to opt their children out of this requirement. However, when my children were in the local state primary school the daily act of worship was just a time when some rather vague 'good behaviours'—such as helpfulness—were taught and announcements were made.

We home schooled Christopher for six months when he was 10. It was a major commitment and took a lot of time. It is probably impossible to home school and for both parents to hold down full-time jobs—even if, like mine, they are home-based. It was made more difficult by the fact that at age 10 Christopher had already discovered the 'joys' of computer games, so he veered very quickly and easily towards his games rather than school work. However we chose to home school him because his time in the local school had become really difficult for him. In his last year of junior school he had a change of teacher. Being a really bright lad he really couldn't get on with the slow pace of teaching and he was incredibly stressed and upset every day before school. This couldn't go on: we felt it would completely put him off learning to continue in this way so we considered home schooling. I was concerned that he might not get enough contact with other friends, but this was solved by him joining the local football club, so he would be able to keep up with his friends and see them at weekends. Home educators who are in it for the long run frequently get together for group activities, and there are many websites and chat rooms so none need feel isolated.

My other main concern was, how would I be able to teach him for a full school day? I was chatting about this with a friend, who made me realise that a large proportion of the day at school is taken up with the teacher having to quieten the class before each lesson, so he probably only had about an hour of actual teaching each day. This was an appalling thought.

---

[232] www.brainyquote.com/quotes/quotes/b/beatrixpot131912.html.

Armed with these answers we took him out of school for the spring and summer terms prior to going to secondary school. It was difficult, and yes, he did spend a lot of time playing computer games, but he also learned things that he still remembers—like what a graviton is, the arrangement of colour on a colour wheel, and how to light a bonfire.

George Bernard Shaw famously said: 'The only time my education was interrupted was when I was in school.'

• **Private Christian Schools**

Another option is to send your children to one of the newly emerging private Christians schools.[233] Some of these are connected to churches and some have been started by groups of concerned parents. Some are fee-paying, some are not, but all try to be affordable. These schools will generally be teaching and modelling the same morality and behaviours that you will be teaching and modelling at home.

> Instruction, and advice, and commands will profit little, unless they are backed up by the pattern of your own life. Your children will never believe you are in earnest, and really wish them to obey you, so long as your actions contradict your counsel . . . Think not your children will practise what they do not see you do. You are their model picture, and they will copy what you are . . . will seldom learn habits which they see you despise, or walk in paths in which you do not walk yourself.[234]

All our children attended our local Christian school—the River School in Worcester.[235] David made the choice that after ten years there he wanted to follow some of his friends into the local secondary school, where he did very well. Our other children stayed at the River School until the travelling and fees become too much for us to continue. Rosannagh then went on to attend the local secondary school, and our two youngest children went to the local primary school. They had all really enjoyed being at the River School so it was a tremendous wrench for them, even more so as the decision was made suddenly in the middle of the school year.

The River School had opted out of the SATS exams that the children were supposed to take, so the curriculum was not aimed at the passing of exams. This meant that the children had enjoyed wonderful creative times while they were learning. Now that they were in the state school system all this changed. Christopher was in year 3 when he moved so only had the benefit of two full school years in the River School, where he had developed a love for maths and a very keen mind that enjoyed learning. He would often come home singing the latest

---

[233] For more info see www.christianschoolstrust.co.uk or the Association of Christian Schools International at www.acsi.org.
[234] J. C. Ryle (Bishop of Liverpool), 'The Upper Room' (1888).
[235] http://www.river-school.co.uk.

songs that he had learned during the worship time. I can remember him singing his heart out, I could almost see his spirit growing. Things changed at the new school, he stopped singing, I could sense that his spirit was no longer being fed, and he came home with tales of how the teacher took so long to quieten the class down that they hardly did any work. And he wanted to work. In addition to this the maths was taught in a different way—one that was aimed at helping the less able to understand but didn't take account of the abilities of the more able. He began to go backwards as he struggled to learn the bizarrely long methods used for simple arithmetic. Rosannagh and Elisia came back with similar tales. It was extremely hard for them in the early days at their new schools and I'm not sure if they ever really settled in.

Some Christians disagree with the idea of sending their children to Christian schools. Rightly believing that we should be an influence for good in the societies where we live, they prefer to have their children involved with local state schools. And it is true that when our children started at the state schools we began to make new friends among the parents in the local area, which was really good. But having experienced both systems I have come to the opinion that sending our children into the state system is a bit like throwing them to the lions.

I like to grow onions. Mainly I like to grow them because I have been successful with onions but not so successful with other veg. Most people grow onions from onion sets—which are small onions that you put in the ground so that they grow bigger. That seems like cheating to me! I like to grow them from seeds. Over the Christmas period I sprinkle the seeds onto compost, cover the tray with plastic and put it on the windowsill. Lo and behold, the fragile little shoots come up, and eventually in a couple of months or so I get round to putting them in the ground. There they grow on into nice big juicy onions.

The point is—I don't put them straight into the ground. They need time in a protected and warm environment in which to start growing and to develop strength before having to cope with all the stresses of being out there surviving on their own in the midst of all sorts of dangers and predators. I feel it is the same with children. If they are well grounded in their early years they will have a strong foundation for life. As it says in the book of Proverbs: 'Point your kids in the right direction—when they're old they won't be lost.'[236]

This applies to the whole of the learning process. It is at these early stages that they will learn the life skills, and, as the educationalists put it, the transferable skills that they will need to go on into life. It is at this stage that they will learn the joy of new discovery, learning, experimenting, and taking risks. They also need to have discipline put into their lives, and learn about good and evil, right and wrong. They need to learn about God, how much he loves

---

[236] Prov. 22: 6, THE MESSAGE.

them, and to be taught his ways. 'Write these commandments that I've given you today on your hearts. Get them inside of you and then get them inside your children.'[237]

In a state school the standards and ethos are so very different from the standards and ethos that we have in our Christian homes. Do we really want to undo all the foundations that we have put into our children's lives by immersing them into such a secular and often ungodly world?

> Dismayed by what they perceive as poor academic and behavioural standards in their local state schools, many parents, teachers and churches have made great personal and financial sacrifices to establish these, their own independent schools.
>
> I can personally testify to the achievements—spiritual, personal and academic—of those new Christian schools which I have visited . . . I was always impressed first and foremost by the ethos; these were places where children were manifestly happy. There was no sense of intimidation associated with bullying or aggressive behaviour. The children were enjoying lessons in an atmosphere of personal engagement with teachers, who clearly cared for them as individuals and were keen to help them on a personal one-to-one basis.[238]

• Independent or public schools

Because of the high cost of private school fees, private schooling is really an option only for the wealthy, although some parents make tremendous sacrifices in order to send their children to these schools. Private or independent schools generally achieve higher academic standards and have a broader curriculum and better outcome for the students, who often go on to become leaders in society. These schools are free to operate outside any government curriculum, can attract the best teachers, and can choose which students to take. Often originating as church schools, many of these independent schools have a Christian ethos and morality. If they were not doing something right the great and good in our society would not be sending their children to them.

• State schools

Most of us, however, will send our children to schools provided by our governments. Our Western societies have changed considerably over time and the requirements of education have had to change with them. Economic realities mean that, more than ever, all children will grow into adults who must be able to provide for themselves and eventually their own families. In order to do this they will need to jump through the hoops of exams and qualifications, as there are few if any jobs nowadays that require no qualifications or commitment to further learning.

---

[237] Deut. 6: 6–7, THE MESSAGE.
[238] Baroness Cox, Foreword to Sylvia Baker and David Freeman, *The Love of God in the Classroom* (Christian Focus, 2005).

If your child's only ambition is to work at McDonalds just so that he can eat lots of burgers and fries he will be in for a rude awakening. McDonalds has a commitment to training and learning that goes way beyond knowing how to eat a Big Mac.

The key aims underpinning the UK's National Curriculum are:

> The school curriculum should develop enjoyment of, and commitment to, learning as a means of encouraging and stimulating the best possible progress and the highest attainment for all pupils. It should build on pupils' strengths, interests and experiences and develop their confidence in their capacity to learn and work independently and collaboratively. It should equip them with the essential learning skills of literacy, numeracy, and information and communication technology, and promote an enquiring mind and capacity to think rationally . . . The school curriculum should promote pupils' spiritual, moral, social and cultural development and, in particular, develop principles for distinguishing between right and wrong.[239]

Sadly these high and lofty ideals are all too often overtaken by the struggle to keep the class from degenerating into total anarchy and keep on top of all the paperwork.

> Silvia Thomas (not her real name) left teaching in the 1970s, to go into educational broadcasting. A while back she signed as a supply teacher and was so taken aback by the ferocity and the frequency of disruption at every school she was sent to that she decided to continue her teaching as an undercover journalist, at randomly selected schools with good Ofsted reports. . . . Partly, the footage she obtained merely shows the visceral difference between knowing something and seeing it. As a mother of young children in one of the most feeble education authorities in Britain, I'm used to regular news and gossip about the antics of the children at local comprehensives, and used as well to the sight of police cars at the school gates.
>
> Yet within seconds of sitting down to watch Classroom Chaos, I was on my feet again, pacing up the room in agitation . . .
>
> Children were simply on their feet, moving around, shouting, bustling, getting on with their own bits of petty social business. The noise was massive and the teacher appeared to be making no impact at all on the crowd. The fact that within 15 minutes they were seated at their desks with books open in front of them, seemed, from this perspective, like a miracle rather than an appalling waste of teaching time.
>
> Until now, I realised, I'd had a rather stagey view of what 'pupil disruption' looked like. Somehow, I imagined, two, three or four people managed to keep up a low-level

---

[239] http://webarchive.nationalarchives.gov.uk/20100202100434/http://curriculum.qcda.gov.uk/key-stages-1-and-2/Values-aims-and-purposes/index.aspx

disturbance that distracted but did not engage the other children. But in this footage, whole classes are routinely reduced to a milling, hysterical mob, sometimes with certain pupils yelling for their fellows to shut up because they want to listen.

Silvia Thomas is aware that as an ageing supply teacher, rusty in her training, she is an easy target for pupils. But other teachers watching her footage, confirm that this really is pretty much par for the course in many English schools (a separate report, cited in the film, also points to declining disciplinary standards in Scottish schools). I've never, personally, seen anything like it, even though I was schooled at a rough comprehensive that mainly served housing estates. This high level of insolence, rebellion, violence and disobedience has to be seen to be believed.[240]

Not limited to secondary schools, this kind of behaviour can also be seen in our junior and primary schools. When corporal punishment in schools was outlawed in 1986 no effective alternative was thought about or put into place. This vacuum means that many schools have now become places of anarchy where teachers are not respected or obeyed and bullies rule. This increasing problem of pupil disruption and violence in the classroom is well documented. But there are also less well-documented agendas that are aimed at our young people.

Global agendas in the classroom

Speaking at an Education Seminar in Denver in 1973, Chester M. Pierce—Professor of Education and Psychiatry at Harvard, had this to say:

> Every child in America entering school at the age of five is insane because he comes to school with certain allegiances toward our Founding Fathers, toward his parents, toward our elected officials, toward a belief in a supernatural being, and toward the sovereignty of this nation as a separate entity. It's up to you, teachers, to make all of these sick children well by creating the international child of the future.[241]

And Josef Stalin, who knew a thing or two about the control of people, said: 'Education is a weapon, whose effect depends on who holds it in his hands and at whom it is aimed.'[242]

There are secret agendas in the classroom and at the root of these is the agenda first set out by Adam Weishaupt, the founder of the shadowy group known as the Illuminati. Weishaupt was a Freemason, occultist, and Gnostic. He spent a number of years formulating a plan to create an organisation aimed at bringing all occultic systems into one powerful organisation which he called the Illuminati or 'enlightened ones'. The Illuminati work from within

---

[240] Deborah Orr, 'Mob Rule In the Classroom' (www.independent.co.uk).
[241] http://www.feariscontrol.com/?p=56.
[242] www.brainyquote.com/quotes/quotes/j/josephstal113988.html.

Freemasonry to promote a New World Order, which will rise out of the destruction of society. They intend to engineer this by the promotion of five main goals.

- The abolition of all monarchies and ordered governments.
- The abolition of private property and inheritances.
- The abolition of patriotism and nationalism.
- The abolition of family life and the institution of marriage, and the establishment of communal education for children.
- The abolition of religion. (In particular the Christian religion.)[243]

These goals are aimed at the creation of chaos from which the New World Order will emerge to 'save us'. We can see this same principle at work in the tightening of security and the resulting loss of our freedom after the chaos caused by recent terrorist attacks. When these goals have been achieved the world will be ruled by the 'enlightened' few—and ultimately by the 'enlightened' one. It is intended that the ordinary population will then become global citizens who will be little more than worker ants.

In schools, colleges, and universities our children are being educated into a belief system designed to change their attitudes, their values, and their faiths so that they will willingly accept the changes that are planned. John Lennon's song 'Imagine', that envisages a future without and countries, religions, or possessions could be seen as the anthem for this new global society.

Most people roll their eyes in disbelief when conspiracy theories are mentioned because the advocates of these theories often seem to be nerdy in the extreme. These theorists often look at the facts available and, like children with wax crayons, they join up all the dots and discover a hidden plan. They discover that the dots join up to make a picture and it is the picture of something very disturbing. Like the prophetic watchmen on the walls they start shouting out and warning us about these visions. Many of the facts that they have assembled are true, but joining all these dots together as if there were a 'human' conspiracy may be a step too far. As Christians we know that there is a conspiracy, but the arch conspirator is the angelic being known as Satan or Lucifer. Desperate to take one last bite at the apple of world domination he uses people and policies like the pieces in an infernal game of chess to set up a world system that will finally acknowledge him as god. At the end of the age—like 'Jack'—he will jump out of the box and announce himself to the world. 'He opposes and exalts himself above every so-called god or object of worship, so that he takes his seat in the temple of God, declaring himself to be God.'[244]

---

[243] Sourced from Pat Robertson, *The New World Order* (Thomas Nelson, 1992).
[244] 2 Thess. 2: 4, NRSV.

Satan's game plan that Adam Weishaupt wrote down in 1776, is now so far along in its implementation that it reads like today's newspapers. And this agenda is coming—or indeed has come—to a school near you where there is a war going on for the hearts, minds, and very souls of our children.

In the last few decades schooling has changed. Most countries now have a national curriculum that is the forerunner to a global curriculum:

> '[I]ncreasing numbers of educators, particularly those in leadership roles, have moved toward cross-national educational concerns,' wrote Professor John I. Goodlad in *Schooling for a Global Age,* funded by powerful globalist foundations such as the Danforth and Rockefeller Foundations as well as the U.S. Department of Education. Their common goal was 'the preparation of better persons for a better world.' Around the earth, they would teach their students the same basic 'global or humankind' beliefs using the same psychological strategies. If they could inspire all children with a common vision of a planet without national boundaries, the battle for global governance would be won.[245]

One of the educational methods used to promote these global agendas is called Outcome Based Education (OBE). To varying degrees Outcome Based Education and its many variants is practised in state schools across the developed world.

> OBE is packaged in a deceptive language that appears to be mischievously chosen to mislead parents. . . . OBE advocates continually use double-entendre expressions that parents assume mean one thing but really mean something different in the OBE context. When they talk about 'new basics,' for example, they are not talking about academics such as reading, writing and arithmetic, but OBE attitudes and outcomes. When they talk about 'higher order thinking skills' or 'critical thinking,' they mean a relativistic process of questioning traditional moral values.
>
> The following statement from OBE literature is typical: 'OBE schools are expected to become "success based" rather than "selection oriented" by establishing the instructional management procedures and delivery conditions which enable all students to learn and demonstrate those skills necessary for continued success.' OBE salespersons don't tell parents that 'success' for all children means 'success' in demonstrating only the dumbed-down outcomes that the slowest learners in the class can attain. OBE means 'success' in mediocrity rather than excellence.[246]

---

[245] http://www.crossroad.to/Books/BraveNewSchools/2-International.htm.
[246] Phyllis Schlafly, Report: 'What's Wrong With Outcome-Based Education?', May 1993 (www.ourcivilisation.com/dumb/dumb3.htm).

In many counties—such as South Africa and Australia—OBE is now falling out of favour and other systems for learning are being introduced. But even these are often based loosely on the OBE system. In the UK instead of OBE, we talk about 'learning outcomes'. These are the whole focus of NVQs,[247] but they also affect the rest of the education system in the UK. These learning outcomes and the language used to describe them are some of the main reasons why we as parents find ourselves completely at a loss when it comes to understanding our children's school reports.

The main premise of OBE is that all children will be able to learn; that schools will set clear goals for achievement and that children will demonstrate those achievements. This all sounds very good and praiseworthy. But before we start jumping up and down with happiness, we should look at what OBE really promotes.

> ■ Outcome Based Education stems from the new 'progressive education' ideas that were being discussed in the early nineteen hundreds by psychologists such as John Dewey— an atheist—who along with his fellow psychologists rejected the teachings of the Bible and instead, placed their faith in science, evolution, and psychology. These men—all members of the Communist Party—considered that man is an animal and can be trained in the same way that Pavlov trained his dogs. In his article 'Dumbing Down America', Dr Samuel Blumenfeld says;

>> To Dewey, the greatest obstacle to socialism was the private mind that seeks knowledge in order to exercise its own private judgment and intellectual authority. High literacy gave the individual the means to seek knowledge independently. It gave individuals the means to stand on their own two feet and think for themselves. This was detrimental to the 'social spirit' needed to bring about a collectivist society.
>> . . . Blinded by his vision of socialism, Dewey was incapable of seeing what was truly happening in the mind of a child and why the teaching of reading and writing was quite appropriate for the children between ages 5 and 7. All children, except the very seriously impaired, develop their innate language faculty extremely rapidly from ages 2 to 6. In fact, by the time they are six they have developed speaking vocabularies in the thousands of words, and can speak with clarity and grammatical correctness without having had a single day of formal education. In other words, children are dynamos of language learning and can easily be taught to read between ages 5 and 7, provided they are taught in the proper alphabetic-phonics way. Also, Dewey's notion that the primary function of language is social

---

[247] National Vocational Qualifications.

communication is debatable. If we accept the Bible as our source of information, it becomes obvious that the primary purpose of language—which was God's gift to Adam—was to permit Adam to converse with God and know God. The second purpose of language was to permit Adam to know objective reality and exercise thought. The third purpose of language was to permit Adam to know Eve, the social function of language. The fourth purpose of language was to permit Adam to know himself through introspection and inner dialogue. For Dewey and his colleagues, only the social function of language was paramount, and therefore children would be instructed in reading and language in a manner that emphasized its social function.[248]

In her book *The Deliberate Dumbing Down of America*, Charlotte Iserbyt tells of a young teacher named O. A. Nelson who, in 1928, with members of the Council for Foreign Relations, attended a meeting of the Progressive Education Association. Later Mr Nelson wrote:

> We were 13 at the meeting . . . The sole work of the group was to destroy our schools! We spent one hour and forty-five minutes discussing the so-called 'Modern Math'. At one point I objected because there was too much memory work, and math is reasoning; not memory. Dr Zeigler turned to me and said 'Nelson, wake up! That is what we want . . . a math that pupils cannot apply to life situations when they get out of school!'[249]

- OBE has at its heart the concept of extreme accountability—so everything requires proof. This proof requires paperwork, and although not part of the OBE agenda, this paperwork leads to league tables of good and bad schools and these in turn create schools where highly motivated parents want to send their children and schools that are the opposite.
- OBE uses the jargon of corporate business and it uses a business model for its basis. The jargon is impressive but often delivers very little. OBE prepares children for life beyond school, so that they are able to fulfil life roles that fit into the performance- (or outcome-)based economy where everything is judged by profit and loss.

> Only a dumbed down population, with no memory of America's roots as a prideful nation, could be expected to willingly succumb to the global workforce training planned by the Carnegie Corporation and the John D Rockefellers, I & II

---

248 Dr Samuel Blumenfeld, 'Dumbing Down America' (www.ordination.org/dumbing_down.htm).
249 Charlotte Iserbyt, *The Deliberate Dumbing Down of America* (3d Research, 1999). See also www.deliberatedumbingdown.com.

in the early twentieth century which is being implemented in the United States Congress in the year 1999.[250]

It speaks in term of outputs or exits, rather than inputs—such as good teaching. OBE does not put any emphasis on the content of lessons and prides itself on being syllabus free. Indeed outputs are often so vague and general that nearly anything a child does can be made to fit one of the outcomes and tick the box. 'The death of knowledge occurs: when evidence of learning becomes more important than the learning itself.'[251]

Evidence suggests that the real outcome being sought by one-world enthusiasts is to control and determine what the adults of tomorrow will do and what they will think.

Behavioural psychologist B. F. Skinner proposed 'a perfect society or new and more perfect order' in which children are reared by the State, rather than by their parents and are trained from birth to demonstrate only desirable behaviour and characteristics. Skinner's ideas would be widely implemented by educators in the 1960s, 70s, and 80s as Values Clarification and Outcome Based Education.[252]

Students are encouraged in lifelong learning so that they can 'do' stuff rather than the lifelong acquisition of knowledge. The teaching of basic skills such as reading and writing is not emphasised.

OBE is a method for concealing and perpetuating the number-one crime of the public school system—the failure to teach first-graders how to read. OBE is wholly committed to the 'whole language,' word-guessing method rather than the phonics method. This ensures that children will learn only to memorize a few words that are massively repeated. Teachers are cautioned not to correct spelling and syntax errors because that could be damaging to the student's self esteem and creativity.
Here are some direct quotations from the official 'Oklahoma State Competencies, Grade One,' pages 15–22, which confirm that first-graders will reach their 'Reading Learner Outcomes' by guessing rather than by reading: 'The student attend[s] to the meaning of what is read rather than focusing on figuring out words. . . . Uses context, pictures, syntax, and structural analysis clues to predict meanings of unknown words. Develops a sight vocabulary of high frequency words. . . . Predict[s] unknown words. . . . Uses predictions in order to read pattern books (stories with a repetitive element). . .

[250] Iserbyt, www.deliberatedumbingdown.com.
[251] Richard G. Berlach, 'Outcomes Based Education and the Death of Knowledge', Paper presented at the Australian Association for Research in Education Conference, University of Melbourne, 2004 (http://www.aare.edu.au/04pap/ber04768.pdf).
[252] http://www.americanchronicle.com/articles/view/20207.

. Uses fix-it strategies (predicts, uses pictorial cues, asks a friend, skips the word, substitutes another meaningful word). . . . The student will interpret a story from illustrations.[253]

- OBE is child-led: the teacher is no longer the one who sets the agenda for learning. OBE seeks to offer individual learning opportunities. This means that the teacher is inundated with trying to provide different 'lessons' and learning outcomes for each child in her class. Teachers weary from controlling a class of disruptive pupils now have the added burden of a mountain of paperwork associated with all this assessment. No wonder my children come home and tell me that their lessons are boring. No wonder so many teachers are leaving the profession.

- Outputs do not differentiate on the basis of quality. If the child has performed the skill they get a tick in the box, even though they may have performed it extremely well or extremely poorly. There is no possibility for individual excellence. OBE believes that every child in a group can learn to the required level. If a child is not able to demonstrate the outcomes for this level the whole group is held back, going round in endless circles until the box is ticked. The faster learners are not allowed to move on to the next level. It is believed that the child failing in outcomes such as reading and writing has been failed by the school or the teacher. There is no allowance for the possibility of failure on the part of the student. OBE believes that every child is a winner—no one fails. This is great for the underachievers, but high achievers and boys in particular often need the impetus that comes from a bit of competition. As such it has been accused of dumbing down education to the lowest common denominator so that all children succeed. It's great that children feel good about themselves and their level of achievement, but this must be grounded in some sort of reality. The singing contest *X Factor* is famous for bursting the bubbles of many of the contestants who have obviously never been told that they are quite simply rubbish at singing.

- OBE does not seek to instil knowledge: instead it focuses on what a child *is* rather than what he knows. Facts and knowledge enable a person to think for himself but in tomorrow's 'brave new world' there will be no room for free thinkers. In tomorrow's societies individual thinking must give way to collective thinking. The education system is being used to achieve this goal.

Knowledge- and fact-based learning has been replaced with OBE outcomes that concern values, attitudes, opinions, and relationships rather than objective information. These values encourage children to reject truth and moral absolutes in favour of tolerance, situational ethics, and consensus.

---

[253] Schlafly, 'What's Wrong With Outcome-Based Education?'

Behaviour modification is fundamental to achieving OBE-type results. OBE uses a 'stimulus–response–stimulus' pattern, a rewards-and-punishment process based on Ivan Pavlov's and B. F. Skinner's programmed learning/behaviour modification techniques. Under OBE, students are recycled through the process until they meet the mandated outcomes.[254]

Already looking toward the year 2000 A.D., the president of the National Education Association, Catherine Barrett, wrote in the Feb. 10, 1973, issue of the Saturday Review of Education, that 'dramatic changes in the way we will raise children in the year 2000 are indicated, particularly in terms of schooling . . . We will need to recognize that the so-called "basic skills" which currently represent nearly the total effort in elementary schools, will be taught in one-quarter of the present school-day . . . When this happens—and it is nearly here—the teacher can rise to his true calling. More than a dispenser of information, the teacher will be a conveyor of values, a philosopher . . . We will be the agents of change.'[255]

Outcome Based Education strategies in the classroom may just be the tip of a very large iceberg, as the elite few seek to indoctrinate us with their agendas.

The 'Common Purpose' Charity is perhaps another of these initiatives. On its website it announces: 'Common Purpose is an independent, international leadership development organization. We give people from the private, public and not-for-profit sectors the inspiration, skills and connections to become better leaders at work and in society.'[256] However some would say that the leadership training on offer has a hidden agenda;

But evidence shows that Common Purpose is rather more than a Charity 'empowering' people and communities'. In fact, CP is an elitest pro-EU political organisation helping to replace democracy in UK, and worldwide, with CP chosen 'elite' leaders. In truth, their hidden networks and political objectives are undermining and destroying our democratic society and are threatening 'free will' in adults, teenagers and children.[257]

So what are the values that this global agenda wants to promote?

---

[254] Schlafly, 'What's Wrong With Outcome-Based Education?'
[255] www.ewtn.com/library/HOMESCHL/HIGHJACK.htm.
[256] http://www.commonpurpose.org/who/about-us
[257] http://www.cpexposed.com/about-common-purpose

Chapter 4
<u>New Values</u>

Children are being taught that there is a coming global catastrophe and it's all their fault. Science lessons are now being invaded by lessons in lifestyle, politics, and even faith.

As the first decade of the twenty-first century nears its end, there is ever more evidence to suggest that, thanks to global warming, the world may be heading towards an unprecedented catastrophe. But it is not the one which has been so widely and noisily predicted by the likes of Nobel Peace Prize winner Al Gore.

The real disaster to be brought about by global warming, it now seems highly possible, is not the Technicolor apocalypse promised by Gore and his many allies—melting ice sheets, rising sea levels, hurricanes, droughts, mass-extinctions. It will be the result of all those measures being proposed by the world's politicians in the hope that they can avert a nightmare scenario which as many experts now believe, was never going to materialize anyway.[258]

Is it possible that the threat to our planet, and our way of life, from global warming has been exaggerated beyond the facts?

While politicians have engaged in an unholy scramble to appear cool and 'green' by promoting costly and impractical policies aimed at reducing CO_2, the truth is that scientists are not in agreement even about the fact of global warming. And if they accept that global warming is happening, they don't all accept that man is the cause, or that global warming is a catastrophe.

However, the science is not settled. Many renowned climatologists strongly disagree with the IPCC's conclusions about the cause and potential magnitude of Global Warming. More than 20,000 scientists have now signed the Oregon Petition which criticises it as 'flawed' research and states that *any human contribution to climate change has not yet been demonstrated.* Dr Chris Landsea resigned from the IPCC because he *personally could not in good faith continue to contribute to a process that I view as both being motivated by preconceived agendas and being scientifically unsound.*[259]

The Oregon Petition states:

---

[258] Christopher Booker, *The Real Global Warming Disaster* (Continuum, 2010).
[259] http://www.green-agenda.com/science.html.

There is no convincing scientific evidence that human release of carbon dioxide, methane, or other greenhouse gasses is causing or will, in the foreseeable future, cause catastrophic heating of the Earth's atmosphere and disruption of the Earth's climate. Moreover, there is substantial scientific evidence that increases in atmospheric carbon dioxide produce many beneficial effects upon the natural plant and animal environments of the Earth.[260]

Thanks in part to the rapid growth of the Chinese economy, figures show that in the last ten years CO_2 emissions have been growing faster than ever before. During this time there has not been an increase in global temperature and some scientists now say that the earth is cooling.

This headline may come as a bit of a surprise, so too might the fact that the warmest year recorded globally was not in 2008 or 2007, but in 1998.

But it is true. For the last 11 years we have not observed any increase in global temperatures. And our climate models did not forecast it, even though man-made carbon dioxide, the gas thought to be responsible for warming our planet, has continued to rise. [261]

This global cooling has highlighted an increasing understanding that global temperatures are governed by solar activity rather than CO_2 emissions. It also highlights the frailty of the computer models used to forecast global warming as none of them predicted this cold spell.

So are the ice-caps melting, leaving polar bears adrift and about to become extinct? According to the well-known broadcaster and botanist Professor David Bellamy there are more polar bears now than there were twenty years ago: 'Why scare the families of the world with tales that polar bears are heading for extinction when there is good evidence that there are now twice as many of these iconic animals, most doing well in the Arctic, than there were 20 years ago?'[262]

But, like those polar bears clinging to ice floes, politicians still cling desperately to the unsubstantiated theories of global warming. Anyone who calls for a debate on the matter is labelled a 'denier' and compared to people who still believe the earth is flat. And plans are still being put in place to teach global warming theories to our children. In the UK a new curriculum has been unveiled by the Qualifications and Curriculum Authority, the Government's exams watchdog.

Children will be put on the front line of the battle to save the planet under radical proposals to shake up the way that geography is taught in schools.

---

[260] http://www.petitionproject.org/index.php.
[261] Paul Hudson, BBC Climate correspondent, 'What Happened to Global Warming'
    (http://news.bbc.co.uk/1/hi/8299079.stm).
[262] http://nzclimatescience.net/index.php?option=com_content&task=view&id=58&Itemid=1

The plans . . . will ensure that, for the first time, issues such as climate change and global warming are at the heart of the school timetable. Pupils will also be taught to understand their responsibilities as consumers—and weigh up whether they should avoid travel by air to reduce CO_2 emissions and shun food produce imported from the other side of the world because of its impact on pollution . . .

The new topics children will study

* Climate change—the impact on pupils, the UK and the rest of world.
* Children's responsibilities—whether to travel by aeroplane or buy food from the other side of the world, and the impact of purchasing a gas-guzzling car or buying new clothes or trainers.
* The impact of the south Asian tsunami and Hurricane Katrina.
* Sustainable development—the importance of recycling waste products and saving energy.
* Global warming—impact of rising sea temperatures and melting ice caps.
* Fieldwork projects—such as studying ways to regenerate east London during preparations for the 2012 Olympics.
* Learning to examine individuals' carbon footprints, and what they can contribute in the fight to preserve the planet's resources.[263]

All very good stuff! We should look after our world as good stewards who will have to give an account to God for the way we have used his beautiful creation.

But climate change and environmental issues are being used to change the worldview of our children by uniting them in the fear of global catastrophe. The fact is that the green agenda is being used to help bring in global policies. According to David Rockefeller II, at a UN dinner in 1994: 'We are on the verge of a global transformation. All we need is the right major crisis, and the nations will accept the New World Order.'[264]

And it seems they found it: 'No matter if the science of global warming is all phony . . . climate change provides the greatest opportunity to bring about justice and equality in the world.'[265]

The fear of a common enemy is a great unifier: based on the so-called 'proof' that mankind is responsible for killing the planet, a framework has evolved to reshape the globe. This fear of a global environmental catastrophe has become one of the largest and most

---

[263] Richard Garner, Education Editor, 'All pupils to be given lessons in climate change', *The Independent,* 2 Feb. 2007 (http://www.independent.co.uk/environment/climate-change/all-pupils-to-be-given-lessons-in-climate-change-434717.html).

[264] http://www.huffingtonpost.com/larry-flynt/common-sense-2009_b_264706.html.

[265] Christine Stewart, former Canadian Minister of the Environment (inter alia: www.green-agenda.com/).

influential of social movements in recent years. It has created a backdoor through which the global agenda can begin to take centre stage, and all this will come about under the noble banner of saving the earth.

While the brave young men and women in our armed forces have been shedding their blood on foreign soil a bloodless coup has been taking over our governments. And it is aimed at denying us our God-given liberty and freedom. In 1992 a gathering of world leaders attended the Earth Summit held in Rio de Janeiro; 179 of those leaders signed a document called Agenda 21. This agreement—though not legally binding—ties governments to the United Nation's plan that will control the way we and our children live, eat, learn, travel, and even how we think. When fully implemented, Agenda 21 will have governments involved in every aspect of the life of every human on earth. This agreement even stretches its tentacles down to the community level.

> At the Rio Earth Summit in 1992, the United Nations agreed that the best starting point for the achievement of sustainable development is at the local level. In fact, two thirds of the 2500 action items of Agenda 21 relate to local councils. Each local authority has had to draw up its own Local Agenda 21 (LA21) strategy following discussion with its citizens about what they think is important for the area. The principle of sustainable development must form a central part of the strategy. [266]

We now have global decisions being taken by the United Nations—which is not a government—and ratified by world governments unaware that their sovereignty is being eroded.

The 'Club of Rome' is a think-tank composed of many leading members from around the world. 'The organization was founded in 1968 by global elite kingpin David Rockefeller and counts amongst its members some of the most influential power brokers on the planet, including current and former Heads of State, UN bureaucrats, high-level politicians and government officials, diplomats, scientists, economists, and business leaders from around the globe.'[267] In 1993, the Club published *The First Global Revolution*. According to this book, divided nations require common enemies to unite them,

> In searching for a new enemy to unite us, we came up with the idea that pollution, the threat of global warming, water shortages, famine and the like would fit the bill . . . All these dangers are caused by human intervention, and it is only through changed attitudes and behavior that they can be overcome. The real enemy then, is humanity itself.[268]

---

[266] http://www.sustainable-environment.org.uk/Action/Local_Agenda_21.php
[267] http://www.infowars.com/club-of-rome-behind-eco-fascist-purge-to-criminalize-climate-skepticism/.
[268] Club of Rome, *The First Global Revolution* (Pantheon, 1991); http://www.canadafreepress.com/index.php/article/49174.

Along with an anti-capitalist mantra, hidden in the climate change message is an anti-man viewpoint that sees man as merely one of many inhabitants of an earth held together by the mother goddess Gaia.

The Gaia hypothesis first formulated by Professor James Lovelock during the 1960s, proposes that the living and non-living parts of the earth form a complex interacting system that acts much like a single organism. The Gaia hypothesis is a thinly disguised pantheistic faith in Mother Earth that is totally opposed to the monotheistic religions of Judaism, Christianity, and Islam. In particular it singles out Christianity as being the cause of all the world's ills.

In the spiritual vacuum of today's society that has cast out the creator God, man is now fully committed to worshipping the creation. 'They exchanged the truth about God for a lie and worshiped and served the creature rather than the Creator, who is blessed forever.'[269]

The Gaia hypothesis and faith has gained credibility in the scientific community and goes under the name of Earth System Science. The Bible does confirm that the earth and her inhabitants are linked together, but they are linked by Jesus Christ. 'For everything, absolutely everything, above and below, visible and invisible, rank after rank after rank of angels— everything got started in him and finds its purpose in him. He was there before any of it came into existence and holds it all together right up to this moment.'[270]

The Bible also speaks of a coming day when the earth will be set free to thrive and prosper: 'The created world itself can hardly wait for what's coming next. Everything in creation is being more or less held back. God reins it in until both creation and all the creatures are ready and can be released at the same moment into the glorious times ahead.'[271]

When this happens all creation will sing for joy;

> So you'll go out in joy, you'll be led into a whole and complete life. The mountains and hills will lead the parade, bursting with song. All the trees of the forest will join the procession, exuberant with applause. No more thistles, but giant sequoias, no more thornbushes, but stately pines—Monuments to me, to God, living and lasting evidence of God.[272]

---

[269] Rom. 1: 25, NRSV.
[270] Col. 1: 16–17, THE MESSAGE.
[271] Rom. 8: 19–21, THE MESSAGE.
[272] Isa. 55: 12–13, THE MESSAGE.

The message of Gaia denies that man is a unique creature made in God's image, possessing a soul and spirit that are uniquely immortal and eternal, and capable of relationship with him. It also denies that there is an external God. 'Adherents of Pantheism understand it as a way of life, a way of viewing a world where human beings are but one of many living things. For the Pantheist, creator and context are one entity, the Universe being experienced holistically.'[273]

Not only does the green movement see man seen as a 'non-unique' dweller on this earth, but he also views him as being the one responsible for all of the earth's woes. 'Mankind is the most dangerous, destructive, selfish and unethical animal on the earth.'[274]

Population control

Your children will learn in school not only that man is bad for the environment but also that there are too many of us and something needs to be done about it. This will prepare them to accept the concept of the culling[275] of human beings in order to restore the 'correct' balance to the mother earth Gaia. These 'culls' are beginning now with an increasing acceptance of contraceptive methods such as the 'morning after' pill, and abortion, euthanasia, mercy killing, and the sterilisation of people with learning disabilities. But there will be a progression that will go hand in hand with the desensitization of people as they become used to these ideas and practices. A population cull could well take place by covert means through vaccination, the release of diseases, poisons in our foods, the rationing of healthcare, and other hidden means. It may even progress on to execution. You may be sure that if such a 'cull' ever happens it will begin with 'undesirables'. But who will determine who these undesirable are?

> In Germany they first came for the Communists,
>> and I didn't speak up because I wasn't a Communist.
> Then they came for the Jews,
>> and I didn't speak up because I wasn't a Jew.
> Then they came for the trade unionists,
>> and I didn't speak up because I wasn't a trade unionist.
> Then they came for the Catholics,
>> and I didn't speak up because I was a Protestant.
> Then they came for me —
>> and by that time no one was left to speak up.[276]

---

[273] http://www.pantheist.net/society/pantheist_world_view.html.

[274] Michael Fox, vice-president of The Humane Society, cited in, inter alia, Ward Clarke, *Misplaced Compassion* (iUniverse, 2001), 35.

[275] To pick out from others; select. To gather; collect. To remove rejected members or parts from (a herd, for example). *n.* Something picked out from others, especially something rejected because of inferior quality (http://www.thefreedictionary.com/culling).

[276] Pastor Martin Niemöller; German anti-Nazi theologian, who spent the war in a concentration camp.

Just for starters the UK-based Optimum Population Trust wants to reduce the population in the UK from 61.8 million[277] to 30 million, a figure similar to that of the population in Victorian times.

> Jonathon Porritt, one of British Prime Minister Gordon Brown's leading environmental advisers, is to warn that Britain must drastically reduce its population if it is to build a sustainable society.
>
> Porritt's call will come at this week's annual conference of the Optimum Population Trust (OPT), of which he is patron.
>
> The trust will release research suggesting the U.K. population must be cut to 30 million if the country wants to feed itself sustainably. [Britain's population is now about 60 million and growing.]
>
> Porritt said: 'Population growth, plus economic growth, is putting the world under terrible pressure. Each person in Britain has far more impact on the environment than those in developing countries, so cutting our population is one way to reduce that impact.'[278]

That means that half my family must be 'cut', half my friends must disappear, and the local town will be even emptier on a Saturday.

God knows the future and he commanded: 'Be fruitful and multiply, and fill the earth and subdue it.'[279] Those who don't understand that God himself has set times and limits in motion believe that the earth will run out of space and resources in the next hundred years or so. Currently however, the population has plenty of room.

I was 16 in 1970 when the Isle of Wight played host to the largest of its famous pop festivals. I was envious of friends of mine who went, along with approximately 600,000 other people. Unknown to me at the time, my birth mother was living on the island then and she was the driver for Jimi Hendrix, who played at the festival. There was an urban myth circulating that the entire population of the world could stand on the Isle of Wight but that it would sink into the sea under all the weight. Let's do the maths and see if the population of the world could have attended that festival.

The Isle of Wight covers 147 square miles; convert this to square feet: $147 \times 27,878,400 = 4,098,124,800$. The population of the world in 1970 was 3.7 billion, that's 37 with 8 zeros

[277] http://www.statistics.gov.uk/cci/nugget.asp?id=6.
[278] http://www.foxnews.com/story/0,2933,510377,00.html#ixzz2XhAa5RJw
[279] Gen. 1: 28, NRSV.

after it.[280] If you divide the area of the Isle of Wight in square feet by the population of the world you discover that each person would have had approx 1.1 square feet. But there would have been no room for a stage, loudspeakers, or loos. Yuk!

The population of the world is now 7 billion, so let's look at another urban myth. Apparently the population of the world could live in some comfort in Texas. Quite why they would want to live in Texas remains to be seen, but let's do the maths for this. The area of the state of Texas is 268,820 square miles, or 7,494,271,488,000 square feet. If this area is divided by the population of the world, there would be 1,071 square feet per person (slightly less than half a tennis court). However most people live in groups. If each family group consists of four people then each family group would have 4,282 square feet. Enough land for a decent sized house (1,000 sq. ft.) with a bit of garden. This is a population density of 26,030 people for every square mile. Building upwards would mean that there would be room for infrastructure such as the Royal Opera House, The Empire State Building, and McDonalds. 'If we all lived like New Yorkers, for example, 7 billion people could fit into Texas. If we lived like Houstonians, though, we'd occupy much of the conterminous United States.[281]

According to these calculations we could all live quite happily in Texas leaving the rest of the world for food, energy production, and exotic holidays. But the amount of land needed to support such a large city would depend on *how* we lived. However an article published in *New Scientist* says that there is enough space in the world to produce the food we need.

DOOM-MONGERS have got it wrong—there is enough space in the world to produce the extra food needed to feed a growing population. And contrary to expectation, most of it can be grown in Africa, say two international reports published this week.

The first, projecting 10 years into the future from last year's food crisis, which saw the price of food soar, says that there is plenty of unused, fertile land available to grow more crops.

'Some 1.6 billion hectares could be added to the current 1.4 billion hectares of crop land [in the world], and over half of the additionally available land is found in Africa and Latin America,' concludes the report, compiled by the Organization for Economic Cooperation and Development and the UN Food and Agriculture Organization (FAO).[282]

In our world, politics and greed cause more hunger and poverty than does lack of space. However, a new threat to the availability of land for food production is the green agenda's

---

[280] 1 billion in world population terms is 1,000 million—the American billion.
[281] http://persquaremile.com/2012/08/08/if-the-worlds-population-lived-like
[282] From a report by the Organisation for Economic Co-operation and Development and the Food and Agriculture Organization of the United Nations (http://www.newscientist.com/article/mg20227143.100-africa-alone-could-feed-the-world.html).

demand for bio-fuels and carbon offsetting through the creation of forests and woodland, which would use valuable arable land.

The desire to reduce the human population stems not from a genuine concern about overpopulation, but from the desire of an elite few to have absolute power and control over mankind. Basing their beliefs on Charles Darwin's ideas of natural selection, a group of intellectuals in the early twentieth century formed the Eugenics[283] Society. They believed that survival of the fittest human beings by natural selection was being impeded by the work of charities set up to help the poor. As far as the Eugenics Society was concerned the poor, the racially unclean, the sick, the disabled, and just about anyone who wasn't part of the social elite should not be allowed to breed, or be given healthcare or any other assistance to keep them alive. Hitler took this one step further when he tried to create a master race. 'History is replete with examples of rulers and elites engaging in eugenics and human population culls. It seems the lessons of history have not been learnt. Our "humanitarian" misanthropes continue to promote their culture of death. The packaging may have been tidied up a bit, but the same hatred of humanity remains.'[284] The family planning clinics, abortion on demand, in vitro fertilization, genetics and the human genome project all stem from the desire to control population.

Marie Stopes, who founded the first family planning clinics, was herself a member of the eugenics movement and her successful campaign to introduce family planning was aimed specifically at the working classes and undesirables. Whilst we see the emergence of family planning methods as an emancipator of women, she saw it as something totally different.

Stopes, a racist and an anti-Semite, campaigned for selective breeding to achieve racial purity, a passion she shared with Adolf Hitler in adoring letters and poems that she sent the leader of the Third Reich.

The feminist also attended the Nazi congress on population science in Berlin in 1935, while calling for the 'compulsory sterilisation of the diseased, drunkards, or simply those of bad character.' Stopes acted on her appalling theories by concentrating her abortion clinics in poor areas so as to reduce the birth rate of the lower classes.

Stopes left most of her estate to the Eugenics Society, an organization that shared her passion for racial purity and still exists today under the new name The Galton Institute. The society has included members such as Charles Galton Darwin (grandson of the evolutionist), Julian Huxley and Margaret Sanger.

---

[283] Eugenics is the science of improving a population by controlled breeding to increase the occurrence of desirable heritable characteristics (http://oxforddictionaries.com).

[284] Bill Muehlenberg, lecturer in ethics and philosophy at several Melbourne theological colleges and a Ph.D. candidate at Deakin University (http://www.mercatornet.com/articles/view/green_eugenics/)

Ominously, The Galton Institute website promotes its support and funding initiative for 'the practical delivery of family planning facilities, especially in developing countries.' In other words, the same organization that once advocated sterilizing black people to achieve racial purity in the same vein as the Nazis is now bankrolling abortions of black babies in the third world.

Several prominent individuals have expressed their outrage that Stopes is to be included on the 50p stamp in Britain.

Chaplain to the Stock Exchange Peter Mullen, who is Rector of St Michael's in the City of London, branded Stopes a 'Nazi sympathiser'.

He said: 'She campaigned to have the poor, the sick and people of mixed race sterilised.

Stopes extended her vile doctrines even to her own family. She cut her son Harry out of her will after he married a near-sighted woman—actually the daughter of Barnes Wallis, inventor of the bouncing bomb deployed by the Dambusters.'[285]

The human genome project—which has mapped every gene in humans— is also aimed at the eradication of the 'unfit'. Far from causing us to live longer, the likelihood is that it will end up helping the rich but enslaving or eliminating the poor and those judged to be undesirable.

The desire to produce better human beings by manipulating heredity and reproduction is not new. What *is* new is that the techniques for reproductive and genetic manipulation are outstripping earlier programs that relied primarily on voluntary, slow efforts at selective breeding—and on occasional involuntary programs for sterilizing or otherwise forbidding the reproduction of those deemed genetically unfit.[286]

Those who don't have the right genetic make-up may be unable to get work, they may be classed as second-class citizens, denied healthcare and health insurance, and perhaps more. There is currently a push to gather the DNA from as many citizens as possible and the Mayor of New York wants to impose DNA testing on all newborns. We may need to consider our response to these kinds of DNA collecting initiatives in order to protect our children.

Along side this collection of our DNA there is also a disturbing rise in the number of patents being applied to that DNA—our DNA.

Since the mid-1940's, genomics and the patenting of genes has grown exponentially. At present, nearly 20 percent of the entire human genome, or some 4,000 genes, are covered by at least one US patent. These include genes linked with Alzheimer's disease, colon

---

[285] http://www.thelabourparty.org/royal-mail-celebrates-eugenicist-marie-stopes.htm.
[286] http://harvardmagazine.com/2000/03/the-eugenic-temptation.html.

cancer and asthma. Myriad Genetics owns the exclusive patent for the BRCA1 and BRCA2 genes. As explained by *The New Yorker*:

'*Anyone conducting an experiment on them without a license can be sued for infringement of patent rights. This means that Myriad can decide what research is carried out on those genes, who can do that research, and how much any resulting therapy or diagnostic test will cost.*'

Needless to say, this has profound implications for medicine. As stated by the American Civil Liberties Union (ACLU):

'*Through its patents, Myriad has the right to stop anyone from using these genes for clinical or research purposes. It has therefore locked up a building block of human life.*' [287]

Conservation

The gaze of the global agenda has also turned itself to look at how human activities impact natural resources. We know that there have been some terrible disasters caused in the name of progress, such as the tragedy at Bhopal, India;

On the night of Dec. 2nd and 3rd, 1984, a Union Carbide plant in Bhopal, India, began leaking 27 tons of the deadly gas methyl isocyanate. None of the six safety systems designed to contain such a leak were operational, allowing the gas to spread throughout the city of Bhopal. Half a million people were exposed to the gas and 20,000 have died to date as a result of their exposure. More than 120,000 people still suffer from ailments caused by the accident and the subsequent pollution at the plant site.

These ailments include blindness, extreme difficulty in breathing, and gynecological disorders. The site has never been properly cleaned up and it continues to poison the residents of Bhopal.[288]

And at Chernobyl:

In the early morning hours of 26 April 1986, a testing error caused an explosion at the Chernobyl nuclear power station in northern Ukraine. During a radioactive fire that burned for 10 days, 190 tons of toxic materials were expelled into the atmosphere. The wind blew 70% of the radioactive material into the neighboring country of Belarus. Almost 20 years later, the people of Belarus continue to suffer medically, economically, environmentally and socially from the effects of the disaster.[289]

Similar 'disasters in the making' are affecting our seas:

---

[287] Mercola, J. "Genetic Testing for Breast Cancer and Radical Mastectomy—Are Women Being Misled into a False Sense of Security?" Retrieved Sep 20, 2013, from http://articles.mercola.com/sites/articles/archive/2013/05/27/angelina-jolie-double-mastectomy.aspx

[288] www.bhopal.org.

[289] www.chernobyl-international.org.

Man-made pollution is spreading a growing number of suffocating dead zones across the world's seas with disastrous consequences for marine life, scientists have warned. The experts say the hundreds of regions of critically low oxygen now affect a combined area the size of New Zealand, and that they pose as great a threat to life in the world's oceans as overfishing and habitat loss.[290]

The list grows longer every year as man's greed flourishes. But it is not only man that is being affected. All living creatures need a place to live, find food, and have young. Man occupies a special place in the heart of God and he gave us the responsibility to look after the environment in which he placed us: 'God took the Man and set him down in the Garden of Eden to work the ground and keep it in order.'[291] The word 'keep' in the original Hebrew means to guard, to preserve, to protect, to hedge about, to have charge of, and to watch over. The account of Noah and how he rescued the animals demonstrates God's desire to preserve not just humankind but animal kind as well. The Old Testament laws governing the use of the land and the years when it was to lie fallow also demonstrate his commitment to the very land itself.

Man, made in God's own image, is called to demonstrate his characteristics of creativity, but sadly, all too often (in his quest for riches and power), destruction has followed in his wake. The Bible puts it well when it says: 'Lust for money brings trouble and nothing but trouble.'[292]

When we take over natural areas for our own use, without any care for the land and the habitat, we take those areas away from other living creatures. We are taking over habitat at an alarming rate to provide ourselves with homes and agriculture, as well as plundering resources from forests, and other natural areas. This habitat loss is a real threat to the natural world.

But because of the environmentalists' pantheistic worldview the rights of the natural world have been elevated over and above the needs of man, who is seen as being just one of the inhabitants of earth. David Foreman said, 'My three main goals would be to reduce human population to about 100 million worldwide, destroy the industrial infrastructure and see wilderness, with it's full complement of species, returning throughout the world.'[293]

The use of land and property has increasingly been restricted because of the needs of endangered animal groups and environments. For instance, in the UK if you are building a

---

[290] David Adam, environment correspondent for *The Guardian*, 'Suffocating dead zones spread across world's oceans'. (http://www.guardian.co.uk/environment/2008/aug/14/pollution.endangeredhabitats).
[291] Gen. 2: 15, THE MESSAGE.
[292] 1 Tim. 6: 10, THE MESSAGE.
[293] Dave Foreman, co-founder of Earth First!, in an interview with Jerry Mason. Cited in Holly Swanson, *Set Up and Sold Out* (1994); 3rd rev. edn. (CIN, 2003).

property you really don't want to find bats, slowworms, great crested newts or any of the other protected species on your site. 'Planning permission is often dependent on developers showing that no protected animals, plants or buildings will be adversely affected by construction.'[294]

But the global plan is to set large tracts of land aside for endangered animals and squeeze humans into small areas of urbanization. Under the guise of sustainable development, natural resources are being 'rationed' and it is the intention to herd people into large communities and 'urbanisations'. People can be controlled far more easily if they live in large groups where transport, housing, work, faith, food, health, and education are all controlled. Land and water are being grabbed for wildlife so that you won't have it.

It makes perfect sense when the objectives of the UN's Agenda 21 are understood, as Agenda 21 is the overarching blueprint for depopulation and total control from the international level all the way down to the individual level, using the environment as the excuse. Most people are unaware that one of Agenda 21 Sustainable Development's goals is to make 50% of America into 'Wildlands' that are off-limits to humans and to herd people into 'Smart Growth' cities. Almost all wealth is derived from land and its resources. The more land the federal government owns, the more control they have. Less than 6% of America is considered developed (with roads and buildings) but the federal government is devoted to reducing these developed areas.[295]

Cute pictures of the human-like orang-utans, polar bears clinging to ice floes, elephants, and fluffy baby leopards will be shown to your children in school and they will become concerned for these endangered animals. But the hidden message is that the land belongs to these animals and we humans have no right to it.

The loss of local amenities in rural areas, such as Post Offices, Village Shops and Bus Services, together with the rise in petrol prices are all aimed at 'encouraging' us to move out of rural areas and into urban areas. These rural areas will then be returned to their true owners—the animals and wild plants.

Agenda 21 leaves no stone unturned and no person outside of its reach. In order to accomplish its goals of sustainable development and to make you into a so-called 'steward of the environment,' Agenda 21 seeks to control you and your life. Once implemented, Agenda 21 will affect you in the following ways:
- Eliminating your right to private ownership (property rights)
- Forbidding you from entering woodland and wetland areas

---

[294] Carly Chynoweth, 'Comfort for creatures puts building on hold', *The Times*, 16 April 2008 (http://business.timesonline.co.uk/tol/business/career_and_jobs/careers_in/article3744870.ece).
[295] http://www.campaignforliberty.com/blog.php?view=37187.

- Punishing you with higher prices at the store
- Restricting your civil liberties
- Restricting the number of children you can have
- Restricting the amount of trash or waste you can dispose of
- Restricting the amount of water you can use
- Telling you how much to harvest on your farm orland
- Forcing you to participate in community projects [296]

Human rights and sexuality

The human rights of a child are being used to promote the idea that children have a right to detailed knowledge about sexuality, sexual practices, and alternative lifestyles. Much of this knowledge may well fall into the category of being just 'too much information too soon'. With tolerance now elevated to godlike status, terms such as 'mum and dad' and 'husband and wife' could well become illegal and those who promote and use such terms could be prosecuted.

> 'Mom and Dad' as well as 'husband and wife' effectively have been banned from California schools under a bill signed by Gov. Arnold Schwarzenegger, who with his signature also ordered public schools to allow boys to use girls' restrooms and locker rooms, and vice versa, if they choose . . . The bills signed by Schwarzenegger include SB777, which bans anything in public schools that could be interpreted as negative toward homosexuality, bisexuality and other alternative lifestyle choices. There are no similar protections for students with traditional or conservative lifestyles and beliefs, however.[297]

Along with a redefinition of the God-ordained institution of marriage, this aggressive tolerance—being promoted by a vocal minority—will soon be taught in your children's school.

It's really good that children are learning about sex, as I can remember the dark ages when as a teenager in 1965 the biology teacher gave our class a photocopy of the male and female body parts and we were supposed to work it out from there. A long time and many 'dirty' jokes later I did finally work it all out. My five children bear testimony to that fact. However, this style of teaching (where we were left to 'fill in the blanks') was really confusing and left a lot to the imagination. My mother, who had attended the same school but in the 1920s, was only given instruction about reproduction in plants! So things had moved on a bit! I do believe that clear and detailed sex education is a good thing—but at the right age and within the right moral framework. My children have all benefited from sex education and are very open and free in their discussions about sex.

---

[296] Agenda 21 and You by The John Birch Society:
[297] http://www.wnd.com/2007/10/44009/.

My husband Mark teaches biology, and within that he is responsible for sex education. On one occasion he asked me to go and buy a pregnancy testing kit which he needed for a lesson. Since I was heavily pregnant at the time the shop staff gave me a very funny look! He taught sex education to a number of different age groups and his observation was that girlfriend and boyfriend relationships within the class would start soon after the sex lessons, no matter what the age of the children.

Children in many other countries have often, for cultural, religious, and economic reasons, been denied the opportunity of sex education and as a result have been poorly equipped to deal with early marriages and parenthood, or with abusive environments and the sex trades that are rampant around the world. For such children the attempt, spearheaded by UNESCO, to ensure that sex education is provided for all is laudable.

The *International Guidelines on Sexuality Education* published by UNESCO in 2009 has six key concepts. The first three are to do with relationships, values, cultures, and human rights. The second three cover human development, sexual behaviour, and sexual health. However, the global agenda is again at work in this Outcomes Based Education curriculum being proposed by UNESCO.

- It promotes the idea that sexual experience is a lifelong right, and that even young children can enjoy sexual pleasure: 'Under the U.N.'s voluntary sex-ed regime, kids just 5–8 years old will be told that 'touching and rubbing one's genitals is called masturbation' and that private parts 'can feel pleasurable when touched by oneself.'[298]
- It is heavily weighted towards total acceptance of all expressions of sexuality, thus heterosexual relationships within marriage are seen as being only one of many valid expressions of love and sexuality: 'By the time they're 9 years old, they'll learn about "positive and negative effects of aphrodisiacs," and wrestle with the ideas of "homophobia, transphobia and abuse of power."'[299]
- The UNESCO learning objectives for children just 9–12 years' old also teach that:

    Respect for human rights requires us to consider others' opinions on sexuality.
    Specific steps involved in obtaining and using condoms and contraception, including emergency contraception.
    Legal abortion performed under sterile conditions by medically trained personnel is safe.
    Human beings are born with the capacity to enjoy their sexuality throughout life.

[298] http://unitedfamiliesinternational.wordpress.com/2009/08/27/sex-education-at-age-5/.
[299] Joseph Abrams, 'U.N. Report advocates teaching masturbation to 5-year-olds', Fox News, Wed., 26 August 2009 (http://www.foxnews.com/story/0,2933,543203,00.html).

Many boys and girls begin to masturbate during puberty and sometimes earlier.[300]

- It is geared towards the prevention of Aids via contraception and considers all kinds of contraception, including abortion, to be equally valid. Children aged 12–15 years are encouraged to identify local sources for condoms and contraceptives. And those in the 15–18 year group are encouraged to view abortion as a right: 'At 12, they'll learn the "reasons for" abortions—but they'll already have known about their safety for three years. When they're 15, they'll be exposed to direct "advocacy to promote the right to and access to safe abortion."'[301]

- It promotes the idea that morals and values promoted by people of faith are the cause of many sexual problems and tensions. For instance one of the learning objectives for children aged 5–8 discusses: 'How harmful cultural/traditional practices affect health and wellbeing.'[302] This has some foundation in truth with regard to the widespread forbidding of sex education, or the prevalence of female circumcision in some cultures. However, this discussion can also be used as the vehicle to undermine the moral training that underpins our Judaeo-Christian societies. 'For SEICUS, Planned Parenthood, and other sex education programs modeled after Kinsey, the problem lies in the Judeo-Christian perspective on marriage and sexuality. In other words, the belief that sexual expression is only adequate in heterosexual marriage is seen as the abnormality and guilt is seen as a disease in need of a cure.'[303]

Faith

In 1933 the first Humanist Manifesto was published. One of the original signatories of this manifesto was John Dewey, a noted philosopher, psychologist, and highly influential educational reformer. He promoted the synthesizing of all religions and 'a socialized and cooperative economic order.'[304] Another co-signer of this manifesto, C. F. Potter, said: 'Education is thus a most powerful ally of humanism, and every American public school is a school of humanism. What can the theistic Sunday schools, meeting for an hour once a week, teaching only a fraction of the children, do to stem the tide of a five-day program of humanistic teaching?'[305]

These early 'pioneers' began a movement to eradicate God from the school curriculum. This aggressive secularism is still on the march, and in particular it is marching into a school near you by increasing the pressure for state schools to become more godless. Secularists believe

---

[300] http://www.foxnews.com/projects/pdf/082509_unesco.pdf.
[301] http://www.foxnews.com/story/0,2933,543203,00.html.
[302] http://www.foxnews.com/projects/pdf/082509_unesco.pdf.
[303] http://www.vidahumana.org/english/family/kinsey.html.
[304] http://constitution.org/col/cuddy_nwo.htm.
[305] http://www.khouse.org/articles/2001/365/.

that teaching a belief system to a child is an abuse of their human rights and that they should be free to make up their own minds when older. The Bible is at complete odds with this concept, believing that children need to be taught about faith and moral values. 'Point your kids in the right direction—when they're old they won't be lost.'[306]

This onward march of secularism is spearheaded by The Campaign for Secular Education:

Humanists, atheists and secularists believe that this life is all we have and that all our efforts should go into making it as enjoyable and satisfying as possible for everyone. We believe that morals are rooted in our human experience and that to teach opinion as fact to children is an abuse of their trust, and their rights. We believe that supernatural beliefs are at best an irrelevant diversion and at worst a dangerous obstacle to peaceful ethical societies. Because of this we want to see our atheist opinions considered and not censored out of philosophical and ethical discussions.[307]

Because of these influences our children now attend schools that have largely banned or sidelined Christianity. Instead, they are immersed in the new global spirituality that is a politically correct blend of all religions. Through role playing, rituals, symbols, and multicultural experiences schoolchildren now experience and take part in a dangerous medley of various new age and false religious activities. UNESCO's Declaration on the role of religion in a culture of peace, closes with an appeal for unity:

Grounded in our faith, we will build a culture of peace based on non-violence, tolerance, dialogue, mutual understanding, and justice. We call upon the institutions of our civil society, the United Nations System, governments, governmental and non-governmental organizations, corporations, and the mass media, to strengthen their commitments to peace and to listen to the cries of the victims and the dispossessed. We call upon the different religious and cultural traditions to join hands together in this effort, and to cooperate with us in spreading the message of peace.[308]

In a world that has seen too many religious wars and acts of atrocity it's no wonder that there are moves afoot to mix all our religions into one lovely 'pic and mix' religious system where no one faith claims to have the only truth, be the best, or provide the only pathway to god. "'There has been a huge outpouring of interfaith effort since Sept. 11," said Padraic O'Hare, director of the Center for Study of Jewish–Christian–Muslim relations at Merrimack College

---

[306] Prov. 22: 6, TM.
[307] http://www.c.s.e.freeuk.com/#Top
[308] http://www.unesco.org/cpp/uk/declarations/religion.pdf

in North Andover, Mass. "This is not a luxury. It's a necessity, whether there is a God or not."'[309]

These initiatives are encouraged and promoted by the good, the wise, the rich, and the unbelievably powerful:

> It involves unlikely support, such as that offered by the Obama White House, which has identified interfaith work as a public policy goal. President Obama's Council on Faith-Based and Neighborhood Partnerships has an 'interreligious dialogue and cooperation' task force that includes a female Hindu priest, an Orthodox Jewish layman, a female Muslim pollster, a nondenominational evangelical Christian pastor, a pastor and black civil rights leader, and a Muslim youth worker.
>
> 'It benefits from some unlikely backing. Some of the biggest movers and shakers in the interfaith movement are governments in Muslim states: Jordan, Saudi Arabia and Kazakhstan.
>
> 'Heads—or former heads—of state are likewise involved. Soon after British Prime Minister Tony Blair retired, he founded an interfaith foundation in London to 'promote respect and understanding about the world's major religions and show how faith is a powerful force for good in the modern world.'
>
> Not since 1950, when the National Council of Churches was founded, has this much energy been aimed toward alliances across religious barriers.[310]

John Lennon's vision, expressed in his song 'Imagine', is truly beginning to take shape through interfaith movements such as these around the world.

Underpinned by the teachings of Darwin, which are now mandatory in schools across the globe, this interfaith movement shores up the idea that religions are all the same, that their only function is to be an emotional prop, and that in reality there is no God at all save the god of knowledge.

Evolutionists believe that man developed the worship of nature, which evolved into the worship of various small gods, and then into the worship of one creator God. Historically nothing could be further from the truth. The worship of one creator God was the start point for all world religions. It was from this original creator worship that all the many gods and the worship of nature originated. 'Their research suggests that tribes are not animistic because they have continued unchanged since the dawn of history. Rather, the evidence indicates degeneration from a true knowledge of God.'[311]

---

[309] http://www.washingtontimes.com/news/2010/apr/05/interfaith-movement-gains-new-strength/?page=all
[310] ibid.
[311] Robert Brow, *Religion—Origins and Ideas* (Tyndale, 1966).

Evolutionists believe that man created his own gods, and is therefore at liberty to cast them aside when he no longer needs them. But the new god worshipped by the new thinkers of this age is this god of knowledge.

Thus the echoes of Eve reaching out for knowledge rather than relationship are still sending their shockwaves through her offspring. The knowledge now taught in our schools as fact has a central focus on the theory of evolution publicised and made popular by Darwin. But as with all things 'there is nothing new under the sun' and the concept of evolution 'has roots in antiquity, in the ideas of the ancient Greeks, Romans, and Chinese as well as in medieval Islamic science.'[312]

However, Darwin did a lot of the scientific legwork to 'prove' his theory and these tenets have become the cornerstone upon which a worldview that is anti-mankind and anti-God has been built. Darwin's gift to the world was:

- *Relativism and the loss of personal accountability:* The theory of evolution promotes the concept of 'life by chance'. If I am merely an object of chance and not the creation of a being with personality and desires then it doesn't matter what I believe or what I do. The end will justify the means, morality is relative to my circumstances, your beliefs are as good as mine, there are no absolutes except that it absolutely is not my fault and I can't be held responsible because I am a victim of my circumstances.
- *The loss of faith and the emergence of man as god:* Most people believe that our evolution from the primeval soup excludes the possibility of an external god. This leaves man as the highest form of being, a 'god' if you like. Thus an external God becomes at best irrelevant and the Bible becomes just another work of literature. Clearly, since God works through laws and principles that he has set up, there is no reason to exclude God just because he may have chosen to create man through a mechanism we call evolution. However, the lines are drawn and a belief in evolution is clearly equated with atheism, whilst belief in God is equated with the belief in a literal six-day creation period. Perhaps this is all a little too rigid.
- *The loss of the family unit:* With the loss of God from our belief systems the structures that he inaugurated are being slowly dismantled. The institution of marriage has now been eroded to the extent that is has become almost meaningless, trivial, temporary, and alternative. With this loss of the marriage unit, the family unit and the safe place for children that it provided has disappeared faster than the Amazonian rainforest. Children are now lost, bereft, cut adrift and without any emotional foundations in a hostile world where the government seeks to become the parent. The family unit

---

[312] http://www.citelighter.com/science/science/knowledgecards/history-of-evolutionary-thought

formed the first social unit and this became the basis for all civilisations. With the loss of the family unit there is a breakdown in society and the loss of civilisation.

- *The loss of a belief in the sanctity of life:* Evolution puts forward the theory of natural selection and survival of the fittest. The fact that you and I were ever born must mean that we are the progeny of those selected by chance, genes, and nature to live. In the future man will be able to cooperate with this natural selection by ensuring that only the fittest and finest specimens of mankind will survive. He will do this through contraception, including enforced contraception and post-conception measures such as the 'morning after' pill and abortion. This will progress on to voluntary euthanasia for all those who are so sick that they really want to die, then onto involuntary euthanasia for those who are sick, disabled, or mentally ill and unable to make their own decisions. Once on a slippery slope it's hard to get off, and the degeneration into a Nazi-like state, where the socially unacceptable are eradicated, is not hard to imagine.

Some say that on his deathbed Darwin renounced his belief in evolution, but others refute this. Whether he fully understood and would now approve of what he unleashed remains to be seen.

Chapter 5
The Will and the Emotions

Our will and our emotions express themselves through our bodily actions and reactions. These actions and reactions are always affected by the emotions. Poker players have to learn how to disguise their feelings—from where we get the term 'poker face'—and how to read the feelings of others. When a player has a good hand he will often betray this fact no matter how hard he tries not to. The other players looks for these 'tells': a 'tell' in poker is a change in a player's behaviour or conduct that gives clues to what that player thinks about his hand. Emotions also have a huge effect on our will, our decisions, indeed everything we do. It is often in the area of our emotions that we need healing in order to be able to function to our full capacity and achieve our dreams.

The will

The will is that part of me that is able to make decisions and implement them. I can decide to go for a walk, change my job, paint the front door red, or only ever eat Haribos. No matter how bizarre my desires, when I have freedom I can turn these desires into actions. When God placed Adam and Eve in that glorious garden he gave them a gift that was far greater and more amazing than the physical world. He gave them free will. They were free to make choices—any choices—even those that would have a negative impact on the world so lovingly prepared for them. He gave them the choice to obey him and be submitted to him or to rebel and be submitted to Satan.

The wrong choice they made plummeted mankind into a world full of mini dictators. With Satan's character now written into our very DNA, we all have the desire not only to make our own choices but to make choices for others and thus take away their free will. Submitting to the ungodly will of others—even unwittingly—reinforces Satan's authority over us. That's a fairly hefty statement but let's have a look at the ways in which people try to make us do what they want.

Domination

Domination (otherwise known as bullying) is the deliberate attempt to control another person or group of people. Often bullies are people who have had bullying or inconsistent behaviour modelled to them as children, or they may have experienced social or academic rejection. But this isn't always the case: they can also be highly popular over-achievers who have come to enjoy the sense of power and affirmation they experience by controlling the lives of others.

This control may be exercised through physical, emotional, and verbal abuse. The bully will often pick out some point of difference such as having red hair, wearing glasses, being small or being large. The whole point of the bullying is about the power the bully gains rather than the differences he is highlighting. Bullying is not just a school phenomenon that people grow out of, it also happens in workplaces, in homes, in the military and in homes for the elderly. Bullies will usually single out an individual for their attention and will attack that person with constant fault-finding, criticism, put-downs, and many other forms of verbal abuse. They will seek to distort that person's perception of reality by undermining them, humiliating them, belittling them, threatening them with false accusations and lies, and by separating them from friends. Their demands are often unclear, leaving the victim in a constant state of fear, and they often cause their victim to become dependent on them. Because the typical bully can be very charming and persuasive, other people are often unable to see the bullying for what it is.

Not necessarily lone individuals, bullies also run in packs, as seen by the recent spate of 'happy slapping' incidents, which is a form of bullying where a group of people attack another and then post the event on social media. Bullies can also be leaders of nations. There are many people in the world today who live under repressive regimes where they have no freedom at all. Such leaders or dictators are often little more than career-ladder bullies who have made it to the top. Consider the leaders of North Korea whose people must praise and worship them despite their terrible crimes:

> Kim Il Sung, North Korea's dead but current head of state and 'Eternal President', and his son Kim Jong Il, the 'Dear Leader' are the subject of worship and veneration unique to political leaders in the world today. Citizens are taught that all good things come from the leaders, who deserve unending loyalty and devotion. Due to the isolation, North Koreans genuinely believe this and worship them, bowing before the enormous statue of Kim Il Sung and memorising his speeches and texts. North Koreans must have pictures of the two leaders in their homes and failure to keep them clean is viewed as a political crime. State propaganda accords the 'Great Leader' supernatural powers and control over nature.[313]

Terrorists are the ultimate bullies, as domination is their political or religious goal and sworn duty. They advocate dominating, humiliating and killing those who believe in other faiths or who have other political beliefs. We have seen too many times the terrible consequences of their actions. This kind of domination is not from any 'god' I want to get to know, or any kind of political system I want to be part of.

---

[313] http://www.asialinkministries.org/resource/country_profile_NK.htm.

The long-term effects of bullying are devastating, as the victim comes to believe that he is not desirable, capable, useful, interesting, or of value and worth. His self-identity has been damaged, self- confidence takes a dive, he feels out of control, he can be beset by ongoing depression and lack the ability to prosper in life. We understand ourselves by what we see reflected back from others. If this reflection shows a negative image then the core of what we believe about ourselves will conform to this negative and destructive image. We will find it almost impossible to realise our full potential.

If your child is being bullied he is likely to be very reluctant to talk about it, but will display other signs, such as becoming withdrawn, refusing to go to school (if that is where the bullying takes place), becoming a bully himself—possibly to his siblings; he may stop eating or there may be physical signs such as bruises. It goes without saying that any form of abuse in the home or any form of sexual abuse are also forms of bullying and may have very similar symptoms. As parents we should do all we can to prevent the bullying by creating a way to avoid the bullies and by helping your child with assertion and self-esteem. There will be an ongoing need for affirmation even after the bullying has stopped.

Manipulation

Bullies will use all kinds of methods in their attempts to dominate and have power. One of these methods is manipulation. Not all manipulators are outright bullies but all want to get their own way by fair means or foul. Manipulation is a covert way of ensuring that you get your own way in a situation. Manipulators believe that they can fool people into giving them what they want and that nobody will realise what is happening. For many manipulators it's such a way of life that they don't even realise what they are doing. And it's probably something that we all do. If you've ever heard yourself saying: 'If you love me, then you'll . . . ', then you've probably done a bit of manipulating yourself.

A manipulator will seek to exploit the weaknesses and vulnerabilities of others. He wants to be in the position where he is right and you are wrong, he wants to be the one that you feel obligated or indebted to, he wants to make you feel responsible for his wellbeing, and he will coerce you into doing what he wants through guilt and fear. If you are being manipulated it's likely that you will feel a sense of rage, anxiety, irritation, confusion, and loss of control. Because the manipulator has a big emotional investment in your responses, you will feel as if you have woken up one morning and found yourself in a war zone. Instead of being true to our own thoughts, principles, and beliefs we often allow ourselves to respond to manipulators with what they want to hear.

Conspiracy theorists believe that a group of people are covertly manipulating events on the global scene in order to gain control and power, and they may well be right. However, Satan is the arch manipulator behind all these schemes as he plans to have absolute control. On an individual level he also wants to coerce you into actions you may later regret and that are aimed at taking away your free will.

Churches too have their fair share of manipulators. When a manipulator is leading a church the members will often equate loyalty to him as minister or leader with faithfulness to God. They are also likely to believe that their 'church' is extra special, better than others, and perhaps the only true church within a given area. There may be a sense of subtle or sometimes not so subtle censorship where members are taught to find fault in other churches; to mistrust other ministers, teachers, and authors; to take counsel only from their own pastor and to limit their contact with those who hold different views. This isolation is a particular feature of the more organized and obvious Christian and non-Christian cults that practise brainwashing. Manipulators can also seek to control churches and Christians from other 'roles' within the congregation. The Bible teaches us that we are all sinners but some of us find it really hard to believe that the seemingly nice, good, gifted, super-spiritual and godly person who has a leadership role in our church could possibly be a devious schemer who is consciously (or subconsciously) using aggressive tactics to get control, adoration, and power.

Because of its reliance on the Gnostic practice of having a ministry and a laity (that's all the rest of us), the Church is particularly open to abuse by those who want power and control. This desire for control sometimes goes under the name of the 'Jezebel Spirit'. Jezebel was the wife of Ahab, one of the kings of Israel; she was known for her worship of pagan gods, her desire to kill the true prophets of God, and her dominating and manipulative character. When a Jezebel spirit is operating in the church, the prophets and the true voice of God will be silenced and members will become dependent on others rather than God for direction. If allowed to run rampant this spirit causes tremendous destruction and pain to communities of believers.

When we are being bullied, dominated, or manipulated we are effectively being brainwashed. Our defence against brainwashing is to have an outside source of information. Countries that brainwash their citizens typically prohibit or severely block services by companies such as Google so that their citizens are kept in a state of misinformation or no information. It is this knowledge or information that helps people rise up and say 'enough is enough', as in the recent uprisings of the Arab Spring.

Recent attempts by the US government to restrict online freedom and grant itself more or less limitless control over the internet and its content were thwarted when millions of people took to the streets and to their computers to protest over the proposed 'Stop Online Piracy Act' (SOPA). This act, together with the Protect IP Act (PIPA), were 'sold' as ways to address online copyright infringement, but both laws contained measures capable of severely restricting online freedom of speech. These bills have now been put on hold.

However, the 'Campaign for Liberty is continuing its fight to stop another government intrusion, warning that this coming December [2012] the United Nations will also be meeting to compile even more recommendations for international internet regulations'.[314]

Dr Mercola warns that the coming censorship of the internet will have far-reaching effects on our freedom:

> Some of you may at this point wonder why I report on an issue such as this, so let me make this point clear. Access to health information could easily be deemed a 'threat' to national welfare—especially when web sites such as this one publish information that contradicts the official government stance. Examples such as advising women against national mammography screening standards, or raising concerns about vaccine safety, or questioning conventional cancer treatments could all be considered a threat to an extremely profitable status quo.
>
> In such a scenario, they could simply shut Mercola.com, and others like us, down; leaving you with no truth-telling, corruption-exposing, alternative voices other than the officially sponsored viewpoint. And it should be quite clear by now that the government-sanctioned stance on most issues relating to health and diet are primarily dictated by powerful lobbying groups furthering financially-driven industry agendas that have absolutely nothing to do with optimizing health and longevity.[315]

As Christians our outside source of information is God. Learning to hear him speak to us and then staying true to what he says is the ultimate antidote to any kind of manipulation. Jesus, who lived a life following God, said: 'I seek to do not my own will but the will of him who sent me.'[316]

When he was confronted with a close friend who sought to manipulate him and sway his resolve to follow God's will, Jesus was both insightful and assertive with his response:

> Then Jesus made it clear to his disciples that it was now necessary for him to go to Jerusalem, submit to an ordeal of suffering at the hands of the religious leaders, be killed, and then on the third day be raised up alive. Peter took him in hand, protesting, 'Impossible, Master! That can never be!' But Jesus didn't swerve. 'Peter, get out of my way. Satan, get lost. You have no idea how God works.'[317]

---

[314] Mercola, J. "If You See This Google Warning, Act Fast: Big Brother is Watching" Retrieved Sep 20, 2013, from http://articles.mercola.com/sites/articles/archive/2012/08/05/internet-security-virus.aspx?e_cid=20120805_SNL_ArtNew_1.
[315] Ibid.
[316] John 5: 30, NRSV.
[317] Matt. 16: 21–3, THE MESSAGE.

In the days to come this closeness to God and the ability to hear his voice must become the source of our life and the safe place for us and our children. We must learn to follow him rather than the manipulations, desires, and fickleness of men. Doing this calls not only for a close relationship with God our Father but also for a high degree of emotional wholeness.

Emotions

Like the engine in a car, emotions drive the decisions that we make and the actions that we take. We find it almost impossible to hide our emotions and those trained in reading body language can often glean all sorts of information from us even when we are trying to hide our feelings. Security forces around the world are typically trained in the behaviour analysis needed to spot a lie because the emotion of lying always betrays itself. Emotions form the basis for desire, and desire—which is an activity of the will—directs our actions. If our emotions have been damaged in some way then our actions will be affected.

Emotions, or feelings, such as love, hate, anger, surprise, joy, panic, fear, or grief can be very short in duration and are usually triggered by events and experiences. Moods are emotions too, but generally they last longer and are not so dependent on circumstances; although they can be affected by our health and diet. Moods such as happiness, sadness, frustration, contentment, or anxiety are underlying feelings that can actually alter the way we experience circumstances. 'A cheerful heart brings a smile to your face; a sad heart makes it hard to get through the day.'[318]

When we are 'in a good mood' we are able to let things go that would have really bugged us, we are lighter in our outlook, and we don't feel so isolated. When darkness clouds our vision then everything seems hopeless and we have a tendency to focus narrowly on the negative and not see the positives in life. Moods are not only affected by our health, they can also affect our health and make us ill: 'A cheerful disposition is good for your health; gloom and doom leave you bone-tired.' [319]

This link between our mood and our health has also been discovered by scientists, who now agree that laughter really is the best medicine:

Laughter really may be the best medicine, according to research presented to the American College of Cardiology. Laughing appears to boost your blood flow and researchers say it may reduce your risk of developing heart disease.

---

[318] Prov. 1: 13, THE MESSAGE.
[319] Prov. 17: 22, THE MESSAGE.

But the benefits of laughing don't stop with your heart: laughing has previously been found to help fight infections, relieve hay fever, ease pain, and help control diabetes.[320]

And:

> Given up to die within a few months in 1965, almost completely paralyzed, Cousins checked out of the hospital, moved into a hotel room and began taking extremely high doses of vitamin C while exposing himself to a continuous stream of humorous films and similar 'laughing matter'. His condition steadily improved and Cousins regained the use of his limbs until he was able to return to his full-time job at the Saturday Review.[321]

Apart from laughter there are many other things we can do to lift our mood, such as listening to music, changing our diet, going for a walk, or reading a good book. 'Summing it all up, friends, I'd say you'll do best by filling your minds and meditating on things true, noble, reputable, authentic, compelling, gracious—the best, not the worst; the beautiful, not the ugly; things to praise, not things to curse.'[322]

When we feel strong emotions we usually have a bodily response such as a flushed face, laughter, muscle tensing, facial expressions, a change in tone of voice, rapid breathing, restlessness, or other body language. Someone who is lying will find it difficult to maintain eye contact, they may lean away from you, they may fidget, they will sweat, and their breathing will alter. All this will come about because they are experiencing emotions—such as guilt—that are uncomfortable.

Love brings a different set of uncontrollable bodily reactions. When Elvis sang of love in his song 'All Shook Up' he was encountering an extreme reaction to being in love. Emotions are also something we share with the animal kingdom. When Maisie our dog used to hear thunder—and she would hear it way before I did—she would come to find me, shaking like a leaf. We had to give her tranquillizers before the Fifth of November (Bonfire Night in the UK) when thousands of fireworks are sent skywards.

> A three-month-old baby died in its mother's arms earlier this month. For hours the mother, Gana, gently shook and stroked her son Claudio, apparently trying to restore movement to his lolling head and limp arms. People who watched were moved to tears— unfazed by the fact that Gana and Claudio were 'only' gorillas in Münster zoo, northern Germany.[323]

---

[320] http://www.bupa.co.uk/health_information/html/health_news/160305laugh.html.
[321] http://www.healingcancernaturally.com/laughter-is-medicine.html#normanCousins
[322] Phil. 4: 8, TM.
[323] John-Paul Flintoff, 'Do animals have emotions?', *Sunday Times*, 24 August 2008 (www.timesonline.co.uk).

We share with animals the basic functions of many emotions. Fear may cause reactions that could save our lives, and our response to anger may be to attack—and so on. But with animals, when it comes to emotions, what you see is what you get. Humans process emotion differently, they can get their emotions all mixed up, they can hide their emotions to some extent and they can also use their emotions to create change.

Emotions are often channelled into the creation of art, music, and literature. They can be the motivations for war and 'man's inhumanity to man'. They can be the motivation for self-help groups, political change, and charity. Jesus himself was motivated by his emotions: 'A leper came to him begging him, and kneeling he said to him, "If you choose, you can make me clean." Moved with pity, Jesus stretched out his hand and touched him, and said to him, "I do choose. Be made clean!"'[324]

Without the motivation of emotions the drive to sustain a plan of action, or follow through with ideas, will be missing. It is emotions that colour people's lives and give them difference and purpose. However, in the same way that our bodies have often been thought of as bad, evil, and unspiritual, so too have our emotions. This has led to an attempt by many Christians to squash, deny, and ignore the very part of us that should motivate and inspire us. No wonder Christians have been seen as such a colourless bunch and have become the butt of so many jokes and characterisations.

Where do emotions come from?

Emotion is a characteristic that we get from God in whose image we are made. When we are born again and God's spirit comes to live within ours, we can often feel the feelings that God has when he looks at individuals and society. We see that God has emotion by looking at Jesus, who freely expressed his emotions, and who said: 'Have I been with you all this time, Philip, and you still do not know me? Whoever has seen me has seen the Father. How can you say, "Show us the Father"?'[325]

Jesus wept at the graveside of his friend Lazarus, he was angry with the moneychangers in the temple, and he felt forsaken on the cross. But he was also humorous: many of his words as recorded in the Bible would have been extremely funny to his audience, after all: 'How do you get a camel through the eye of a needle?' Likewise God the Father is described as having emotions. The first and greatest of these is love: 'This is how much God loved the world: He gave his Son, his one and only Son. And this is why: so that no one need be destroyed; by believing in him, anyone can have a whole and lasting life.'[326]

---

[324] Mark 1: 44, NRSV.
[325] John 14: 9, NRSV.
[326] John 3: 16, THE MESSAGE.

But He also laughs and gets angry:

> Why do the nations conspire, and the peoples plot in vain? The kings of the earth set themselves, and the rulers take counsel together, against the Lord and his anointed, saying, "Let us burst their bonds asunder, and cast their cords from us." He who sits in the heavens laughs; the Lord has them in derision. Then he will speak to them in his wrath, and terrify them in his fury, saying, "I have set my king on Zion, my holy hill."'[327]

He hates the things that harm us: 'be most careful, for God hates dishonesty, partiality, and bribery'.[328] And he gets sad: 'God was sorry that he had made the human race in the first place; it broke his heart.'[329]

The Holy Spirit too has emotion, as it says: 'do not grieve the Holy Spirit of God'.[330] The Holy Spirit, who dwells in our spirits when we are 'born again', seeks to replace our fallen and damaged human emotions with His healthy Godly emotion.

> But what happens when we live God's way? He brings gifts into our lives, much the same way that fruit appears in an orchard—things like affection for others, exuberance about life, serenity. We develop a willingness to stick with things, a sense of compassion in the heart, and a conviction that a basic holiness permeates things and people. We find ourselves involved in loyal commitments . . .'[331]

Because these gifts of Godly emotion come from the Holy Spirit they are placed first in our human spirit but then spill over into our souls and our bodies. If our emotions have been damaged we may not be able to express these God emotions and will feel spiritually blocked and constrained. When we are able to express these God emotions they will motivate or drive us into God actions. This work of the Holy Spirit within us is deeply emotional, and the more we are able to let him work in us the more we come to feel the very emotions and heart of God, his longings and his love for mankind. 'We do not know how to pray as we ought, but the Spirit himself intercedes for us with sighs too deep for words.'[332]

It was this deep-felt God emotion that caused Wilberforce to fight for the abolition of slavery; it caused Martin Luther King to use non-violent protest against the segregation of black people; and it was a the emotional response to a divine call that inspired Florence

---

[327] Ps. 2: 1–6, NRSV.
[328] 2 Chr.19: 7, THE MESSAGE.
[329] Gen. 6: 6, THE MESSAGE.
[330] Eph. 4: 30, NRSV.
[331] Gal. 5: 22, THE MESSAGE.
[332] Rom. 8: 26, NRSV.

Nightingale to revolutionize the care of patients and the nursing profession. We are equipped with emotion from our mothers' wombs:

> As it is with the establishment of physical settings in utero, the emotional system is also organizing itself in relation to the range and varieties of experiences encountered. A baby surrounded with anger, fear, and anxiety will be adjusting itself to that world and may carry those settings forward unless something changes. Patterns of fearful reaction already visible via ultrasound before birth can be seen after birth.[333]

The Bible also refers to babies in the womb having emotions: when Elizabeth met Mary the mother of Jesus the baby John in her womb 'leaped for joy'.[334] and Jacob and Esau were described as 'struggling together' in the womb.[335]

Soon after conception the baby does not have the mind with which to process emotion, but he does have a spirit which is capable of emotion and he can be deeply affected by his parents' emotional state and through them the circumstances into which he has been conceived.

> In writing our new book on preventing depression in very young children one of the things we noted was how kids could be born depressed or anxious depending on their mothers' experiences—especially negative relationship stressors—during pregnancy.
> Now new research published in the May edition of the *Journal of Clinical Endocrinology and Metabolism* shows that pregnant women who witnessed the September 11 World Trade Center collapse have passed on markers of posttraumatic stress disorder to their unborn babies through transgenerational transmission. The findings strengthen the evidence for in utero or early life risk factors for the later development of adult mental or physical disorders.[336]

The emotion that God intended us to be surrounded by is love: from conception through love, to love of the new life within, to love of the baby, the child, and the adult. Love, acceptance, respect, care and all that is good should be the environment for the lives of our children. Love should have been the environment for us too as we grew up and began life as a parent. Too often there are gaps in this love.

A gap or absence of love through any of these stages will almost certainly produce fear in one of its many manifestations. For fear (not hate) is the true opposite to love and just as light

---

[333] http://birthpsychology.com/free-article/when-does-parenting-begin-introduction
[334] Luke 1: 44. NRSV.
[335] Gen. 25: 22.KJV.
[336] http://www.upliftprogram.com/h_stress.html#h27

banishes darkness so love banishes fear: 'There is no room in love for fear. Well-formed love banishes fear. Since fear is crippling, a fearful life—fear of death, fear of judgment—is one not yet fully formed in love.'[337]

As we allow God's love to touch us at a very deep level so we can be healed of the lacks in love that were our experience as children, only then can we love our own children more and prevent the vicious circle that a lack of love sets in motion.

Healing for our emotions

The secular world offers help for those with painful and dysfunctional lives, but this help often takes no account of the human spirit. Trained in secular colleges with humanistic outlooks, counsellors, psychologists, and psychotherapists are taught that the answers to life's difficulties are within man and he can solve them on his own—or with a little pharmaceutical help. Add to this a value system that is variable at best and totally denies any absolutes of right or wrong at worst and you can see that looking for healing might be like chasing the wind.

Psychological theories and the science of understanding the mind are comparatively new kids on the block. Labels of mental illnesses are given to people—and they are then treated for this illness—even though these labels are subjective and constantly being revised.

In an unprecedented move for a professional body, the Division of Clinical Psychology (DCP), which represents more than 10,000 practitioners and is part of the distinguished British Psychological Society, will tomorrow [13 May 2013] publish a statement calling for the abandonment of psychiatric diagnosis and the development of alternatives which do not use the language of 'illness' or 'disorder'.

The statement claims: 'Psychiatric diagnosis is often presented as an objective statement of fact, but is, in essence, a clinical judgment based on observation and interpretation of behaviour and self-report, and thus subject to variation and bias.'[338]

In addition to this, the same article in *The Guardian* also says that new conditions are constantly being 'discovered,' and that the link to the pharmaceutical companies cannot be discounted.

Critics claim that the American Psychiatric Association's increasingly voluminous manual will see millions of people unnecessarily categorised as having psychiatric disorders. For example, shyness in children, temper tantrums and depression following the death of a

---

[337] 1 John 4: 18, THE MESSAGE.
[338] http://www.guardian.co.uk/society/2013/may/12/medicine-dsm5-row-does-mental-illness-exist.

loved one could become medical problems, treatable with <u>drugs</u>. So could internet addiction.

Inevitably such claims have given ammunition to psychiatry's critics, who believe that many of the conditions are simply inventions dreamed up for the benefit of pharmaceutical giants.

Psychological therapies that are on offer from your medical practitioner generally fall into three categories;

- *Behavioural therapies;* focusing on cognitions and behaviours.
- *Psychoanalytical and psychodynamic therapies;* focusing on unconscious relationship patterns evolving from childhood.
- *Humanistic therapies;* focusing on self-development in the 'here and now'.

• Behavioural Therapies

Behavioural therapy is based on the idea that behaviour is learnt, and so can be unlearnt, or reconditioned. It concentrates on the 'here and now' and does not try to find reasons for the behaviour by looking at past events and experiences. So for instance; therapy may include the rewarding of desired behaviour, and the lack of reward for undesired behaviour.

Cognitive therapy is a form of behavioural therapy that concentrates on the way we think. Based on the idea that the way we perceive situations influences how we feel about them it seeks to change our perceptions, especially where they are distorted. It comes from the idea that we all play 'tapes' in our subconscious minds that say things such as 'I'm stupid', 'I always fail', 'I can't do that', etc. It does not try to get at the root of these negative thoughts but seeks to replace them so that the individual can experience a more positive life, and be less afraid of situations that confront their negative beliefs.

To some extent the Bible also teaches this approach: we are taught to 'give thanks in all circumstances',[339] and Paul, in his letter to the Philippians, tells us; 'you'll do best by filling your minds and meditating on things true, noble, reputable, authentic, compelling, gracious—the best, not the worst; the beautiful, not the ugly; things to praise, not things to curse'.[340] In Christian counselling we are often taught that our thoughts need to come into line with the things that God says about us—which don't include rants about how stupid we are.

These two therapies combine to form Cognitive Behavioural Therapy. This involves not only changing the way you think (cognitive), but also how you respond to these thoughts

---

[339] 1 Thess. 5: 18, NRSV.
[340] Phil. 4: 8, THE MESSAGE.

(behaviour). It focuses on the 'here and now' rather than looking for any root causes, and it does this by breaking down seemingly overwhelming problems into smaller parts, making them easier to deal with. These smaller parts may be emotions, physical feelings, or actions that may interact with each other and that ultimately affect the way we behave.

Suitable for people with anxieties, phobias, sleep problems, relationship problems, and many more, the therapist will try to help you understand your thoughts and fears. Over a course of treatment you will work together to find ways of dealing with these. You may be asked to keep a journal, practice coping mechanisms, or even gradually expose yourself to the source of your fears.

The rewarding of desired behaviours and the lack of reward—or punishment—for undesired behaviours are forms of 'therapy' that we practise on our small children. It is quite normal for us to help our children to realise that inappropriate behaviour is connected to undesirable consequences, such as time spent on the 'naughty step', and that appropriate behaviour brings rewards. We do the same with their thoughts, teaching them to be positive and happy and to understand how loved and lovely they are.

The Old Testament law has a very similar function to these forms of therapy. Acting as a very strong deterrent, some of the laws seem to us to be totally barbaric. It can appear that the God of the Old Testament is full of wrath and judgement, whilst the God of the New Testament is full of love and mercy: but, these two are one. However, before Jesus came there was little possibility for the inward change of an individual, so God in his mercy gave a set of rules that, as one of its outworkings, would keep the social structure of society from falling into decay. Before Jesus came the only way to deal with 'transgressors' was to remove them from society either by exile or death, and thus prevent the spread of rebellion and evil.

Jesus' death on the cross makes it possible to access the mercy of God, so that we can receive forgiveness and healing. 'I will put my law within them, and I will write it on their hearts; and I will be their God, and they shall be my people. No longer shall they teach one another, or say to each other, "Know the Lord," for they shall all know me, from the least of them to the greatest, says the Lord; for I will forgive their iniquity, and remember their sin no more.'[341]

---

[341] Jer. 31: 33, NRSV.

• Psychoanalytical and Psychodynamic Therapies

Freud is usually regarded as being the founder of modern psychology and he developed the therapy known as psychoanalysis. He believed that an individual's behaviour and thoughts are not within their conscious control but stem from childhood experiences. These repressed feelings may result in depression and other negative symptoms.

In psychoanalysis the 'patient' will talk freely about their thoughts and memories and the therapist will seek to interpret and make sense of these. These interpretations will, of course, be extremely subjective. This kind of therapy is an intensive process and clients can attend therapy sessions for years.

Psychoanalytic therapy is based upon psychoanalysis but is less intensive, and there are fewer therapy sessions. It is often helpful for individuals who want to understand more about themselves. The aim is to work through any issues so that they can have a more satisfying life.

Psychotherapy evolved from psychoanalytic therapy, but tends to focus on more immediate problems. It aims to increase the client's self-awareness and understanding of how past experiences have influenced their present thoughts and behaviours. Patients are encouraged to explore unresolved issues and conflicts, and to talk about important people and relationships in their life.

The experience of talking through deep inner pains and issues can in itself bring some degree of healing. The Bible confirms that talking helps. The Roman Catholic practice of confession is a form of this talking, but we can talk to God directly and receive relief, forgiveness, and healing: 'if we admit our sins—make a clean breast of them—he won't let us down; he'll be true to himself. He'll forgive our sins and purge us of all wrongdoing.'[342]

We are also encouraged to share with other Christians: 'Confess your faults one to another, and pray one for another, that ye may be healed.'[343] Very few of us have such a group of people around us with whom we can share our hearts on a deep level. Perhaps this is why we have seen the emergence of Christian groups dedicated to the ministry of this kind of healing.

• Humanistic Therapy

There are various therapies grouped under the heading of humanistic therapies, these are: Person Centred Counselling, Gestalt Therapy, Transactional Analysis, Transpersonal Psychology, and Psychosynthesis and Existential Therapy.

---

[342] 1 John 1: 9, THE MESSAGE.
[343] James 5: 16, KJV.

Humanistic therapy was developed comparatively recently and it holds that people are inherently good. It focuses on recognising human capabilities in areas such as creativity, personal growth, and choice. The aim is to find out how an individual perceives himself and to recognize areas for growth, self-direction, and responsibilities. In this therapy it is the client who is responsible to find a way to improve, rather than the therapist. However, a good rapport with the therapist is essential to the process. This method is optimistic and attempts to help the client discover for himself his strengths by offering a non-judgemental, understanding experience.

In addition to these therapies pharmaceutical drugs are routinely used along with a variety of medical interventions.

Whilst some of these therapies undoubtedly do work, the healing of the mind and the emotions cannot truly take place in isolation from the understanding that the human spirit needs to come back into relationship with God. It is only through this renewed relationship that healing for the mind and the emotions can become part of our experience.

Bear Hug

Bear Hug

MATERIALS
2 x 50g ball Rowan Belle Organic Aran shade 223 Marina. 2 x 50g ball Rowan Belle Organic Aran shade 212 Zinc for trousers and bow tie, (90 metres per 50g ball). Oddment of brown for the face.
2 sets (of 4) no 4 mm double pointed needles 2 buttons for the trousers.

TENSION
Over garter stitch on no 4 mm needles 20 sts and 36 rows = 10cm (4 in) square.

ABBREVIATIONS
See page 305

SIZE
The bear is approx 51 cm (20 in) tall.

Note: When working in rounds garter stitch is worked as alt rows of knit and purl.

LEGS
Cast on 3 sts (1 on each of 3 needles)
Work in rnds of g st as follows;
1st round: Knit twice in each stitch. (6sts)
2nd round: Purl twice in each stitch. (12sts)
3rd round: Knit twice in each stitch. (24sts-8 on each needle)
4th round: *p3, purl twice into next st, rep from * to end of rnd. (30sts)
Rearrange the sts so that there are 10 sts on needle 1, and 7 sts on needles 2 & 3.
5th round: knit
6th round: purl

7th round: k6, k2tog, k to end of rnd. (29sts)
8th round: purl.
9th round: k5, sk2po, k to end. (27sts)
10th round: purl.
11th round: k4, sk2po, k to end. (25sts)
12th round: purl.
13th round: k3, sk2po, k to end. (23sts)
14th round: purl.
15th round: k2, sk2po, k to end. (21sts-7 on each needle)
Now cont in g st on these sts for 58 rnds. Cast off knitwise. Work 2nd leg to match.

ARMS
Cast on 3 sts (1 on each dpn)
1st round: Knit twice in each st (6sts)
2nd round: Purl twice in each st. (12sts)
3rd round: Knit twice in each **alt** st (18sts-6 on each needle)
Work in rnds of garter stitch for 48 rnds. Cast off knitwise.
Work 2nd arm to match.

BODY
Cast 15 sts onto each of 3 needles. (45sts)
Work two rnds in g st
Next round: k22, m1, k1, m1, k22 (47sts)
Work three rnds in garter stitch.
Next round: k10, k2tog, k10, (k1, m1) x 2, k11, skpo, k10. (47sts - 19 sts on needle 2 and 14 sts needles 1and 3)
Work five rnds in garter stitch.
Next round: k23, m1, k1, m1, k23 (49sts)
Work three rnds in garter stitch.
Next round: k9, k2tog, k12, (k1, m1) x 2, k13, skpo, k9. (49 sts-23 sts on needle 2 and 13 sts needles 1and 3)
Work three rnds in garter stitch. (49 sts)

Next round: k10, k2tog, k to last 12 sts, skpo, k10. (47 sts-23 sts on needle 2 and 12 sts needles 1and 3)
Work five rnds in garter stitch.
Next round: k9, k2tog, k to last 11 sts, skpo, k9. (45 sts - 23 sts on needle 2 and 11 sts needles 1and 3)
Work five rounds in garter stitch.
Next round: k8, k2tog, k to last 10 sts, skpo, k8 (43 sts - 23 sts on needle 2 and 10 sts needles 1and 3)
Work five rnds in garter stitch.
Next round: k7, k2tog, k to last 9 sts, skpo, k7. (41 sts - 23 sts on needle 2 and 9 sts needles 1and 3)
Work five rnds in garter stitch. (41 sts)
Now working on needle 2 only work 9 rows in garter stitch.
Next row: k5, k2tog , k3, sk2po, k3, k2tog, k5. (18sts)
Break yarn and rejoin to needles 1 and 3.
Work across all these 16 sts for 10 *rows* in garter stitch.
Break yarn.

HEAD
Rejoin yarn to needle 1 at centre of back as before, and work 3 rnds across all three needles in g st. (34 sts)
Next round: k17, m1, k17. (35 sts)
Work three rnds in garter stitch.
Next round: k8, m1, k9, m1, k1, m1, k9, m1, k8. (39 sts)
Work three rnds in garter stitch.
Next round: k19, m1, k1, m1, k19. (41sts)
Work three rnds in garter stitch.
Next round: k9, m1, k11, m1, k1, m1, k11, m1, k9. (45 sts)

Work three rnds in garter stitch.
Next round: k10, k2tog, k21, skpo, k10. (43sts) Work one rnd in garter stitch.
Next round: k10, k2tog, k 19, skpo, k10. (41sts) Work one rnd in garter stitch.
Next round: k9, k2tog, k19, skpo, k9 (39 sts) Work one rnd in garter stitch.
Next round: k9, k2tog, k17, skpo, k9 (37 sts) Work one rnd in garter stitch.
Next round: k8, k2tog, k17, skpo, k8 (35sts) Work one rnd in garter stitch.
Next round: k8, k2tog, k15, skpo, k8 (33sts) Work one rnd in garter stitch.
Next round: k7, k2tog, k15, skpo, k7. (31sts) Work one rnd in garter stitch.
Next round: k7, k2tog, k13, skpo, k7. (29sts) Work one rnd in garter stitch.
Next round: k6, k2tog, k13, skpo, k6. (27sts) Work one rnd in garter stitch.
Next round: k6, k2tog, k11, skpo, k6. (27sts) Work one rnd in garter stitch.
Next round: k5, k2tog, k11, skpo, k5. (25sts) Work one rnd in garter stitch.
Cast off loosely.

EARS
Working with two needles only
Cast on 6 sts, turn.
1st row: k4, wrap and turn.
2nd row: knit back
3rd row: k2, wrap and turn.
4th row: knit back
Rep these 4 *rows* six *more* times.
Cast off. Work 2nd ear to match.

NOSE
Cast on 3 sts (1 on each dpn)
1st round: Knit twice in each stitch (6sts)
2nd round: Purl twice in each stitch. (12sts)

3ʳᵈ round: Knit twice in each stitch. (24sts -8 on each needle) work 6 rnds in garter stitch. Cast off.

TO MAKE UP

Stuff legs firmly. Place into lower edge of body with RS together, (pull the body down over the legs) and making sure toes point to front. Work small back stitches through all 4 layers.

Stuff arms and place into the slits for armholes. Sew in as for the legs. Stuff the body and the head from top. Sew up the head seam.

Sew ears into place on curve of head. Partially sew nose into place and stuff then complete sewing. Using photo as a guide and with contrast brown yarn embroider nose mouth and eyes.

DUNGAREES

Using set of 4 mm needles cast on 39 sts – placing 13 on each needle.

Work in rnds of g st for 4 rnds. Now work in rnds of st st for 9 rnds.

Next round: knit 11, k2tog, rep from * to end of rnd. (36) sts.

Now cont in st st until 24 rnds have been worked. Leave on needles and set aside.

Work 2ⁿᵈ leg to match.

Body

Next round: With needle 1 work across 1ˢᵗ 18 sts of 2ⁿᵈ leg and 1ˢᵗ 6 sts of 1ˢᵗ leg, with needle 2 work across next 24 sts of 2ⁿᵈ leg, with needle 3 work across last 6 sts of 1ˢᵗ leg and last 18 sts of 2ⁿᵈ leg. 24 sts on each needle. (72 sts)

Work in rnds of st st for 36 rnds. (Work may be a little 'tight' to begin)

Next round: purl
Next round: Knit
Next round: cast off purlwise, the 24 sts from needle 1, and 12 sts from needle 2, (36 sts cast off for front) cast off a further 9 sts from needle 2, k4 (counting the stitch already on the needle as one on these), cast off 10 sts, k4 (counting the stitch already on the needle as one of these), cast off rem 9 sts. Break yarn.

Rejoin yarn to 1ˢᵗ group of 4 sts and work in rows of garter stitch for 70 rows. Cast off. Work 2ⁿᵈ strap to match.

BOW TIE

Cast on 6 sts and work in g st for 40 *rows*.
Next row: k2tog, k2, k2tog, (4 sts)
Cont in g st on these 4 sts for a further 60 *rows*. Cast off. Fold into a bow tie shape, wrap round neck and sew into place.

Spirit

Chapter 1
<u>All you need is love</u>

Almost from the time when he was merely a twinkle in daddy's eye, our brand new little person has needs. But in that unbelievable moment when baby is first placed in our arms, the task of growing him into wholeness and maturity can seem overwhelming. At that moment we are launched into a loving and nurturing process that is intended to provide for all his needs—but often we feel ill equipped for the task. His body has needs, and into this we will stuff spaghetti bolognaise. His soul has needs, and into this we will stuff learning, skills, guidance and healthy emotions. And his spirit has needs—whatever do we stuff into his spirit? We may feel that we don't know where to start with growing his spirit or even understand the relevance of doing so. And there may be precious little time to even think about this aspect of his nurture as the urgent needs of the body and the very strong demands of the will take precedence.

Yet as we instinctively cuddle him and sing to him, rock him and communicate our love to him, we are already feeding his spirit in the very best way. Although we will make many mistakes as we take this journey into parenthood, these will have far less negative impact on our children if they are enveloped in unconditional love and are able to feel it and receive it: 'love covers a multitude of sins.'[344] Just being there is already the best thing you can do for your child.

Perhaps this ability to love and to be loved is mankind's most defining characteristic. Defying science which cannot isolate, dissect, or even point to its substance, love is one of the greatest forces at work on the earth. When we are in love we are 'over the moon', when we are loved we can function, create, grow, imagine, and generally thrive. When we are not loved our world 'falls apart': we lose the ability to focus, to create, to function and even to live.

When God made humans in his own image this characteristic of love was one of the primary family traits that he passed on to us. So whilst love can be expressed physically and emotionally, it is essentially spiritual. We know this because God who is pure spirit is also love. Everything that God does has love written through its DNA. His very essence and all that he does is love.

A person, or being, who loves needs to have an object for that love. We are the object of God's love. We do not deserve it and we cannot make ourselves worthy of it. We cannot make

---

[344] 1 Pet.4: 8, NRSV.

him love us any more and we cannot make him love us any less. His love for us is not connected to how we perform or how much we 'do for him'. His love is unconditional.

Our love for our children, although immensely strong, is only a poor reflection of the amazing love that God the Father has for you and me. God's love is a love that rescues the despairing and lonely, binds up the broken and finds the lost.

I crawled through a very long dark tunnel during my twenties. A tunnel of despair, that seemed to have no light at its end. As though a battle of cosmic proportions was being fought over my life I reeled punch drunk from disaster to disaster, unable to get my life on track. Stuck in the middle of this battle I tried desperately to hang in there and make some sense of it all. I struggled with everything. The past—not just my own past but my generational history—had all come up and hit my present. Severely depressed, twice I tried to commit suicide. Both times something miraculous happened to keep me here. There seemed to be no way of escape. Conversely, I can see that my spirit was going from strength to strength. I was hearing God, dreaming dreams and seeing visions, and I could spend hours in prayer and Bible study. God became my main friend. But God does not intend us to be isolated or to wake up every day wishing that life would end. He stepped in and rescued me.

I didn't really want to go out that evening because it was rather cold, but my friend phoned and asked me to go to a church meeting being held in the local school. I followed her in and as I went to sit next to her, she told me to go and sit somewhere else. The words were strangely hostile and I couldn't take them in. I felt as though I had been kicked in the stomach. My instant reaction was: 'Help—get me out of here, I'm going to cry,' so I pulled myself together as much as I could and headed towards the loo. As I walked down the corridor I could see a stranger coming in the other direction. I thought maybe he was the caretaker so I looked up, determined to give him a really good Christian smile to make him feel at ease.

But it was God who looked back at me. In that brief moment time stood still and eternity crashed in. I saw God's love for me. Love like nothing I could ever explain, love that went on for ever and ever, back into my past, forward into my future, and here in the present. God looking at me with overwhelming compassion and love: just for me. I had never experienced such a thing: it was awesome, it was frightening, it only lasted a millisecond but it went on for eternity. It coloured my past, my present, and my future. I would never be the same again. I had a Father who loved me. I couldn't bear it and I had to look away. But his love has never left me.

How did this happen? God looking at me through the eyes of a stranger? I only know that's what happened. I had experienced something from out of this world and it changed my life. I later discovered that this 'caretaker' was in fact the visiting speaker. At the end of the meeting he had some words from God for me that reinforced what had just taken place. Now, even though many of my problems remained, I had a foundation to stand on. A foundation of love. 'I waited patiently for the Lord; he inclined to me and heard my cry. He drew me up from the desolate pit, out of the miry bog, and set my feet upon a rock, making my steps secure. He put a new song in my mouth, a song of praise to our God.'[345]

In our love for Jesus and our joy at the new life he has given us, many of us have missed the point. Jesus' life and death on earth were all about bringing us back into relationship with God the Father who loves us. Until we find this relationship with him as our Father we have not fully grasped all that Jesus did for us. The heart of God our Father is love and although many people will eagerly deny the existence of God, we all believe in, and long for, love.

How do we express love?

Because love is spiritual food, the love that we have for our children goes deep into their spirits bringing life which then flows out to sustain them in both body and soul. For most of us the love for our newborn is instinctive and almost overwhelming. But for all sorts of reasons the communication of that love can get lost in translation. In a counselling situation we may ask, 'Did your father love you? Did your mother love you?' Invariably the answer is yes and indeed often the counsellee will have had very loving and caring parents. But when we probe further they may not be able to describe how they were loved or talk about any one experience that made them feel loved. Yes, their parents loved them, they were committed to them, they fed them, they provided a home for them, and birthday parties and presents, but the feelings of being loved were not adequately communicated. It would be wrong to say that they were not, or are not, loved. But effectively, for many people, their need for love has not been met. This unmet love need creates a spirit starved and unable to grow into wholeness.

Love does not just come from 'nowhere', it has to be modelled to us—'We love because he first loved us.'[346] But living in societies that are epitomized by stress, financial worries, and the breakdown of the family, the model has all but broken, leaving countless numbers of us adrift and lonely. With this loss of connectedness, belonging, and love, the compassion and care in society has been increasingly squeezed out. Women who used to be the backbone of a caring society—unselfishly looking after sick relatives and elderly neighbours—now go out to work just to keep the roof over their heads and enough food on the table. The caring professions have become 'careers' rather than 'vocations' and we no longer help each other on a day-to-day basis as we used to. I can remember as a child how my mum would often go next door and take the neighbours' washing off the line because it had started raining. But like the little birds in

---

[345] Ps. 40: 1–3, NRSV.
[346] 1 John 4: 19, NRSV.

spring that exhaust themselves flying in and out of the nest, we scurry around barely stopping to breathe as we juggle our commitments. Single parents have to be truly superhuman: they need all the help, support, and encouragement that can be given to them in their overwhelming task. When Jesus was talking about the end of the age he said 'the love of many will grow cold'[347]. Or as The Message translation puts it, 'the overwhelming spread of evil will do them in—nothing left of their love but a mound of ashes'.[348] He could have been talking about today—perhaps he was. Love in our society, like the vapour trail left by a jet in the sky, is gradually fading as we push God further and further out of the picture.

Amidst all our busyness as parents it can be hard to remember to actually communicate love. Like Tevye in the musical *Fiddler on the Roof* our children need to know and feel love. When he questions her love, his wife Golde replies that she has been looking after him, having his children, cooking, cleaning, and milking the cow for 25 years so she doesn't understand why he needs to ask the question.

Like Golde many of us express love to our children through the food we provide, the clothes we give them to wear, the activities we take them to, and the education we give them. And often we shower them with treats and gadgets. Whilst these are valid expressions of love they may not be the expressions that your child needs or is looking for to 'fill up' his love needs. The way you express—or perhaps don't express—love may be born out of your own failings and needs. It may be that the way you express love to your child is not the way he can receive it. According to Gary D. Chapman and Ross Campbell in their book *The Five Love Languages of Children*, each child feels love in a different way:

> For a child to feel love, we must learn to speak her unique love language. Every child has a special way of perceiving love. There are basically five ways children (indeed, all people) speak and understand emotional love. They are physical touch, words of affirmation, quality time, gifts, and acts of service. If you have several children in your family, chances are they speak different languages, for just as children often have different personalities, they may hear in different love languages. Typically, two children need to be loved in different ways.[349]

As adults and parents we all have different ways to communicate love, some of us like Golde express our love through services provided, some of us may be more touchy-feely, others may be good at 'quality time', gifts, and words of encouragement. Our Rosannagh needs quality time. It doesn't matter how much time and energy we put into supplying her needs, organising

---

[347] Matt 24: 12, NRSV.
[348] Matt. 24: 12, TM.
[349] From Gary D. Chapman and Ross Campbell, *The Five Love Languages of Children* (Moody Press, 1997).

her education, sorting out her travel and accommodation, she still needs time spent just with mum and dad, talking and cuddling. Without this quality time she feels adrift in a hostile world and unable to make her way. Conversely Chris doesn't want quality time or all the cuddly stuff. What he really wants is to have his bed made and be constantly supplied with pasta.

The likelihood is that whatever our normal ways of expressing love, we may have got into a rut. And whilst we may express love one way, our children may well experience love in a different way—so there is a mismatch. Certainly as children they don't understand love in the same way that we do as adults. Indeed, as babies our children process love in their soul and spirit as pure emotion expressed physically, emotionally, and spiritually. They are touched by love through hugs and kisses, care and kindness, laughter, and perhaps most importantly the loving 'vibes' that come from you. Whilst 'vibes' may not be a very technical term, they are something we have all felt when we have been around people that love us. These vibes are true spirit to spirit communication. It's only as they grow up and develop that our children learn to appreciate other, perhaps more cerebral expressions of love. It can be a very long time before they realise that all the hours you spent at the office desk were because you loved them so much you wanted to provide for them. By that time, sadly, they may have started trying to fulfil their unmet love needs in other places.

If your child has a spirit that is full up with your unconditional love he will be open to new ideas, learning, and all the other stuff that will equip him for his journey into adulthood. This includes being open to learning about, and relating to, God. Even though as Christian parents we may want to prioritise this learning about and knowing God, we need to realise that if their spirits are shrivelled for lack of love, they will find it really hard to appreciate and experience how much God loves them. Many adults find it hard to relate to God as a loving Father because fatherhood has been poorly modelled to them. With marriages now failing so frequently this can only get worse.

Apart from an overwhelming feeling of love for each of my children, I have to admit that I gave little thought to the nurture of my children's spirits and their spiritual needs. If I'm honest I had no clear understanding of what the human spirit is, or its job function. It was all rather haphazard and fuzzy round the edges. I assumed that the growth of their spirits would happen through the mainly religious activities of praying for and with them, reading them Bible stories, and taking them to church. This was the model that I received from my parents, who believed that praying and reading the Bible were the only ways to grow spiritually. And this was a good model, although perhaps rather limited.

I can look back now and see so many ways in which God guided us in the choices we made for our children, often despite our lack of prayer and listening to him. I have become amazed at his great love for each one of my children as I have seen how he has guided their paths despite a rather haphazard approach on our part.

Love then is the most important characteristic of this God we are getting to know. And because his very nature is love the spiritual world that he inhabits must also have at its very heart the principle of love. What then is this spirit world to which we are so inextricably linked?

The spirit world

On my first trip abroad one of the hotel meals began with a bowl of clear soup, in the middle of which was a whole hard-boiled egg. It was absurdly difficult to get a hold of this egg, every time I prodded it with the spoon or fork it spun around wildly threatening to leap right out of the bowl. Trying to give definition to the spirit world and the spirit within us is much like trying to extract the egg from the soup. Just when you think you've got it, it spins away and you discover that you haven't.

We know from the Bible that God inhabits a place that we can't see. And although God is so big that his presence reaches everywhere, the Bible refers to the place where he lives and has his throne as 'heaven'. The heaven that God inhabits is one of three heavens that are referred to in the Bible. The first two are physical places, that is; the sky and outer space. The third heaven is the place where God dwells and is not part of the physical universe. Paul in his second letter to the church at Corinth says that he visited this third heaven,

> I know a man who, fourteen years ago, was seized by Christ and swept in ecstasy to the heights of heaven. I really don't know if this took place in the body or out of it; only God knows. I also know that this man was hijacked into paradise—again, whether in or out of the body, I don't know; God knows. There he heard the unspeakable spoken, but was forbidden to tell what he heard.

There are those today who report that they have visited heaven either in near death experiences or in visions like that of Paul.

If this place called heaven is not in our physical realm then where is it, and perhaps more importantly what is it, and does it have any relevance for us? Heaven is not a fluffy cloud inhabited by dead people playing harps, it is a very real place and people who have had visions of heaven often describe it in very tangible and real terms.

For the last hundred years or so scientists have increasingly looked at smaller and smaller particles that make up our physical universe. They have begun to realise that the building blocks from which our world is created can behave in quite bizarre ways. According to Phillip Day in his book *Origins*:

> Quantum physics declares that the fundamental particles of matter are not matter. That sub-atomic particles can be everywhere and nowhere at the same time. Einstein believed that the speed of light set limits on how fast a material entity could travel. Now we learn that space-time is an illusion.
>
> . . .That cells respond to belief by the sender is now a fact in the laboratory two millennia years after a carpenter from Nazareth proved the selfsame phenomena in the vineyards of Israel. In the bible we find Jesus using quantum language and concepts two thousand years before Karl Pribram and Cleve Backster, even telling his spellbound audiences that the universe is taking notes: *'Every idle word that men shall speak, they shall give account thereof in the day of judgement. (Matt 12: 36)*[350]

This study of quantum physics has led to the growing belief that there are other laws in the universe that operate on a far deeper level than the ones we know and experience. It has also led to a growing conviction that there are other dimensions.

We live in a world that can be described or defined by four properties or dimensions. These are: length, width, height, and time. But science now proposes that there may be as many as eleven or more dimensions all existing alongside each other and with the possibility of some overlap. For the unscientific this is all a bit mind boggling and hard to grasp. But the Bible confirms the existence of at least one other dimension—the heavenly dimension where God lives. And the Bible is proof itself that there is some overlap. Essentially inspired by God and then 'received' by men (and women) the Bible is a message to us from the dimension—or dimensions—where God lives. Often when we read the Bible we just don't see this other dimension. We have become so heavy with tradition that the language used in the Bible sometimes seems to be unreal, mythical, and lacking any current relevance. It goes 'in one ear and out of the other'.

This winter I managed to roll my car on some ice and completely write it off. It was a really good car, with low mileage and very reliable. The funny thing is that before I bought this car I had never seen any like it before, but after buying it suddenly the road was swarming with blue Peugeots. It's like that with the Bible. When I began to see that God dwells in a different dimension I began to see things in the Bible confirming this. Take, for instance, Jesus' response to Pilate's questions: 'My kingdom is not from this world. If my kingdom were from

---

[350] Phillip Day, *Origins* (Credence Publications, 2009).

this world, my followers would be fighting to keep me from being handed over to the Jews. But as it is, my kingdom is not from here.'[351]

Jesus came to restore the interaction between God who lives in this other dimension and humankind. But what kind of dimension does God live in and how does it affect us?

What is the Spirit World like?

There may be any number of dimensions that together make up the spirit world, but one of these is heaven. We are told that heaven contains a city, thrones, precious stones, gold, silver, a river, trees, and more. In the various descriptions of these commodities there is a sense of them being altogether different to anything found on the earth. So for instance: 'Coming from the throne are flashes of lightning, and rumblings and peals of thunder, and in front of the throne burn seven flaming torches, which are the seven spirits of God.'[352]

There are mythical creatures in heaven which may be representative of the animals on earth, and there are also earthly animals such as horses: 'Then I saw heaven opened, and there was a white horse!'[353]

Heaven is also home to human beings in the form of 'elders' and departed saints. Predominantly though, the spiritual realm and in particular heaven is inhabited by God—that is God the Father, God the Son, and God the Holy Spirit, together with various other spirit beings and ranks of angels.

All these other spirit beings were created by God as his messengers and workers. They have names, personalities, and free will, and they exist in time and space. Although they can appear in a body they don't have permanent physical bodies. These angels have various ranks and each of these ranks has a different job function, such as the Seraphim who are the highest in rank and who continually praise and worship God, the Cherubim, and the Archangels, of whom Gabriel is one.

Lucifer, originally one of the Seraphim, was probably in charge of the worship of God. He held a very high rank possibly the highest rank among the angels. But he rebelled against God and his name and nature were changed from Lucifer the Light Bearer to, among others, Satan which means 'adversary' and Devil which means 'accuser'. In the Bible Satan is also referred to as 'the god of this world',[354] 'the prince of this world',[355] and the 'ruler of the power of the

---

[351] John 18: 36, NRSV.
[352] Rev. 4: 5, NRSV.
[353] Rev. 19: 11, NRSV.
[354] 2 Cor. 4: 4, NRSV.
[355] John 14: 30, KJV.

air'.[356] He took with him into his rebellion angelic beings from all the angelic ranks. They formed themselves into a highly organized hierarchy of fallen angels, probably mirroring the heavenly ranks. The ranks of these fallen angels are referred to in the Bible as authorities, principalities, powers, rulers of darkness, wicked spirits, and demons. Led by their commander-in-chief, Satan, they are involved in a spiritual war that centres on the human race and seeks to influence it at every level of personal, social, and political life. Currently, the world system is being 'groomed' to accept a global leader through whom Satan hopes to finally achieve his five stated aims: 'I'll climb to heaven. I'll set my throne over the stars of God. I'll run the assembly of angels that meets on sacred Mount Zaphon. I'll climb to the top of the clouds. I'll take over as King of the Universe!'[357]

It seems that Satan, in his role as accuser, is still able to come into God's throne room in heaven, but this access may be limited to those times when God commands him to do so. It is generally believed that Satan was thrown out of heaven, but the when, where, and how of this fall are not clear. It may be that this fall from heaven is a process that began at some point in history and will reach its climax at the end of the age before Jesus returns.

Striking at the very heart of God who gave all his created beings free will, Satan continually seeks to turn human beings away from serving God into the worship of himself as the 'Supreme Being'. Using deceit and trickery, he and his angelic followers disguise themselves and their activities so that we do not understand who we are following. 'Satan does it all the time, dressing up as a beautiful angel of light. So it shouldn't surprise us when his servants masquerade as servants of God.'[358]

His masterstroke of genius was to deceive Adam and Eve into eating the forbidden fruit. Through this one act of disobedience Satan gained dominion over the earth. We know this because Satan offered Jesus all the kingdoms of the world in exchange for worship. Jesus did not correct Satan's statement of ownership but reminded him that only God is to be worshipped. Now Satan's serried ranks of destroyer angels are continually influencing the political systems, the religious systems, the business systems, the health systems, the education systems, and all other systems right down to the town or village where you live, and you yourself as one person on this planet. Working behind the scenes they tirelessly seek to put a spanner in the works of all our best-laid plans for peace, prosperity, and blessing.

We know that Jesus came to destroy all the works of the Devil and that he finished this work. But though Satan is a defeated enemy he is still fighting. We live in the overlap between

---

[356] Eph. 2: 2, NRSV.
[357] Isa. 14: 13–14, THE MESSAGE.
[358] 2 Cor. 11: 14–15, THE MESSAGE.

Jesus' finished work on the cross and the time when Satan is eventually silenced in a lake of fire. Why Satan is still fighting is a bit of a mystery—perhaps he still thinks he can win. However, since he lives in time and space, every day that he continues his fight puts off the day of his end.

In the process of this battle Satan has unleashed a terrible war against both the Jews and the Christians in his efforts to delay and prevent the end time prophecies from coming to pass. The atrocities that have been perpetrated against the Jewish people down through the ages demonstrate to us the hatred that Satan has for them. Anti-Semitism is a spiritual force that has nothing to do with rational thought processes. This same hatred also reaches out to Christians: according to Konrad Szymański MEP (ECR Group[359]): '75% of deaths linked to religion-based hate crimes affect people of the Christian faith, which makes Christians the most persecuted religious group in the world.'[360]

Satan's war to retain dominion on the earth is raging all around us in the spiritual realm and it affects us in ways that we do not see and often do not understand. The wars, famines, injustices, and natural disasters that affect planet Earth are a direct result of this spiritual war. An enemy who is unseen or misunderstood is a dangerous enemy. In his letter to the Corinthians Paul says that he is aware of Satan's strategies: 'we don't want to unwittingly give Satan an opening for yet more mischief —we're not oblivious to his sly ways!'[361]

Characteristics of the Spirit world

We know that angels live in and are limited by the dimension of time because Jesus said that they do not know the day when he will return, 'But about that day and hour no one knows, neither the angels of heaven, nor the Son, but only the Father.'[362] So whilst heaven and all the angels are bound by the dimensions of time and space, God is not. God lives outside time in the ever-present; he is 'the high and lofty one, who inhabits eternity'.[363] He even refers to himself in that way: 'God said to Moses, "I am who I am."'[364]

Jesus infuriated the Jews when he too refers to himself as 'I am'; 'Jesus said to them, "Very truly, I tell you, before Abraham was, I am."'[365] Because of this quality of being outside time God can see the whole of history laid out before him: he knows how it began and he knows how it will end.

---

[359] European Conservatives and Reformists Group.
[360] http://www.comece.org/site/en/activities/events/conferenceonpersecution.
[361] 2 Cor. 2: 11, THE MESSAGE.
[362] Matt. 24: 36, NRSV.
[363] Isa. 57: 15, KJV.
[364] Exod. 3: 14,NRSV.
[365] John 8: 58, NRSV.

The heavenly realm where God lives is a spiritual dimension, and if we want to relate to God it must be on a spiritual level. 'God is spirit, and those who worship him must worship in spirit and truth.'[366] The Bible tells us that we must be 'born again' or we will never be able to interact with God. Referring to this new birth Jesus said; 'I tell you, no one can see the kingdom of God without being born from above.'[367]

Our world is governed by certain natural laws—such as the law of thermodynamics—that can be observed, measured, and relied on. But some scientists say that there may be other laws in the universe operating in different ways and in different dimensions and that some of them—and the law of gravity may be one of these—can leak into our dimension. Heaven is a place governed by the character and laws of God that are capable of leaking onto the earth through those who are open to hearing God and doing what he says.

God's Kingdom has laws and principles that are totally different to the laws that we see operating on the earth. Because these laws and principles emanate from God himself—who *is* love—they are never negative, fearful, or selfish. When the Bible talks about the fruit of the spirit it is talking about the operating system of the heavenly realm. 'the fruit of the Spirit is love, joy, peace, patience, kindness, generosity, faithfulness,'[368] These laws are not just nice 'optional extras' to a life that is busy with paying the mortgage and changing nappies. They are not the topping on the cake. They are the cake.

Jesus' primary teaching when he was on earth was about the Kingdom of God. Whilst the Jews of Jesus' day were waiting for a Messiah to come and establish a kingdom with a geographical location, Jesus talked not so much about a place on earth as an attitude of the heart and God's rule in the lives of people. In his parable about the mustard seed Jesus says that the Kingdom of Heaven rather than arriving with a fanfare will start quite humbly and grow: 'The kingdom of heaven is like a mustard seed that someone took and sowed in his field; it is the smallest of all the seeds, but when it has grown it is the greatest of shrubs and becomes a tree, so that the birds of the air come and make nests in its branches.'[369] However, this fact, that God's Kingdom is growing from small and humble beginnings, doesn't negate what the Jews believed—that the Messiah, Jesus will one day come and oust the newly formed Roman or global Empire from Jerusalem before taking his place as King.

Before that climatic event in the future, we, who are born again, are part of a kingdom that just keeps on growing. Newspapers often highlight the apparent decline in numbers of those who would call themselves Christian; according to a recent article in *The Telegraph*, 'Secular

---

[366] John 4: 24, NRSV.
[367] John 3: 3, NRSV.
[368] Gal. 5: 22–3, NRSV.
[369] Matt. 13: 31–2, NRSV.

campaigners said the new figures showed that Christianity had now dropped below "critical mass", making the case for disestablishing the Church of England stronger.'[370] However, whilst the established church may be in decline in certain parts of the world, Christianity is growing at an incredible rate. According to this article from the BBC,

> It is impossible to say how many Christians there are in China today, but no-one denies the numbers are exploding.
>
> The government says 25 million, 18 million Protestants and six million Catholics. Independent estimates all agree this is a vast underestimate. A conservative figure is 60 million. There are already more Chinese at church on a Sunday than in the whole of Europe.[371]

The same could be said of many other parts of the globe, including Africa and Latin America. Even in the Western world there is growth in the more evangelical church groups. Ed West writing in *The Telegraph* says of this growth, 'The happy clappy thing is not my scene—I'd need at least four Stellas before I could get up and dance in a church without dying of a cringe-related stroke—but it's easy to see why Evangelical Christianity is rapidly spreading in the UK.'[372] This growing movement, which relies more on heart change than nominal adherence, places an emphasis on small gatherings of people who connect as a close-knit community and seek to allow God's Kingdom to flow in and through them.

Characteristics of God's Kingdom

God's Kingdom has different operating principles and values to those we experience in the world, but what are they? According to the book of Romans, 'God's kingdom isn't a matter of what you put in your stomach . . . It's what God does with your life as he sets it right, puts it together, and completes it with joy.'

This change in our way of living and behaving is not something that happens to us overnight—it's a journey. As we seek God and get to know him better, his life will flow in us and through us creating change. This change will begin to encompass our, thoughts, our desires, our words, and our actions. While we remain on the earth our job specification is purely and simply to allow this change so that these heavenly characteristics can flow out of us. Characteristics such as:

- Love rather than hate, violence and self-centredness.
- Meekness not aggressiveness.

---

[370] http://www.telegraph.co.uk/news/religion/10062745/Christianity-declining-50pc-faster-than-thought-as-one-in-10-under-25s-is-a-Muslim.html.
[371] http://www.bbc.co.uk/news/magazine-14838749.
[372] http://blogs.telegraph.co.uk/news/edwest/100019857/im-not-surprised-evangelical-christianity-is-on-the-rise/.

- Humility rather than pride.
- Sincerity not hypocrisy.
- Faith in God.
- Dependence on God rather than self-dependence.
- Hearing God and doing what he says.
- Forgiveness of those who do us wrong.
- An emphasis on inward realities rather than outward show and appearance.

When these values begin to flow through us we bring a little piece of heaven into our corner of earth, adding flavour through creativity, wisdom, faith, and love, creating thirst for God, and frustrating Satan's plans.

Allowing God's kingdom to flow out of us in this way is often easier said than done because the world system, peer pressures and our own inner brokenness all exert a tremendous pressure on us to conform. Paul says in his letter to the church in Rome; 'Don't become so well-adjusted to your culture that you fit into it without even thinking.'[373] Or as it is put in the Bible translation by J. B. Phillips: 'don't let the world around you squeeze you into its own mould'[374].

This world that we have been born into, its ruler, its systems and its way of operating will all pass away. It is only temporary.

Are we giving our children only an earthbound perspective or are we giving them a glimpse into the heavenly realm? Are we teaching them how to become citizens of this heavenly kingdom that will last into eternity? And are we teaching and modelling Gods ways to them? These are the only ways that will last. Paul puts it this way; 'for what can be seen is temporary, but what cannot be seen is eternal.'[375]

---

[373] Rom. 12: 2, THE MESSAGE.
[374] J. B. Phillips, "The New Testament in Modern English", 1962 edition, published by HarperCollins.
[375] 2 Cor. 4: 18, NRSV.

Chapter 2
<u>The Human Spirit</u>

It is with our spirits that we communicate with God who is Spirit and who lives in the spiritual dimension. But the human spirit is different to all other spirits because it is clothed with a body through which it relates to other human beings and the creation around. This body is not merely a suit of clothes that can be removed at will, the union of the body and the spirit were intended to be for all time. The spirit was originally created to sustain the body, energising it, healing it, and sustaining it so that the two would be totally inseparable. Only when sin made its entrance onto the scene did we begin to see the 'unnatural' separation of body and spirit that we call death.

The Bible tells us about the human spirit, its condition, and its job function, and about God who is Spirit. It describes the human spirit in a variety of different ways:

- *It talks about our 'inner being':* 'I pray that, according to the riches of his glory, he may grant that you may be strengthened in your inner being with power through his Spirit'[376] And: 'You desire truth in the inward being;'[377]
- *It talks about our heart:* more than just a physical organ, 'heart' is the word we use to describe our deepest emotions and motivations. We talk about getting to the 'heart' of a matter. It may be that this 'heart' is the interface or crossover point between our souls and our spirits, having, as it were, a foot in both camps. In the Hebrew the word 'heart' also means inner man and in the Greek it means 'the centre and seat of spiritual life'.[378] The apostle Paul says: 'so that, with the eyes of your heart enlightened, you may know what is the hope to which he has called you.'[379] And the prophet Ezekiel said: 'A new heart I will give you, and a new spirit I will put within you; and I will remove from your body the heart of stone and give you a heart of flesh.'[380]
- *Jesus even referred to a man's belly as being that innermost or spirit part of a man:* 'He that believeth on me, as the scripture hath said, out of his belly shall flow rivers of living water.'[381]

---

[376] Eph. 3: 16–17, NRSV,
[377] Ps. 51: 6, NRSV.
[378] From Strong's *Greek Lexicon*.
[379] Eph. 1: 18, NRSV.
[380] Ezek. 36: 26, NRSV.
[381] John 7: 38, KJV.

Modern man prides himself on living in a technological age full of electronic gadgets and gizmos. He sees everything through the eyes of science. And science is god. This embracing of science, knowledge and laboratory proof, has contributed to the difficulties that we have when it comes to understanding, seeing, and experiencing our human spirit. Because the scientific method has never isolated a substance or state of being that can be identified as a soul or a spirit, an angel or a demon—that can be experimented upon—scientists say these things are not real and do not exist beyond the minds of the men who invented them. And we have believed them. We have been sold the lie that the spirit world is non-existent and irrelevant.

Many people vigorously believe that the lack of proof for the existence of God is proof in itself that there is no God. Despite the fact that all people groups have beliefs in the non-material spirit world, science says that any thoughts of a spirit world are the mass delusion of the uneducated and uncivilized. This spirit world is primarily understood and experienced by faith, but according to Richard Dawkins author of 'The God Delusion', 'Faith is the great cop out, the great excuse to evade the need to think and evaluate evidence. Faith is belief in spite of, even perhaps because of, the lack of evidence.'[382] With this denial of the spiritual it's not surprising that scientists have been unable to define what 'life' is and how it is created. They understand so much about the building blocks of life: the amino acids, the DNA, the chemicals, and all the processes necessary for life, but the life principle itself eludes them. According to Tim Radford in the Observer, 'One hundred and fifty years of serious, secular study have brought us to a better understanding of what constitutes all living organisms, but the why and how of life itself remain elusive.'[383]

The Bible answers this question by telling us that life comes from God: 'Then the Lord God formed man from the dust of the ground, and breathed into his nostrils the breath of life; and the man became a living being'[384]

But this breath was not just fresh air. Had this been the case, then with the benefit of today's advances in medicine it would be a simple process to bring people back to life. It takes more than air to bring someone to life. The very spirit of God was breathed into Adam and it was this spirit that created life in him: 'The spirit of God has made me, and the breath of the Almighty gives me life.'[385]

When God breathed his Spirit into the lifeless form of Adam a soul was created through which he could interact with and understand the world around him and the God who made him. In the same way that hydrogen and oxygen come together to form water, or blue and

---

[382] http://www.positiveatheism.org/hist/quotes/dawkins.htm.
[383] Tim Radford, *The Observer*, Sunday, 27 April 2008, at http://www.guardian.co.uk/science/2008/apr/27/genetics.evolution.
[384] Gen. 2: 7, NRSV.
[385] Job 33: 4, NRSV.

yellow come together to make green, so man's soul was created when God's Spirit came into his body. This soul develops through the processes of life and becomes 'who we are today'. When the spirit leaves the body, not only does the body start to decay and go smelly, but the soul leaves also. The Bible refers to this as sleep. The body is put in the ground, the soul sleeps, and the spirit goes back to God. There will come a day when for all those who have died the three parts of their being: body, soul, and spirit, will come together again.

> But we do not want you to be uninformed, brothers and sisters, about those who have died, so that you may not grieve as others do who have no hope. For since we believe that Jesus died and rose again, even so, through Jesus, God will bring with him those who have died. For this we declare to you by the word of the Lord, that we who are alive, who are left until the coming of the Lord, will by no means precede those who have died. For the Lord himself, with a cry of command, with the archangel's call and with the sound of God's trumpet, will descend from heaven, and the dead in Christ will rise first. Then we who are alive, who are left, will be caught up in the clouds together with them to meet the Lord in the air; and so we will be with the Lord forever.[386]

This spirit then, is the life source that so eludes the searching of the scientists. And this spirit contains the attributes of God. Just as he had said: 'Let us make human beings in our image, make them reflecting our nature . . .'[387]

With one breath God uniquely gave to Adam his own attributes and the power to pass these on to his offspring. Adam truly became God's son: like him with the same talents, abilities, and desires. He was a 'chip off the old block'. We see these Godlike qualities such as creativity, music, laughter, the love of beauty, love for each other, love for our children, in all the races of mankind. The desire to live together in family units is also innate, as are other characteristics such as righteous anger, the desire to see justice done, and the desire for vengeance. We also share in common the desire to relate to God. Almost all societies believe in the existence of invisible supernatural or spiritual beings who influence human life and who need to be appeased or to whom we should pray. It's just part of our DNA.

So the human spirit is the source of life, but how does it flow through us and how does it affect us? Jesus responded to this question when he was talking to the man Nicodemus:

> When you look at a baby, it's just that: a body you can look at and touch. But the person who takes shape within is formed by something you can't see and touch—the Spirit—and becomes a living spirit . . . You know well enough how the wind blows this way and that.

---

[386] 1 Thess. 4: 13–18, NRSV.
[387] Gen. 1: 26, THE MESSAGE.

You hear it rustling through the trees, but you have no idea where it comes from or where it's headed next. That's the way it is with everyone 'born from above' by the wind of God, the Spirit of God.[388]

We can see the wind by observing how it moves in the trees. We can see the Holy Spirit by seeing what he does. Similarly with the human spirit we can see the spirit in a man by looking at his actions. When a man has love in his spirit it can be seen as sacrifice, bravery, courage, and heroism. The Hollies famously sang, 'the load doesn't weigh me down at all, he ain't heavy, he's my brother'. Times of war provide plenty of proof that this sentiment is true. There have been many medals for bravery awarded to UK soldiers:

> L/Cpl Clarke was severely injured while on foot patrol when her unit came under heavy fire from insurgents who pinned them down with rocket-propelled grenades (RPGs). Shrapnel from one of the exploding grenades sliced into L/Cpl Clarke's shoulder blade, but [she] refused to be evacuated by helicopter and continued to treat wounded comrades under open fire.[389]

And in the United States President Barack Obama recently presented the Medal of Honor to 25-year-old Staff Sgt Salvatore Giunta:

> Sgt Giunta pursued the enemy under heavy fire across an open clearing. His only cover was the dust kicked up by bullets and grenades. He killed one of the Taliban fighters—a sought-after foe known as Mohammed Tali—and the other fled. Sgt Giunta carried the badly wounded Sgt Brennan to safety, where they remained for half an hour until a medevac helicopter arrived.[390]

But courage and bravery are not limited to soldiers, who are perhaps more prepared for it:

> By any measure, Irena Sendler was one of the most remarkable and noble figures to have emerged from the horrors of World War II. But, until recently, her extraordinary compassion and heroism went largely unrecorded.
>
> When the Germans finally caught her, the Roman Catholic social worker had managed to save 2,500 Jewish babies and toddlers from deportation to the concentration camps.
>
> She had spirited them out of the heavily-guarded Jewish ghetto in Warsaw, and hidden their identities in two glass jars buried under an apple tree in her neighbor's

---

[388] John 3: 6, 8, THE MESSAGE.
[389] http://www.telegraph.co.uk/news/worldnews/asia/afghanistan/7534938/Army-medic-to-receive-bravery-medal-for-rescuing-comrades.html.
[390] http://www.bbc.co.uk/news/world-us-canada-11770442.

garden.

She was beaten, tortured and sentenced to death by the Gestapo—who even announced her execution. But Irena survived, her spirit unbroken, her secrets untold.

She died last week, in her modest Warsaw apartment, aged 98. What a woman she was. For once, the term 'heroine' is no exaggeration, though such plaudits did not sit easily with her.

She said: 'I was brought up to believe that a person must be rescued when drowning, regardless of religion and nationality.'[391]

It is the spirit that is at work when a mother displays almost superhuman strength to rescue her child from need or danger. But its not just mothers who can display this strength. An unlikely hero, young Austin Smith lifted a car off his grandfather:

It was more like something you would see in a Superman movie or one of the world's strongest man competitions. But, fueled by pure adrenaline and love for his grandfather, 15-year-old Austin Smith, from Michigan, was able to lift a two thousand pound Buick Century off his grandfather after it fell on top of him.[392]

The work of the human spirit

The human spirit that is not in relationship with God has a greatly reduced ability to function. That it does still have some limited ability can be seen from many examples of almost superhuman acts of love and bravery. Apart from courage, there are many other qualities that flow from our human spirit.

The human spirit can be seen at work in creativity. Many of the arts such as painting, sculpture, music, and poetry flow from the artist's spirit. There are examples of cave paintings, decorated pottery and jewellery from the earliest known times and it seems that man has always had the need to surround himself and express himself with beauty and pattern.

This creativity often goes hand in hand with a deep desire to communicate. Within us we have the strong desire to share our lives with others—spirit to spirit. This communication can take many forms: it can be musical, visual, structural, written, or verbal. It may be practical and useful or purely aesthetic: it may be religious or secular. It may have an overt message or it may be purely decorative but it will always convey something of the individual creator's spirit. Each 'creator' has a different 'voice'. And these voices call to us resonating with our own inner selves and a spirit-to-spirit communication takes place.

---

[391] http://thegatheringplacehome.myfastforum.org/viewtopic.php?t=2741&start=0.
[392] http://www.dailymail.co.uk/news/article-2104495/Fueled-love-adrenaline-Teen-15-lifts-2-000lb-Buick-grandfather-fell-him.html.

The Bible says that man's spirit comes from God, it is separate from God, and it only really comes alive when in communication with him. As Paul says, 'God's Spirit touches our spirits and confirms who we really are.'[393]

The human spirits breathed into each one of us by God have their characteristics and job functions. Just as there are an infinite number of shades of colour so the spirits in each of us are infinite in variety and focus. This gives us our individual innate talents and desires. God wants to give us the desires of our hearts [394] because he was the originator of those desires.

Being made in the image of the triune God, the human spirit within us is modelled on the Holy Spirit and has the same purpose and abilities. We can understand more about our own human spirit by looking at some of the characteristics of the Holy Spirit.

• The Holy Spirit brings life

He took part in creation, he was the agent of Christ's virgin birth, he brings new birth at salvation, and he cleanses a person from sin giving them a new nature. Without the Holy Spirit we cannot have a relationship with God as Father.

In the same way our human spirit brings life to our body. When the human spirit comes into our body at, or soon after conception, the body comes alive. When the spirit leaves the body, the body is dead and it starts to decompose. Since Adam's fatal bite of the apple the human spirit in every person has been a malfunctioning spirit. It is this malfunction that causes sickness and ultimately death to conquer our bodies. When our spirit has sickness and pain held within it the expression of that sickness and pain will flow through every part of our being, often causing both emotional and physical pain. As parents we must nurture the spirit in our children so that life, rather than pain and sickness, can flow into their soul and body.

• The Holy Spirit is eternal

Being God, the Holy Spirit is eternal: that is, he has no beginning and no end. The Bible teaches that the human spirit came from God and goes back to God[395] until being reunited with its body at the resurrection. This eternal human spirit was originally meant to inhabit a body that would live forever. The body we inhabit has an end in death, but our human spirit remains eternal. Where that human spirit goes after the body has died, is a decision that we must make while we are alive. Those who choose to have a relationship with God as Father will go to be with him and embrace all the good stuff he has planned for eternity, those who do not

---

[393] Rom. 8: 16, THE MESSAGE.
[394] Psalm 37:4 NRSV
[395] Ecclesaistes12:7

choose this relationship will be judged and then go to the place of punishment that God has prepared for the Devil (to whom they have chosen, by default, to belong).

Then I saw a great white throne and the one who sat on it; the earth and the heaven fled from his presence, and no place was found for them. And I saw the dead, great and small, standing before the throne, and books were opened. Also another book was opened, the book of life. And the dead were judged according to their works, as recorded in the books. And the sea gave up the dead that were in it, Death and Hades gave up the dead that were in them, and all were judged according to what they had done. Then Death and Hades were thrown into the lake of fire. This is the second death, the lake of fire; and anyone whose name was not found written in the book of life was thrown into the lake of fire.[396]

• The Holy Spirit is a communicator

As part of the triune God the Holy Spirit lives in harmony with God the Father and Jesus Christ. They have perfect communication between each other, though with differing job functions. The Holy Spirit also communicates with Mankind.

- *He speaks:* 'Then the Spirit said to Philip, "Go over to this chariot and join it."'[397]
- *He teaches:* 'But the Advocate, the Holy Spirit, whom the Father will send in my name, will teach you everything, and remind you of all that I have said to you.'[398]
- *He bears witness:* 'When the Advocate comes, whom I will send to you from the Father, the Spirit of truth who comes from the Father, he will testify on my behalf.'[399]
- *He guides:* 'They went through the region of Phrygia and Galatia, having been forbidden by the Holy Spirit to speak the word in Asia.'[400]
- *He hears:* 'When the Spirit of truth comes, he will guide you into all the truth; for he will not speak on his own, but will speak whatever he hears, and he will declare to you the things that are to come.'[401]
- *He lives in us:* 'Do you not know that you are God's temple and that God's Spirit dwells in you?[402]

This eternal human spirit that inhabits you and me was designed to act as the interface between God's world and our world. When we are born again the Holy Spirit comes to live in us and we begin to hear what he is saying, and even feel what he is feeling. He also engages

---

[396] Rev. 20: 11–15, NRSV.
[397] Acts 8: 29, NRSV.
[398] John 14: 26, NRSV.
[399] John 15: 26, NRSV.
[400] Acts 16: 6–7, NRSV.
[401] John 16: 13, NRSV.
[402] 1 Cor. 3: 16, NRSV.

with our spirit to produce worship. Worship is perhaps the primary function of the human spirit as it is the primary method of communicating with God. We worship God because we love him and are incredibly aware of how much he loves us. But worship is not just about singing, dancing, and generally being enthusiastic in a meeting setting. We worship God when we present our bodies to serve him and allow him to change us.

As Christians our task is to allow the Holy Spirit to change us and flow through us bringing healing and wholeness not just to us but to those around us. The Holy Spirit has an insatiable desire to leak out through us, changing the world we live in. Often because of our inner brokenness, stubbornness, and pride we block this flow.

The human spirit in us also reflects the Holy Spirit's characteristic of wanting to communicate and be communicated with. We all long for someone to touch us spirit to spirit, heart to heart, and walk with us awhile. But all too often in our relationships we fail to connect in this way because the gulf that separates us from God also separates us from each other. Much of people's pain and malfunctioning comes from this deep inner need. Whilst secular counselling can help enormously it cannot satisfy a thirsty spirit. Jesus said that not only could he satisfy this thirst but that through us he would satisfy the thirst of others: 'On the last day of the festival, the great day, while Jesus was standing there, he cried out, "Let anyone who is thirsty come to me, and let the one who believes in me drink. As the scripture has said, 'Out of the believer's heart shall flow rivers of living water.'"'[403]

Our children need this spiritual intimacy as much as they need to be fed. And indeed it's often as we feed our babies and have meals together that this takes place.

When the Holy Spirit communicates with us our spirit is the part of us that receives and hears that communication which is then processed in the mind. The mind is capable of dismissing, ignoring, or accepting and believing these communications. We hear him in all sorts of ways: through impressions and gut feelings, through the visual input of pictures, visions, and dreams, through someone else speaking to us, through the Bible which is God's word, and indeed in many other creative ways. And how do we know that he is speaking to us? To start with it may be just that something in us just goes 'zing'! And we have a light bulb moment. At other times we have a growing certainty about a course of action. Or we may take a course of action even though we don't realise at the time that it is the Holy Spirit leading us. As parents we should be modelling this ability to hear God and do what he says. And we should be speaking words from the Holy Spirit to our children so that their spirits grow.

---

[403] John 7: 37–8, NRSV.

• The Holy Spirit has personality

The Holy Spirit is not some cosmic or impersonal force that just does God's bidding. In the Bible the Holy Spirit is always referred to as 'he'. Specifically Jesus himself speaks of the Holy Spirit as 'he': 'When the Spirit of truth comes, he will guide you into all the truth.'[404] The Holy Spirit also demonstrates all the characteristics of personality such as:

- *Emotion:* 'the love of the Spirit,[405]—'And do not grieve the Holy Spirit of God'.[406]
- *Mind:* 'God, who searches the heart, knows what is the mind of the Spirit.'[407]
- *Knowledge:* 'no one comprehends what is truly God's except the Spirit of God.'[408]
- *Will:* 'All these gifts have a common origin, but are handed out one by one by the one Spirit of God. He decides who gets what, and when.'[409]
- *He can be lied to:* 'why has Satan filled your heart to lie to the Holy Spirit'[410]
- *He can be opposed:* 'you are forever opposing the Holy Spirit.'[411]

Similarly the human spirit is not an impersonal life force but has personality:

- *Emotion:* Mary Jesus' mother had joy in her spirit: '. . . my spirit rejoices in God my Saviour'.[412]
- *Understanding:* 'But truly it is the spirit in a mortal, the breath of the Almighty, that makes for understanding.'[413]
- *Will:* 'the spirit indeed is willing, but the flesh is weak.'[414]

Our personality can be whole and full of life and joy or broken and diseased, holding deep, painful emotions. What is in our spirits will always flow out through us.

• The Holy Spirit has a job to do

When the Spirit of truth comes, he will guide you into all the truth; for he will not speak on his own, but will speak whatever he hears, and he will declare to you the things that are to come. He will glorify me, because he will take what is mine and declare it to you.[415]

---

[404] John 16: 13, NRSV.
[405] Romans 15: 30, NRSV.
[406] Eph. 4: 30, NRSV.
[407] Rom. 8: 27, NRSV.
[408] 1 Cor. 2: 11, NRSV.
[409] 1 Cor. 12: 11, THE MESSAGE.
[410] Heb. 10: 29, NRSV.
[411] Acts 7: 51, NRSV.
[412] Luke 1: 47, NRSV.
[413] Job 32: 8, NRSV.
[414] Matt. 26: 41, NRSV.
[415] John 16: 13–14, NRSV.

Within our human spirits there is the desire to do something effective and lasting with our lives. Since man fell, this has been dominated by the need to provide food and shelter. These needs often take precedence over the desire to follow the dreams written in our hearts. When the pressures of work decrease many men—and women—gravitate towards these dreams: the production of works of art, lobbying for change, good works, and so on.

I'm a great people watcher and the more I have looked at people the more I have seen the tremendous diversity in the things to which people are drawn. The sportsman will invest hours and hours perfecting a skill. He will be up at dawn running round the track. There is an inner drive that motivates him. Others may have the inner drive to help people, or create art, cakes, or music. Still others just want to organise everything and everyone.

When Christopher was just 4 we had free tickets to a new cinema that was opening. I took him along to watch the cartoons that were on offer. But he didn't watch them. Instead he spent the whole time running around reading the numbers on the seats and working out how many seats there were in the cinema. Something deep inside him was calling him to numbers. Likewise Elisia has to cover everything with pattern.

I have the deep desire to design. My favourite part of any project is the design part: setting the table for dinner, wrapping the presents, choosing and designing what to wear. God has put within all of us these deep desires and callings.

• The Holy Spirit is creative

The Holy Spirit is the way God gets things done. He was the cause of Mary's pregnancy: 'The Holy Spirit will come upon you, and the power of the Most High will overshadow you; therefore the child to be born will be holy; he will be called Son of God.'[416]

He inspired David to write the poetry and songs found in the psalms. He is the source of Godly dreams and visions. And although we don't put much emphasis on it, he encourages us to be creative when we get together: 'Speaking to yourselves in psalms and hymns and spiritual songs, singing and making melody in your heart to the Lord.'[417]

The Holy Spirit also inspires and enables craftspeople: 'I have called by name Bezalel son of Uri son of Hur, of the tribe of Judah: and I have filled him with divine spirit, with ability, intelligence, and knowledge in every kind of craft.[418]

---

[416] Luke 1: 35, NRSV.
[417] Eph. 5: 19, KJV.
[418] Exod. 31: 2–3, NRSV.

As human beings we too are highly creative; we love to make things such as cakes and curtains, beautiful gardens and labour-saving devices. We love to surround ourselves with pretty things, designed interiors, and amazing technology. Over the last century there has been a technological explosion driven by the imagination of creative geniuses. This creativity, despite being a God-given quality, has been heavily underrated in the Church.

The fallen human spirit

How sad it is that we reflect so very little of all this capacity in our spirits: they are damaged, broken and reflect only a part of all that God made them for. And all because of a piece of fruit.

On the day that Adam and Eve ate the forbidden fruit there was a physical change in their bodies—some say that they had been covered in a glow that now disappeared—and they became mortal. There was a change in their souls—now they were afraid. And there was a change in their spirits—they were ashamed, they hid, and they didn't want to talk to God. This was death. Death that started in their spirits but affected their souls and bodies as well. It changed the order of things. Adam and Eve's spirits, once dominant in their human 'trinity' and once able to communicate with God, were now destined to become shrivelled, empty, and diseased. Now the ability to communicate with God had gone and a vacuum was left in the place where God had been. Now they had to find a new source for their intelligence, a new source for their authority, a new source for their wisdom, a new source for their happiness, and, indeed, a new source for everything that had previously originated, in their spirits, from God.

Heroically the body and soul now stepped up to do the job. Without the leading of a spirit in communication with God, the functions of the mind, the will, and the emotions began to lead and guide Adam and Eve. Building on the wisdom and knowledge that they had already received from God they now had to build up their experience and understanding of life by trial and error.

And oh what a merry dance our now dominant emotions have led us on. We have come to the point in our 'evolution' where we now follow our feelings as though they confer unstoppable human rights. Aleister Crowley (described by many as 'the most evil man who ever lived'), received from his spirit guide the words: 'Do what thou wilt shall be the whole of the law.'[419]

If it feels good, 'just do it' has become the unwritten law of the day. Our young people stumble around on Saturday nights in and out of pubs and clubs just 'doing it' but not 'getting

---

[419] http://www.brainyquote.com/quotes/quotes/a/aleistercr156787.html

any satisfaction'. We, the older generation, have not given them a good example to follow as we have grasped for more and more. How different to the attitude Jesus had when he said: 'My food is to do the will of him who sent me and to complete his work.'[420]

But the really big bully that now began to dominate was the body. Whatever the body wanted it had to have. Over and above the legitimate needs for fuel and oxygen, shelter and clothing the body now began to want more. Throughout history whenever food was plentiful and people lived at ease they began to indulge themselves in all manner of excess. They filled themselves with nice things to see, nice things to hear, nice things to smell, feasting and gluttony, all manner of sexual practices, the pursuit of power, and lots and lots of money.

Sodom and Gomorrah have become a byword for this kind of excess. 'This was the guilt of your sister Sodom: she and her daughters had pride, excess of food, and prosperous ease, but did not aid the poor and needy.'[421]

Very few leaders, kings, and world rulers have lived lives of poverty and self-denial and many have taken excess to the limit. These excesses were for the physical desires such as food, sex, money, homes, and possessions. But they also exhibited a lust for power and control through corruption, murder, and torture for which lots more money was needed.

A recent study by the Carnegie Institution for Science[422] has labelled Genghis Khan the greenest invader in history because his slaughter of more than forty million people meant that the forests could grow back. Well that's OK then. Perhaps they didn't realise that he also undid his green credentials by his amazing success at repopulation.

Khan had a great many children, both with his wives and with other women. His sons, who expanded the Mongol Empire into Europe, had many children of their own. Although the empire broke up in the decades following Khan's death in 1227, his male descendants ruled large chunks of it for centuries. And like their ancestor, they had many children as well. If the geneticists are right, Khan and his descendants spread his distinctive Y chromosome to about half a percent of the world's male population alive today, or some 16 million men.[423]

The Roman Empire was known for excess and corruption, much of what they did was truly gruesome and some was just bizarre.

---

[420] John 4: 34, NRSV.
[421] Ezek. 16: 49, NRSV.
[422] http://carnegiescience.edu/news/war_plague_no_match_deforestation_driving_co2_buildup.
[423] http://www.forbes.com/2007/02/25/genghis-khan-descendants-lead_achieve07_cz_cz_0301khan.html.

Nero celebrated by staging yet wilder orgies and by creating two new festivals of chariot-racing and athletics. He also staged musical contests, which gave him further chance to demonstrate in public his talent for singing while accompanying himself on the lyre. In an age when actors and performers were seen as something unsavoury, it was a moral outrage to have an emperor performing on stage. Worse still, Nero being the emperor, no one was allowed to leave the auditorium while he was performing, for whatever reason. The historian Suetonius writes of women giving birth during a Nero recital, and of men who pretended to die and were carried out.[424]

More recently a list of the world's most corrupt leaders has been produced. Ten of them from the last two decades are listed according to the amount of money they have embezzled from their people, a terrible total of between twenty-eight and fifty-six billion US dollars.[425] Number two on the list is Ferdinand Marcos, president of the Philippines from 1972 to 1986. His widow Imelda has recently opened a shoe museum where her collection of over a thousand pairs of shoes is the main exhibit.

Religion has not held back when it comes to excesses either. In the middle ages the 'church' sold relics and free passes into heaven—known as indulgences. It also raised money from pilgrimages, tithes, and enforced labour. In this way the Roman Catholic Church grew massively wealthy, powerful, corrupt and corrupting. At the same time many of its clergy were leading lives of utter depravity as exemplified by the popes at this time.

Pope Alexander VI epitomizes this corruption. Born as Rodrigo Borgia in Spain in 1431, he was elected Pope in 1492, an event that spawned rumors that he had spent a considerable fortune bribing the appropriate Cardinals to assure his success.

The new Pope loved the good life. He sired at least twelve children through a number of mistresses. The most famous of his offspring were his son Cesare, noted for the murder of political rivals, and his daughter Lucrezia who was married off to a number of husbands for political gain.

Pope Alexander VI was in constant need of money—to support his lavish life style, to fill the coffers for his political bribes and to fund his various military campaigns. The sale of Cardinalships was a major source of cash, so too was the sale of indulgences. An indulgence was a written proclamation that exonerated—for a fee—the individual (or his relatives) from punishment in the after-life for sins that had been committed, or in some cases, may be committed in the future.[426]

---

[424] http://www.roman-empire.net/emperors/nero-index.html.
[425] http://www.infoplease.com/ipa/A0921295.html.
[426] http://www.eyewitnesstohistory.com/alexanderVI.htm

But you don't have to be a despot or religious leader to be ruled by the desires of your body and soul. The most popular song sung at funerals is Frank Sinatra's 'I did it my way'. As we have seen 'doing it my way' may well be a chorus line inspired by demonic spirits.

When man is governed by the needs and desires of the body or soul he lives a life that is out of balance and all of his thoughts and actions are corrupt. This 'life out of balance' has been the default setting for all human beings since Adam and Eve. Because of this, over the millennia man's human spirit and soul have all but merged into one so that we find it really hard to hear or distinguish anything that comes from our spirit. It's as if the clear water in our spirits has mixed with the earthiness of our bodies and souls and become a muddy puddle whose components can no longer be separated.

The God-shaped hole

With our human spirit unable to communicate with God and so dominated by the body and soul it has all but vanished, leaving only an empty space filled with a nameless ache. As Bruce Springsteen sang, 'Everybody's got a hungry heart'. This empty, God-shaped vacuum has been filled with all the evil characteristics of Satan. Shame, fear, guilt, and separation have now taken up residence in our spirits and from there emanate out into our souls and bodies. The human race now in pain has been unable to satisfy the deep longings within.

Aided and abetted by Satan, our bodies and souls are now driven with the constant desire to fill the empty places in our lives with stuff. The spirit of man has become like an empty garage—the car has driven off and the space is being filled with all sorts of things we don't need or want but lack the courage to throw away.

- *We fill our emptiness with noise*: Where can you go now to find some quiet? Our whole lives, like a movie, are lived to the soundtrack of other people's commentaries, in songs and words. Never far away from some sort of noise, we are all filled up.
- *We fill our emptiness with work*: Legitimate needs to provide for ourselves and our family become addictive forces. We spend our lives hoping to land the 'big catch', or win the Lotto so that we can be released, but if the big win does happen it causes us to get back in touch with our core emptiness and we lose our way.
- *We fill our emptiness with food, drink, and chocolate*: Along with naughty little chocolate breaks, comfort eating is probably something we all do. And many of our young people spend Saturday nights getting 'wasted'.
- *We fill our emptiness with things:*

    The land of a rich man produced abundantly. And he thought to himself, 'What should I do, for I have no place to store my crops?' Then he said, 'I will do this: I will pull down my barns and build larger ones, and there I will store all my grain and my goods. And I will say to my soul, Soul, you have ample goods laid up for many years; relax, eat, drink, be merry.' But God said to him, 'You fool! This very night your life is being demanded of you. And the things you have prepared, whose will they be?' So it is with those who store up treasures for themselves but are not rich toward God. [427]

- *We fill our emptiness with religion:* Because Satan is determined to fill this God-shaped gap with himself he will take on any identity in order to receive worship and simultaneously prevent us from finding God. He has been hard at work throughout history setting up religious systems and diverting Christianity away from Jesus. As Jeremiah says; 'My people have committed two evils: they have forsaken me, the fountain of living water, and dug out cisterns for themselves, cracked cisterns that can hold no water.'[428] These religions take on the characteristics of their creators, both spiritual and human. 'No good tree bears bad fruit, nor again does a bad tree bear good fruit; for each tree is known by its own fruit. Figs are not gathered from thorns, nor are grapes picked from a bramble bush.'[429]

  Many religions have characteristics that are hostile, legalistic, controlling, manipulative, and judgmental—including Christianity when it becomes man-centred and religious—because they all emanate from Satan in partnership with fallen man. But God has not called us to be religious. Religion is the enemy of life. Or as Karl Marx rightly said: 'Religion . . . is the opium of the people.' It stuffs us full and keeps us from the truth. Worse than that, it is responsible for tremendous evil in the world. It was responsible for the first recorded murder in history when Cain killed his brother Abel, and that was just the beginning.
- *We fill our emptiness with pride:* stubbornly refusing to listen to the inner voice that would call us back to God.

And all the while our spirits are ignored and lie shrivelled within us. We ignore our very life source and take no care of it by filling ourselves up and blocking out its cries with all this useless stuff.

When Jesus looked on the crowds it says that 'he had compassion for them, because they were harassed and helpless, like sheep without a shepherd.'[430] He might have been looking at the crowds on any typical street today.

---

[427] Luke 12: 16–21, NRSV.
[428] Jer. 2: 13, NRSV.
[429] Luke 6: 43–4, NRSV.
[430] Matt. 9: 36, NRSV.

Apart from being separated from God and motivated by a huge vacuum, the human spirit, the Bible also says, can be troubled, anguished, sorrowful, sad, broken, wounded, grieved, overwhelmed, failing, breeched, heavy, defiled, fainting, and fearful. It can hold huge pain that goes far deeper than any pain the soul can experience. Because the job function of the human spirit is to be a well of life, the life that flows from a spirit affected in this way will be a life coloured by this pain. It is this 'dis-ease' in our spirits that leads to our physical and emotional sicknesses. Our spirits can become sick like this for many reasons often linking back to a lack of love, care, understanding, and nurture at key times in our lives. The Holy Spirit longs to get to the root of our troubles and bring the healing of Jesus into the places that are traumatised, despairing, guilty, and shameful.

Chapter 3
<u>Hope for the human spirit</u>

The story of Jesus is the story of God's plan to restore us in body, soul, and spirit. But it starts with the spirit. When our spirit comes back into relationship with God it can bring order and health to our souls and bodies. Before our spirit can fulfil its purpose this new life from God must flood into it, swell it, and grow it. This is exactly the same process and miracle as when our physical body was created at conception. Jesus explained this when he was talking to Nicodemus; 'I tell you, no one can see the kingdom of God without being born from above.'[431] Nicodemus was mystified and replied:

> 'How can anyone be born after having grown old? Can one enter a second time into the mother's womb and be born?' Jesus answered, 'Very truly, I tell you, no one can enter the kingdom of God without being born of water and Spirit. What is born of the flesh is flesh, and what is born of the Spirit is spirit.'[432]

If we want to see our children grow up whole, live well, and go on into an eternal life that starts now, then bringing our children to the place where they can accept for themselves this new life from God has to be our primary aim.

What is being born again?
Many people believe the incredibly successful lie that in order to go to heaven when we die we must be good. This is a performance-orientated belief. God loves us and nothing we can do will alter that fact. However, God is often portrayed as being a bit like Father Christmas who will only give gifts to those who have been good.

But being good or nice are not the criteria for a heavenly free pass. Those who are going to heaven will get there because they have a relationship with God, and this relationship must start before we take the trip. Since we don't know when that will happen we need to get it sorted now, as a matter of urgency.

A relationship with God is the starting point from which life will flow now and on into eternity. There may well be many people with a reputation for goodness and kindness but because they didn't get their relationship with God sorted out they will not be in heaven. Perhaps their goodness and kindness was just their way to fill up the emptiness. We may

---

[431] John 3: 3, NRSV.
[432] John 3: 4–5, NRSV.

equally be shocked to find that all sorts of unkind and evil people do get their relationship with God sorted and make it to heaven. It's not about what we do, it's about relationship. God intended our good works to flow from relationship with him. Good works in themselves do not create a relationship with God.

Someone who is born again—a Christian—is not just someone who leads a good life, or who was baptised as a baby or who was born into a Christian country. And because God has no grandchildren, being born into a Christian family does not provide us with an instant 'get out of jail free' card either.

Because we all share in the guilt of our ancient ancestors we all share in the consequences. Understanding this, a Christian is someone who realises that they have been judged as guilty and sentenced to death. But they have taken hold of God's remedy for this.
God's remedy was to send a human being—whom he loved dearly—to take the death sentence on behalf you and me: 'For God so loved the world that he gave his only Son, so that everyone who believes in him may not perish but may have eternal life.'[433]

Most religions in the world focus on the struggle to better oneself in order to earn eternal life and a place in heaven. Christians have accepted that we can do nothing to better ourselves or climb up towards God by our own efforts, we need God to come down to us. And he did. As a result of what Jesus achieved by taking our punishment we can now come into relationship with God the Father. Jesus confirmed this when he said: 'No one comes to the Father except through me.'[434]   If we accept this gift from God with faith then immediately three things happen:

- *We are forgiven and all our debt and guilt is cancelled:* 'everyone who believes in him receives forgiveness of sins through his name.'[435] And 'He has rescued us from the power of darkness and transferred us into the kingdom of his beloved Son.'[436]
- *The Holy Spirit comes to live in our spirit:* 'In him you also, when you had heard the word of truth, the gospel of your salvation, and had believed in him, were marked with the seal of the promised Holy Spirit'[437] So we now become the place where God the Holy Spirit dwells, or as the Bible puts it: 'Do you not know that you are God's temple and that God's Spirit dwells in you?'[438] Because of this we are able to relate to God.

---

[433] John 3: 16, NRSV.
[434] John 14: 6, NRSV.
[435] Acts 10: 43, NRSV.
[436] Col. 1: 13–14, NRSV.
[437] Eph. 1: 13, NRSV.
[438] 1 Cor. 3: 16, NRSV.

- *Thirdly we get a sparkly new life:* 'I came that they may have life, and have it abundantly.'[439]

Imagine that your human spirit is like a balloon that has become deflated and shrivelled with no air. When we are born again it's as if God begins to inflate this old balloon with air. The balloon begins to swell and grow. Sometimes it's hard to allow this growth and that's why the apostle Paul talks about the struggle between the 'flesh' (the old habits) and the new habits that are flowing through us from the Holy Spirit.

[E]verything—and I do mean everything—connected with that old way of life has to go. It's rotten through and through. Get rid of it! And then take on an entirely new way of life—a God-fashioned life, a life renewed from the inside and working itself into your conduct as God accurately reproduces his character in you.[440]

This new life is a free gift from God to us and is activated by faith. In order to have faith we first need to hear about God's gift and take it to heart. Then we talk to God. Of course the concept of speaking into 'thin air' can be a bit daunting to those not brought up to pray to any kind of spiritual being, but it really is the same as talking to a friend. You open your mouth and you speak some words. If you have not spoken to God before you could do so now saying something like this:

God, I have not lived up to your standards but I know that I need you. I am sorry for all the wrong things I have done [you might want to be specific here] *and I want to change. Thank you for sending Jesus to take my punishment so that I can be forgiven. I want to receive this forgiveness and the gift of the Holy Spirit. I ask you to come into my life so that I can live a new life in relationship with you.*

That's it! You don't even have to say Amen!

Praying for our children

Because our children are born fallen they have a default setting that will veer them off the right course and away from right actions.

My dad made me a bicycle. It was a really great bike and I used it a lot. Every week I would cycle a couple of miles to the library and change my books. But the one thing I really wanted to do eluded me. The local boys, who all seemed very old and mature at 15 or 16, could ride their bikes no-handed; they could even ride no-handed with someone sitting on the

---

439 John 10: 10, NRSV.
440 Eph. 4: 22–4, THE MESSAGE.

handlebars. Try as I might I could not ride my bike no-handed. The bike always veered out of control. I tried and tried but I never achieved my goal. It was years later before I realised that the bike was never going to ride straight because the frame—being second-hand—was bent and this always made it ride crookedly. I needed a new bike.

Just like my beloved bicycle we are all are set up to veer off course. This is called 'iniquity'. The Bible talks a lot about sin and iniquity, but if you're anything like me you don't see these words as having different meanings. So when we read in the Psalms: 'Wash me thoroughly from my iniquity, and cleanse me from my sin,'[441] we tend to think that this is just two rather poetic ways of saying the same thing. But they are two different words with two completely different meanings.

We are born with iniquity. And like the bent bicycle frame this iniquity veers us towards wrong actions or a lack of actions, wrong thoughts, and wrong attitudes. This iniquity can never be repaired; there is no band-aid that will fit and no pill that will cure it. What is needed is a new—or renewed—spirit. Only a new spirit will wash away this iniquity and create in us the inclination to do what is right. This is why we need to be born again—and so do our children.

But sin follows on from iniquity as surely as night follows day. We sin when we don't come up to God's standards.

So our brand new baby in all his loveliness has iniquity and this iniquity will bear fruit. You know this, of course, because you know that you won't have to teach him to throw his dinner across the room, or to have tantrums, or to lie, or disobey, or steal, or any of the other things the little chap will get up to quite soon.

But is it possible that this squeaky clean new baby has already sinned? Of course he hasn't gone to the bank with a shotgun and demanded money. He hasn't been discovered behind the bicycle sheds with Polly Smith. And he hasn't bullied someone on Facebook.

But there are far more subtle ways of sinning than the obvious lying, cheating, stealing, gratuitous sex, or violence. We also sin when the pain and brokenness in our lives overflows so that we do, or don't do, the things we should do, or when we allow bitterness and judgements to engulf us.

Just because an action or lack of action or an attitude stems from pain does not mean that it is without sin. It is highly likely that your lovely baby or my lovely baby has been born with

---

441 Ps. 51: 2, NRSV.

attitude— the wrong attitude. Wrong attitudes are the result of wrong responses that we make because we veer towards what is wrong and negative. Wrong attitudes are always the starting point for sin.

I was conceived into a world that didn't want me and didn't have room for me. I was told that being adopted made me extra 'special' and 'chosen', and on the surface I believed it. But there was a flip side to this coin. Underneath all the goodness and acceptance of adoption lay another truth—the truth of rejection. I started life 'over' at the age of eight weeks, but my inner self carried with it the scars and loss of basic trust that coloured my future health, wealth, wellbeing, and all my onward relationships.

When rejection like this happens iniquity causes us to respond with anger, bitterness, and all manner of wrong attitudes towards ourselves, towards God, and towards others. In these distortions lies the death of our potential. In prayer I have had to undo and repent of attitudes that almost certainly stemmed from this rejection and my prenatal reaction to it.

Like a stick of Brighton rock that has 'Brighton' written all the way through it, 'not welcome here' was written through all the layers of my life. But I have found in Jesus that *I am* welcome here. Echoes of the old words are beginning to fade and new loved-up words are taking their place. However, I'm still in process and God hasn't finished with me yet—as many will confirm. 'There has never been the slightest doubt in my mind that the God who started this great work in you would keep at it and bring it to a flourishing finish on the very day Christ Jesus appears.'[442] Right from conception, iniquity veered me towards wrong attitudes: so, yes, I sinned, and it is through repentance and deep inner healing that I have found release from some of these deep pains and harmful behaviour patterns. This pattern of having to deal with prenatal attitudes is discussed by John and Paula Sandford in their book *Healing the Wounded Spirit*:

> In the womb every adopted child has in his spirit experienced rejection from his natural parents. He has absorbed all the elements of his environment: the fear, tension, uncertainty, anxiety, guilt, shame, confusion, hatred, anger and pain of his mother . . . he may have been reacting in his spirit with resentment, tightening up in defensiveness, punishing with aggressive anger, or withdrawing in fear or rebellion against life. Certainly rest and trust are neither born nor formed in him.[443]

Jesus was born into a similar maelstrom of conflicting emotions as Mary struggled with her illegitimate pregnancy, but he was without sin. He didn't become bitter, or make wrong

---

[442] Phil. 1: 6, THE MESSAGE.
[443] John and Paula Sandford, *Healing the Wounded Spirit* (Victory House, 1985).

judgements, vows, and decisions. He was born with the right attitude towards God and towards life. Because he was born without iniquity he demonstrated a life without sin. And thus he completely fulfilled his potential.

While some of us have been rejected from the womb, many more were conceived and born into an environment full of love and acceptance. However, all of us suffer from faulty parenting and painful experiences that can lead to damage in our souls and in our spirits. It seems that the earlier the damage the deeper it runs. Unlike Jesus, we all walk a crooked path marred by judgements, bitterness, vows, sins, and serial wrong attitudes. For some the path is more crooked than for others.

But all is not doom and gloom. Although not a 'quick fix', we can ask God to step in and bring healing, restoration, and new life. There are many Christian people, groups, and organisations[444] that specialise in bringing help and hope to thousands of discouraged and deeply wounded people.

As parents we are in the unique position of being able pray for and with our children to catch things in the bud before they become life-altering habits and expectations. Because we have authority over our children, we have the authority to deal with some of these issues—with or without their cooperation. We will lose this authority when they individuate and leave our care. Just what that age is will differ from child to child. With this in mind, I had an interesting dream concerning our son David. At that time he was 16 and about to choose his career options, he was interested in Sports College or the British Army.

In the dream I was standing in a field near the front line of a battle. A bus pulled up full of young lads in army uniform. An officer stepped out followed by these young men. The officer was huge—really huge—he towered above me and he started ordering these soldiers into the front line of the battle. I saw that David was one of these young men. I stood between this officer and David and took authority, saying to the officer, 'You will not command David into battle, I have authority over him, he will not be sent to the front line, and I take authority over you and forbid you to speak to him.'

I woke up in the morning somewhat disturbed and began to pray, but the Lord said to me that I had done all the praying that was necessary and the battle had been won in the dream. Oh that all praying were always that easy . . . perhaps it should be! That same day I was due to take David to look round the local sports college. The young man showing us round was very nice, and after the tour he began to fill out some paperwork. At the end of this process he said that David had now been enrolled in the college. We later learned that this was a most unusual

---

[444] See page 303.

way to enrol, and nobody understood how or why it had happened this way. What a miracle! The decision was made and David took this route through Sports College getting a few more years under his belt before starting his army career.

I know that it was prayer, and in particular, the fact that I took authority over the demonic forces represented by the huge officer in the dream, that ordered this career path and kept him out of the war zone until he was older. I had declared my authority over David, who at 16 was a young man with his own mind.

Whilst we cannot dictate the choices that our children will make we can influence them through our actions and through our prayers. In the midst of all the business of life, cleaning, preparing the meals, the parental taxi service, homework and exam revision, we *must* pray for our children. There are all sorts of circumstances for which they will need prayer. We will need to pray about their schooling, the friends they make, the hobbies and sports that they get involved with, their health, their safety and their relationship with God. This prayer will need to be regular, intense, specific, and often take the form of warfare. It may involve fasting and should involve both parents and sometimes the children themselves.

Even if the path they are travelling at the moment is pretty smooth we have no idea what's up ahead, what sort of pressures our children will face, who will influence them, and the state of the world around them. As parents if we pray for them we have a unique ability, responsibility, and authority to change attitudes and circumstances and to bring blessing, prosperity, healing, and balm into their lives. We can even pray for their future spouses, jobs, work colleagues, and friends.

We have a friend who talks about 'prayer dumps'. The logistics of providing for an army in combat are quite amazing, requiring provisions to be left at various sites in and around the war zone. We can pray in this way for our children, providing not only for their present needs but also for their future needs. Like dumps of spiritual blessing these supplies will be ready for them as they meet life's challenges, even reaching out to them after we have gone.

These prayers, and the prayers of the wider family, will continue to be crucial as our children develop their own relationship with God and decide to worship and follow him. While we—and they—are on this earth, this kind of praying will not end.

Chapter 4
<u>Preparing the Way</u>

In much the same way that the Secret Service prepares the way before the President of the United States visits, so John the Baptist prepared the way for Jesus to come.

> The good news of Jesus Christ—the Message!—begins here, following to the letter the scroll of the prophet Isaiah. 'Watch closely: I'm sending my preacher ahead of you; He'll make the road smooth for you. Thunder in the desert! Prepare for God's arrival! Make the road smooth and straight!'[445]

John's mission was to prepare people for the arrival of Jesus and the primary outcome of this work was repentance. The people of his day flocked to see him in the wilderness and to be baptised as an expression of the repentance of their sins.

By extension you could say that before our children or indeed anyone asks Jesus into their lives a similar preparing work must take place. As parents wanting to see our children take this step it will fall primarily to us to prepare them. The way that John prepared people to meet Jesus can be an example to us in this task. So what did John do to prepare people to meet Jesus?

He got himself ready

Beginning with his miraculous conception John was a man called and prepared by God. The Bible says that he lived in the desert and tradition says that this was from quite a young age. As a wandering hermit he was unencumbered by the social and religious pressures of the time. He was a man who lived, thought, prayed, and heard God from 'outside the box'. As a result his message was fresh, new, and relevant.

As parents we need to get ourselves ready to have children. Ready physically, emotionally, and spiritually. This may mean taking time out to really seek God for wholeness and healing and for his Spirit to come into our lives. As we have already seen, our physical wellbeing needs to be at its peak before conception and during pregnancy. But there will also be spiritual and emotional issues that need to be addressed so that we can parent our children unencumbered by our own baggage and certainly not pass it on for them to carry. 'The best gift you can give your children is your own emotional, physical, spiritual and intellectual health.'[446]

---

[445] Mark 1: 1–6, THE MESSAGE.
[446] Sherrill and Prudence Tippins, *Two of Us Make a World* (Henry Holt, 1996).

Time spent before God dealing with our sins and our pains is going to be time well spent, both for parenting, being a spouse, and a life in relationship with God. As David wrote: 'Search me, O God, and know my heart; test me and know my thoughts. See if there is any wicked way in me, and lead me in the way everlasting.'[447] Whilst we know that God loves us just as we are we also know that we are not perfect.

I had a dream. In the dream I was looking at the most beautiful and exquisite vase. It was covered in a pattern of beautiful flowers, leaves, and swirling stems. As I looked closer I saw that there was a small part where the surface seemed chipped and was breaking away. I pulled at this and I began to see that underneath there was something else, also really beautiful. I pulled away at the outer layer and eventually another vase was revealed even more beautiful than the first, and amazingly it was bigger than the first vase. I looked closer and again there was a small chipped place which I began to pick away. Again a new vase was revealed of even more beauty and even bigger than the previous vase. This went on a few times and then I woke.

God loves you and me just the way we are. He sees us as very, very beautiful. And yet there is more to be revealed in and through us. It is time to cast off our limitations and move on to the more. The good can be the enemy of the best. We need to allow the process of change to happen, not clinging on to the life that we see as being good, even beautiful, but allowing God to bring forth all that he has put within us. We know that we all have issues in our lives that need to be put under the spotlight, but this can be a quite daunting or even painful process. And how do we even know where to start?

The Bible uses the imagery of fruits to talk about the things that flow out from us. Fruit is the visible product of mature growth, or the end result of a process. That process can either be good or bad. We can either have good fruits flowing from processes in our lives or bad fruits. As human beings we usually have a mixture of good and bad fruits. Depending on the proportions of that mixture, and the skill with which we cover up the bad fruits—and we do— we may think of ourselves, or be thought of by others, as a good person or a bad person, a lucky person or an unlucky person. But we are all a mixture, even Mother Theresa, Hitler, and my mum (who could do no wrong).

Obviously the good fruits in our lives are those things that are good, such as peace and joy, health and wealth, good relationships and happy children. They flow from good things that come into our lives such as love, good parenting, health, happiness, self-discipline, and from our good reactions to adversity. Good fruits do not harm us or others and they are the basis for

---

[447] Ps. 139: 23–4, NRSV.

happiness, health, and prosperity. Good fruits will produce good fruits in others around us. We want our children to experience and produce these good fruits.

Good fruits are also the primary result of the Holy Spirit coming into our lives when we are born again.

But what happens when we live God's way? He brings gifts into our lives, much the same way that fruit appears in an orchard—things like affection for others, exuberance about life, serenity. We develop a willingness to stick with things, a sense of compassion in the heart, and a conviction that a basic holiness permeates things and people. We find ourselves involved in loyal commitments, not needing to force our way in life, able to marshal and direct our energies wisely.[448]

We can identify good fruits in our lives because they are founded on what God says and on his character which, as we have seen, is love.

Love is patient; love is kind; love is not envious or boastful or arrogant or rude. It does not insist on its own way; it is not irritable or resentful; it does not rejoice in wrongdoing, but rejoices in the truth. It bears all things, believes all things, hopes all things, endures all things. Love never ends.[449]

In contrast, bad fruits are all the negative things that mar our enjoyment of life. They can also block the flow of the Holy Spirit in us and through us. Bad fruits reach out to affect those around us, our families, friends, workmates, and societies. Similarly we can be affected by the bad fruits of others. Like good fruits, bad fruits can affect our bodies, our emotions, and our spirits. They are usually the product of disobedience to God, either in our own lives, or the lives of our parents, ancestors, town, or nation. These fruits will display characteristics of Satan, such as pride, jealousy, domination, manipulation, control, hatred, prejudice, fear, violence, and separation. They may present as circumstances that have happened to us often as repeated patterns. They will produce limitation, frustration, division, and loss in our lives. Some bad fruits, in no particular order, are:

- Hatred, violence, murderous thoughts, desire to inflict pain, and abusive behaviour.
- Bitterness, unforgiveness, cynicism, judgementalism.
- Pride, self-centredness, egotistical behaviour, lack of compassion, lack of love.
- Robbery, theft, the desire to have what others have, jealousy.
- Lust and sexual appetites that are out of control or misdirected.

---

[448] Gal. 5: 22–3, THE MESSAGE.
[449] 1 Cor. 13: 4–8, NRSV.

- Fears and all kinds of phobias, fear of people, fear of rejection, fear of life.
- Addictions: we can be addicted to almost anything, such as, cigarettes, alcohol, chemical substances, chocolate, TV, sex etc.
- Compulsive and obsessive behaviour patterns.
- Withdrawal, isolation, separation, and lack of emotion.
- Uncontrolled emotion or anger.
- Things that happen to us such as sickness, poverty, accidents, and relationship breakdowns.
- Difficulty experiencing the spiritual: such as God's love, the desire or ability to worship, pray, or read the Bible.

Generally bad fruit will flow and grow from lack of love and care, poor parenting, sickness, sadness, lack of discipline, and so on. They can form vicious circles that perpetuate themselves in us and through us and down the generations. Families with generational bad fruits often live with poor resources, poor health, poor living standards, and no idea why they see these patterns being repeated in their children. Bad fruits affect all of us and we need to be prayerful and hear God when he tells us to deal with issues in our lives, otherwise they may flow down the generations affecting our children and our grandchildren. 'Keep a sharp eye out for weeds of bitter discontent. A thistle or two gone to seed can ruin a whole garden in no time.'[450]

Obviously it's a lot easier to see the bad fruit in other people than in ourselves; 'Why do you see the speck in your neighbor's eye, but do not notice the log in your own eye?'[451]

We need to cultivate a lifestyle that is open to hearing the Holy Spirit—directly or through others—when he points out our areas for change. Whilst this will be an ongoing process it is essential that we have started this process before we are thrust into the busyness of raising children.

However, we all have fruit of different kinds in our lives. Whilst there may be much in our lives that is pleasing and good we also have things that are difficult, painful, and destructive. Often we try to hide these issues from ourselves and from others. But the mouldy fruits at the bottom of the fruit bowl have a way of contaminating the glossy new fruit on the top.

As individuals we have to deal on a daily basis with those things that we find difficult or painful. Things like debt, dealing with a difficult boss, sickness or disability, addictions, managing our anger, trusting others, and much more. And all of us have families in which there are individuals who we treat with 'care' because they frequently explode, or because they

---

[450] Heb. 12: 15, THE MESSAGE.
[451] Matt. 7: 3–4, NRSV.

are nervous, because they talk too much, because they are poorly, and so on. That's what families do: they cover over each other's weaknesses, mistakes, and foibles.

As Christians we should be addressing the bad fruits in our lives and beginning to see change. Like water flowing down a rocky ravine the Holy Spirit in us will begin to dislodge these boulders of bad fruit in order to bring healing. We may experience a rather 'bumpy ride' as God creates a succession of circumstances and experiences that highlight the area he next wants to heal. God is far more interested in bringing our bad fruits to the light so that they can be removed or healed than in presenting a polished outward appearance. So it's likely that these experiences will keep coming until we either harden over or find this healing. As Christians we are all are in this process whether we are aware of it, and cooperate with it, or not.

Being born again is not the end of a process but the beginning. It's the beginning of a process of change that will see God's good fruits flowing out of us more and more. Traditionally we have been taught that producing fruit means 'making disciples', by bringing people to church and getting them to become Christians. If we have never led anyone to Jesus we can feel as though we have failed by producing no fruit. However, the analogy of the church as a body shows that we are not all called to do the same job, although we are all witnesses we are not all evangelists, we do not all make the tea after church, if I have an itch, unless I am disabled, its my hand not my foot that scratches it.

Producing good fruit has a much wider application than just soul-winning. In fact Jesus tells us that we know if a person is Godly not by his popularity or even by his apparent effectiveness as a preacher or prophet, but by the fruit of good character in his life: 'Beware of false prophets, who come to you in sheep's clothing but inwardly are ravenous wolves. You will know them by their fruits. Are grapes gathered from thorns, or figs from thistles?'[452]

All these kinds of fruit in our lives—both the good and the bad—are an outward expression of inner growth. These fruits, supported by a system of hidden roots, originated with a single, often tiny, seed.

The seed

Jesus told a story about a man who went out into his field to sow seeds. The seeds in Jesus' story represented the words that God speaks, and the story was about the way these seeds grow. Seeds can be either viable—they will grow into a plant given the right environment—or non-viable—they have no life in them. All God's words have life in them and the Bible says that they will all bring forth fruit.

---

[452] Matt. 7: 15–16, NRSV.

For as the rain and the snow come down from heaven, and do not return there until they have watered the earth, making it bring forth and sprout, giving seed to the sower and bread to the eater, so shall my word be that goes out from my mouth; it shall not return to me empty, but it shall accomplish that which I purpose, and succeed in the thing for which I sent it.[453]

God's words and actions always ultimately bring good. But because we are made in God's image all *our* words—whether casual and throwaway or laden with meaning and purpose—have creative or destructive abilities.

You brood of vipers! How can you speak good things, when you are evil? For out of the abundance of the heart the mouth speaks. The good person brings good things out of a good treasure, and the evil person brings evil things out of an evil treasure. I tell you, on the day of judgment you will have to give an account for every careless word you utter; for by your words you will be justified, and by your words you will be condemned.[454]

There are many things that we say or that are said to us that are laden with potential pain, sickness, limitation, and death. The words that we speak to ourselves also have incredible power in our lives. These inner tapes that run in our heads and the words that we speak often side with Satan rather than God. Phrases such us 'I'm not important, nobody loves me, I can't do it, I won't be able to pay my bills, I'm a loser, what's wrong with me? I'm not clever, I'm afraid, it's all my fault' are all things we repeatedly say to ourselves like a demonic mantra. Running these tapes in our head take us out of agreement with God, who does not say these things about us or to us. And he does not say them to our children. For the same reason we need to be very careful about the casual throwaway words that we say to our children. Words that are spoken by people in authority such as parents, teachers, pastors, and doctors can be particularly powerful.

Experiences that are painful, sorrow that continues, frustration at lack of success, and all the negative stuff that happens to us, also have the ability to act as seeds that will grow and produce bad fruits.

But it's our reactions to such negative words and experiences that are a key to the growth of these negative seeds. If we react to them in a godly way with forgiveness, love, prayer, and faith in God then negative seeds that would try to take root in our lives will just not germinate. But given the right environment and the right nourishment these kinds of seeds will grow up into bad fruits.

---

[453] Isa. 55: 11, NRSV.
[454] Matt. 12: 34–7, NRSV.

We did not allow our children to watch TV soaps (such as *Eastenders* and *Coronation Street* in the UK) because their storylines seem to rely so much on the many negative reactions of the characters. Anger, unforgiveness, deceptions, lies, fear, pride, and the whole gamut of negative emotions may make for explosive storylines that will generate good viewing figures, but they model wrong reactions. These same TV programmes then go on to demonstrate the effect of bad reactions by the escalating chaos that follows. The chaos then goes on to produce more negative reactions in an endless spiral. Negative seeds can be sown into our lives through:

- *Negative words:* that are spoken to us or about us. In particular the words that are spoken by people in authority over us, parents and grandparents, teachers, doctors, ministers of religion, lawyers and police officers, social workers and people that we really admire.
- *Negative actions*: such as: violence and abuse, emotional abuse, bullying, theft, slander, and false accusations.
- *Accidents and traumas*: whether physical, like falling off a ladder or being in a car accident; or emotional, such as the death of a loved one; or spiritual, such as being dominated by a church leader.
- *Sickness*: our own sickness or that of a close family member or friend.
- *Cultural and family actions*: such as being born in a country or family that is predominantly given over to the worship of false gods. Those growing up during a time of war, or into a country or family that has suffered a major disaster, such as those living in Chernobyl after the reactor blew up or those living in Japan devastated by the recent massive earthquake and tsunami.
- *Our own sins.*
- *Demonic influences:* that can attach to any of the above or that can in some cases be purely external, such as poltergeist activity.

Good seeds can be sown into our lives through:

- *Positive words*: that are spoken to us or about us. In particular the words that are spoken by people in authority and people that we really admire.
- *Positive actions:* such as love, help, encouragement, respect, and gifts.
- *Good health.*
- *Good circumstances*: such as being brought up in a place of peace and prosperity.
- *Success.*
- *The Holy Spirit talking to, encouraging, and guiding us.*

We may not see the fruit of these actions immediately but—depending on the species—seeds can lie dormant for a very long time without germinating: 'An ancient seed that germinated after being recovered from the rubble of King Herod's pleasure palace has been dated as 2,000 years old, smashing the record for the oldest seed ever grown.'[455]

So it is with the seeds that grow in our lives, they can lie dormant for some time before the right conditions cause growth. Inside every seed there is an embryo and a food supply. This baby plant has the capacity to grow both roots and a shoot, but it needs—and will wait for—favourable conditions before beginning to germinate and start growing.

Thus roots, shoots, and ultimately fruits grow from seeds that have been given the right environment in which to germinate. In our children we want to create the right environment for seeds that will produce good fruit to grow.

In Jesus' story about the man scattering seeds he talks about the ground on which the seed lands and how it has an influence on the growth of the seed. We know that the right kind of environment for good stuff to grow in our children is a loving, caring environment that has encouragement and stimulation to promote growth. Bad seeds will germinate well in ground that is harsh, critical, unloving, frightening, and inconsistent. Its not rocket science: good stuff grows in good ground, bad stuff grows in bad ground. In our own lives as grown-ups we will already have many fruits that come from both types of ground. We should be encouraging the growth of plants bearing good fruit in our lives and the lives of our children, but pulling up and destroying the plants bearing bad fruit.

So often we try to remove these bad fruits from our lives by picking all the fruit. Anyone who harvests fruit in the autumn will tell you that picking fruit is an exhausting process. You may become so consumed with picking off the bad fruit in your life that there is no emotional energy left for anything else. But as soon as our focus is diverted to some other activity, back come all those bad habits. If it were easy to stop bad habits there would be no market for products to help stop smoking, taking drugs, or eating too much.

Likewise, traditional childcare has focused on the removal of bad traits in our children so that they learn to do those things needed to live in a social society and stop doing those things that would alienate them. Willpower and behaviour modification are the main mechanisms by which we remove these bad fruits, and they do have their place. Both these actions focus on altering behaviour by learning to behave in a new way. This learning is often reinforced by punishment such as 'time out' or the 'naughty step' and by rewards such as points-for-presents charts or some other way of monitoring and rewarding 'good behaviour'. This is called discipline. We commonly use behavioural modification methods on our toddlers and small children and it works very well when it comes to keeping them out of the road or away from

---

[455] http://www.guardian.co.uk/science/2008/jun/12/ancient.seed

the fire. The Bible reinforces this position, 'Train children in the right way, and when old, they will not stray.'[456]

God's laws are like this behaviour modification process. They concentrate on removing fruit but don't get down to the root of the problem. They highlight the problems without having the ability to sort them out. When the Holy Spirit comes into our lives we are transformed so that these laws—now written on our hearts and in our spirits—can change us from the inside out.

Healing

Sometimes God will just bring healing to us as we go about our everyday life. He may prompt us to forgive someone, remind us of his love for us, or call us to repent, and it can be all done and dusted by lunchtime. At others times we will need to set aside time for this process.

This process which is often called 'prayer counselling' or 'prayer ministry' can take place on our own as we pray, with a trusted friend, or with a professional Christian counsellor. However, we usually start this process with some idea of what we need to achieve. But we will have to realise that whilst we can have a mental list of things we really need to change in our lives, the Holy Spirit may well start from the inside out and in his own particular order. In my experiences of healing I have discovered that God rarely deals with the things at the top of my list first. Often he starts with smaller seemingly trivial issues. These more trivial issues may need addressing before any more weighty ones can be dealt with. Climbing a hill or mountain is a process of small steps. But these small steps take you, one by one, to the summit and then you can look back, see how far you have climbed, and be amazed at the view. It's the same with the process of healing. The cumulative effect of dealing with lots of seemingly small issues can also be really great as you look back and see the release that has come into your life.

But however God deals with us, it's true to say that we usually start with a wish list for change. This is often the starting point to finding out root causes that need to be addressed. But discovering these root causes may require a bit of detective work. As the Holy Spirit leads us it may be good to ask;

- When did I first feel unhappy, cross, angry, etc.?
- When did I first do this?
- What does doing this make me feel?
- What need does it meet?
- Do I need to forgive someone, or myself, or God?

---

[456] Prov. 22: 6, NRSV.

- Did I make any inner vows, such as 'I will never trust, be weak, get married' etc.
- Did I make any judgements? Such as 'bad luck always happens to me', 'men are only interested in one thing', or 'women can't be trusted?'

These kinds of questions—and perhaps more importantly their answers—may provide release in themselves. Sometimes we just need someone to talk to and the cathartic or healing process of letting it all out in a safe place. But the answers to these questions will also point the way forward in terms of any prayer and help that may be needed. In my experience all prayer for healing involves confession of our sins and faults, repentance that opens the way for us to receive God's forgiveness, and our forgiveness, of others. These can sometimes be very painful to do.

- *Confessing:* Confession is a deep awareness of our sin; it involves taking responsibility and saying 'yes it was me . . . it was my fault'. Often it brings into the light things that were hidden in darkness. These hidden sins, which may be actions, reactions, or attitudes, can be the root cause of much distress in our lives. Sometimes we may also need to confess the sins of our fathers or even our people-group.
- *Repentance:* Repentance takes confession one step further as we ask God for forgiveness and seek to change. It too is a deep emotion, but it is not something to be avoided because it brings great change and healing. 'Godly grief produces a repentance that leads to salvation and brings no regret, but worldly grief produces death.'[457]

> A simple but vivid example comes to my mind. In a home prayer meeting, I found myself next to a young man in his early twenties. We had not met before, but I felt led to ask him, 'Have you received the Holy Spirit?'
>
> 'Yes,' he replied, but then added rather wistfully, 'but I don't speak in tongues.'[458] Clearly he felt there was something lacking in his experience.
>
> Without discussing any further the issue of tongues, I asked him, 'Did you ever visit a fortune-teller?'
>
> He reflected for a moment, and then said, 'Yes, once, when I was about fifteen. But I only did it as a joke. I didn't really believe in it.'
>
> 'But still,' I pressed him, 'you actually did have your fortune told?'
>
> 'Yes,' he acknowledged rather reluctantly, and then added defensively, 'but I didn't mean anything by it.'
>
> 'Would you be willing to confess that as a sin,' I said, 'and ask God to forgive you and release you from its consequences?'

---

[457] 2 Cor. 7: 10, NRSV.
[458] Speaking in another language not known to the speaker but inspired by the Holy Spirit.

When he agreed to this, I led him in a simple prayer, in which he confessed his visit to the fortune-teller as a sin, and asked God to forgive him and release him from its consequences. Then without a further word of explanation, I put my hand on his shoulder and asked God to release the Holy Sprit within him. Instantly, without hesitation or stammering, he began to speak clearly and fluently in an unknown tongue. In a few moments he was lost in the presence of God, oblivious to all that was going on around him. The invisible barrier in his life had been removed![459]

- *Forgiveness:* Just as we need to ask God to forgive us, we also need to forgive others. Forgiveness can be very hard to do, but the prayer that Jesus taught us to pray; 'forgive us our debts, as we forgive our debtors',[460] links our forgiveness, by God to our willingness to forgive others. Forgiveness can be a deliberate choice or an act of the will and may need to be a repeated action. It is also is linked to our heart understanding of a situation: when Jesus was on the cross he prayed: 'Father, forgive them; for they do not know what they are doing.'[461]

Emotional healing

Often we will need to pray through deep emotions that come to the surface during these times of prayer. Jesus' ministry on earth concentrated on allowing the Holy Spirit to move through him, bringing healing to those that needed it. He said; 'The Spirit of the Lord is upon me, because he hath anointed me to preach the gospel to the poor; he hath sent me to heal the brokenhearted, to preach deliverance to the captives, and recovering of sight to the blind, to set at liberty them that are bruised, to preach the acceptable year of the Lord.'[462]

We are all born with emotional baggage, brought up by parents with emotional baggage, into a world full of emotional baggage. Sadly we have often been encouraged to forget about this baggage in the past and press on to the future. Much of the fuel for this idea comes from what Paul wrote to the Philippians: 'forgetting what lies behind and straining forward to what lies ahead, I press on toward the goal for the prize of the heavenly call of God in Christ Jesus.'[463] Mistakenly believing that this means we should not even think about troubling stuff in the past, many Christians have been condemned to limp through life unable to achieve any goals at all. But while we remain tied to unresolved pain we will never walk free. As Leonard

---

[459] Derek Prince, *Blessing or Curse: You Can Choose* (Chosen Books, 2006).
[460] Matt. 6: 12, KJV.
[461] Luke 23: 24, NRSV.
[462] Luke 4: 18–19, KJV.
[463] Phil. 3: 13–14, NRSV.

Cohen so aptly wrote in his song *'Bird on a Wire'*, things from the past have a way of holding us back.

But God is in the business of setting us so free that often we no longer even remember the event and certainly don't feel the pain of it anymore. That is true forgetting. If you're struggling to forget then you haven't forgotten! I have received lots of healing over the years and there are in particular a number of issues in my life that were deeply painful and affected my life for many years. Now, however, because those memories have been healed I can barely remember them and the same old feelings just don't come back when I do remember. They no longer have any power to affect my life. It's as if they just didn't happen—that's what forgetting is all about.

Each of us has in our lives a storehouse of memories. These memories are absolutely vital to life because it is through all these past experiences that we make sense of the world around us in the present. But these memories aren't just a list of events. Stored with each one are all the emotions, feelings, and even the smells and sights associated with that memory. When you pull that memory card out of the filing system in your mind all these feelings and emotions come flooding back. Sometimes these are happy memories triggered by such thing as the smell of new-mown grass, the sight of the sea, the warmth of a hug, but there are some memories that are dark and painful. The mind is very clever at hiding these away in the file marked 'M' for missing. Every once in a while an event will come along that triggers this memory, and the old feelings and emotions will threaten to come flooding back. It's then that we sometimes react in a really over the top kind of way, becoming angry or sad, bursting into tears, or becoming violent. We've all met people who reacted like this leaving us wondering what on earth we said or did. These inappropriate reactions come from unresolved memories that just won't stay down.

It can take a lot of courage to open up some of these deep wounds, but while they remain hidden within us they do us no good. It's only when we bring them to Jesus and talk them through with him that we can receive the healing that he wants for us.

If praying about these issues brings back deeply painful memories it may be helpful to imagine Jesus with you when you were suffering and see what he is saying and doing. I have found that using my imagination in this way has been an incredible help. Imagination is the ability to form pictures in the mind. In our mind's eye we can envisage events from the past, events in the future, ideas, pictures, and designs. When God uses the screen of our imagination to bring healing he often shows us where he was, what he was doing, and how he felt while we were in pain. These 'imaginations' can be tremendously powerful, rewriting our past from God's perspective and healing our emotions. Our imagination can also be like a screen on which God shows us what he wants to do now.

243

Jesus saw what his father was doing and only did those same things: 'I tell you, the Son can do nothing on his own, but only what he sees the Father doing; for whatever the Father does, the Son does likewise.'[464] Because imagination can act as an interface between the soul and the spirit, I think that Jesus may have seen these things on the screen of his imagination.

The imagination has been largely ignored and downgraded by Christians, because it is another of those God-given gifts that can also be used in a bad way. I believe and know from experience that God wants to show us about himself and his love for us on these inner screens and it is through this gift of imagination that I have received much healing from past hurts.

One of the first times I ever prayed in this way was soon after I realised the effect of my adoption. I was praying with a friend and we each had something to share and pray about. When it came to my turn to see what Jesus was doing I imagined my cot after my birth-mother had left and before my adoptive parents arrived. I could see myself abandoned and alone. In the picture I saw Jesus walk in, come over to the cot and pick me up. A very simple picture, and yes, it could have been a figment of my imagination, but it had lasting repercussions in my life, building me a foundation and assuring me of God's love.

Generational blessings and curses

It is also likely that you will have to pray about negative patterns in your family line. We are the generation above our children. Just as we have inherited family habits and traits from our parents and their ancestors, so too our children will receive those same things from us. These influences can and do affect all three parts of our personality: our body, our soul, and our spirit. We hope that these influences will be all good—we would call these 'blessings'. But all too often we see patterns of pain, sickness, poverty, and spiritual darkness repeated through our family line—the Bible calls these curses. In his book *Blessing or Curse*,[465] Derek Prince talks about generational blessings and curses.

There may be forces at work in our lives that have their origin in previous generations. Consequently, we may be confronted with recurrent situations or patterns of behaviours that cannot be explained solely in terms of what has happened in our lifetime or personal experiences. The root cause may go back a long way in time, even thousands of years.

And he describes the effects of curses:

---

[464] John 5: 19, NRSV.
[465] Derek Prince, *Blessing or Curse: You Can Choose* (Chosen Books, 2006).

There is one word that sums up the effects of a curse: *frustration.* You reach a certain level of achievement in your life and everything looks set for a bright future. You have all the obvious qualifications—and yet something goes wrong! So you start all over again, and reach the same level as before, but once again things go wrong. After this happens several times, you realize that this is the pattern of your life. You cannot see any obvious reason for it.

The Bible makes it clear that blessings that bring life, enlargement, and multiplication can flow down a family line for a thousand generations. Curses that are the penalty for breaking the law bring death, reduction and division but God in his mercy has limited their effect to only four and at the most ten generations.

A curse will stop operating if the sin is not repeated during those four or ten generations. However because of the effect of the sin it is likely that a repeated pattern will be set up before the curse has reached the fourth or tenth generation. And so the curse begins again. We see this repeated pattern working particularly in the lives of those who have worshipped false gods, or who have had occult involvement. The good news is that we can be released. 'Christ redeemed us from the curse of the law by becoming a curse for us.'[466]

However just as we don't see all Christians physically well, so not all Christians are whole or free from curses—and the two are often linked. The fact is we can't just make the grand assumption that everything that Jesus did for us on the cross became effective in our lives the moment we were born again. We often have to apply the work of Jesus to specific issues. We do this by confessing these specific sins, repentance from our involvement with that sin, and by completely renouncing it.

We will know if there are curses operating in our family if we see repeated patterns emerging even in our own generation. According to Derek Prince these patterns may include: mental health issues, repeated sickness, barrenness, miscarriage and 'female problems', breakdown of marriages, alienation, poverty, being accident prone, and untimely deaths.[467]

Having traced my birth family in order to find my parents and my roots, I discovered all sorts of repeated patterns working their way through the family line. A predominant one was the abandonment of children, even those born within marriage or who had been adopted. There was also abandonment by spouses and a number of rather strange money issues.

---

[466] Gal. 3: 13, NRSV.
[467] Derek Prince, *Blessing or Curse: You Can Choose* (Chosen Books, 2006).

I first saw the need to deal with these issues when I was 13, way back in the swinging sixties. I was on a Christian youth camp and for some reason the verse about bastards not entering the congregation was read out. I remember nothing more about the weekend other than the totally dominating feeling that I needed to get this dealt with. I prayed with the guest speaker and believe I received release. It marked the beginning of my journey into wholeness.

You may need to do some digging into family history, perhaps completing a family tree, to work out the causes of any negative patterns you see in your family. Ask the Holy Spirit to be involved in this process. If you believe that these patterns come from curses operating in your family you will need to pray. Derek Prince[468] recommends a seven-step approach to release:

- Confess your faith in Christ and in his sacrifice on your behalf.
- Repent of all your rebellion and your sins.
- Claim forgiveness of sins.
- Forgive all other people who have ever harmed you or wronged you.
- Renounce all contact with anything satanic or occultic.
- Pray a prayer for release from any curse.
- Now believe that you have received, and go on in God's blessing.

Conclusion

As we begin to see the benefit of praying for our own healing we will be able to help others and in particular we will be able to help our children, praying with them as difficulties arise and teaching them about repentance, forgiveness, and right attitudes. In this way they will be able to go on into a future unencumbered by long-term guilt, unforgiveness, bitterness, judgements, and wrong attitudes.

For a list of resources about prayer for healing see page 303.

---

[468] Ibid.

Chapter 5
<u>Following our Calling</u>

John the Baptist did what God had told him to do and he spoke what God had called him to speak. He lived out his calling, and he didn't care what people thought of him. Of course, preparation is the key here. If we want to follows in John's footsteps we are likely to be less affected by our peers and more able to fulfil God's calling on our lives if we have some degree of emotional wholeness. We also need to know what God's calling is, both in terms of the big picture and of the daily tasks.

Learning how to hear God in the quiet of time with him and in the noisiness of life is crucial. All the more so as we rush towards the end of this age and all the changes that it will certainly bring.

Often we swing wildly between the two opposite positions of not doing what we should be doing or of doing it but taking it too far. And we often do what we shouldn't be doing at all! And all the while our children are watching and learning from us as we model for them the fulfilled and Holy Spirit-led Christian life.

With all of our faults we are the book they read. Through us they will see God. So what are they seeing? Is it a balanced and good picture or sketchy and full of inconsistencies? Are we fulfilled, have we found the calling that God has for us that fits us perfectly? Are we being led by the Holy Spirit? Or are we just filling our own emotional needs with a lot of stuff and busyness that strokes our damaged egos?

It's so very easy within the Christian scene to end up doing all the 'jobs' in the church just because there seems to be no one else to do them. But filling up the gaps in your local church may block someone else from seeing the need and moving into their purpose. Or, of course, you may be a person frustrated because someone else is busily doing the job you feel called to. This is often a leader in the church. Sadly many leaders find it really hard to let other people do stuff in the church in case they get it wrong, not willing to allow them to learn on the job. The hierarchy often acts like a cork in a bottle of wine. And while the cork remains in the bottle the wine cannot be poured out.

Am I wrong in thinking that a lot of this is down to peer pressure? We are all under huge pressure to appear to be getting it right—all the time. If we live in the real world—and yes, we do—we will make mistakes but we will never learn from them if we deny their existence.

Church leaders need to make sure that the right things are said and done within the church but not to the extent that fear of what people think leads the church. Although they must be humble and loving they also need to cultivate assertiveness and authority to say if something has gone wrong so the whole church family can learn from it.

John the Baptist didn't give a fig for what people thought and he was very happy to tell people when they had gone wrong. The consequence was that people were then able to repent and prepare themselves for Jesus.

As Christian parents we want our children to be seen to perform well. We want them to go to youth group and have a good social life with nice Christian friends. We don't want them to smoke, wear too much make-up, or have relationships with dubious people. We would really like it if they would become part of the worship group or the media group or help in the crèche.

These may be fine ambitions, but we need to be very wary about what drives them. Is it that our own need for acceptance is the driving force behind the way we lead our children? Do we really love them for who and what they are? Are we really helping them to deal with root issues in their lives and find their own way? Loving means giving them room to grow even by making mistakes. Mistakes that others will see.

You don't dig up the seeds in the garden to see if they're growing. So too with our children we shouldn't push uninvited into their personal space in order to check up on them—that kind of intrusion is usually for our benefit not theirs. Rather we should water them with prayer, warm them with love, and above all exercise faith in God for them.

So John the Baptist did the right stuff and wasn't pressurised by other people. But he also spoke what God wanted him to speak. Not too little and not too much. And the people flocked to hear him because he scratched where they itched.

He waited for the hungry people to seek him out

John could not be accused of spoon-feeding his audience, of cosseting them, or of stuffing them full of religion. He didn't run around after people trying to convert them. He knew when someone was not ready or willing to really hear what he had to say. Lets not Bible-bash our children: how hard is it to wait until they ask or until God really does nudge us to speak? They will learn far more from our actions than our words. 'The right word at the right time is like a custom-made piece of jewelry.'[469]

---

[469] Prov. 25: 11, THE MESSAGE.

And does our relationship with Jesus match up to our words? 'Like billowing clouds that bring no rain is the person who talks big but never produces.'[470]

We vastly underestimate the motivating power of hunger. But hunger is not just about physical food. There can be an inner hunger that drives us on. As Jesus said: 'Blessed are those who hunger and thirst for righteousness, for they will be filled.'[471]

Babies learn because of inner hunger. It drives them towards movement, walking, reading, and achieving success as they grow up. As they learn to reach out and a grab a toy, or begin to roll and move, we know that we mustn't do these things for them or they will never learn and achieve success. Just as it is important for them to have that hunger that spurs them on physically, so also they need hunger in their souls and in their spirits.

We have so much entertainment on hand that there is a real danger that our children won't learn how to fill empty moments creatively, how to be still, or how to be lost in a sense of wonder. It's really important to give them spaces that are not all filled up with activity and noise. We should leave empty places in their schedules because it's during these times, when they are moaning and stomping about because they are bored, that they will eventually discover how to make their own choices, follow their own creativity, and produce their own pleasures. And these are incredibly important life skills.

In the same way we shouldn't overfill them with Christian stuff. By that I mean dead, religious stuff. Reading them Bible stories and surrounding them with a living faith is essential to their spiritual growth. But they need to develop a sense of hunger and we do need to be wary of stuffing them so full that they feel sick, especially as they grow into the teenage years.

Our son David didn't seem to make the connection between that funny pain in the tummy—called hunger—and the need to eat. He was 2 and he had hardly ever eaten a whole meal. But he would get really cross and crotchety because he was hungry. So we taught David about hunger and how and when and what to eat. We tried to provide the right kind of food and present it in the right kind of way. But, of course, mostly we fed him crisps and pudding just to get him to eat. It's amazing that he hasn't grown up with a disproportionate love of puddings!

It's the same with their spirits. Our children need to learn to recognise hunger, how to fill it, and what to fill it with. Our part in this process is the same as with the physical. We feed

---

[470] Prov. 25: 14, THE MESSAGE.
[471] Matt. 5: 6, NRSV.

their spirits with bits of spiritual food such as Bible stories, praying (especially the kind that produces visible results), music, creativity, and relationship with other Christians. When they see us excited about some new understanding of the Bible, they are learning that it's not a dull and boring book. When they are old enough, just as they take over physically feeding themselves, so they will also learn how to feed their own spirits. Children who grow into adults unable to feed their bodies with the right kind of food are disabled and do not go on to thrive and prosper.

We want our children to thrive and prosper spiritually by knowing how to feed and grow their own spirits. We certainly don't want them to become spiritually anorexic by avoiding spiritual input altogether.

He hated dead religion

John wouldn't have anything to do with people who were religious and was even quite rude to them. In this respect, John was very childlike. Children seem very quickly to pick up the true 'vibes' from a situation, otherwise known as having 'discerning of spirits'. They are particularly good at discerning the spirit of 'hypocrisy' and 'bullshit'. Take your child to a church that has a name for being lively but is in reality full of hypocrisy and he will squiggle and squirm to get away.

Our children, it seemed, were particularly sensitive to this. And, in this respect, they were particularly expressive. Like litmus paper that turns pink in the presence of an acid, they would become quite disruptive if the Holy Spirit was left out of a meeting. Even when armed with masses of drawing and play things they still didn't want to be in some churches no matter how short the service. At other times they would sit quietly for hours through a meeting or conference—albeit they were drawing or playing games—but also really enjoying being there. On one occasion I discovered that Christopher was drawing a picture of a donkey. The pastor was preaching about Jesus going into Jerusalem on a donkey. Could it be that he was even listening? They seemed to really know when they were in a church where the Holy Spirit was moving and his presence was real.

We really need to encourage them in this discernment and teach them how and when to express it. Hitting me during the sermon and saying very loudly, 'I'm bored now, can we go?' is, I have learned, not the right time and place. However we can go too far when it comes to making them 'behave'. In his book *Children of Revival*, Vann Lane (the children's pastor of Brownsville Assembly of God church), says that from a young age he held an important position in the church. 'When I was a child, I even had a position in the church—my position was to sit still and be quiet.'[472]

If we don't encourage and talk to our children about their experience of the church we belong to then this discernment may well be switched off. They will deaden the hunger pains and they will grow up into young adults who couldn't care less about Jesus, God, church, and all that stuff. Or perhaps even worse they will learn to play the hypocritical smiley-smiley plastic Christian game.

Churches are often far too grown-up. On the whole they do not cater for small children, seeing them as a distraction from the real business of hearing God. When my children were small I can remember being embarrassed if they cried or made a noise, and I remember one mother being asked to take her child out of the service. Imagine how our children must feel being taken every Sunday to a place where they are not really welcome and they must be quiet, shut up, and stop fidgeting! Whatever does that say about God as a loving father? I don't think Jesus is very happy about this state of affairs:

> At that time the disciples came to Jesus and asked, "Who is the greatest in the kingdom of heaven?" He called a child, whom he put among them, and said, "Truly I tell you, unless you change and become like children, you will never enter the kingdom of heaven. Whoever becomes humble like this child is the greatest in the kingdom of heaven. Whoever welcomes one such child in my name welcomes me. If any of you put a stumbling block before one of these little ones who believe in me, it would be better for you if a great millstone were fastened around your neck and you were drowned in the depth of the sea."[473]

Children too are part of the church and have a legitimate need and right to be filled with the Holy Spirit, hear Jesus speak to them, and begin to do the things Jesus is telling them to do. However, ministry in the church usually only involves 'important' grown-ups, and there is no place for children to express what they feel God is saying and doing. In the sort of churches I have attended these 'important' people have usually been middle-aged, middle-class, and successful. Certainly the people that minister do not include children, except possibly at Christmas when a nativity play may be produced. This merely reinforces the whole idea that church is a performance where other people do stuff.

If we are to grow our children's spirits then they must learn that they are a valuable part of the church community with a valuable contribution to make. They are not the church of

---

[472] Vann Lane, *Children of Revival* (Destiny Image, 1998).
[473] Matt. 18: 1–6, NRSV.

tomorrow; they are part of the church today. But all too often they are shoved out of the service while the important work of listening to what God is saying takes place. They go out to 'Sunday school' or 'children's church' where they will be entertained with Bible stories, sweets, games, and perhaps a bit of hilarity so that they will actually enjoy themselves. Geared towards giving the adults a few minutes of peace and quiet, children's groups are often more about babysitting than about hearing God speak and moving in the gifts of the Spirit.

Rather than having a children's church where we minster *to* our children, we should be seeking to minister *with* them. In that way their relationship with Jesus will grow. They will hear him speak, see what he does and grow in faith. Only that way will we raise a generation of children who don't abandon Jesus, the minute they head off to college or university, because they have a real living experience of his power in their lives.

As soon as our children were old enough they voted with their feet and absolutely refused to go to any children's groups at all. This means that as they have grown older they have lacked Christian mates with whom to socialize, which has had both positive and negative outcomes for them. The group of Christians that we attach to as 'our church' is vitally important in the spiritual life and growth of our children. As they grow up and begin to individuate, the friends they form in church and these older family friends will become important voices in their lives.

Jesus' ministry was not performed in hallowed churches, but in the open air. It was in the public places where he did his teaching, healing, and deliverance, and yet there is no record of him telling the mothers to take their children away because they weren't old enough. Quite the reverse is true. 'One day children were brought to Jesus in the hope that he would lay hands on them and pray over them. The disciples shooed them off. But Jesus intervened: 'Let the little children come to me, and do not stop them; for it is to such as these that the kingdom of heaven belongs.'[474] Perhaps if our churches were more child-friendly they would be more Jesus-friendly too and he would come and visit more often.

He called people to repent and get ready for God

Having been brought up with an understanding that God accepts us just as we are it seems strange to discover that John's message was intended to get people to change their lives before Jesus came. He was of course preaching to a pre-Christian Jewish people, but as parents do we need to learn from his example? We know that Jesus died for us while we were still cut off from God. And in his letter to the Romans the Apostle Paul says: 'But God proves his love for us in that while we still were sinners Christ died for us.'[475]

---

[474] Matt. 19: 13–14, NRSV.
[475] Rom. 5: 8, NRSV.

But John was sent to get people ready for Jesus' coming even to the point of baptising them. And we too get our children ready to hear the message that Jesus brings as we talk to them, as we model the Christian life to them, by being part of a local church, and by having friends who are Christians. But there are other ways that we can get them ready.

We need to make sure that the eyes and ears of their spirits are open. Jesus himself talked about this in the parable of the man sowing seeds, which I have already mentioned. He pointed out that the good news he came to bring is like seeds—full of potential—but the reception and fruitfulness of them depends on the ground where they fall. The soil is the heart or spirit of people in various states and stages of life and a person's reception of God's words is determined by the condition that it is in.

• The Hardened ground

The first batch of seed falls on the pathway round the edge of the field that had been baked hard in the sun. Jesus said that the seed that falls here doesn't even get a chance to penetrate into the soil before the birds snatch it away to eat. The people hearing these words do not even begin to understand what he is saying. Since we can only understand God's words in our spirits these people have human spirits that are just not able to hear, they are shrivelled and hardened. Hardened spirits are not the result of love, kindness, and goodness, but rather, as the parable implies, they are hearts or spirits that have been walked all over and have finally dried up. If you have children like this at home it is not too late to water them with love so that they can become softened ground ready and able to hear God when he speaks. The prophecies spoken by the angel who announced John's prospective birth specifically said that restoring family relationship was part of the preparation needed before Jesus would come. 'With the spirit and power of Elijah he will go before him, to turn the hearts of parents to their children, and the disobedient to the wisdom of the righteous, to make ready a people prepared for the Lord.'[476] Paul also talks about parents' relationships with their children: 'Fathers, do not provoke your children, or they may lose heart.'[477]

In Mark's gospel, we are told that Jesus looked at the religious leaders of the day and was 'grieved for the hardness of their hearts'. The word translated 'hardness' is also the word 'calloused'. The Pharisees had a calloused attitude to God and to others. Physically calluses are caused by repetitive action that causes dead skin cells to form on the part of the body affected. These skin cells form a thick layer that is defensive in nature. Emotionally we can develop calluses when we try to defend ourselves from constant criticism, negativity, or any other painful experience. It is also possible to become deliberately calloused, by repeated actions and

---

[476] Luke 1: 17, NRSV.
[477] Col. 3: 21, NRSV.

253

reactions that we know to be wrong. Unfortunately these calluses affect our human spirits and ability to hear God because they make us stubborn and dulled in our spiritual perception. God doesn't want us to develop hard, untouchable areas in our lives. He wants to heal us.

Hard hearts can also be hearts that have been hoodwinked by belief in false gods. Freemasonry in particular can bring whole families into spiritual darkness where they cannot see the truth. Right from the first stage of the freemasonic rituals a man will commit himself to following a false light.

At the time that he is led in the oath, the candidate is disoriented, blindfolded, half naked, confused, afraid, and humiliated. He has been stripped of all his clothes and his wedding ring, and has put on something similar to pajamas, with one leg rolled up and the shirt half off his torso. He has been blindfolded with a hood, and had a rope put around his neck. He has been led around during the initiation ritual like a blind dog on a leash. He has no idea who is watching him or how many men there are. He has been told that he is in darkness and must depend on Masonry to give him light.[478]

If you have family involvement in any false religion you will need to repent of it specifically: undoing all wrong vows, oaths, and rituals so that you and your children can reap the benefit of ears and eyes that are open to God. We undo these vows verbally by renouncing them and declaring that we are no longer in agreement with them. There are people and groups that can help with this. (See page 303)

Jeremiah the prophet called the children of Israel to break up the fallow or unploughed ground, and just as the farmer ploughs up the hard ground before planting seeds, so we too must be proactive in preparing our hearts and the hearts of our children to hear and receive God's word.

• The Stony Ground

The stony ground is very much like the hard ground but scattered with good bits of soil. The seed begins to sprout when it lands on a good part of the ground bringing a lot of very quick growth. However it is unable to put down deep roots because the stones get in the way. As soon as the sun comes up the plant dries up and withers away. People like this receive the words that God speaks but they are received only by the soul. The mind, will, and emotions latch on to the word with great enthusiasm, but as soon as there is any difficulty they give up. Their human spirit has not received the life of the Holy Spirit and they have not been born again so they have no depth and no sustenance.

---

[478] http://www.crossroad.to/articles2/006/freemasons.htm.

Given that these people are likely to have joined a church and be in an environment where they are hearing God's word there is hope that they will suddenly see, understand, and be born again in their spirits. I certainly wouldn't knock it if my children suddenly became wildly enthusiastic about church. But this is not the time to stop praying for them. They too need to have their fallow ground broken up, specifically concentrating on removing the stones so that the words of Jesus can take root in their spirits.

• The Thorny Ground

'Those sown among the thorns: these are the ones who hear the word, but the cares of the world, and the lure of wealth, and the desire for other things come in and choke the word, and it yields nothing.'[479]

This ground is actually fertile ground that is ready to receive God's word. Unfortunately it has been planted with weeds. This is the ground that is full of the other 'stuff' we talked about before. Stuff such as making money, hobbies, being anxious, and false religious ideas. This stuff fills up and takes pride of place in all the empty places of our lives. We are stuffed so full that we are not hungry but are rather busy with all sorts of other things that come first before God. These things choke out the word of God. This was Jesus' attitude to these things;

What I'm trying to do here is to get you to relax, to not be so preoccupied with getting, so you can respond to God's giving. People who don't know God and the way he works fuss over these things, but you know both God and how he works. Steep your life in God-reality, God-initiative, God-provisions.[480]

Unfortunately these people too have only received God's words in their souls. We know this because there has been no change of attitude stemming from new life in the spirit. They still prefer all their 'stuff' more than their relationship with God, and they have not grown any fruit in their lives.

Our children will learn from us about our priorities, passions, stresses, and concerns. If we plant carefully into their fertile lives and do the occasional bit of weeding they will hear the word and it will take root, producing fruit.

• The Good Ground

We want our children to have this kind of ground in their lives so that they hear God, understand in their hearts what he is saying, and are born again. These are the ones who will

---

[479] Mark 4: 18–19, NRSV.
[480] Matt. 6: 31–4, THE MESSAGE.

grow into fruitful and fulfilled human beings. It falls to us to prepare this ground of our children's hearts so that it is soft and receptive to the things of God.

He pointed out where Jesus was and what he had come for

'The next day he saw Jesus coming toward him and declared, "Here is the Lamb of God who takes away the sin of the world! This is he of whom I said, After me comes a man who ranks ahead of me because he was before me. I myself did not know him; but I came baptizing with water for this reason, that he might be revealed to Israel."' [481]

We too need to help our children discover who Jesus is, what he is doing, and how he is speaking to them. We might be tempted to think that only after they have made a decision to follow Jesus will they hear Jesus speak or have any true spiritual growth or gifts. A study of the Bible quickly dismisses that theory, as many non-believers heard God speak to them in ways that had a massive effect on history.

- *God spoke to Abraham:* Abraham was brought up in the city of Ur. Ur at that time was very much like our modern cities in that it had libraries and schools, and a system of laws. Jewish tradition says that Terah, Abraham's father, was an idol maker. At some point Terah decided to take his family from Ur to Canaan. However, when they got to Haran the family stopped and settled down. Later, after Terah died, Abraham heard God speak to him saying: 'Now the Lord said to Abram, "Go from your country and your kindred and your father's house to the land that I will show you. I will make of you a great nation, and I will bless you, and make your name great, so that you will be a blessing. I will bless those who bless you, and the one who curses you I will curse; and in you all the families of the earth shall be blessed."'[482] When God spoke to Abraham like this he was in no doubt that this call was from the one true God and not an idol. The book of Hebrews records that: 'By faith Abraham obeyed when he was called to set out for a place that he was to receive as an inheritance; and he set out, not knowing where he was going.'[483] This act of faith became the starting point for a people who were called by God to bring forth the King of Kings and Saviour of the world—Jesus.
- *God spoke to Pharaoh:* We all know the story of Joseph and his multicoloured coat. In the story Pharaoh the king of Egypt had a dream. Being a man whose spirit was not awake he had no idea what the dream meant and so he sent for all the wise men to come and interpret it. They were not able to do so, but his cupbearer remembered that Joseph, who was in prison, was able to interpret dreams. Joseph was sent for and

---

[481] John 1: 29–31, NRSV.
[482] Gen. 12: 1–3, NRSV.
[483] Heb. 11: 8, NRSV.

God gave him the interpretation of the dream. Through the interpretation God made Pharaoh aware that seven years of plenty would be gobbled up by seven years of famine. Some say that this was historically played out during the reign of Djosar and that Imhotep, his next in command, was actually Joseph. If this is so it is possible that the profit made from selling grain during the famine was the beginning of Egypt's massive wealth and power. It was also instrumental in keeping Abraham's family line safe during the famine.

- *God spoke to Nebuchadnezzar:* Nebuchadnezzar, like Pharaoh had a dream that troubled him. Again, like Pharaoh, he called for the wise men and magicians, asking them not only to interpret his dream but also to tell him what it was in the first place! Of course none of them had a clue, so as is the way of rulers he decided to have them all killed, including Daniel and his friends. Daniel stepped in, saving the day by interpreting the dream. The dream painted a prophetic picture of the future kingdoms of the earth.

- *God spoke to Cyrus:* Cyrus, a heathen king, was chosen by God to help fulfil His purposes and resettle the Hebrew people in their homeland. Some 150 years before he conquered Babylon Isaiah prophesied about him. The prophesy was very long and very specific, and according to Josephus the Hebrew exiles in Babylon—possibly Daniel himself—showed it to king Cyrus who was then prompted to fulfil what was written. Imagine reading a prophecy that spoke about you by name but was written 150 years earlier! Historically the prophecy that Isaiah had was extremely accurate and the return of the Jews to their homeland was a key part of God's plan for the coming of Jesus.

- *God spoke to Pilate's wife:* Tradition says that Pilate's wife was called Claudia Procula, that she was the granddaughter of Augustus Caesar, and that she became a Christian soon after Jesus' death. In the Eastern churches she is regarded as a saint, known under her name of Saint Claudia or Saint Procula. She had a moment of fame that, depending on your translation, is less than forty words long! She is remembered, of course, for a dream that is so compelling that she disturbs her husband when he is already in session at the court where Jesus is being tried: 'While he was sitting on the judgment seat, his wife sent word to him, "Have nothing to do with that innocent man, for today I have suffered a great deal because of a dream about him"'[484] Pilate may well have taken her warning very seriously, as he seems to have tried all means possible not to condemn Jesus to death. Eventually, however, he washed his hands of the case and handed Jesus over to the Jews, knowing that they would put him to death. What a cop-out!

---

[484] Matt. 27: 19, NRSV.

As we have seen, people can hear God speak way before they make any decision to follow him. God is not silent but sometimes we are deaf. We don't know why these people were open to hear God because we can't see their hearts, but we do know that what they heard was not just personal but also had historical importance, particularly with respect to the coming of Jesus.

Today many unchurched people are hearing and seeing God in dreams and visions and they are coming to know him. There are tales coming from the Middle East of individuals and even whole villages who are hearing from Jesus and turning to him.

I was a very devoted Muslim but I began to feel that there was something missing in my faith as a Muslim. I started praying to God to show me if the Muslim faith was the truth and soon after that I began to have strange dreams. In one of these dreams I saw some Christians standing in line to get into Heaven. I tried to get into this line also, but a very tall being blocked my path and I started to cry because the side I was on was really horrible but the side they were on was a beautiful place, so beautiful, so blue.[485]

It is just as likely that God will speak to children whether or not they have been brought up in a Christian home. What is needed, as in the case of Pharaoh and Nebuchadnezzar, is someone to help them understand that it is God who is speaking to them, what he is saying, and what response is needed. This is what happened when God spoke to the child Samuel:

Then the Lord called, "Samuel! Samuel!" and he said, "Here I am!" and ran to Eli, and said, "Here I am, for you called me." But he said, "I did not call; lie down again." So he went and lay down. The Lord called again, "Samuel!" Samuel got up and went to Eli, and said, "Here I am, for you called me." But he said, "I did not call, my son; lie down again." Now Samuel did not yet know the Lord, and the word of the Lord had not yet been revealed to him. The Lord called Samuel again, a third time. And he got up and went to Eli, and said, "Here I am, for you called me." Then Eli perceived that the Lord was calling the boy. Therefore Eli said to Samuel, "Go, lie down; and if he calls you, you shall say, 'Speak, Lord, for your servant is listening.'" "So Samuel went and lay down in his place. Now the Lord came and stood there, calling as before, "Samuel! Samuel!" And Samuel said, "Speak, for your servant is listening."[486]

Like the old man Eli, we need to have our ear tuned to God so that we know when he is speaking to our children and can then help them to respond. The way that God speaks can be creative, different, out of the box, and childlike. He can use our ears, our eyes, our sense of smell, our imagination, our artistic abilities, our bodies, our dreams, and our emotions. We

---

[485] Leah's Testimony at http://isaalmasih.net/isa/dreamsofisa.html.
[486] 1 Sam. 3: 4–10, NRSV.

need to help our children so that they can understand when God is speaking to them, just as Eli did.

Our daughter Elly is a very empathetic and compassionate person. When she was quite young she would get all sorts of aches and pains. Some of these were undoubtedly growing pains and the like. However I felt impressed to say to her that it was possible that she was picking up on other people's emotional and physical ills. I encouraged her to pray for others when she had these pains. I don't know if she remembers it now, but it highlighted to me the importance of being able to see how God is speaking to our children.

He decreased so that Jesus could increase

When John had prepared himself, prepared others, and pointed the way to Jesus, he retired from public speaking and the ministry of Jesus grew.

> The one who gets the bride is, by definition, the bridegroom. And the bridegroom's friend, his 'best man'—that's me—in place at his side where he can hear every word, is genuinely happy. How could he be jealous when he knows that the wedding is finished and the marriage is off to a good start? This is the assigned moment for him to move into the centre, while I slip off to the sidelines.[487]

While our children are small we take centre stage in their lives. We are the centre of their universe and everything that we teach them and all that we model has a direct effect on the way that they will grow up. However, the umbilical cord that was physically cut at birth remains as an emotional tie and has to be gradually unravelled until our children completely individuate and take off into life as complete, whole, happy, spiritually alive adults. It's our job to release them into this freedom and not to hold on to them in order to keep our own emotional needs fed. But it can be a frightening process.

From the moment that baby is born he is leaving us. He begins by learning to move and talk and understand in his world and his environment and then he begins to explore other worlds and other environments. Finally there comes that day when he dons his oversized school uniform and his clean shiny shoes and you take him to school and leave him there. When David began to go to pre-school I would walk him there in the buggy and then walk home alone. Nathan had recently died and now I had 'lost' David too—the house felt so empty that I often spent the morning crying.

Soon those new shoes were scuffed and needed replacing, the uniform seemed to shrink and my requests for news about what he had done at school remained unanswered. He thrived

---

[487] John 3: 29–30, THE MESSAGE.

in this new world with these new relationships. How hard it is to let go and experience that empty—'what shall I do now?'—feeling.

What I did then of course was to have three more beautiful children, Rosannagh, Elisia, and Christopher. And so I had to go through the whole process again. Just this week, Christopher left school for the last time. He is now a fully fledged adult teetering on the brink of living in the real world. Job done!

It doesn't end there of course, as we all know 'love never ends'. But all my children can talk, they can walk, they have come out of nappies and given up their bottles, they sleep through the night, can swim and ride bicycles, can read and write, and are capable of earning a living and paying their own bills! And they all love Jesus. At one time these were all seemingly impossible things.

> Alice laughed. 'There's no use trying,' she said: 'one *can't* believe impossible things.'
> 'I daresay you haven't had much practice,' said the Queen. 'When I was your age, I always did it for half-an-hour a day. Why, sometimes I've believed as many as six impossible things before breakfast.'[488]

On both sides the letting-go process can be difficult. There are times when our children run happily off into the playground leaving mum a blubbering wreck, and there are other times when you are desperate for some 'me' time but they won't leave your side. Christopher would never go to parties, the only way I could get him there was to go to them as well. I had to join in all the games and eat lots of cake. Invariably by the end of the party he was just beginning to join in! I always hoped that I would be able to pop to the shops or go home and put my feet up but it rarely happened.

But mums too can find it difficult to let go. Risking being called 'helicopter parents', sometimes we try to keep control of our children's environment to such an extent that they never face obstacles and always have mum or dad hovering over them even when they don't want or need it. Helicopter parenting is fine while the children are little but inappropriate when they are older.

I can remember the Sunday school at the church we were part of decided to take the children for a walk along the river. David, being hyperactive, was quite likely to end up in the river. I was appalled and convinced that they had no idea what they were doing. I snuck along behind just to make sure that he was OK and discovered that he behaved really well with other people!

---

[488] Lewis Carroll, *Alice's Adventures in Wonderland* (1865).

We all know the story of Moses in the bulrushes, but his mother deserves a mention because she too was a helicopter parent. She sent her daughter Miriam to hover over him:

> When she could hide him no longer she got a papyrus basket for him, and plastered it with bitumen and pitch; she put the child in it and placed it among the reeds on the bank of the river. His sister stood at a distance, to see what would happen to him.[489]

Being a helicopter parent is fine and good while they are little, but the helicopter needs to be dismantled and taken out of commission by the time they hit their teens.

As we see with John the Baptist and Jesus, as they grow older our involvement in our children's lives should decrease. Then we will have all the 'me' time that we want—perhaps more than we can cope with!

We have conceived them, grown them, given birth to them, fed them, cared for them, cried with them, laughed with them, and led them to Jesus. Now it is time to let go and let Jesus take that dominant role in their lives, leading them on into all that he has for them.

It was an amazing day, the sun was shining, there wasn't a cloud in the sky, the birds were singing clear as a bell, and the water looked fresh and inviting. Rosannagh had chosen to be baptised in the local river with just a few friends and family around her. We got the BBQ going, sang a few songs, and then she was baptised by a family friend, Paul, and her dad. Paul 'accidentally' fell in and floated downstream with much laughter. It was all just how she wanted it. Everybody had something to contribute, there were readings and memories, prophecies and words of encouragement, and we prayed for her. Her early life had been really difficult because of David's hyperactivity. But he stood there and asked her forgiveness for all the ways in which he had hurt her. This amazing moment washed away all the struggle and turmoil of those early years, drawing a line under a saga that had played out for so long.

They're brilliant, my kids. And all of them, including Nathan, will be there on that day when we stand before Jesus.

Although written prophetically about the Hebrew nation and their return to Israel, God's word to me was that I'm 'going to put on all my children just like jewellery, I'm going to use them to dress up like a bride'. They're my pride and joy. And they're the apples of their father's eye.

---

[489] Exod. 2: 3–4, NRSV.

'Lo, these shall come from far away, and lo, these from the north and from the west, and these from the land of Syene. Sing for joy, O heavens, and exult, O earth; break forth, O mountains, into singing! For the Lord has comforted his people, and will have compassion on his suffering ones. But Zion said, "The Lord has forsaken me, my Lord has forgotten me." Can a woman forget her nursing child, or show no compassion for the child of her womb? Even these may forget, yet I will not forget you. See, I have inscribed you on the palms of my hands; your walls are continually before me. Your builders outdo your destroyers, and those who laid you waste go away from you. Lift up your eyes all around and see; they all gather, they come to you. As I live, says the Lord, you shall put all of them on like an ornament, and like a bride you shall bind them on.'[490]

---

[490] Isa. 49: 12–18, NRSV.

Love Hearts

SIZE
The finished cushion measures 30 cm (12 in) square.

MATERIALS
2 x 50g ball of Debbie Bliss Cashmerino Aran shade 009 Grey (A) and 1 x 50g ball shade 101 Ecru (B) (90 m/100yd per ball)1 x 50g ball of King Cole Merino Blend DK shade 858 Pink (112 m/125yd per ball)

4.5 mm (US7) knitting needles & 4 mm (US 6) circular needle (100 cm long)

Wool sewing needle, 3 x 25 mm buttons and a 30 cm (12 inch) cushion pad

Love Hearts

TENSION

Over colour pattern 20 sts and 24 rows = 10 cm square. Over st st 20 sts and 28 rows = 10 cm square.

ABBREVIATIONS

See page 305.

Note: Strand the colours not in use behind the work *very loosely* so that the tension is not affected (pulled in) by these strands.

FRONT

Using no 4.5 mm needles and Grey, cast on 61 sts and knit 1 row. Now work from the chart the 1st row being:

1st chart row: *k2B, (k3A, k1B) x2, rep from * to last st, k1 B.

Cont to follow the chart for 63 rows (there are 9 rows of hearts). Work 1 row knit. Cast off loosely.

BACK

Using no 4.5 mm needles and Grey, cast on 61 sts and starting with a knit row, work in st st for 30 rows.

Back Opening

Next row: knit 55 sts, turn.

Next row: purl 49 sts turn.

There are now six unworked sts at each end of work. Cont on these 49 sts in g st (every row knit) for 6 rows. Cast off these 49 sts.

With RS facing rejoin yarn to last group of 6 sts and knit 6 ending at side edge.

Next row: (WS) knit 6, turn and cast on 49 sts, then knit first group of 6 sts. (61 sts)

Work 4 rows in g st.

Next row: (RS)   k12, *k2tog, yo x 2, skpo, k12, rep from * once more, k2tog, yo x 2, skpo, k13.

Next row: Knit across row knitting into the back of each of the 2nd yo loops.

Now cont in g st for 4 more rows, (end with a WS row).

Now work in st st starting with a knit row for 30 more rows. Cast off

TO MAKE UP

Pin out and press each piece so that they are the same size and shape. Sew in all ends.

Using Pink, work Swiss Darning stitch over one of the hearts to create one pink heart.

Sew side edges of back opening into place on the WS of the back. Sew buttons into place to correspond with buttonholes.

Edging

Working from the RS of the front and using no 4 mm circular needle and pink yarn, join to a point halfway along lower edge of work then *pick up and knit 30 sts to corner, pick up 3 sts in corner and place coloured thread for marker in the centre st of these 3 sts, pick up and knit 30 sts to centre point of side edge, rep from * three times more. (240 sts) Now work in rounds of reverse st st (that is every row knit with the purl side to the front.) for 2 rounds. **Next round:** *work to within 1 st of marked st at corner, sk2po, rep from * three times more, then work to end of round. Cast off purlwise.

Place the WS of the back to the WS of the front, pin the edges together and over sew the two pieces of the cushion together under the curl of the edging. Allow the curl of the edging to roll over this seam.

Stuff the cushion with a cushion pad

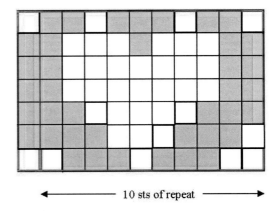

← 10 sts of repeat →

Extras

This section contains more detail about specific vitamins and minerals, what they do and why they are so vital to our health. I will then go on to talk about the effects of the different vaccinations your child will be offered—so that you can make more informed decisions about when and if you want your child to be vaccinated.

Finally there is a list of useful resources and for those of you who want to make the projects the abbreviations used in the project patterns together with a list of stockists can be found on page 315

1.   <u>Vitamins</u>

Vitamin A

Vitamin A helps keep the skin, hair and teeth healthy. It is also essential for bone growth, is a powerful antioxidant and keeps the immune system healthy. It plays an important role in vision development. According to the World Health Organization: 'vitamin A deficiency (VAD) is the leading cause of preventable blindness in children and increases the risk of disease and death from severe infections. In pregnant women VAD causes night blindness and may increase the risk of maternal mortality.'[491]

Less severe symptoms of vitamin A deficiency include dry eyes, conjunctivitis, poor night vision, mouth ulcers, acne, dry skin, broken fingernails, dandruff, thrush and cystitis. During World War two our pilots were given extra carrots for their vitamin A content to help them see in the dark when flying at night.

Sources of Vitamin A include: liver, oily fish, dairy products, carrots, sweet potatoes and spinach. Too much Vitamin A can also be a problem during pregnancy as it can cause birth defects.

Vitamin B

This is a large family of vitamins that includes vitamins B1 (Thiamine), B2 (Riboflavin), B3 (Niacin), B6 (Pyridoxine), B12, folic acid and pantothenic acid. This group of vitamins is important for a whole range of different body processes such as cell repair, digestion, and production of energy and it is essential for normal red blood cell production.

Vitamin B deficiencies can cause muscle weakness, fatigue, migraine, brain and nerve disorders, diarrhoea, depression, poor concentration, anaemia, and dermatitis. Pregnant

---

[491] http://www.who.int/nutrition/topics/vad/en/.

women are often given folic acid supplements to prevent foetal abnormalities such as spina bifida and cleft palate. Vitamin B is found in most foods especially grains, leafy green food, red meat and dairy products.

Vitamin C

Vitamin C helps to reduce cholesterol levels: it regulates blood pressure and helps with the absorption of calcium and iron. It is beneficial in healing wounds and is very important for a healthy immune system. Vitamin C helps the body fight against infection and illness. It aids in collagen formation and is needed for healthy teeth and gums. Vitamin C is a powerful antioxidant. Foods that contain vitamin C include, red berries, citrus fruits, tomatoes, spinach and broccoli.

Signs of deficiency include scurvy, poor wound healing, sore gums, leaky capillaries and heart problems. It is quite hard to take too much, but the early warning sign of this is diarrhoea.

A New Zealand dairy farmer is being called the Miracle Man after doctors tried to force the family to cut off life support, because he would not survive his case of swine flu. Not only did the farmer have swine flu but a form of leukemia. Using the vitamin C therapy he recovered from the brink.

While the medical specialist had given up hope, his family had not. They demanded the doctors try high doses of Vitamin C. Of course, the hospital refused but finally agreed to try it for a couple of days after the family pleaded. After only two days of vitamin C treatment, the farmer's condition improved. One week after the start of the vitamin C therapy he was taken off life support.

Ever adamant, the doctors stopped the vitamin C treatment several times. Ultimately, the family had to constantly watch and fight the doctors to keep the treatment going. Finally going to court. The recovery is now being called a medical miracle. [492]

You can see this story on you tube at: http://www.youtube.com/watch?v=qUSwjOwIDT0.

Vitamin D

'Vitamin D is not really a vitamin at all—it is a pre-hormone that's produced in your skin in response to sunlight exposure. As such, it is an integral part of human health and longevity'.[493] Vitamin D is crucial for the development and maintenance of strong, healthy teeth and bones

---

[492]http://www.naturalmedicine.com/news/community-news/new-zealand-man-uses-high-dose-vitamin-c-to-survive-swine-flu-after-doctors-give-up/.
[493] http://www.vitamindcouncil.org/.

and in the prevention of osteoporosis. It allows your body to use and absorb calcium. It is also needed to keep the immune system strong and to maintain healthy nerves and muscles. Severe deficiency can cause rickets, tetany, osteomalacia and other problems with bones; less severe, it also causes: backache, muscle cramps, tooth decay and hair loss. It has also been linked to many other health issues: 'But beyond bone and muscle problems, some evidence suggests a dearth of vitamin D may be associated with an array of more serious illnesses, including many forms of cancer, high blood pressure, depression, and immune-system disorders such as multiple sclerosis, rheumatoid arthritis and diabetes.'[494]

The primary source of this vitamin is the sun. Recommendations say that we need to be uncovered in the sun for at least ten to fifteen minutes three times a week in order to process the required amount of this vitamin. This is not so difficult in the summer months, but for those of us who have cold and cloudy winters it can be difficult to maintain during the winter months. The need to top up our Vitamin D levels could provide the perfect excuse for a winter holiday in the sun.

Over the last few decades there has been a furore about skin cancer and the need to avoid the sun at all costs. As parents we have been targeted and manipulated by the makers of sunscreen products, and even health professionals, who by filling us with fear would have us keep our children out of the sun or covered in toxic chemical products. This has led to an increase in vitamin D deficiency disorders. As someone who has been treated for malignant melanoma I know only too well the dangers of sunburn. However, the knee-jerk reaction of avoiding the sun altogether can be equally damaging to our health.

Few health recommendations have had as damaging an effect as the advice that you should never leave your house without sunscreen. Wearing sunscreen effectively blocks your body's production of vitamin D, which happens naturally when your skin is exposed to sunlight. In fact, sunscreens reduce vitamin D production by as much as 97.5 to 99.9 percent.

The widespread acceptance and adoption of this faulty doctrine has contributed to severe vitamin D deficiency on a grand scale, which in turn claims about one million lives a year from 16 different types of cancer and other common diseases such as: heart disease, diabetes, inflammatory bowel disease, rheumatoid arthritis, multiple sclerosis and osteoporosis.'[495]

---

[494] http://www.washingtonpost.com/wp-dyn/articles/A43711-2004May20.html.
[495] Mercola, J. "Four Out of Five Sunscreens May Be Hazardous to Your Health" Retrieved Sep 20, 2013, from http://articles.mercola.com/sites/articles/archive/2008/07/01/four-out-of-five-sunscreens-may-be-hazardous-to-your-health.aspx.

A lack of Vitamin D during pregnancy can also lead to pre-eclampsia, and premature birth. 'Women should take up to 10 times the current recommended dose of vitamin D during pregnancy to protect against premature birth, researchers have urged. The higher dose was found to halve their chance of suffering from one of a number of problems including having the baby before term and pre-eclampsia.'[496]

Vitamin D can be found in oily fish and eggs. Some countries add vitamin D to various foods such as cereals, and of course it can be taken as a supplement.

Vitamin E

This is essential for growth of the body. It helps in maintaining healthy cells and tissues and acts as an anti-blood-clotting agent. It promotes healthy functioning of the eyes, the liver and the skin. It plays a major role in the prevention of external damage to the lungs by air pollutants and it protects DNA, fats, cell membranes and enzymes from damage. It is also important in the production of red blood corpuscles and in the development of the immune system. Vitamin E is found in many foods, such as oils, nuts and seeds, dried apricots, spinach and broccoli. Because it is a fat-soluble vitamin, deficiency is found in people who have disorders that affect their absorption of fat, such as premature babies or those with coeliac disease. Extreme low fat diets can also lead to vitamin E deficiency. Deficiency of vitamin E can lead to poor muscle coordination and shaky movements, the inability to walk, decreased sensation to vibration, lack of sex drive, exhaustion, lack of reflexes, and paralysis of eye muscles. Children with this deficiency can have difficulty with reading and fall behind in other intellectual skills during their early school years.[497]

Vitamin K

Most of us only become aware of vitamin K when the doctor wants to stick a needle into our precious newborn in order to top him up with vitamin K. Vitamin K is essential to the blood-clotting mechanism and newborns need it as they are often low on this vital vitamin. If you don't want your baby to be injected it can be given orally. A deficiency of vitamin K can lead to a serious bleeding disorder called Hemorrhagic Disease where internal bleeding affects the brain and other organs. In newborns the clotting mechanism doesn't come in until day five or so and this comment on Dr Mercola's website is yet another ratification of the God's laws;

> As pointed out by one Mercola reader, it is interesting to note that a newborn's natural prothrombin levels reach normal levels between days 5 and 7, peaking around the eighth day of life, related to the buildup of bacteria in the baby's digestive tract to produce the

---

[496] http://www.telegraph.co.uk/health/healthnews/8444739/Health-benefits-of-vitamin-D.html.
[497] Facts from http://medical-dictionary.thefreedictionary.com/vitamin+E+deficiency.

vitamin K that is necessary to form this clotting factor. Day 8 is said to be the only time in a baby's life when his prothrombin level will naturally exceed 100 percent of normal.

As it turns out, Genesis 17:12 of the Bible mandates the circumcision of infant boys on the eighth day after birth—a recommendation pronounced long before we had the science to back it up.[498]

Vitamin K deficiency has also been linked to Alzheimer's in old people and recent studies suggest that there is also a link between deficiency of vitamin K and hardening of the arteries.

One of the undisputed benefits vitamin D provides for you is improved bone development by helping you ABSORB calcium. This is not news—we have known about vitamin D and the absorption of calcium for many decades.

But there is new evidence that *it is the vitamin K* (specifically, vitamin K2) that directs the calcium to your skeleton, while preventing it from being deposited where you don't want it—i.e., your organs, joint spaces, and arteries. A large part of arterial plaque consists of calcium deposits (atherosclerosis), hence the term 'hardening of the arteries.'

. . . In other words, without the help of vitamin K2, the calcium that your vitamin D so effectively lets in might be working AGAINST you—**by building up your coronary arteries rather than your bones.**[499]

The best sources of this vitamin are liver, green leafy vegetables and members of the cabbage family. So you really should eat your greens.

2.   <u>Minerals</u>

<u>Essential Minerals</u>
Calcium

Calcium is the most abundant mineral in the human body. Most of it is stored in the bones and teeth and the rest is in the blood, muscles and extracellular fluid. It is necessary for strong bones and teeth, and it plays an important role in blood-clotting. It is essential for the nervous system as it helps with cell to cell communication. It lowers cholesterol levels and helps prevent heart disease: is an effective treatment for PMS, and is recommended for attention deficit

---

[498] Mercola, J. "The Dark Side of the Routine Newborn Vitamin K Shot" Retrieved Sep 20, 2013, from http://articles.mercola.com/sites/articles/archive/2010/03/27/high-risks-to-your-baby-from-vitamin-k-shot-they-dont-warn-you-about.aspx.

[499] Mercola, J. "The Missing Nutrient to Blame for Heart Attacks and Osteoporosis (Nope - NOT Calcium or Vitamin D)" Retrieved Sep 20, 2013, from http://articles.mercola.com/sites/articles/archive/2011/03/26/the-delicate-dance-between-vitamins-d-and-k.aspx.

disorders and migraine headaches. It reduces the risk of colon cancer by neutralizing the toxic effects of cancer-promoting fats. It lowers blood pressure, prevents leg cramps and helps prevent insomnia and anxiety. A deficiency may lead to aching joints, brittle nails, eczema, raised blood cholesterol, heart palpitations, high blood pressure, insomnia, muscle cramps, nervousness, numbness in the arms and legs, rheumatoid arthritis, rickets, and tooth decay. As we have already seen, the vitamins D and K are needed to help in the absorption of this mineral and to prevent calcium from being deposited in places where you really don't need it, such as your arteries. A high protein diet, caffeine from coffee, carbonated beverages, alcohol, and antacids can diminish calcium levels in your body. Calcium is found in milk, cheese, butter, vegetables, and hard water.

Phosphorus

This is needed for blood-clotting, bone and teeth formation, cell growth, the storage of energy, the maintenance of healthy blood-sugar levels, for the health and proper working of the heart muscle, and for kidney function. It helps the body to use vitamins properly and to convert food into energy; it is involved in virtually all chemical reactions in the body.

Deficiencies of phosphorus are rare as phosphorus is found in most plant and animal foods; however some drugs and foods can interfere with absorption of this mineral. Specifically the long term use of antacids and the consumption of large amounts of fructose—which is used as a sweetener in soft drinks and fast foods—may cause phosphorus deficiency.

Symptoms of a lack of phosphorus include loss of appetite, and anaemia, fatigue, numbness and tingling, difficulty in walking, weakness, rickets, osteomalacia, and having a decreased attention span.

Magnesium

This is required for hundreds of biochemical reactions in the body. It is needed for energy production, and is crucial for normal muscle and nerve function. It helps to maintain a regular heart-beat. You also need magnesium for strong bones and a healthy immune system and it is essential in allowing your body to control insulin levels in your blood.

Magnesium deficiency is rare as it is found in many plant and animal food sources, but it is thought that the intake of magnesium has been dropping and many people may now have borderline deficiencies. Deficiency of magnesium may result in calcium depletion, heart spasms, nervousness, confusion, calcium deposits in soft tissue and kidney stones. The elderly, those with diseases such as Crohn's diseases or diabetes, alcoholics, and those who take diuretics, may be at risk of low magnesium levels. Good sources of magnesium are fish, dairy products, lean meat, dark green leafy vegetables and unrefined grains and nuts. Magnesium is sometimes prescribed in therapeutic doses for a number of health problems such as high blood pressure, migraines, diabetes and asthma.

Sodium

Sodium is vital to human life. Together with potassium and chlorine, it forms a very important part of blood plasma. Sodium also allows our bodies to maintain the right blood chemistry and the correct amount of water in our blood. Without sodium, our cells could not get the nutrients they need to survive. It allows our muscles to contract normally.

Our bodies need sodium to digest the food that we eat and our nervous system also depends on sodium to work properly. Symptoms of sodium deficiency include headaches, nausea and vomiting, muscle cramps, drowsiness, fainting, fatigue and possibly coma. Too much sodium in the blood can result in swelling, high blood pressure, difficulty in breathing, heart failure, and may be fatal.

Sodium usually comes in the form of sodium chloride that we call salt. Salt is so essential to life that not long ago it was a highly prized and expensive commodity, much like oil is today. Roman soldiers received a salt allowance with their wages and from this we get our word 'salary'. We might also refer to someone who doesn't work very well as being 'not worth his salt'. In the Western world we often eat far too many salty snacks and sodium deficiency is rare. However if you sweat a lot because of sports or physical work you will lose sodium and in severe cases the outcome can be fatal.

Similarly sodium can be lost through prolonged bouts of illness or diarrhoea. It occurs naturally in most foods as well as being added to processed foods, ready meals, snacks and fast foods. Sodium also comes in the form of monosodium glutamate, sodium bicarbonate and sodium benzoate.

Sulphur

Sulphur is used to detoxify the body, by cleaning the blood and helping to protect against toxic build-up. It assists the immune system and fights the effects of ageing and age-related illnesses such as arthritis. It is found in the hair, nails and skin. Sulphur is an essential element of several key amino acids, and vitamins. Not much is known about deficiency of sulphur but deficiency symptoms may include skin problems or disorders, muscle pain, nerve disorders, circulatory trouble, arthritis, inflammation, damage resulting from free radicals, stress, infection, constipation and wrinkles. Dietary sources include most proteins: lean meats, poultry, fish, eggs and milk. Vegetable sources include legumes, garlic, cabbage, brussel sprouts, onions, turnips, kale, lettuce, kelp and seaweed, and some nuts also contain sulphur.

Potassium

Potassium is extremely important for a healthy nervous system and heart rhythm and it aids muscle contraction. It works together with sodium to control the water balance in the body, helping to maintain a stable blood pressure. It helps to prevent the build-up of plaque in the arteries, aids clear thinking by sending oxygen to the brain, keeps the heart muscle strong and helps to prevent leg cramps. The Western diet is thought to be quite low in potassium and this may play a role in the prevalence of some of our modern-day diseases. Deficiency in potassium is associated with a risk of low blood pressure, irregular heartbeat, pins and needles, irritability, swollen abdomen, and general weakness. The richest sources of potassium are fruits and vegetables, with baked potatoes coming in at the top of the list: one baked potato (eaten with the skin) contains approximately 926 mg of potassium. Bananas, plums, lima beans and tomato juice are also high in potassium.

3.   Trace Minerals

These are minerals that are essential to body maintenance but are only needed in very small amounts. There are many trace minerals and a deficiency in any of them can cause issues ranging from the minor to the severe.

- *Arsenic:* despite Arsenic's reputation as a highly toxic substance, it is thought to be necessary for the functioning of the nervous system and for people to grow properly.
- *Boron:* this is needed in minute amounts for the proper absorption of calcium, magnesium, and vitamin D, especially in older people. It helps to maintain healthy bones and prevents osteoporosis; slows the loss of minerals through urination; plays an important role in joint health and has helped those with rheumatoid arthritis. It can help to raise oestrogen levels, which has been shown to prevent bone loss; is needed for proper muscle growth; and enhances brain function promoting mental alertness. In places where there is little boron in the soil there is a higher incidence of arthritis.
- *Chromium:* this is involved in the metabolism of glucose and is vital in the breakdown of cholesterol, fats, and proteins. It maintains stable blood-sugar levels through proper insulin utilization. It promotes a healthy circulatory system and has been used as a treatment for migraine headaches, psoriasis, acne, anxiety and fatigue. It is used extensively by athletes and dieters because it promotes fat loss and increases lean muscle tissue. Lack of chromium can cause cold sweats, dizziness, the need for frequent meals, cold hands, drowsiness, thirst and the love of sweet foods.
- *Cobalt:* without cobalt, Vitamin B-12 could not exist.
- *Copper:* along with vitamin C, copper is needed for wound healing and for the body to make connective tissue, which is needed for strong blood vessels, cartilage and bones.

Copper is also necessary for some <u>antioxidant</u> reactions to occur, as well as for the metabolism of iron (another trace mineral). It is also a major component of the oxygen-carrying part of blood cells. It is involved in hair and skin colouring and taste sensitivity.

- *Fluoride:* When compounded with other minerals, fluoride is considered to be a trace mineral that is good for developing strong bones and teeth. As a result of this some parts of the world have fluoride added to the water as a form of compulsory medication. But fluoride is a very dangerous toxin and can have detrimental side effects. 'Recent studies in the peer-reviewed medical literature indicate that fluoridated water can have detrimental side effects. Health risks associated with low-to-moderate doses of fluoride include: dental fluorosis; bone fracture; bone cancer; joint pain; skin rash, reduced thyroid activity; and IQ deficits.'[500]

To add insult to injury: 'Most recent, large-scale studies have found that fluoridated water provides only a minor benefit to teeth, or no demonstrable benefit at all.'[501] But naturally occurring fluoride which may have some nutritional benefit is very different to the fluoride that is added to our water. An article on the website Dr Mercola.com states:

> The fluoride added to 90% of drinking water is hydrofluoric acid which is a compound of fluorine that is a chemical byproduct of aluminum, steel, cement, phosphate, and nuclear weapons manufacturing.
>
> Such fluoride is manmade. In this form, fluoride has no nutrient value whatsoever. It is one of the most caustic of industrial chemicals. Fluoride is the active toxin in rat poisons and cockroach powder.
>
> Hydrofluoric acid is used to refine high octane gasoline, to make fluorocarbons and chlorofluorocarbons for freezers and air conditioners, and to manufacture computer screens, fluorescent light bulbs, semiconductors, plastics, herbicides,— and toothpaste.
>
> . . . Once in the body, fluoride is a destroyer of human enzymes . . . Since enzymes are proteins, once they've been changed, they're now foreign-looking. The body now treats them as invaders, even though they're part of that body. This is known as an autoimmune situation—the body attacks itself . . .
>
> Fluoride prematurely ages the body, mainly by distortion of enzyme shape. Again, when enzymes get twisted out of shape, they can't do their jobs. This results in

---

[500] http://www.fluoridealert.org/faqs.aspx#A8.
[501] http://www.fluoridealert.org/faqs.aspx.

collagen breakdown, eczema, tissue damage, skin wrinkling, genetic damage, and immune suppression. Practically any disease you can name may then be caused.

. . . Millions of tons of this poison are produced every year. Imagine the cost of containing and disposing of those mountains of waste every year. It's in the billions.

But what if lobbyists from these industries could present 'scientific studies' paid for by the industries, and provide for a continual stream of media presentations about the health benefits of fluoride, and create unimaginably lucrative positions for 'research' and 'education' within the American Dental Association and the AMA, and do all these things in a consistent and unending way, year after year?

What are the economic advantages of that? Simple: instead of paying money to dispose of toxic waste, money could now be made by selling fluoride to the water companies of the nation.

They'll use the public water supply as a sewer for industrial wastes. And now with these new billions added instead of subtracted, there's plenty to go around, for everyone involved. Out of the Red, into the Black.

Somewhere Machiavelli smiles.[502]

Dr Mercola goes on to comment:

Over time, fluoride accumulates in many areas of your body, including areas of your brain that control and alter behavior, particularly your hippocampus and other limbic areas. More than 124 studies linking fluoride to brain damage in animals and reduced IQ in children have been published.

One particularly striking animal study published in 1995 showed that fluoride ingestion had a profound influence on the animals' brains and altered behavior. Pregnant rats given fluoride produced hyperactive offspring. And animals given fluoride after birth became apathetic, lethargic 'couch potatoes.' This study was particularly powerful because the effects were measured using objective computerized evaluations of behavior, to rule out subjective bias by the researchers observing the animals.

For the past 60 years, pregnant women have ingested fluoridated water and used fluoridated water to reconstitute infant formula for their babies. If these effects were true for humans as well, we'd expect to see a striking change in human behavior at this point as well. And we most definitely do.

---

[502] Mercola, J. "Is Fluoride Really As Safe As You Are Told?" Retrieved Sep 20, 2013, from http://articles.mercola.com/sites/articles/archive/2002/02/02/fluoride-safety-part-one.aspx.

Today, an estimated one in 10 children has ADD/ADHD . . .

According to the British Fluoridation Societies' website, countries who add fluoride to the water are: the UK, Chile, South Korea, Singapore, Spain, Ireland, the United States, Canada, Brazil, Malaysia, Vietnam, Australia, and New Zealand. More information about your area can be found on the web. However, most of Western continental Europe has rejected, banned, or stopped fluoridation due to environmental, health, legal, or ethical concerns. China has banned the addition of fluoride to water supplies and India is taking steps to reduce the naturally occurring fluoride in water because of the widespread problem with fluorosis. 'Water fluoridation delivers a drug to infants at a level which would be gross malpractice if prescribed by a physician or dentist.'[503]

- *Germanium:* Germanium is a trace element that some believe is highly beneficial to good human health. In fact, germanium has many important medicinal properties. In the body, germanium attaches itself to oxygen molecules. This has the unexpected effect of making our bodies more effective at getting oxygen to the tissues in our body. The increased supply of oxygen in our bodies helps to improve our immune system. It also helps the body excrete harmful toxins. Germanium can stimulate the human immune system to fight cancer cells without damaging the rest of the body. Many people go to Lourdes in France to drink the healing water. These waters are said to contain very high levels of germanium. Other sources of germanium are: garlic, shiitake mushrooms, onions, bran, whole wheat flour, vegetables, seeds, meats, dairy products, aloe vera, comfrey and ginseng.

- *Iodine:* This is needed to keep the thyroid gland healthy and control the metabolism. Iodine deficiency can result in a thyroid condition called goitre. In the UK we have the term 'Derbyshire Neck' to describe someone who has the large swelling typical of iodine deficiency. This was caused by a lack of the mineral Iodine in the local soil— especially in Derbyshire. Iodine deficiency during pregnancy can result in various kinds of mental health retardation. Iodine is found in large amounts in seafood, seaweed and iodized salt.

- *Iron:* Iron acts as an oxygen carrier supplying it to the various parts of the body. It is also essential in the production of blood. Iron deficiency results in a reduced amount of oxygen that is delivered to the cells and leads to fatigue and anaemia, loss of appetite, and sensitivity to the cold. Not getting enough iron can also negatively affect your immune system. Pregnant women who suffer from a lack of iron may develop a

---

[503] (Source: Dentist David Kennedy, International Academy of Oral Medicine and Toxicology (IAOMT). IAOMT is a network of dental, medical and research professionals which supports the effort to inform consumers about health risks from water fluoridation.) http://www.wmaf.org.uk/index.php?content=content&parent=42&read=42&keyword.

bizarre disorder called 'pica' where doctors have reported cases of people eating dirt, chalk, clay, paste, paper, cardboard, ice chips and Styrofoam. Deficiency can occur from lack of iron in the diet, difficulty absorbing enough iron from the foods you eat, or from chronic blood loss. Dietary iron is found in meat, fish, poultry, oats, legumes and spinach.

- *Manganese:* along with calcium, manganese is required for the production of sex hormones and the development of the skeletal system. It is important for production of enzymes and antioxidants that fight free-radical damage. It supports the immune system, regulates blood- sugar levels, and is involved in the production of energy and cell reproduction. Additionally, manganese works with vitamin K to support blood-clotting. Working with the B-complex vitamins, manganese helps to control the effects of stress while contributing to one's sense of wellbeing. Deficiency may lead to paralysis, convulsions, dizziness, ataxia, loss of hearing, digestive problems, growing pains, fits and convulsions, joint pain, blindness and deafness in infants. Birth defects can result when an expectant mother doesn't get enough of this very important element. Some researchers are also looking into a link between poor manganese intake and higher skin cancer rates. Foods high in manganese include avocados, berries, nuts and seeds, egg yolks, whole grains, green leafy vegetables and legumes (such as peanuts, peas and beans).

- *Molybdenum:* This is necessary for good health, though in extremely small amounts. It provides energy and vigour by helping with carbohydrate and fat metabolism. It has a role to play in alcohol detoxification and in the detoxification of cancer-causing chemicals: it helps prevent tooth decay, promotes normal cell function and activates the enzyme that produces uric acid. Uric acid helps carry excess nitrogen out of the body when you urinate. A deficiency of molybdenum in our diets can cause mouth and gum disorders and may contribute to cancer. A diet high in refined and processed foods can lead to a deficiency of molybdenum, resulting in anaemia and loss of appetite and weight. The amount of molybdenum in plant foods varies significantly and is dependent upon the mineral content of the soil that the plants are grown in. Nevertheless, the best sources of this mineral are beans, legumes (peanuts and peas), dark green leafy vegetables, and grains. Hard tap water can also supply molybdenum to the diet.

- *Selenium:* Despite selenium's reputation as a toxic heavy metal, this element is actually very important to good human health. It is an important part of a molecule in the body that protects blood cells from certain damaging chemicals and together with vitamin E, it helps our immune system produce antibodies. Selenium helps keep the pancreas and heart functioning properly and is also needed to make our arteries and skin elastic. Deficiency can result in premature ageing, a family history of cancers, cataracts, heart disease, psoriasis, dandruff, loose skin and eczema. The amount of selenium in food is dependent on the amount in the environment where the food is grown. Fish, grains and Brazil nuts are considered to be good dietary sources of selenium.

- *Silica:* This is necessary for the formation of collagen for bones and connective tissue: it promotes healthy nails, skin, and hair. It helps to maintain flexible arteries and plays a major role in preventing cardiovascular disease. It counteracts the effects of aluminium on the body, and is believed to be important in the prevention of Alzheimer's disease and osteoporosis. It stimulates the immune system and inhibits the ageing process in tissues, is important for calcium absorption and improves the elasticity and thickness of the skin. Foods rich in silicon include whole grain breads and cereals, alfalfa, beets, bell peppers, beans and peas.

- *Zinc:* your body uses this trace mineral in small amounts. You need zinc for normal growth and healthy immune system function as zinc is involved in protein production, DNA synthesis and cell division. Zinc is necessary for over 300 enzymes to function properly and in many different chemical reactions in the body, and is also crucial for a normal sense of smell and taste. Zinc is also required for the proper healing of wounds, it helps prevent and reduces the length and severity of the common cold, helps decrease cholesterol deposits, helps heal stomach ulcers, relieves symptoms of rheumatoid arthritis, prevents acne outbreaks, regulates the activity of oil glands, promotes a healthy immune system, has beenshown to be important in brain function and in the treatment of schizophrenia, makes your fingernails strong (getting rid of white spots on your nails), helps prevent loss of appetite, taste and smell problems, dermatitis, and binge-eating. It is also believed to retard the ageing process: possibly as many as 20 percent of the over-sixties do not get enough zinc from their diets. Deficiency may result in delayed sexual maturity, prolonged healing of wounds, white spots on finger nails, white hair, retarded growth, stretch marks, fatigue, decreased alertness, poor sense of taste and smell and susceptibility to infections. Your body doesn't have a good storage system for zinc, so you need to eat foods that contain zinc every day. Zinc is found in foods that also contain protein such as meat, poultry, fish and seafood. Legumes, nuts, whole grains and dairy products contribute smaller amounts of zinc.

4.   Vaccination

Here are some of the various vaccinations that will be offered to your child. Currently these are not mandatory in the UK and you can choose whether to have your child vaccinated, select which vaccinations you want him to have or delay them until he is older.

The 5-in-1 single jab

This vaccination has been around since about 2004. It contains vaccination for diphtheria, tetanus, pertussis, polio and haemophilus influenzae type B. The various components are:

- *Diphtheria:* The diphtheria vaccine was the first to become part of a national vaccination programme and as such it began the era of mass childhood vaccination. At that time—in 1941—deaths from diphtheria had been dropping and it was becoming a less severe disease, however the vaccination successfully prevented diphtheria and the numbers of those getting the disease fell significantly. But it doesn't end on that happy note as it seems to have had a tragic side effect. 'When diphtheria and pertussis vaccines were introduced in the 1940s, cases of paralytic poliomyelitis skyrocketed.'[504] Diphtheria is quite rare in the West but there are often outbreaks in places where there is poor sanitation, poverty and crowded living conditions. There was a major outbreak in Russia in the early 1990s that spread across all of the countries of the former USSR.

- *Tetanus:* We don't catch tetanus from other people because it comes from a poison in the spores of the Clostridium tetani bacterium. These spores are found in contaminated soil all over the world. Tetanus is not very common in the West but in the third world it is a major killer of the newborn, possibly because of the use of unsterile instruments when cutting the umbilical cord, or—even worse—the practice of putting animal dung on the cord once it is cut. Like the diphtheria disease the number of deaths from tetanus fell throughout the twentieth century.

> During the 2nd World War, only 5 American soldiers died of tetanus, despite being up to their eyes in mud in the trenches. All five of these soldiers had been vaccinated against tetanus, one had received a full programme of shots, the others had been partially vaccinated.
>
> The British Army had 22 cases of tetanus in which 11 people died. All of the deaths were in tetanus vaccinated soldiers. The 11 survivors were unvaccinated.
>
> …Unlike childhood diseases, it isn't possible to gain natural immunity to tetanus. If you've had it once, you can have it again. The body does not produce antibodies to Clostridium Tetani. Vaccination is the act of injecting a viral or bacterial substance into the body to make it produce antibodies to that disease. However, since no natural antibodies can be made, then there is no possible way that artificial antibodies could be made either.'[505]

---

[504] http://vaxtruth.org/2012/03/the-polio-vaccine-part-1-2/
[505] http://www.vaccineriskawareness.com/Tetanus-Vaccine

The only trial of the tetanus vaccine was conducted on soldiers from the UK and USA during World War Two. The fact that our soldiers have been used for medical experimentation is quite frankly appalling. And it seems this situation has not changed as evidence now exists that the anthrax vaccine was recently tested on soldiers in both the UK and the USA.[506] Since the tetanus vaccine trial on soldiers in WW2 there have been few further trials of the tetanus vaccine and it is not known how effective this vaccine is or much about any side effects. According to the National Vaccine Information Centre:

> The most common reactions reported to occur following DT vaccine include swelling and pain at the injection site; sleepiness; irritability; vomiting; loss of appetite; persistent crying; and fever. Paleness, cold skin, collapse, rash, and joint pain have also been reported.
>
> In 1994 the Institute of Medicine concluded that there is compelling scientific evidence to conclude that tetanus, DT and Td vaccines can cause Guillain-Barre syndrome including death; brachial neuritis; and death from anaphylaxis (shock).[507]

In 1961 the tetanus vaccine was incorporated into the new triple vaccine along with whooping cough and diphtheria. It is now part of the 5-in-1 vaccination.

▪ *Whooping Cough—Pertussis:* Whooping cough—also known as the hundred-day cough— has the distinctive symptom of a whoop-like sound made between coughs when the patient tries to catch his breath. In the nineteenth century many children died of the disease, especially those under the age of 10. The number of deaths from whooping cough fell during the first part of the twentieth century but despite high vaccination rates is rising again, particularly in newborn babies under the age of eight weeks—possibly due to the loss of the mother's natural immunity. The vaccine was developed in the 1920s but only introduced as part of the childhood immunisation programme in the 1950s. In 1961 it was launched as part of the new triple vaccine. However doctors were divided about its need, effectiveness and, most importantly, its side effects. From the 1930s on there had been increasing numbers of reports about convulsions, permanent physical and metal disability and death following immunization for whooping cough.

In 1973, Dr Wilson [consultant paediatric neurologist at Great Ormond Street Hospital, London], stood up at the annual meeting of the British Paediatric

---

[506] 'Vaccine A: The Covert Government Experiment That's Killing Our Soldiers—And Why GI's Are Only The First Victims' by Gary Matsumoto ISBN-10: 046504400X.
[507] http://www.nvic.org.

Association and described, to the medical audience, thirty six of the children he had seen at Great Ormond Street. The majority of these children were left mentally retarded and with persistent fits. The cause of the brain damage in these children was, he felt, the whooping cough vaccine.[508]

As a result of this news many parents refused the vaccination, and the government was forced to offer separate vaccines in place of the triple vaccine. There followed a period when, despite aggressive government propaganda, the uptake of the whooping cough vaccine was very low. During this time of low vaccination rates, deaths from whooping cough did not increase.

> The total number of children dying from whooping cough in the two epidemic years with low immunisation rates (well under one in two uptake) is identical to the number of children who died in the 1974/5 epidemic when over three quarters of children had been immunised. What is more, the number of deaths is far fewer than in the 1970 epidemic when, again, four in five children were immunised. This shows convincingly that the number of children immunised has little bearing on the numbers of children dying from whooping cough.[509]

Children who receive the whooping cough vaccine are also more likely to go on to suffer from asthma, hay fever, eczema and ear infections, and during the fall in immunisation rates of the late 1970s fewer children died from meningitis.

> Certainly in the 'natural experiment' that took place in this country when the acceptance of the vaccine fell so dramatically in the mid 1970s to the mid 80s there was an accompanying fall in the number of deaths of children aged four years and less from invasive meningococcal disease. The numbers began to rise again as vaccine uptake increased.[510]

Originally the pertussis part of the triple vaccine was made from the whole bacterium which was killed and then injected. However half of all babies had a reaction of some sort, so research began to find a safer vaccine. This resulted in a vaccine made from only certain parts of the bacterium, called an acellular vaccine. This was taken up by Japan as early as 1981 and by most West European countries and the USA by the year 2000. Great Britain didn't catch up with this development until 2004 when the new 5-in-one vaccination was introduced. These new acellular vaccines have fewer side

---

[508] The Truth About Vaccines—Making the Right Decision for Your Child—by Dr Richard Halvorsen, ISBN 9781906142445.
[509] Ibid.
[510] http://www.whale.to/w/donegan.html.

effects but according to Dr Mercola there is still a risk: 'Acellular pertussis vaccines do not contain mercury preservatives and have reduced amounts of bioactive pertussis toxin and endotoxin. They appear to cause fewer cases of brain inflammation and permanent brain damage but are still not entirely safe for every child.'[511]

In addition to this he goes on to report that the vaccine loses its effectiveness in just three years. So that in America five doses are given to children under age 6, with boosters for teenagers and adults. With all this vaccination going on there is evidence to suggest that the *B. pertussis organism has evolved to become vaccine resistant so that whooping cough outbreaks are now occurring in highly vaccinated populations.*

* *Polio:* In the early part of the twentieth century, polio was of little concern. Compared to huge numbers of deaths from diseases like measles and whooping cough that were killing thousands of children a year, polio accounted for only a couple of hundred deaths. It was considered to be a minor illness which at that time was called infantile paralysis because it affected mainly those under 1 year old. In the summer of 1947 the UK had its first polio epidemic, which caused nearly 700 deaths, and over 7,000 people were paralysed. During the next ten years polio killed and maimed thousands. This was not a new disease but one that seemed to have changed and now had more serious consequences. And it was mainly affecting the middle classes and the well-to-do in society. As people became more hygiene conscious they were less likely to catch the milder form of the disease in infancy. Catching the disease so young gave them lifelong immunity and the girls were then able to pass it on to their children. At the same time that all this hygiene was going on the diphtheria vaccination was rolled out across the UK. Subsequently it was found that deep injections into the muscle could trigger full-blown polio with severe complications if the person already had the early stages of the mild form of polio: '...a Medical Research Council report concluded that the risk of paralysis from polio within a month of a diphtheria or whooping cough vaccination was three times the normal rate. Between 1951 and 1953, 1 in every 37,000 diphtheria and whooping cough immunizations in the UK resulted in a case of paralysis from polio.'[512]

Despite the fact that the disease was now in decline there were frantic attempts to find a vaccine that would work against this new form of polio. In the late 1950s two vaccines were created: one that used the inactivated polio virus (IPV) and one that used the activated or live polio virus (OPV). Most countries decided to use the inactivated version. Initially the UK made use of the inactivated version, but in 1962

[512] Mercola, J. "Red Alert: The Vaccine Responsible for Half the Awards for Injury and Death" Retrieved Sep 20, 2013, from http://articles.mercola.com/sites/articles/archive/2011/11/02/why-is-this-vaccine-causing-increased-infant-mortality.aspx.
[512] The Truth About Vaccines—Making the Right Decision for Your Child—by Dr Richard Halvorsen, ISBN 9781906142445.

changed to the live vaccine. It was known that the live polio virus would be excreted from vaccinated children thereby passing into the community and on to others who had not been vaccinated. This was expected to raise immunity levels in the population. However, it was not known if these live vaccines, which were quite unstable, would, when released into the community mutate and cause more cases of polio. It turns out that this is exactly what it did. The UK government refused to change to the inactivated version until the introduction of the 5-in-1 vaccine in 2004. 'To this day, doctors and parents remain unaware that the mass vaccination of children between 1962 and 2004 with the cheaper OPV may not have been the great success story claimed, but instead a dangerous misjudgement, contributing no extra to the decline in polio, yet paralyzing dozens of children.'[513] The live vaccine is still used in poorer countries. As Dr Mercola reports;

> Nigeria and many other nations use an oral polio vaccine because it's cheaper, easier, and protects entire communities. But it's made from a live polio virus which carries a risk of causing polio. In even rarer instances, the virus in the vaccine can mutate into a deadlier version that ignites new outbreaks. Genetic analysis has proven that such mutated viruses have caused at least seven separate outbreaks in Nigeria.

> . . .In the United States, every case of polio that's occurred since 1979 has been the result of the live-virus vaccine.[514]

- *Haemophilus Influenzae Type B:* By now governments around the world were well and truly in love with the vaccination process and so in 1992 another vaccination was rather hastily added to the childhood schedule. According to the World Health Organization:

> *Haemophilus influenzae* type b, or Hib, is a bacterium estimated to be responsible for some three million serious illnesses and an estimated 386 000 deaths per year, chiefly through meningitis and pneumonia. Almost all victims are children under the age of five, with those between four and 18 months of age especially vulnerable . . . Contrary to what the name Haemophilus influenzae suggests, the bacterium does not cause influenza . . . Industrialized countries, with sophisticated health-surveillance systems, became aware of the threat posed by Hib

---

[513] Ibid.

[514] Mercola, J. "Polio Vaccine Blamed for Outbreaks in Nigeria" Retrieved Sep 20, 2013, from http://articles.mercola.com/sites/articles/archive/2009/12/01/polio-vaccine-blamed-for-outbreaks-in-nigeria.aspx.

as much as 50 years ago. Before immunization programmes began in the early 1990s, Hib was demonstrated to be the leading cause of childhood bacterial meningitis in nearly all countries in which appropriate studies were performed, including Australia, Canada, Finland, the Netherlands, Sweden and the United States of America. (The rate of Hib-caused pneumonia in developed countries was not clear, although it was considered to occur less often than meningitis—the opposite of the situation in the developing world). Systematic vaccination has now virtually eliminated Hib disease in industrialized nations. [515]

I well remember the introduction of the HIB vaccine as it was commonly thought that this vaccine would prevent all forms of meningitis and I often had to tell friends that this was not the case. It would not have prevented Nathan's death from meningitis. Nathan died from pneumococcal septicaemia caused by pneumococcal meningitis. In 2006 a vaccine was introduced to prevent pneumococcal meningitis, and in 2010 the number of strains that this protected against was increased; however, according to the Meningitis Research Foundation:

'. . . there are vaccines that protect against some forms of meningitis and septicaemia, but although these vaccines provide excellent protection, they can't prevent all strains of these diseases. As yet there is no vaccine that can prevent all forms of meningitis and septicaemia.'[516]

Sadly one of the side effects of the HIB vaccine seems to be the loss of immunity to this bacterium in the general population and after a brief honeymoon period when the vaccine seemed to be effective at preventing HIB disease in the young, there are now increasing numbers of adults and the elderly who are going down with HIB related illnesses. And adults are far more likely to die from these HIB diseases. There is also evidence to suggest that since the introduction of the HIB vaccine more children are developing diabetes.

Pneumococcal infection

This is not part of the 5-in-1 vaccination, but is also now given to babies at 2 months. This vaccine was introduced in the United States in 2000, and according to a study published by *Science Daily* it has been extremely effective. 'According to the study, incidence rates for pneumococcal meningitis in all age groups declined 30.1 percent from 1998–1999 to 2004–2005. After PCV7 was made available, the incidence of meningitis decreased by 64 percent in

---

[515] http://www.who.int/mediacentre/factsheets/fs294/en/index.html.
[516] http://www.meningitis.org/disease-info/types-causes/pneumococcal.

children and by 54 percent in older adults.'[517] However as with all vaccines this success story does not come without risks, and there have been extreme reactions to this vaccine.

Data from the Vaccine Adverse Events Reporting System, or VAERS, which includes 'coincidental' events and those that were confirmed to have been caused by vaccines revealed a total of 28,317 adverse reactions related to the Prevnar vaccine since it was approved and released in 2000. The statistics included 558 deaths, 555 life threatening conditions, 238 permanent <u>disabilities</u>, 2,584 hospitalizations, 101 prolonged hospitalizations, 8,166 emergency room cases, and 16,155 mild reactions. These are big <u>numbers</u> considering that the vaccine should protect the children rather than cause harm.[518]

One of the side effects of pneumonia vaccination, however, is that more people, both children and adults, now get infected by rarer and more drug-resistent forms of pneumonia.

The use of the vaccine Prevnar, which has successfully curbed pneumonia, meningitis, and deadly bloodstream infections in young children for the past seven years, has now unleashed a superbug that is resistant to all currently available drugs.

Prevnar covers seven of the 90-odd strains of the strep bacteria, and although diseases from the seven covered strains have declined dramatically, one strain called 19A has developed super resistance and is spreading.[519]

Meningitis C

On the back of scare stories in the press about new cases of meningitis in babies and teens, the government launched the new meningitis C vaccine in 1999. This was only five years after it had gone into development and before any significant trials could be done. Thus the children in the UK were all turned into guinea-pigs in one huge trial of this vaccine.

The risk of Meningitis C disease was perceived to be so great that it [the government]took the unprecedented step of introducing the new Meningitis C vaccine without any evidence that it actually worked.

. . . On 1 November 1999, the day the campaign began, the government's chief medical officer (CMO), Professor Liam Donaldson, declared the campaign to be a

---

[517] http://www.sciencedaily.com/releases/2009/01/090114172308.htm.
[518] http://pneumoniavaccinesideeffects.com/pcv-vaccine/.
[519] Mercola, J. "News Alert: Common Childhood Vaccination Promotes New Superbugs" Retrieved Sep 20, 2013, from http://articles.mercola.com/sites/articles/archive/2007/10/06/news-alert-common-childhood-vaccination-promotes-new-superbugs.aspx

'tremendous success.' To do this before the first vaccination had been given might have seemed somewhat premature . . .[520]

The vaccine was effective and deaths from meningitis C were reduced; however' it was soon discovered that even though doses were given at two, three and four months these only provided children with protection in their first year. It became clear that booster doses would be necessary. And all this for a strain of the disease that is not very common. In his article titled 'Perhaps One of the Most Unnecessary Vaccines Ever', Dr Mercola explains;

> The meningococcal vaccine is already recommended for young teens, 11–12 years old, and again at 16 years of age or as college freshmen. Now they want to add anywhere from three to four more doses at two months, four months, six months and 12 months of age.
>
> *'Here is the situation with this vaccine,'* Fisher says. *'Neisseria meningococcal is only associated with about 1,400 to 3,000 cases [of meningitis] per year in the United States, out of 308 million Americans. There are five strains (serotypes): A, B, C, Y, and W135. A third to half of the cases of Neisseria meningococcal disease is caused by strain B. And that strain is NOT in the vaccine.'*
>
> In children under the age of five, strain B is responsible for *66 to 70 percent of the cases* of meningitis. Infants under the age of one are now the new target age group being considered for this vaccine recommendation—despite the fact that:
>
> a. The bacterial strain responsible for the vast majority of the cases is NOT included in the vaccine, and
>
> b. In the last nine years, there has been an average of 16 fatalities per year from the Neisseria meningococcal infection in children under the age of 12 months.
>
> The proposed policy is now to vaccinate EVERY child at two, four, six and 12 months, and then again at 11 to 12 years of age, and at 16 years of age. That's six doses of a meningococcal vaccine that *does not* cover 30 to 70 percent of the cases that actually occur, depending on the age group![521]

MMR—Measles, Mumps and Rubella

In 1988 almost 'out of the blue' the MMR vaccination was launched on the UK public. It is the only one of the childhood vaccinations to contain three live viruses, and the effects of this combination were unknown.

---

[520] The Truth About Vaccines—Making the Right Decision for Your Child—by Dr Richard Halvorsen, ISBN 9781906142445.
[521] Mercola, J. "Perhaps One of the Most Unnecessary Vaccines Ever" Retrieved Sep 20, 2013, from http://articles.mercola.com/sites/articles/archive/2011/07/14/barbara-loe-fisher-on-the-meningococcal-vaccine.aspx.

A new study into children who were allegedly damaged by the MMR vaccine claims safety tests for the triple jab were massively inadequate. The study shows that children who developed autism after receiving the MMR vaccine did so on average two and a half years after their jab. But doctors checked children for reactions for only three to six weeks after vaccination before giving the go-ahead to licensing the controversial treatment for use in the UK in 1988.[522]

The MMR also heralded a change in the way the UK government thought about vaccination: whereas vaccination had been all about eradicating serious diseases, now the spotlight was on the more minor childhood diseases.

■ *Measles:* In the late 1950s and through the 1960s it was considered quite normal to get childhood illnesses. I was no exception, having measles, mumps and German measles (rubella) all between the ages of 5 and 10 years or so. I can remember having these illnesses and although unpleasant it meant time off school spent with mummy, lots of cuddles and being 'spoiled'. Having all these diseases gave me lifelong immunity which I then passed on to my children. My breast milk effectively kept them immune to these diseases until their own immune system developed.

In rare cases measles can lead to pneumonia, ear infections, and lung infections. These in turn can be fatal. Complication arising from measles is usually a   result of poor nutrition and in particular a lack of vitamin A. For this reason measles is far more severe in developing countries, according to WHO:

Vitamin A deficiency (VAD) is the leading cause of preventable blindness in children and increases the risk of disease and death from severe infections . . . For children, lack of vitamin A causes severe visual impairment and blindness, and significantly increases the risk of severe illness, and even death, from such common childhood infections as diarrhoeal disease and measles.[523]

It has recently been discovered that having measles may actually confer some health benefits;

Measles may be good for children after all. Researchers have discovered that African children who catch measles tend to suffer less from allergic conditions, such as asthma, eczema and hay fever.

---

[522] http://www.ias.org.nz/vaccines/mmr-safety-tests-flawed-and-invalid/
[523] http://www.who.int/nutrition/topics/vad/en/.

This is in contrast to children in developed countries who, while supposedly protected from the usual childhood diseases by vaccination, go on to suffer a range of allergy related (atopic) conditions in increasing numbers.

Earlier research has indicated that the childhood diseases, such as measles, mumps and German measles (rubella), might provide natural desensitization against atopy.[524]

The measles vaccine has been found to be fairly ineffective, giving protection for only a short time; it pushes up the age at which measles is now being caught and the disease is far more severe in older people. The measles vaccine has also been linked to vaccine induced measles: 'Live virus measles vaccine, which is licensed for use in the U.S. today, can sometimes cause vaccine strain measles virus infection, which is very severe and can end in death.'[525]

In addition to this the measles part of the MMR has been linked to an increase in bowel disease and Autism. Most people are aware of the controversy surrounding Dr Wakefield and his findings connecting the MMR to these diseases. However few realise that his findings have been verified in other studies.

New American research shows that there could be a link between the controversial MMR triple vaccine and autism and bowel disease in children.

The study appears to confirm the findings of British doctor Andrew Wakefield, who caused a storm in 1998 by suggesting a possible link.

Now a team from the Wake Forest University School of Medicine in North Carolina are examining 275 children with regressive autism and bowel disease—and of the 82 tested so far, 70 prove positive for the measles virus.

Last night the team's leader, Dr Stephen Walker, said: 'Of the handful of results we have in so far, all are vaccine strain and none are wild measles. 'This research proves that in the gastrointestinal tract of a number of children who have been diagnosed with regressive autism, there is evidence of measles virus. 'What it means is that the study done earlier by Dr Wakefield and published in 1998 is correct. That study didn't draw any conclusions about specifically what it means to find measles virus in the gut, but the implication is it may be coming from the MMR vaccine. If that's the case, and this live virus is residing in the gastrointestinal tract of some children, and then they have GI inflammation and other problems, it may be related to the MMR.'

The 1998 study by Dr Wakefield, then a reader in gastroenterology at the

[524] http://www.wddty.com/measles-makes-healthier-children.html.
[525] http://www.nvic.org/Vaccines-and-Diseases/MMR.aspx.

Royal Free Hospital in North London, and 12 other doctors claimed to have found a new bowel disease, autism enterocolitis.

At the time, Dr Wakefield said that although they had not proved a link between MMR (measles, mumps, rubella) and autism, there was cause for concern and the Government should offer the option single vaccines—instead of only MMRs—until more research had been done.

. . . This is the second independent study to back up Dr Wakefield. In 2001 John O'Leary, Professor of Pathology at St James's Hospital and Trinity College, Dublin, replicated his findings.

Last night Dr Wakefield said: 'This new study confirms what we found in British children and again with Professor O'Leary. The only exposure these children have had to measles is through the MMR vaccine. They were developing normally until they regressed. They now suffer autism and bowel disease.'[526]

- *Mumps:* The mumps component of the MMR was quite controversial, as mumps was not considered to be a serious childhood disease. The possible complications of mumps are viral meningitis—which is not the same as the bacterial meningitis that we all fear—and encephalitis, but these are rare and rarely serious. There is also the very slight possibility of permanent hearing loss and sterility in men. However most children had mumps quite early on in life and were only slightly poorly. Many did not even know that they had mumps, but the result was immunity for life.

  The immunity that the vaccination gives only lasts a few years and a booster is now given to all children at around the age of 3. As with the measles vaccine, the net effect of this vaccine has been to push up the age of those who now catch mumps. There have been outbreaks of mumps among the teenage population and mumps at this age can be much more severe. 'Researchers investigating a large outbreak of mumps in 2006, when 6,584 cases were reported among college students, have discovered that virtually every sufferer had been vaccinated twice against the disease.'[527]

- *Rubella:* Rubella or German measles is a mild childhood illness. Symptoms include low- grade fever, swollen glands and a pinkish rash. Recovery is quick and afterwards immunity is usually for life. Complications can occur, and these include brain inflammation and chronic arthritis which can cause permanent damage. The main concern with rubella is that a woman in the first few months of pregnancy, who

---

[526] From an article in the Mail on Sunday 28 May 2006, by Sally Beck, at: http://www.dailymail.co.uk/news/article-388051/Scientists-fear-MMR-link-autism.html.
[527] http://www.wddty.com/mmr-major-mumps-outbreak-proves-the-vaccine-doesn-t-work.html.

catches the disease, has a 20 to 25 per cent greater chance of giving birth to a deformed baby and is also at risk of suffering a miscarriage because the rubella virus attacks the developing foetus. This is called Congenital Rubella Syndrome (CRS), and birth defects caused by CRS can include blindness, damage to the heart and major arteries, deafness, abnormally small brain, and mental retardation. The rubella vaccination was originally given to young girls at the age of 12 years so that they would have immunity during their childbearing years. This was scrapped when the MMR was introduced, as the MMR was supposed to confer long-term immunity. At the time that the MMR was introduced there were very few cases of CRS.

Unfortunately, as with the mumps and measles vaccines, the rubella vaccine has merely succeeded in raising the age when this infection is caught.

> The manufacturers of the vaccine had warned in the late 1970's that, for mass vaccination of pre school children to work, the vaccine had to be more effective than the natural disease at producing immunity—something the rubella vaccine clearly isn't. It otherwise risks pushing up the age at which most people get infected into the very group we are trying to protect—childbearing women.[528]

> It seems that this has now happened: . . . a study from Finland that showed that one third of girls given the MMR twice, at one year and six years of age (very similar to the current UK schedule) had lost all the protection they may have had by fifteen years of age.'[529]

Along with the risk to the unborn child measles in this older age group is likely to be more severe. Other side effects of the rubella vaccine are typically, the symptoms of the rubella infection, together with painful or inflamed joints; it has also been linked to chronic fatigue syndrome and ME.

HPV

The HPV vaccines with the trade names 'Gardasil' or 'Cevarix' are comparatively new. It will be given to girls aged between 12 and 13 in order to protect against human papillomavirus types 6, 11, 16 and 18, which cause most cervical cancers and genital warts. Given that this vaccine has not been proved to prevent cancer, but only the 'pre-cancer' state and then only if it is connected to one of a few HPV types, it would seem that the furore surrounding the launch of this new 'wonder vaccine' has been rather overplayed. 'As the US National Institutes

---

[528] The Truth About Vaccines—Making the Right Decision for Your Child—by Dr Richard Halvorsen, ISBN 9781906142445.
[529] Ibid.

of Health (NIH) is at pains to point out, HPV does not lead directly to cervical cancer. Rather, the virus can cause cell abnormalities, or dysplasia, and it is this state that may, over time, develop into cancer.'[530] According to an article on the website *What Doctor's Don't Tell You*:

Of the 26.2 million people with HPV infections, the chances of developing any sort of cancer related to HPV in any given year are 0.08 per cent, and the chances of getting cervical cancer are 0.04 per cent—in other words, out of every 10,000 people with HPV, four will progress to cervical cancer. To put this in perspective, the chances of getting cervical cancer due to HPV infection in any given year are eight times greater than your risk of being struck and killed by an asteroid or about the same as being fatally electrocuted.[531]

However the chances of severe side effects ranging from seizures and numbness to dizzy spells, fainting and paralysis are very high, as Dr Mercola reports; 'As of July 11, 2012, the Vaccine Adverse Events Reporting System (VAERS) has more than 23,000 Gardasil-related adverse events listed in it. Between May 2009 and September 2010, the adverse reactions included 16 new deaths, including four suicides, according to Judicial Watch. Between September 1, 2010 and September 15, 2011, another 26 deaths were reported.'[532]

Alarmingly Dr Mercola also reports that there have been concerns over the ongoing fertility of girls vaccinated with the HPV vaccine and the possibility that these vaccines may contain hidden sterilising agents. He questions the real reason behind the fact that Gardasil has been added to the list of vaccinations that all female immigrants ages 11 to 26 *must* get before they can obtain a green card and whether it is linked to the known population control agenda.[533]

Additives in Vaccinations

Perhaps even more shocking than the safety of the vaccines themselves, is the fact that these vaccines come packaged with many harmful additives.

- ## Animal Viruses

---

[530] http://www.wddty.com/gardasil-selling-out-our-children.html.

[531] Ibid.

[532] Mercola, J. "Don't Give This to Your Daughter - Despite What Your Doctor Says" Retrieved Sep 20, 2013, from http://articles.mercola.com/sites/articles/archive/2010/11/05/gardasil-vaccine-is-a-flop-for-good-reasons.aspx.

[533] Mercola, J. "Prominent Scientist Warns of HPV Vaccine Dangers" Retrieved Sep 20, 2013, from http://articles.mercola.com/sites/articles/archive/2008/10/25/prominent-scientist-warns-of-hpv-vaccine-dangers.aspx.

Vaccines are grown on animal and human tissue and there is a very real possibility that DNA and viruses from those tissues remain in the vaccine.

A growing number of medical researchers fear that a monkey virus that contaminated polio vaccine given to tens of millions of Americans in the 1950s and 60s may be causing rare human cancers. For four decades, government officials have insisted that there is no evidence the simian virus called SV40 is harmful to humans. But in recent years, dozens of scientific studies have found the virus in a steadily increasing number of rare brain, bone and lung-related tumors—the same malignant cancer SV40 causes in lab animals. Even more troubling, the virus has been detected in tumors removed from people never inoculated with the contaminated vaccine, leading some to worry that those infected by the vaccine might be spreading SV40. The discovery of SV40 in human tumors has generated intense debate within the scientific community, pitting a handful of government health officials, who believe that the virus is harmless, against researchers from Boston to China who now suspect SV40 may be a human carcinogen. At stake are millions of research dollars and potential medical treatments for those afflicted with the cancers SV40 may be causing.[534]

And now there is news of a pig virus:

> One million U.S. children, and about 30 million worldwide, have already received GlaxoSmithKline's Rotarix vaccine. Now a research team has discovered it is contaminated with 'a substantial amount' of DNA from a pig virus.
>
> What is pig virus DNA doing in a vaccine intended to prevent rotavirus disease, which causes severe diarrhea and dehydration?
>
> It's anybody's guess, although CNN reported that GlaxoSmithKline detected the substance in the cell bank and the seed used to make the vaccine, 'suggesting its presence from the early stages of vaccine development.'
>
> It is actually common for vaccines to contain various animal matter, including foreign animal tissues containing genetic material (DNA/RNA) . . .[535]

Because of the potential for animal DNA to cross-transfer into humans many vaccine scientists prefer to culture their vaccines in human tissue. This human tissue comes from human foetal remains.

> Currently, the following vaccines in the UK contain aborted foetal tissue: MMR II, MMR (Priorix), MR, Rabies (Imovax), Hepatitis A (Havarix and Avaxim brands). Old style single

---

[534] http://www.vaccinetruth.org/sv40.htm.
[535] Mercola, J. "The FDA Shuts Down Common Infant Vaccine After Startling Discovery" Retrieved Sep 20, 2013, from http://articles.mercola.com/sites/articles/archive/2010/04/17/major-vaccine-suspended-due-to-contamination-with-pig-virus.aspx.

rubella vaccines contained foetal tissue, as well as some brands of single measles vaccines and the Medeva polio vaccine which was withdrawn for safety reasons.

In the USA, there is also an injectable polio vaccine by Connaught Labs which contains foetal tissue, as does the Varicella (Chickenpox) vaccine.

This practice began in the 1960s when lung tissue was taken from an aborted female foetus, for use in the rubella vaccine, after she was terminated for mental health reasons by the mother. They also took tissue from a 14 week old male foetus, aborted for the same reason.

Newer cell lines from fetal tissue includes PER.C6 cell line from Merck, which used tissue from an 18 week old baby whose mother aborted it because she didn't know who its father was. They also used tissue from a 21 week baby and this line is being used in flu and TB vaccines as well as experimental vaccines that researchers are still working on, including malaria and rabies vaccines, cancer and HIV vaccines. The tissue used was from both babies' eyes.[536]

• Preservatives

Once the vaccine has been made it then needs other additives. Preservatives are used to prevent contamination of the vaccine and to keep it pure. This is all very well but the preservative of choice until recently was Thiomersal which is registered as an antibacterial and antifungal. Thiomersal contains about 50 per cent ethyl mercury. Mercury is a toxin in all its forms even in extremely low doses and is known to cause damage to the brain, the nervous system and the immune system. Even in small doses it can impair speech, attention and memory. Of course the governments and pharmaceutical companies are quick to point out that the dose received by any child is a very minute percentage of the vaccine and hardly worth bothering about. Dr Richard Halvorsen says that there are no safety levels for mercury in vaccines, and that the only official safety levels are given for food which is taken in through the mouth and not injected directly into the blood stream. These safety levels are for *methyl* mercury and governments say that the ethyl mercury used in vaccines is much safer than the methyl mercury found in foods. Some studies point to quite the reverse.

> Health officials often claim that ethylmercury—the type of mercury found in vaccines containing thimerosal—should not be compared to methylmercury, a well-established neurotoxin. However, a Russian study found that adults exposed to much lower concentrations of ethylmercury than those given to American children still suffered brain damage years later. In 1985, the Archives of Toxicology published a comparative study that administered similar doses of ethylmercury and methylmercury to rats. The

---

[536] http://www.vaccineriskawareness.com/Vaccination-And-Abortion-.

ethylmercury-treated rats had higher amounts of inorganic mercury in their kidneys and brains. In August 2005, a study funded by the National Institutes of Health also found that ethylmercury is more toxic to the brain than methylmercury. It crosses the blood-brain barrier quicker and converts to inorganic mercury—which is more difficult to excrete and stays in the brain longer—at much higher levels.[537]

And all those small doses in the various vaccines add up to quite a big dose:

> I was alarmed that no one else appeared to have done the calculations for British babies, so I researched the issue. In the first jab at two months, an average sized baby received 49 times the maximum safe daily dose if one adopts the safety levels of the FSA for methyl mercury found in fish. A small baby would have received over 60 times the maximum recommended daily intake. A baby born prematurely, being particularly small, may have received up to 100 times the maximum safe daily intake in a single injection. It is also probably that intermittent large exposures pose more risk than small daily doses.[538]

In addition to the mercury overload that babies receive from these vaccines they may also have received mercury whilst in the womb or breastfeeding. Mercury from the mother's amalgam fillings or from food sources is known to cross the placenta and can be passed to the infant through breast milk. Thanks to the National Health Service in the UK who provide free dental treatment for all pregnant women, I had all my dental work done during the times when I was pregnant. Being unaware of the problem with dental amalgam this would have involved much refilling of these dental amalgams.

> Amalgam emits mercury vapor even after it is implanted into the body. This mercury is bioaccumulative, and it crosses the placenta to accumulate in fetuses as well. Dental amalgam's mercury is a known health risk, especially for children, fetuses, nursing infants, and people with impaired kidney function especially. Even the U.S. Food and Drug Administration concedes that the developing neurological systems of children and fetuses are more susceptible to 'the neurotoxic effects of mercury vapor'—and that there is no evidence that amalgam is safe for these populations.[539]

Thiomersal has now been removed from most childhood vaccines but is still found in the Flu vaccine which is offered to children. When Thiomersal was removed from childhood vaccines another preservative had to be found. This new preservative is 2-Phenoxyethanol (2-PE);

---

[537] Quoted from [2010] MAKE an INFORMED VACCINE DECISION by Mayer Eisenstein, MD, JD, MPH (with Neil Miller) p.128 on the website http://www.whale.to/vaccines/ethyl_vs_methyl.html.

[538] The Truth About Vaccines—Making the Right Decision for Your Child—by Dr Richard Halvorsen, ISBN 9781906142445.

[539] http://www.toxicteeth.org/.

2-Phenoxyethanol (2-PE) is a chemical substance presently used as a preservative in several vaccines. 2-PE contains phenol, which has the ability to inhibit phagocyte activity, meaning it is toxic to all cells. The phenol in 2-PE is capable of disabling the immune system's primary response mechanism. It can also cause systemic poisoning, headache, shock, weakness, convulsions, kidney damage, cardiac failure, kidney failure, or death. 2-PE also contains ethylene oxide, which is an irritant causing dermatitis, burns, blisters, and eczema.[540]

• Adjuvants

Adjuvants such as aluminium, other heavy metals and squalene are put into vaccines to kick-start the immune system into producing more antibodies. These substances are basically contaminants that cause the body to create a more intense immune response. The great thing for the vaccine manufacturers is that when an adjuvant is used, less of the antigen—the active ingredient—needs to be used and this makes the vaccine cheaper, quicker to produce and more profitable. Commonly used adjuvants are;

▪ *Aluminium:* Aluminium has been put into vaccines for many years. It is all around us and we ingest it from many sources such as water, foods, medicines and vaccines. Tea and aluminium cooking pans are in particular considered to be a source of aluminium. Recently there have been scares regarding aluminium in deodorants as there is a possibility that they contribute to breast cancer. Aluminium has also been suggested as a cause for Alzheimer's disease and, in children, hyperactivity and learning disorders. Speaking of aluminium Dr Richard Halvorsen says: 'So I calculated an average baby's intake of aluminium on vaccination day. This revealed a big problem: The intake was between 44 and 71 times the US 'minimal risk' level, and up to one hundred and fifty times the WHO advised maximum at that time. However in 2006, after I made this calculation the WHO reduced its safety level.'[541]

A new disease caused by this aluminium has been discovered:

> There are three basic aluminum salts used in vaccines: aluminum hydroxide, aluminum phosphate and potassium-aluminum sulfate, or alum. The three forms are not interchangeable as they each have their own chemical properties.
>
> A new disease has been identified, first in France, called macrophagic myofasciitis (MMF). The condition manifests with spread out muscle pain and chronic fatigue. One third of the patients develop an autoimmune disease, such as

---

[540] http://www.vaccinetruth.org/2-phenoxyethanol.htm.
[541] The Truth About Vaccines—Making the Right Decision for Your Child—by Dr Richard Halvorsen, ISBN 9781906142445.

multiple sclerosis (MS) or amyotrophic lateral sclerosis (ALS or Lou Gehrig's disease). Even if they don't have an obvious autoimmune disease, most of them are part of a subgroup called HLADRB1*01 that puts them at risk of developing polymyalgia rheumatica and rheumatoid arthritis.

Doctors have identified that the aluminum-hydroxide in the vaccines stays at the site of the injection for years. The whole time it is there, it is stimulating an immune response. Which is exactly why the vaccine makers include it in the vaccine, so that the immune system will react more strongly to the virus or toxoid. But switching the immune system on without turning it off is not good for the body. This appears to be what causes the chronic fatigue seen in MMF.

. . . MMF has now been identified in children, and was characterized by motor delay, hypotonia (diminished muscle tone), and failure to thrive. They concluded that MMF should be considered in the evaluation of children with failure to thrive, diminished muscle tone, and muscle weakness.[542]

Squalene: Squalene is an adjuvant added to the swine flu (H1N1) vaccine. It has not been passed for use in the USA although if a public health emergency was declared it could, and possibly would, be used. It is however licensed for the H1N1 swine flu vaccine in Europe. In an epidemic mass swine flu vaccinations would begin, starting with children and those who are vulnerable. According to Dr Mercola sqaulene in vaccines is not good news;

Your immune system recognizes squalene as an oil molecule native to your body. It is found throughout your nervous system and brain. In fact, you can consume squalene in olive oil and not only will your immune system recognize it, you will also reap the benefits of its antioxidant properties.

The difference between 'good' and 'bad' squalene is the route by which it enters your body. Injection is an abnormal route of entry which incites your immune system to attack *all* the squalene in your body, not just the vaccine adjuvant.

Your immune system will attempt to destroy the molecule wherever it finds it, including in places where it occurs naturally, and where it is vital to the health of your nervous system.

Gulf War veterans with Gulf War Syndrome (GWS) received anthrax vaccines which contained squalene. MF59 (the Novartis squalene adjuvant) was an

[542] From the December 2007 Idaho Observer: 'Aluminum-hydroxide in vaccines causes serious health problems' by Tenna Merchant at: http://www.proliberty.com/observer/20071206.htm.

unapproved ingredient in experimental anthrax vaccines and has since been linked to the devastating autoimmune diseases suffered by countless Gulf War vets.[543]

- *ASO4:* Cervarix and Gardasil are both trade names for the HPV vaccination which is used to prevent cervical cancer. They are given to girls in the 11 to 12 year old age bracket. Cervarix contains ASO4 which is a combination of aluminium hydroxide and monophosphoryl lipid A (MPL). MPL is a purified fat-like substance similar to squalene. 'MPL is identified in declassified documents as one of two squalene emulsions used in the Army's new 'recombinant protective antigen anthrax vaccine (rPA) which the FDA, the National Institutes of Health (NIH) and the Department of Defense fast-tracked into clinical trials in1998.'[544]

Other Additives

- *Antibiotics:* These are routinely put into vaccines so that the child doesn't get an infection at the site of the injection. These antibiotics tend to suppress the immune system leaving the child more open to colds and viruses, and some children are allergic to them. The overuse of antibiotics has been suggested as one of the reasons for the emergence of antibiotic resistant illnesses such as meningitis.
- *Formaldehyde:* according the American FDA:

> Formaldehyde has a long history of safe use in the manufacture of certain viral and bacterial vaccines. It is used to inactivate viruses so that they don't cause disease (e.g., influenza virus to make influenza vaccine) and to detoxify bacterial toxins, such as the toxin used to make diphtheria vaccine. Formaldehyde is diluted during the vaccine manufacturing process, but residual quantities of formaldehyde may be found in some current vaccines. The average amount of formaldehyde to which a young infant could be exposed to at one time through vaccines is considered to be safe.[545]

However the Vaccine Awareness Network sees it differently:

> Formaldehyde is a class 1 carcinogen, labelled by the Environmental Protection Agency in the US as a 'hazardous waste.'
>
> According to Dr. Penny Stanway, famous author of 'Breast Is Best' and 'Green Babies', 'sensitivity to formaldehyde has been linked with eye, nose, throat

---

[543] Mercola, J. "Squalene: The Swine Flu Vaccine's Dirty Little Secret Exposed" Retrieved Sep 20, 2013, from http://articles.mercola.com/sites/articles/archive/2009/08/04/squalene-the-swine-flu-vaccines-dirty-little-secret-exposed.aspx.
[544] http://www.whale.to/vaccine/ceravix_contents.html.
[545] http://www.fda.gov/BiologicsBloodVaccines/SafetyAvailability/VaccineSafety/ucm187810.htm.

and lung irritation, headaches, depression, memory loss and dizziness. 1 in 5 people exposed to formaldehyde may be affected…

▪ *Polysorbate 80:* This helps with the delivery of the vaccine but according to Dr Mercola;

> Polysorbate 80, also known as Tween80, is a detergent (surfactant) used to deliver certain drugs or chemical agents across the blood-brain barrier. This season's flu vaccine for the US market made by GlaxoSmithKline, called Fluarix, contains polysorbate 80, as does Novartis' Agriflu. The HPV vaccine, Gardasil, and a number of other childhood vaccines that carry the potential for serious side effects also contain polysorbate 80.'[546]

> Polysorbate 80 can cause anaphylactic shock and has been linked to loss of fertility. The packet leaflet that comes with Fluarix states that the manufacturer (GlaxoSmithKline) cannot guarantee that your fertility will be unharmed. 'According to the World Intellectual Property Organization, which is part of the United Nations, scientists from the organization are developing vaccines specifically to damage fertility as a method of contraception. A suggested ingredient for the vaccine is tween 80 (polysorbate 80).'[547]

▪ *Octoxynol 9:* This is a known spermicidal! It 'has been used in experiments to 'strip' sperm so that they are no longer capable of fertilizing an egg'.[548] It is also used in the production of vaccines. 'Octoxynol 9 contains glycol ether which is toxic and has been directly linked to infertility problems in men. Namely low sperm count, abnormally shaped sperm and sperm with poor motility. Painters and decorators in particular have been warned not to work with paints containing glycol, yet it is happily injected into male babies.'[549]

▪ *Sodium Borate:*

> Sodium Borate is neuro toxic and not meant for internal use, yet it is used in some vaccines, including the new Gardasil vaccine for cervical cancer. At a cellular level it can cause changes to DNA. Symptoms include nausea, vomiting, diarrhea, flushed skin, changes in respiration and pulse, lethargy, seizures, shock, metabolic acidosis, vascular collapse and death. It can also cause mental illness such as

---

[546] Mercola, J. "What is In the Flu Vaccine that Can Cause Infertility?" Retrieved Sep 20, 2013, from http://articles.mercola.com/sites/articles/archive/2010/10/15/fluarix-flu-vaccine-that-can-cause-infertility.aspx.

[547] Read more at Suite101: Polysorbate 80 Causes Infertility: An Emulsifier That Can Damage Your Reproductive Health | Suite101.com http://joanna-karpasea-jones.suite101.com/polysorbate-80-causes-infertility-a60320#ixzz1d8yrVdKf.

[548] http://suite101.com/article/the-secret-sterilizing-ingredients-of-vaccines-a376233.

[549] http://www.vaccineriskawareness.com/Vaccines-And-How-They-Are-Made.

depression, mental confusion and hyperactivity. It may be a clue as to why there are so many children with depression and behaviour disorders. 'The British Pediatrics Association called for sodium borate not to be used during infancy, yet it is sometimes in vaccines.[550]

- *Gelatin:* Gelatin is used in some vaccines to protect the vaccine viruses from adverse conditions such as freeze-drying or heat. Gelatin which is used in Jelly/Jell-O and many other 'set' foods, is a protein formed by boiling skin or connective tissue. Gelatine used in vaccines usually comes from pigs and may be offensive to people of some faiths. Children can become allergic to foods containing gelatine as a result of gelatine in vaccines.

5.   Resources

All references throughout the book are given in the footnotes and these represent an incredible resource for further research.

For those seeking healing here is a list of counselling organisations that seek to follow Christian principles. They are all groups or individuals that I know and in the case of Ellel Ministries and Elijah House, have trained with. However I can't really make any recommendations as organisations, and the people within those organisations, change. Whilst it's not good to become someone who hops from one counsellor to another, there is a place for recognizing when a particular counsellor is just not 'right for me' and moving on.

The Association of Christian Counsellors: http://www.acc-uk.org
The Association was founded in 1992 to provide a nationwide umbrella organisation. Since then the original vision has been fulfilled in the following ways:

- The provision of nationwide standards for Christian counselling and care.
- The provision of a nationwide system for the accreditation of Christian counsellors broadly acceptable to Christian churches, counselling organisations and the wider community.
- The provision of a nationwide system for the recognition of training in Christian counselling and pastoral care.
- The provision of a body which represents Christian counsellors and develop relations with institutions such as the social services and health authorities, and with denominations and professional bodies.

---

[550] Ibid.

- The encouragement, training and resourcing of Pastoral Carers.
- The Association recognises that among Christians there is a great variety of approaches to counselling. Whereas it aims at high standards in practice and training it does not seek uniformity.

CWR: www.cwr.org.uk
Crusade for World Revival was founded as a Christian ministry in 1965 by Selwyn Hughes, changing its name to **CWR** in the mid 1980s. Since then, it hasgrown into an international publishing and training organisation which seeks to enable people to apply God's word to everyday life and relationships. In addition to the variety of courses on offer, they produce a wide range of high-quality resources including daily devotionals, books, ebooks, DVDs and CDs.

Deep Release: www.deeprelease.org.uk
Their website states: We believe in the centrality of Christ's redemptive work on the cross, the power of the Holy Spirit and the authority of the Word of God as essential to our ministry. We seek to integrate Christian faith with appropriate psychological and psychotherapeutic understanding, skills and practice.

Elijah House: www.elijahhouse.org
Elijah House prayer ministry was founded through the pioneering work of John and Paula Sandford. It is primarily pastoral in nature, based on scriptural principles and led by the Holy Spirit. Prayer ministry at Elijah House will always include looking for the root causes that lie beneath the surface of most problems.

Ellel Ministries: www.ellelministries.org/uk
The mission statement for Ellel Ministries states: Our mission is to fulfil this vision in accordance with the Great Commission of Jesus and the calling of the Church to proclaim the Kingdom of God by preaching the good news, healing the broken-hearted and setting the captives free. We are, therefore, committed to evangelism, healing, deliverance, discipleship and training.

The Harnhill Centre of Christian Healing: www.harnhillcentre.org.uk
Established in 1986 out of the vision of a local vicar, Canon Arthur Dodds, The Harnhill Centre of Christian Healing brings the healing love of Jesus to all who visit.

Restoring the Foundations: www.restoringthefoundations.org.uk
Restoring the Foundations UK & Europe(RTF UK&EU) is a Christian charitable Organisation registered in the UK, passionately dedicated to bringing the healing message of Restoring the Foundations to the greater Body of Christ in the UK, Europe and Scandinavian region.

Wholeness Through Christ: www.wholenessthroughchrist.org
Wholeness Through Christ is a gentle balanced scriptural, powerful ministry which enables people to receive God's freedom release and peace into their lives and to realise NOW is the time of God's favour. THIS IS GOOD NEWS. Through 4 distinct Prayer Ministry Courses they provide teaching and ministry to help people experience God's healing work in their lives, releasing them from brokenness to wholeness and equipping them to take this freedom to others.

6.   Abbreviations and Stockists

UK abbreviations are used for all the patterns. American equivalents are given below.

Knitting Abbreviations

k	-	knit
p	-	purl
st(s)	-	stitch(es)
st st	-	stocking stitch
g st	-	garter stitch
reverse st st	-	work so that the purl side is at the front
yo	-	yarn over needle to make one stitch
k2tog	-	knit two sts together
skpo	-	sl1 one st, k one st, pass the slipped st over this stitch
sk2po	-	slip one st, k2tog, pass the slipped st over this stitch
m1	-	make 1 st by lifting the horizontal bar before the next st, place it on left needle, then knit into the back of this stitch
WS	-	wrong side
RS	-	right side
cont	-	continue
dec	-	decrease
dpn's	-	double pointed needles
rem	-	remaining
rep	-	repeat
rnds	-	rounds

Crochet Abbreviations

ss	-	slip stitch
ch	-	chain
dc	-	double crochet

tr	-	treble
sp	-	space
htr	-	half treble
dtr	-	double treble
shell	-	when making the basket on page 16 this is a group of 5 trebles, when making the rose on page 318 this is a group of 8 trebles
cont	-	continue
rem	-	remaining
rep	-	repeat
magic circle	-	Work as given below;

1) Begin to make a slip knot but do not pull up tight - see fig a.
2) Using the loop on the hook and working into the loose loop ring work stitches as given in the pattern- see fig b.
3) Pull up the short end of the yarn to close the circle- see fig b.

a.

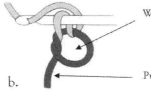

Work into this ring.

Pull this short end to close.

b.

Measurements

mm	-	millimetres
cm	-	centimetres
m	-	metres
in	-	inches
yd	-	yards

American Terms

cast off	-	bind off
tension	-	gauge
dc	-	double crochet = US term single crochet
tr	-	treble = US term double crochet
htr	-	half treble= US term half double crochet
dtr	-	double treble= US term treble

Stockists

Nesting Baskets - p18
Rico Essentials Soft Merino Aran available online at: www.deramores.com.
To Substitute: use correct length of any Aran weight yarn that has a standard knit tension of 18 sts and 24 rows to 10 cm square.

Pitter Patter - p108
Debbie Bliss Cashmerino DK. Now discontinued, but a selection of alternatives can be found in my online shop: www.lupinandrose.co.uk.
To Substitute: use correct length of any DK weight yarn that has a standard knit tension of 22 sts and 28/30 rows to 10 cm square.

Bear Hug - p196
Rowan Belle Organic Aran. Now discontinued, but a selection of alternatives can be found in my online shop: www.lupinandrose.co.uk.
To Substitute: use correct length of any Aran weight yarn that has a standard knit tension of 18 sts and 24 rows to 10 cm square.

I love you - p274
Debbie Bliss Cashmerino Aran. available online at : www.lupinandrose.co.uk.
To Substitute: use correct length of any Aran weight yarn that has a standard knit tension of 18 sts and 24 rows to 10 cm square.

Red Red Rose - p318
Shetland Wool 2 ply Lace Weight available online at: www.shetlandwoolbrokers.co.uk
To Substitute: use correct length of any 3 ply weight yarn that has a standard knit tension of 32 sts and 40 rows to 10 cm square.

Yarn information is correct at time of going to print. Please contact me via my website for more information.

Errata
Any pattern corrections will be uploaded to my website: www.motheringsundae.co.uk

Red Red Rose

<u>MATERIALS</u>
1 x 25g ball each of shade L68 (red)& L101 (pink) Jamieson & Smith 100% Shetland
Wool, 2 ply lace (169 m per ball)
Oddment of green yarn in DK weight
3.5 mm hook (USE/4)
Brooch pin
Wool sewing needle

Red Red Rose

TENSION
Tension is not important.

ABBREVIATIONS
See page 305.

THE BROOCH
Using no 3.5 mm hook and red, make a length of 122 chain.

1ˢᵗ row: 2 ch, (=1 dc and 1 ch), 1 dc into 4th ch from hook, * 1ch, skip 1 ch, 1 dc into next ch, rep from * to end. (61 chain spaces)

2ⁿᵈ row: 2ch, (=1 tr), 7 tr in 1ˢᵗ ch sp, * (1ch, 1 dc in next ch sp) x 4, 1 ch, 8 tr in next ch sp, rep from * four times more ** (1ch, 1 dc in next ch sp) x 3, 1 ch, 8 tr in next ch sp, rep from ** four times more, *** (1ch, 1 dc in next ch sp) x 2, 1 ch, 8 tr in next ch sp, rep from *** four times more. (16 shells)

3ʳᵈ row: 3 ch (= 1 tr and 1 ch), skip 1ˢᵗ tr, (1 tr in next tr, 1 ch) x 6, 1 tr in next tr, * skip 1 ch sp, 1ch, 1dc in next ch sp, (1 ch, 1 tr in next tr) x 8, rep from * four times more, ** skip 1 ch sp, (1ch, 1 dc in next ch sp) x 2, (1 ch, 1 tr in next tr) x 8, rep from ** four times more, *** skip 1 ch sp, (1ch, 1dc in next ch sp) x 3, (1 ch, 1 tr in next tr) x 8, rep from *** four times more.

4ᵗʰ row: 1 ch (=1 dc), (1 tr in next ch, 1 tr in next tr), x 7, * skip 1 ch sp,(1ch, 1 dc in next ch sp) x 2, 1 ch, (1 tr in next tr, 1 tr in next ch), x 7, 1 tr in next tr, rep from * four times more, **skip 1 ch sp,1ch, 1 dc in next ch sp, 1 ch, (1 tr in next tr, 1 tr in next ch), x 7, 1 tr in next tr, rep from ** four times more, 1 dc in next dc. Turn omitting the last five shells.

5ᵗʰ row: 2 ch, * 1 tr in each of next 15 tr, 1ch, 1dc in next dc, 1 ch, rep from * four times more, 2 tr in each of next 14 tr, 1 tr in next tr, 1 ch, skip 1 ch sp, 1 dc in next ch sp, 1 ch, rep from * four times more, 2 tr in each of next 14 tr, 1 tr in last tr. Draw contrast yarn through last loop worked.
Break main yarn and continue with contrast as follows:

6ᵗʰ row: 2 ch, (= 1 dc and 1 ch), skip 1ˢᵗ tr, * (skip next tr, 1 dc in next tr, 1 ch) x 14, 1 dc in next dc, 1 ch, 1 dc in next tr, 1 ch, rep from * five times more ** (1 dc in next tr, 1 ch) x 14, 1 dc in next dc, 1 ch, 1 dc in next tr, 1ch. Rep from ** four times more. *** (1dc in next tr, 1 ch) x 7, 1 dc in next dc, 1 ch, 1 dc in next tr, 1 ch, rep from *** three times more. (1dc in next tr, 1 ch) x 6, 1 dc in last tr. Fasten off.

The Leaf (Make 5)

With 3.5 mm hook and green make a length of 9 ch.

1st side of leaf: 1 htr into 3rd ch from hook (1st 2 ch counts as 1st htr),1 tr in each of next 2 ch, 1 dtr in next ch, 1 tr in next ch, 1 htr in next ch, work 3 dc into last ch, and turn work.

2nd side of leaf: continuing along other side of the same length of ch work as follows; 1 htr in next ch, 1 tr in next ch, 1 dtr in next ch, 1 tr in each of next 2 ch, 1 htr in each of last 2 ch.
Fasten off and leave a long end (about 30 cm) for sewing.

The Stem

With no 3.5 mm hook and green, make a length of 30 ch.
1st row: ss in 2nd ch from hook, ss in each ch to end.
Rep 1st row once. Fasten off.

To Make

Roll the rose into a flower shape and sew from WS to fix. Attach leaves to one end of the stem, and two at each side as in a rose. Attach the stem of leaves to the back of the flower, then sew brooch back into place